Forever, That's How Long I'm Going To Love You

To My Brother Nathan Hill who has been support & inspiration. Let the story you read shed more light on my journey.

Zeke Smith

May 19, 2012

Forever, That's How Long I'm Going To Love You

16 Years

Zeke Smith

Library of Congress Control Number:		2012903562
ISBN:	Hardcover	978-1-4691-7365-8
	Softcover	978-1-4691-7364-1
	Ebook	978-1-4691-7366-5

To order additional copies of this book, contact:
Xlibris Corporation
1-888-795-4274
www.Xlibris.com
Orders@Xlibris.com
111920

GOOD AFTERNOON SAINTS, believers, and any non believers. And for those non believers who are here, just to honor my Pastor and First lady! I invite you to hear my testimony, and you will know there is a living God, and Jesus is the way.

My first knowledge of the Pastor and First lady came from my wife Eileen and daughter Zoriah, Eileen spoke with such affection and admiration I wondered if he was married. Zoriah talked about the additional guidance first lady had added to her life.

My wife was so proud of her service to the church. She was so involved that, it made me know that this dynamic Duo, was having a major impact on her spiritual life,

When I first heard preach, I felt the strong presence of The Lord, in every word he uttered. I would know when God was around because He had healed me before. God ushered me here, when I came to love my wife.

In subsequent sermons, I saw a pattern that revealed to me, that it wasn't just about this Flock. God revealed that it wasn't just about my family or the pain I was feeling from recent deaths, at that time.

I immediately committed to allow this Spiritual, Heavenly, Godly, appointed (not just anointed) Couple to lead me, up a righteous path, to a higher level with God.

The foundation of their existence rests on the Word. The actions of their hearts are motivated by the Word. Any intervention into someone's life is guided by the Word. When I gaze upon their strut I see the Word. When I peer into their eyes, I feel the word.

They embraced my family and me. Now I embrace them and their ministry.

Happy Anniversary! May your journey be long and stay blessed with the Word.

That was a tribute to my Pastor and First Lady as they celebrated their 13th anniversary, in the ministry. I stood alone this day, because my teenage daughter was too shy to stand with me. My wife, who was the reason for me being here, had gone on to a greater glory. We had rediscovered Love and Commitment that came with marriage. We both grew to love and respect each other, in a manner that couldn't be achieved, before our mutual separation. On this day I not only gave honor to the presence of our Pastor. I also gave honor to my wife. She had the courage to send for me in her darkest hour. She needed my strength, courage, love and commitment to help her endure. It has been three months since my wife laid next to me. Let me tell the story that brought her to this town and this church, without me. I am the man who promised to love her for ever and ever. I did not break my promise. Cancer claimed her life, but it didn't claim my love. Now let us go back to April 23, 2002. This begins the rest of their story.

It was early evening and book sales were brisk. I was having a good time helping out one of my closest friends. Van was great! She was helping me pay some bills and I was helping her sell some books. I had been at her house earlier taking a shower. That's the way it was for me now. I had to rely on my friend's homes or an all night laundry mat, to keep my ass clean. I was back to living out of my car. The reconciliation with my wife ended the way the last two did. Once things got better for her, she showed me the door. She always tried to make it seem like, it was my idea. My wife was real good at exempting herself from the rules she made. They applied to everyone but her. She even tested God, when she made herself exempt from the marriage vows. According to the last condition of my return, we were not supposed to separate again. This was going to be our last reunion. I trusted her this time, as I gave up relationships that had supported me. I was taken off the streets and given a home with steady employment. I had even been promised a job with the Dept. of Health, in N.Y.C. We had got back together, right after 9/11/2001. It was my 48th birthday celebration, and I was trying to invite her friends. I had become close to most of her friends, because I always attended functions with her. My wife Legs was always complimented, about my presence and my devotion to her. We didn't do as much together after our daughter was born, but we still loved each other. Legs had asked if it would be alright if she came too. I reluctantly said yes. I was concerned about Legs jealous nature, even though we were separated for the past year. We were in contact regularly, because I had been babysitting my daughter after school, and on weekends during the summer. I was living in the back of the Sports Bar that I managed. The owner was an old friend that saw me grow up. I used to travel great distances to gamble at him. His name was Ruby, and he was the most successful gambler I knew. It was always a great feat whenever I beat him, which didn't happen often. Now Ruby was my benefactor and we no longer tried to bust each other. He took me in when my car was the only home I knew. He listened to my hurt caused by being separated from my family. He stood by me as he seen the viciousness of my wife, whenever I wanted my daughter on my terms. I began to accumulate some money and my social life was very satisfying. When I got back with my wife, I lost Ruby and a remarkable friend. I couldn't stay at home and watch the bar too. Sells begin to suffer as my absence caused a drop in business. The birthday party was quite an event. I shared the spotlight with our top barmaid. She was also celebrating because our birthdays fell on the same day. My sisters were there except the oldest, Big Mama. My wife came with her new young girlfriend. I made mistakes that weekend, which caused so much pain. God would begin to speak to me again, as I searched for answers.

The party was off the hook as the music blared and I mingled with my guests. I had started early on getting the place decorated properly. My co-celebrant was nowhere to be seen. I was not concerned because this was my big day. I was not going to let anyone spoil it for me. I knew people expected the food to be good, because of my known culinary skills. I prepared a salad and a large array of chicken wings. My boss, who was also my best friend, was very cooperative in helping with the preparations. I put on an outfit that hid the bulges but accented the muscle. My mind returned to the present as I continued to greet my guests. I was nervous with anticipation of my wife's arrival. I also was anxious to see her new girlfriend. Legs had let me know earlier that, the friends I knew would not be coming. I was disappointed but hopeful that at least she would be cumming, I mean coming. The drinks started pouring in but I was determined to pace myself. I was not going to get drunk or sick. My sisters were coming, so I had to be able to maintain security and peace. I was a celebrity in this place because of my after hours shows. I also entertained on the dance floor and was known to make the ladies get over-heated. I could roll my belly and bend my legs in ways few had witnessed. Favorite after favorite walked in and I feasted on the attention. A few times I took a moment to dance, just so my joint didn't spend, too much time limp. "There goes my sisters" I shouted to myself as their entourage entered the bar. I quickly went over to the doorman and woman, to let them know, who they were. I also let them know how I expected them to be treated. I led my sisters and their friend over to a table. They had brought me a gift wrapped up professionally. I was impressed and summoned for the waitress to come and take their orders. This was a safe and clean establishment but gangsters were known to hang out here. The down fall of being separated from my wife, caused me to return to a world, I had swore off. My dislike for having to be out here prostituting myself would often cause anger at any moment. The party was in full swing but my co-host still had not come. I grabbed "Baby Sis" and began to dance. My sister loved to dance and I wanted to make sure she was comfortable. The friend they brought with them was a bit shy. She was no spring chicken but easy to look at. Her name was Carol. I wondered what tune she would sing, when she hit her high notes. I danced thru three songs with Baby Sis before we stopped. I turned my attention to the door as I heard a voice shout "there he is." Looking a little thin and frail but beautiful was Legs. She had on her signature dress that clung to her like second skin. "Excuse me that's Legs" I politely told my sisters. They didn't appear delighted to see her. They knew about the way she had tried to bury me. They disliked her for not communicating with them. My sisters never understood why Legs rejected them, when they showed nothing but love to her. I was horny for some old stuff, and I was going to get some tonight. "Hey looking good, and who is this other woman you got with you?" My eyes were wide open as I continued to question Legs. "What is everybody drinking? "Nothing Legs responded. What are you drinking? I started to respond but she handed me an envelope at the same time. "This is for you Honey." She stated as she pulled up close and planted a kiss on my lips. My joint started a commotion as her thigh slide between my legs. I turned to her friend and asked her name. This is Tease and she lives next door to me. Tease seemed so nervous in this atmosphere. I gently grabbed her hand and assured her that she was safe. I thought to myself that she wasn't safe from me. My wife Legs had promised to turn the party out. I kept looking at Tease and imagined her sitting on my face, while Legs played with my dick. Yes my dick because that's what it was feeling like. I finally told Legs that I would like a "Baileys" and she went to the bar to order. I watched Tease hand slide out of mine as she floated away behind Legs. I couldn't help but wonder if the two of them was fucking. I was still planted near the door as two regulars walked in. I had a real crush on this girl and had made it to third base with her. Most times she traveled with another little cutie that had just as much potential. Everyone at the sports bar knew I was a pig. They also knew that I was separated from my wife. They often heard the story of the break-up and how it made me homeless. Some would have sympathy and speak of a reunion and others just wanted me to fuck them. The one thing that was certain was God would make the decision. My boss didn't like me talking about God around him. I was in a moral dilemma because my life-style was a sin. I was still worshipping the Lord and trusting in His word. I remained prayerful and faithful. My boss Ruby used to use me as his ambassador to the local churches. He didn't want to hear about God but he believed in God's existence. He was funny and uncomplicated because he let you know, exactly where he stood.

I went up to the bar and waited for my drink with the girls. I took this time waiting to inspect Tease more closely. She looked young and displayed an unnatural attraction to Legs. She had a nice body with a plumb ass and ample breasts. Her hands were soft to the touch with beautiful skin tone. She had a walk of confidence that said; I know you're watching me. The dress she wore was just above her knees but the material was clingy. It fell over her body like it was painted on. Tease was standing so close to Legs that her breasts were pressed up against Legs shoulders. I leaned over Tease to get my drink from the bar. I was a little off balance as gently brushed up against Tease. She tilted her body forward a little, causing her butt to protrude out. The lights were very dim so no body noticed me, positioning my right leg just under her buttocks. I leaned forward and the softness of her buttocks caused my dick to slide right between her ass. I held this position for some time. I started to fumble with the drink as my cock began to grow. She didn't seem bothered by what was going on behind her. I slowly drew the glass toward me as she began to grind her ass against my bulging cock. I held the drink in my right hand as my left hand gently held her waist. Legs had finished paying for the drinks. She was beginning to pay attention to us. "I see you two like each other." Legs stated while she pressed her body up against Tease as she turned to face her. That action forced Tease to press her body even closer to mine. My cock and her ass was now one as she continued to let me feel her softness. Legs had her back to the bar as I reached around to rub her ass. We had become a sandwich cookie with vanilla crème in the middle. I could no longer hold this position without my sexual urges being satisfied. Legs wanted to use the bathroom, so I sent her to the back where I lived. I grabbed Tease and began to dance. Tease was very flirtatious and continued to let me feel the softness of her body. I went and placed my drink down at my sisters table and returned to Tease. She continued to do a swirling motion with her body as I pressed forward. I placed both hands on her waist and pulled her to me. I had a firm grip as my fingers clinched the insides of her thighs. She rocked back and forth as her hair flared wildly. I glanced at my sisters and realized I had to tone it down. The DJ switched songs and I switched partners. I watched Tease return to the bar and finish her drink. I took this opportunity to go check on Legs. I slipped into the back without being seen. I locked the door and approached Legs in the bathroom. She was in there washing up, to my surprise. "What are you doing? Didn't you take a shower before you left home?" I asked in a very soft tone so as not to alarm her. "Yes I did Honey but I want you to have this now. I'm making it fresher for you." I stopped talking and led her out of the bathroom. She had her clothes on but the panties were in her hand. I leaned her against the arm of the leather sofa I had. The music could be heard in the back. It provided some background noise to muffle her moans. She flinched as I squatted before her and began searching underneath her skirt. The aroma was fresh and she was so willing. She began to spread her legs wide for me. My tongue began to lubricate every area it touched. I pushed her backwards as her legs flung up in the air. Her skirt slide down to her belly button, and my mouth tried to smother her warm pussy. There was no resistance as the tip of my tongue dove deep inside her. I palmed her ass and pushed her further down the sofa. My knuckles were burned, as they slid across the leather, pushing its cargo. Legs knees were straight up in the air and I began groping for my zipper. I slide my pants down to my and stepped out. I knelt down on the floor and turned Legs around to face me. I easily slid into her wet pussy as I pulled her closer to me. She moaned softly as I sung deeper inside her. The pussy was wet and warm, and made a slurping sound, as I rose and dove inside her. "Yes Zeke, this is just for your birthday. I miss this dick Oooooo, but I don't want you hurting me again. Oh Zeeeke keep fucking me I'm gonna cum." I continued my steady strokes but became more forceful with them. She tried to speak again but I buried my tongue in her mouth. She placed her hands down on the couch and raised her body in the air. She started matching my thrusts with some thrusts of her own. I placed my right hand around her waist and held her in the air. I put my knees on the edge of the sofa and pushed her hard against the back of it. She reached out and put her arms around my neck, as I ducked walked on the sofa with my knees. I pinned her to the back and began to pile her hard. She wanted to scream but couldn't as my mouth covered her own. "Huh, huh, huh, I grunted as I continued to slid back and forth in this now dripping pussy. She had cum and was still cumming as I began to drop my load. We matched thrust for thrust and tensed at the same time as the last drops left our organs. That was so good Honey, she cooed softly in my ear. My dick was still hard so I grind on her some more. Oh it felt so good to be inside her again. I was just wishing that Tease was back here too. I slopped around in the pussy, some more before withdrawing. I shuffled over to the bathroom and began my patented, just fucked wash up. I didn't take long so Legs came over with her skirt high above her waist. I got turned on some more as she started washing her pussy. I quickly pulled my dick back out, and greased it up. I began massaging it as it continued to grow. I just stared at what Legs was doing to those bottom lips of her. Emmm it got good fast as Legs began to watch too. My absence from the house seemed to have made her freaky. I continued to massage my dick as Legs began to rinse the soap off her pussy. I rushed into the bathroom past Legs and leaned over the toilet. I was just in time as semen gushed out of my cock. "Oooooo see how you made me cum. Come over here and squeeze the rest out for me." Legs was very obedient as reached out and took a firm hold of my cock, and began squeezing and massaging the head. "Yeahhhh that's it get it all out." I demanded as she began to apply a more gentle touch to it. I grabbed a rag and wiped myself off. Legs finished what she had started and we returned to the party. I went upstairs to the apartment above the bar to bring the food down. I made three trips before everything was spread out. I looked around and my sisters had left. They called me later to say good bye, but I was made they didn't have any food. I made some plates before allowing anyone else to be served. My co-celebrant finally walked in and I asked if she would oversee the feeding. Legs and Tease had disappeared for a few minutes and was just returning. My sisters had left sop it was time to get my freak on. I wanted to do more than just lean on Tease. I wanted her to feel what my wife was missing. Legs had already told me not to let Tease know we were fucking. I got in the middle of the floor and started shaking my ass. I then began to roll my belly and Legs stepped up behind me. She then told Tease to take the front and they began to give me another birthday gift. Tease put the pussy right up on me as I reached out to grab her. I had to hold on for balance as Legs was pressing hard up on my ass. I held Tease by the waist and pulled her tightly up against me. Happy Birthday to ya I began to chant, as my dick tried to dig a hole in the front of Tease's body. Tease reached around me and began to pull Legs in even closer. Legs than reached around and began doing the same thing to Tease. I started pumping my body back and forth as I tried to make both girls cum on that dance floor. I worked myself around so I could face Legs. I wanted her to feel how hard my dick was. Legs began to act shy as I pressed hard against her body. My cock was planted firmly between her legs. Iput my hand on the middle of her back and began to grind hard. Tease was feeling it too as my ass worked itself over her box. Sweat was now pouring down my face and people started to chant "Go Counselor, Go Counselor" I made like a snake and squirm around to face Tease again. She was in a zone now and I was prepared to take advantage of it. Tease hemline began to rise as I sunk lower to get between her legs. I began my gyrations now as my moment started to pick up. This time I put my hands on her ass and she didn't object. I grabbed both cheeks as she reached around and grabbed Legs' ass. We were now a threesome on the dance floor and my boss began to take notice. He had a grin on his face, like he was trying to hide a banana. If this wasn't a public party, I could get him to dig deep for me to increase the action. Oh this was getting good, as Tease began to give back what I was giving her. My cock became very tender. My knees started to get limp. I started to breathe heavier as cock stiffened to an unbelievable hardness. I began to felt warmth in my pants as cum began to slide down my leg. Tease buried her head in my neck as her body began to shake. She licked and sucked on my neck as wave after wave of pleasure flowed through her body. She loosened the grip on Legs and began to slowly pull away. I turned to face Legs as Tease disappeared into the bathroom. Legs wanted to leave too, but she wanted to go home for something. Legs had been introducing herself to everyone I spoke to as my wife. She made sure all the women there knew who she was. She never emphasized the fact of the separation. A friend of mine that listened to me more than once talk about my wife, offered me her truck. I didn't want to leave the party and neither did my friend. We left with Tease still in the bathroom. On the way to the house, I had Legs lift her skirt up, so I could play with the pussy. Legs wanted to get some money. She had got her rebate check and that was the money she was spending. She changed her drawers before she left. While there I studied the surroundings to see any evidence of another man. I saw none but house keeping still wasn't her strong point. The place was a little untidy but clean. It looked like it got that way, from her getting ready for her date out tonight. Legs went to her stash and got the money. I cautioned her not to bring too much because it wasn't necessary. We were now headed back to the party.

I was careful with the truck, because I still couldn't believe she had loaned it to me. I parked the truck outside the Sports Bar and continued inside. Tease met us at the door in a panic. I excused myself as she spoke to Legs. "Hey big girl "I hollered at my friend as I approached her at the bar. Yes, she was a big girl but I called her Ms. T.A. We had become close friends since I began working at the bar. I used to sometimes wish she was more my type. She had her own place with a teen age son. The men in her life were crap. That's one of the things we had in common, too many failed relations. Ms. T.A. was a down to earth woman. She had a good job making nice money, but couldn't budget properly. That was usually the case with so many of my people. They made good money but couldn't manage it right. I learned early how to stash those funds. I used to hide my money and forget that I had it. Many times my sisters would find my dough and dip in it. Most if not all of the time I didn't miss it. It was different now when you live alone. If you lose your money in the house, you will eventually find it. Ms. T.A. brought me a drink as she often did. This time she had me pay for it with a $50.00 dollar bill and keep the change. I was probably some type of whore for her. I was either talking nasty to her about some conquest, or saying what I would do to her. She loved every story I told and we would wind up on the dance floor. She was well over six feet, which presented quite a challenge. I was all equal opportunity when it came to, making the ladies cum on the dance floor. She used to get so excited watching me. Sometimes I didn't even touch her before she was shaking all over her body. I stated with my patented belly roll, which even made the men stop and look. I couldn't always reach the pussy. I had to improvise with my head and my knee. I won't describe what it look like but you could just imagine. Being drug free made me cum free. I stopped charging and I rarely missed an opportunity to discharge. Legs and Tease finally finished their discussion and came over. "Hey what are you two talking about?" Legs asked in a mellow voice. She wasn't about to get pushy with Ms. T.A. "You" replied Ms.T.A. I grabbed both ladies and returned to the dance floor. I wanted my two honeys to make me another sandwich. We hit the dance floor and started doing our thing. The party had started toning down, as morning started its journey from the night. We didn't need an audience as we all got nasty on that dance floor. Clean-up was starting and I didn't want my cake to be destroyed. We had forgot to cut it so we stopped dancing. The remaining guests began to sing happy birthday. It just didn't feel right with so few people left standing. I put the big smile on my face and began to pass out slices. I hid my anger at having to stop my freak to cut a cake. Everyone there was satisfied with their slices. The girls Legs and Tease started packing the food and cake that was left. They also started cleaning up the bar. I assisted under protest until my boss said I should leave. I had to use my car now to get us home. I was hoping that the party would continue at Legs house, where I used to live. It was no simple task leaving with so much stuff. I wanted to have some food to eat at Legs house and I wanted to save my cake. When we got to the block, it felt very strange. I hadn't come thru that front door in over a year. Last night didn't count because no one saw me. Legs let me in and helped with the packages. Tease went right next door to her house, which left me disappointed. Legs was a bit agitated as she searched around her house. She then left hurriedly. I began to take off my clothes and get ready for bed. It was dawn now and light was coming through the windows. I began to wonder, why Legs left and why was it taking her so long. I neatly folded my pants and hung my shirt up in the closet. It was more cluttered than I remembered it. Legs finally walked back in. What she brought with her left me stunned and disappointed. I had heard the rumors that my wife was back out there. I never had any concrete proof. I had even filed a petition against her that summer, claiming she was using drugs. The petition was dropped after she agreed to stop her petition. I watched as Legs started to come out of her clothes. She went into the bathroom and washed up and returned with a small package. Legs placed it on the bed next to me and changed into a short night gown. She didn't bother to put on any panties underneath. Yes I wanted to play with the pussy but the drugs she started pulling out, had me more concerned.

I laid there on the bed with pussy in front of me and desire going out he back. I was a freak no doubt, but drugs made me cringe. Since being separated and living in the streets, I had dove back into that forbidden world. I didn't use right away but I positioned myself to fail. I became a godfather to the young drug dealing thugs. I started out mentoring on how to get the money and maximize their success. I was their driver, look-out, big brother, or friend. It didn't matter as long as they had my back. The young bucks loved their weed and mixed mine with crack. I needed something to keep me sane and numb. I wasn't happy living the way I was, but there was nothing else available. I wanted to be with my family so I slept with the devil to survive. Drugs were always around and soon I was taking advantage of that fact. At first it was in secret but that didn't last. I began accepting crack for payment. Now I needed a mentor so my world flipped. The lower I sung the less respect I received. Now here I was after surviving those times and regaining my self respect, being tempted again. Legs sprawled herself across the bed and began fumbling in a small sandwich bag. "Honey could you roll up this joint? I never could roll weed." I listened to her speak but couldn't believe what I was hearing. I had to play this right, if I wanted to know how deep she was in these drugs. "Sure Baby, hand me the paper." It hurt like hell and I fought back the tears, as I struggled to roll up the weed. "Here baby put some of this in it." Legs had pulled out some white paper that was filled with cocaine. A knot had started to form in my stomach. Legs started looking like thrash to me. Who was this bitch? Now the freak started to wake up as I prepared our

ZEKE SMITH

high. Yes our high because now I was going to turn this bitch out. I thought about all the lies I heard and the rejection I dealt with. I thought about a marriage I put a lot in but got little in return. She was just a hooker to me now. I had brought some of my special mix of alcohol from the bar. It had a aphrodisiac effect on females. It was tried tested and proven to work. I pulled myself a drink as the Devil took possession of my soul. "Here Baby light up the joint while I pour you a drink." My dick began to swell up as she reached over to take the joint. She fell back against the headboard with one leg stretched out. The other leg was bent with her right knee resting in the air. The hem of her short gown had fallen to the crevice near her pussy. I strained to look as I became more turned on thinking about fucking her. Legs began to slur her speech, as she tried to talk about the gap in our lives. I was not feeing sentimental. I wanted some revenge now for the shit I went through in these streets. I never wanted to even move into that neighborhood. I knew it would be a problem because of my past. We had been married seven years plus months, when she put me out. Yes I fucked up but you just quit without even trying to keep it together? I don't think that's what God intended. I watched Legs take a deep drag off the joint and begin to choke. She was looking pitiful now but it wouldn't stop me from cumming. I urged Legs to finish her drink as I took a few pulls off the weed. She had only taken a few sips before she began fumbling with her cocaine. Legs emptied half a cigarette and filled it with cocaine. She had a match book that she used to take some snorts in her nose. This girl was wide open. I began, seeing me engaged in a three-some. The higher she got the more pain I felt. This was a moral dilemma for me until move the drugs aside and reached for the pussy. I took off all my clothes but the tee shirt. I grabbed Legs' ankles and pulled her down to the middle of the bed. She smiled as I reached under that gown and began to massage the pussy. My eyes watered as I thought about the times we had in this room. Such memories don't go away easy. Legs started to slither around the bed as I kept affirm grip on her pussy. It was still soft to the touch but some hairs were graying. I used my free hand to remove that gown. It wasn't covering up much and I wanted to see her butt naked. I continued to work my hand around that pussy. I was so hyped by her movement. My palm was pressed hard against her vulva as my fingers reached out for her ass. Legs started to moan as I tried to swallow her tittie whole. "I miss you Honey but I don't trust you anymore." She was talking but I wasn't listening. The freak was loose and I didn't know when he would leave. I continued my sucking as she responded to my every touch. Yes she missed me but I couldn't stop thinking that it wasn't the dick she was missing. Why do women think we men believe they did without? I know what I left behind. She couldn't resist the drugs, so why should I believe she resisted the dick. Someone had been in there, I just didn't know who. I became more relentless as I assaulted every pleasure point on her body. Legs couldn't stop moaning as my hands began to engulf her wet pussy. I started to pity her, because I knew another man wouldn't treat her as good as I did. Why couldn't she have more patience and allow our differences to work themselves out. I promised to love her forever and I did. I mistreated me because that's who suffered the most. I didn't want to leave but I can't stay where I'm not welcome. I began to slow my movements across her body. She started to squirm like a snake as I stopped for a moment to watch. Look at my Baby enjoying this moment with me. It never had to stop if she had just believed. Just believed that what happened were an accident, and not the beginning of things to come. I returned to her body gentler than when I left. I couldn't hurt that which I loved the most. Legs was weak and I knew that when I married her. Why couldn't I have been stronger? Stronger to resist temptation! Stronger to resist the pain from being left alone often! We stopped going places together for our joint pleasures. I thought we had a baby sitter but that was the evil that brought us apart. There is no sense in reliving that tragedy but I would do things different. I needed to be back with my family. I needed to show God and my wife that it won't happen again. My love making became more passionate as I held her in my arms. I inserted myself inside her. I began slow rhythmic strokes as she held me a little tighter. "Legs I'll love you forever." I meant every word as I continued to whisper in her. "I never meant to hurt you. I want to come home now. I want to be the man you expect me to be. Please Baby just believe and trust God." Legs began to cry as I continued to move in and out of with such gentleness. "Oh I love you to Honey and I don't want to be alone anymore." I believed those words she spoke and began to visualize our lives together again. I wanted her juices to explode against my thrusts, so I began to plunge deeper and faster inside her. Legs dug her nails into my side as she began to release. The tears continued to roll down her cheeks as my streams of cumm gushed inside her. "Don't ever send me away again Baby please don't ever send me away." It was my turn to cry as I held her tight and collapsed on top of her. The room was silent as the sun shone bright thru the windows. The only music playing was in our hearts as we pledged to try love again. We both fell into a deep sleep as the cares of the world seemed so far away.

ZEKE SMITH

I awakened to the escaping sunlight coming thru the windows. It was early evening and I was well rested. It had been years since felling asleep with a woman. I felt like a whore's john waking up expecting to leave a tip on the dresser. Legs didn't budge as she was experiencing the crash after a long coke binge. I went and took a long hot shower thinking of the glory years of the marriage. I wondered to myself if this would be the final make-up? Legs had done this before only to have a change of heart. She was the only who understood the reasons. I was going to have faith after all this was my birthday. I buried my mother three yeas ago on this day. It was time I had something more joyful to connect the date with. In fact this was the first time I even celebrated my birthday, since the funeral. I tried again to wake up Legs but she didn't budge. I was dressed and ready to go. I gathered my belongings and cut a big slice of the birthday cake, we brought back from the party. I put the night lock on the door and left. I stepped out onto the street feeling a bit embarrassed, knowing other men had done the same.

I had trouble getting the car to start. It had been giving me trouble lately and mechanics just took advantage of me. I was a pretty smart guy but I wasn't smart enough to learn about cars. I couldn't complain though because this car had been my life line when I was homeless. Many nights and days this was the only shelter I had. I remember parking far enough not to be seen, but close enough to see what I was missing. It was very painful spying on my family, always dreaming of a reunion. It wasn't just the pussy I was missing but also the companionship. Legs had finally become my best friend. We were able to share our struggles in life. We started thinking more about our future when our daughter was grown and on her on. I loved to cuddle and Legs were an excellent cushion. What the hell was I thinking to let the Devil slip into my thinking, with the aim of destroying me? I had good intentions but I let my feelings of loneliness overtake me. I lowered my guards for a second because the moment was feeling good. I was supposed to know better. I allowed myself to be manipulated and fall victim to my own lust. I immediately felt remorse and expressed it but it wasn't enough. People wanted blood and they got it. That one weak moment cost me everything I had worked so hard to build. I confessed my sins to god and my wife. Only God forgave me. My wife took that opportunity to go solo. My honesty was repaid with her own betrayal. Instead of supporting me and helping me get through the turmoil, she went to the other side. She would regret it one day but the damage was done. Her single act was more devastating to us than anything I did. I was stripped of my dignity and placed in the company of animals. I was repulsed by the course I had to take. Still I accepted it because it was by my actions. I dealt with what the system through at me. My momma made me strong and in her memory I would survive. The details are not as important as the results. I see no need in retelling that story to cause more pain. I'm not the only person that had to heal. We live in a world now where so many of the values that make us decent have disappeared. RRRRR VAROOM! My daydreaming and reflecting has been interrupted by the starting of the engine. I thought I would never get this car started. I pulled out of my spot and made my way back to the bar. I saw them cleaning up when we left. I still knew that something would be left for me to do. I wondered how my boss felt about me staying out all night. He wasn't used to me not being there. He even stopped putting the alarm on since I started living in the back. Night fall was creeping up on the neighborhood. Even though I slept most of the day, I was still feeling very tired. It was probably the come down from the cocaine. Against my better judgment I had engaged because of the sex. Now I had to deal with the aftermath and hope it doesn't bring me back down. There was plenty of parking as usual for a Sunday evening. I pulled into my spot in front of the bar and proceeded inside. The place was locked up but my boss had left the alarm off. I used my key to come in through the side door to my back apartment. I was feeling horny wondered if any of my local girls were out and about. I always could get some good rates on Sunday because traffic was slow. Sometimes I felt like I was taking advantage of them but those feelings quickly passed. Once inside I realized that I couldn't go any further. My boss had locked the other door so I was confined to my back apartment. I wouldn't be watching any porn on the wide screen T.V., unless he decided to come by later on. It was no guarantee that he would open up after such a successful party. I settled myself down and made sure the garbage outside was stacked neat. I stood outside for awhile, hoping I would see Bare Ass. Bare was my most trusted female on the track. She took care of me like I was family and I did the same. She had a petite body with extra meat. Her look was a bit different but cute just the same. She was so agreeable to my sickness and never tried to expose me. I felt safe with her and she felt safe with me. Bare Ass was realistic in her price. Still I usually found reasons to tip her anyway. I can recall the first time I met Bare Ass. I used to watch all the girls walk past the Bar. I never tried to have any conversations but I did say hello. It didn't matter what they did for a living, I spoke to all. Sometimes the Boss and I would be out there together saying hello. This particular night it was raining and money was slow on the strip. The police was busy with their chasing and most of the girls called it a night. Bare Ass was out there having some success but needed a break from the rain. She asked if she could my bathroom. I told her yes if it remained our secret. I ran inside first and made sure there were no security concerns before I let her in. This was an off night, so the Boss wouldn't be stopping by. I let her inside and she raced to the back as I directed her to the bathroom. I made her keep the door open because of all my personal items inside. I also wanted to watch, as my dick swelled just at the thought of her being here. She let out a sigh of relief as she sat down and started to piss. The urine leaving her splashed hard inside the commode. She had her ass raised in the air to avoid contact with the toilet seat. What I sexy sight she was as her skirt was tucked in arms in front of her. I had to go in and show her where the tissue was. She was not embarrassed or ashamed as I leaned over to see the back of her ass. "You are so nasty! What's that bulge in your pocket? You got a gun?" Bare Ass had a voice like a little girl, but she was every bit a woman. I noticed when she finished pissing, that there were no panties to pull up. She wiped her ass and pussy and let the skirt fall back into place. She kept staring at my pocket as if she really wanted to know what was inside. "Come closer so you can see what's in my pocket. Here put your hand in there and pull it out." Bare Ass reached inside my pocket but it was empty. Instead of pulling something out her hand stayed inside playing with my dick. "Damn this shit is hard. Can I take a hit while I'm back here?" I wanted to say no but she was doing such a good job of keeping the dick hard. "Sure but I'll put your ass out quick if you start acting stupid. You also have to wash that pussy first. I want to have something to do while you're smoking." She looked up at me with a warm smile on her face. She seemed relieved that she didn't have to rush back out in that weather. "I don't mind you playing with my pussy, just don't stick your fingers inside." Bare Ass had some smarts and boundaries when it came to her body. Dirty fingers did more to contaminate a pussy than a dirty dick. She took off her skirt and was naked from the waist down. I was sorry my video wasn't set up. I would have loved to have this moment on film. I asked her to use a lot of lather to make sure the pussy was real clean. Bare Ass acted like she enjoyed me giving her instructions. She began to rinse the soap off her. She arched her back as she wiped her lower lips clean. I stepped inside the bathroom and took the rag from her hand. She stared straight into my eyes as she wondered what I was about to do. It had been so long since I had any pussy. It was even longer since I was in private space with a naked pussy. I took the rag and finish wiping the suds from her body. I threw the rag in the sink and began to stroke her body. I told her how soft her body was and she pulled me closer to her. I think at that moment she sensed my loneliness. She began rubbing her nakedness up against me. She put her arms under mine, and placed the palms of hands on my shoulder blades. I did the same to her but my reach was long enough to caress her neck. I lowered my and softly kissed her cheeks. She responded by pumping her body hard against mine. My dick began to swell to an unbelievable length. It was trying to escape the confines of my pants. The head became tender, as it began to pulse against her thrusts. "Bare Ass, are you trying to make me cum?" "No!" She replied. "I'm trying to make me cum. I like how this hard ass dick feels against my pussy. Come on Man grind with me." She was becoming very bossy as she struggled to have an orgasm. I took my hands off her neck and grabbed a chunk of her ass. I was going to help her reach her goal. I started banging my body against her as I reposition dick inside my pants. I stuck my right leg in between hers. I raised her up by the ass and placed her on top of my dick, as it lay along on my right thigh. It was my turn to move and move I did. I kept her pussy pressed tight on my thigh as I pumped my pelvis against her. She rapped her arms around me to seal our bodies tight against each other. "Oh yeah that's it. Oh yeah that's it. Please don't stop. Ah shit yeah, please keep going. My pussy is getting so wet. I'm getting close. That's it right there. Keep your dick right there. Ohhhhhhh! Oooooooo! Ahhhhhhhh! Emmm oh damn that was nice. Thank you so much. Shit I don't even know your name." "Call me Zee, but don't speak to me when the boss Ruby is here." I had to make that plain. Ruby was no fool. I didn't need him thinking that I was walking on the dark side. I look down at the front of my pants. Her juices had run all over me. She slid her body off me and went to her bag. She pulled out her tools and a small capsule. She took her time as she emptied the contents of the capsule, into a long glass tube. She raised the glass in the air. She put a flame from a lighter to the top of it. She waited a brief moment before inhaling deeply. The little white rocks she placed in the glass began to crackle. She continued to inhale and then abruptly stopped. Her cheeks puffed up as she began to slowly exhale. She trembled as she reached out for me to take the glass. I thought for a moment how a hit would make me react. Could I risk exposing myself to this hooker? I chose not to and waved it off. The smoke filled the room and I began to spray Lysol to mask the smell. I looked at this beautiful young woman that had so much potential. I enjoyed every minute with her and wanted to play some more. I had to start her dressing as she fired up the

ZEKE SMITH

glass one more time. They all say it's alright and nothing to worry about. The truth is even they don't know how they might react, after sucking on that glass dick. I rubbed on the pussy some more as she finished off her drugs. I followed her instructions and didn't put any fingers inside. The pussy was so soft and warm to the touch. Her juices had a silky feel to it. I wished she hadn't taken that hit. I wished even more that she hadn't offered any to me. It was time for me to let her out but I knew she would be back. They always came back because I treated them with so much respect. I knew it was the drugs that made them different. I knew without the drugs I couldn't play as much. One day the world would be healed, but that day wasn't it. That's my memory of the first time meeting Ms. Bare Ass.

I kept playing with the garbage to justify still standing out here. It looks like Bare Ass won't be coming today. Just as well though. Look who's pulling up! I looked quickly up the block to make sure Bare Ass wasn't coming. I didn't need any suspicions falling on me now. The boss knew I was a freak. Hell, he helped bring it out into the open. Sometimes I felt like some sex slave with all the shit he had me do to different woman. He loved to watch because my dick would get so hard and his couldn't. He wasn't gay, nowhere close. He was just a freak that couldn't get it up anymore but still love to be around pussy. The easiest way to get him to come out his pocket was to present some sick sexual fantasy that I could play out in front of him. He knew I was still celebrating my birthday. Plus I knew he wanted to hear about my sexual escapades. Yes, he was still freaky even though he couldn't get it up.

"Boss! What's up? What brings you to the neighborhood? You came to give me my gift?" Ruby looked at me out of the corner of his eye. Sunday was payday so I had money coming anyway. I was looking forward to the double bonus. I wanted to get hit off for the party and the extra for my birthday. Ruby hated to give up that money. I bet if you cut his heart out you would find fifty dollar bills and female pubic hair. Money and pussy was his greatest loves and gambling is the route he took to get it. "Come on counselor you know I got some money for you so stop the bullshit! Let me get this gate up and unlock this door. What you gonna do tonight? You staying here or going back to your wife's house?" When he said that, I thought for a moment about returning. Then I thought about the drugs and the men she had when I wasn't there. "Nah Boss, I'm staying here tonight. I'm in no hurry to start playing house again. You my future Ruby, I'm not trying to leave you." Ruby looked at me with his little boy grin and started talking. "Counselor, your breath is stinking with all that bullshit you talking. You know you miss that woman and probably wanna be there now? I don't care what you do just let me know. I don't want you leaving without the alarm being on. I also want to make sure all the right doors are locked." Ruby was right I did miss that bitch and want it to be with her right now. I could never tell Ruby about the drugs. He knew first hand about the ordeals I would go through. Ruby's main other woman loved that cocaine and that's the only time he tolerated it. She had been with him through some hard times but wasn't a good enough earner to be number one. She also loved to play with that dick and had patience to wait for it to grow. It took the longest for ruby's dick to get hard. That's why he kept me around so much. I used to stand in with my massive erection while his tried to catch up. The girls didn't mind because he always had some paper for them when it was over. There also were those times when I broke in the potential hookers and strippers for the after hours. These were the times when me and ruby really bonded. This taught me not to take my dick for granted because one day I would struggle just like Ruby. Ruby was finishing up counting the till and I was done cleaning off the tables they missed earlier. I had started sweeping the floor when Ruby called me. "Here Counselor don't fuck up, I know it's your birthday." In spite of everything we did and didn't do, we had grown to really care about each other. We both were too manly to talk about it. Ruby and everyone else in this area called me counselor because of my profession. I let the name stick so that I never had to reveal my real name. I began to count the knot he just gave me. Damn it was much more than I expected. He really did care about me or had made a stupid sum of money last night. Ruby said his goodbyes after we had one drink together. I walked with him to the front door. I heard him pulling down the gate as I walked back to the bar. I wanted to pour myself one more before I started searching for a porn tape. I loved watching porn on the big wide screen. We had plenty of chocolate to look at. It was almost like they were right there with you. I had to much money to trick. I threw my covers on the pool table. I made it ready for sleeping before I got too tired. I went for the baby oil from behind the counter as a fat ass flashed across the screen. The movie was about to start and I wanted to get me a nut quick. I made the dick slick and it shined in the dim light. I started seeing nothing but ass and pussy on the screen. They were all new to me and I worked my dick like I was fucking a bunch of virgins. It wasn't long before I came and my juices shot across the floor. I was tired now. I switched the DVD off and let the T.V. play. I was sleep before I knew what hit me.

ZEKE SMITH

Oh my back, I need more cushion this. I didn't know what time it was but it looked like the news was on. I was waking up from a deep sleep. My back was hurting. I was afraid I might catch a cramp, if I moved the wrong way. I focused more on the television as I watched a movie about a plan crash. I got up and took a piss. When I came back they were showing this crash again. I turned the volume up and learnt this wasn't any movie. A large jet had crashed into the World Trade Center and a traffic copter had captured it all on tape. Smoke was billowing out the side of the building as some people started jumping out the windows from very high up. Oh my God I couldn't believe what was happening. I immediately called Legs to tell her what was happening. She answered the phone quickly only to tell me what she was hearing and seeing from downtown Brooklyn. We continued to talk and right there before my eyes another jumbo jet crash into the building. "Oh my God Legs, this is no accident we're under attack." The newsman reporting the story was in shock as pandemonium was breaking out in the city. You could see large columns of smoke billowing up from Brooklyn. All you could hear was fire engine sirens all over the place. I stayed glued to the TV. unable to move. Tears began to stream down my face as I thought about the horror of what I was witnessing. You could see some people on the TV screen jumping from the windows. Then like the sound of a freight train rushing by, one of the towers began to collapse. It happened just as the newsman questioned the possibility. A giant cloud of dust rushed toward the TV screen as the camera man was obliterated. I began to cry uncontrollably as people emerged from the dust cloud almost unrecognizable as human. I had to hang up on Legs as news of the tower collapse spread across the city. In an instant they began to suspect the jailed Arab from the earlier World Trade Center bombing. I thought about the subway system as the authorities began to isolate the city. Power was shut off in subways and traffic into the city was halted. I sat watching all this unfold before me and I wanted to do something. I thought about driving to the city to help out. I wanted to witness more of the events up close. I reasoned I could even drive downtown and walk across the bridge. I called Legs back but couldn't get through. There were no signal the circuits were jammed. Everybody and their momma were trying to make a call. The city was in shock and as reality set in they began to turn their attentions towards the Arabs. I finally stepped outside to check on the climate of the neighborhood. The Arab store on the corner had pulled their shutters down. The one across the street had done the same thing. I would later learn that this was being repeated all over the hood. Stores that we believed to be Spanish were actually Arabs. When night fall came the all night stores were also closed. What had happened in America? What had happened in the hood? It came to everyone's awareness that the bodega was gone and the Arabs had implanted themselves in the hood. If it happened here, then at what other levels was it happening? The young boys were ready to tear something up. Money was short in the street unless you had a package to sling. Take that look off your face. You know what package and slinging means. Its all drug related. These all night grocery stores also provided some cover for the users and the dealers. It was a delicate balance that was now interrupted by the collapse of the Towers. The after midnight commerce of the city was in a panic like everything else. The mayor might have been taking care of Manhattan, but the folks in the outer boroughs were on their own. I went back inside because there was nothing I could do. I began to check the numbers in my phone. If this was the beginning of the end, then I wanted some pussy over here with me. I did not want to leave this world with a soft dick. I called one of the dancers we had auditioned. I had my fun with her but Ruby paid for it. There was no Ruby here now to pick up the bill. I would be on my own this time. The phone continued to ring until the voice mail kicked in. "Hi this is Delicious, I'm busy now but leave a message and you could be next." The voice was so tantalizing I wished I could play it over until I came. I left a brief massage wondering if I would get the same attention as my boss. I tried another number only to be told that they were in for the night but should check with them tomorrow. This wasn't working out. I became agitated at not being able to find a cheap thrill. I called Legs again and discovered she had made it home after walking most of the way. She told of the horror that took place in Manhattan. Legs was excited as she talked about people coming from the city covered in soot. Cab drivers were charging crazy rates as they took advantage of the situation. She told me how someone let her ride in their cab when she was halfway home. I wanted to go to her but was more concerned with making some more money. I decided to try a local gambling spot with some of the money I had. If things went good I would start my hunt for some pussy again.

The place was bustling with activity. It was hard to tell that money was short in the streets with so much of it floating around in here. I slid out one of the small bankrolls in my pocket and started betting. My luck was good as I won my first three bets. I started doubling up on what I put down and continued to be blessed by the dice gods. The money started to pile up quickly as I began to hide my winnings in different pockets. Now people started to notice me as they tried to cash in on my luck. One thing I hated was for someone else to bet with me. If the gods were blessing me, I didn't want someone else's bad luck to affect me. I started to make some enemies as I refused to let others put their money with mine. It was time for me to leave while the getting was good. I sent someone to the store with a five dollar bill as other people placed orders. I then faked a move to the bathroom and snuck out the door. This was a regular maneuver of mine to keep the stick-up men off guard. I was amazed that no one had ever caught on, with me doing it so many times before. You had to time it right when everybody was more focused on money than the winners. I made my way back to the bar to stash my earnings. There were so many places to hide money that you just had to remember where you put it. I had more money to trick with so I made another phone call. This time I hit pay dirt but decided to pop in on Legs instead. Legs was happy to hear my voice and wondered if I could bring some drugs with me. When I asked if she was horny and ready to let me play with it, she responded yes. I told her to get it cleaned up and I would be there in a hour. I didn't like buying drugs in the area. There was one guy I could cop some powder cocaine from but he had to swear to secrecy. He was a regular customer at the bar and a friend of the Boss. I took the short walk to his place and he was happy for the sale. Things were slow in the street with all the excitement from the Twin Towers collapsing. The best I could negotiate cost me fifty dollars. It was alright because I was almost five hundred ahead from my trip to the gambling spot. I made it a point not to count my money until I left. That's why I hid so much in different pockets. I stayed with Chico the dealer long enough to drink a beer. It took him almost twenty minutes to come outside. If I took my time driving, I should arrive within the hour I told Legs.

I found a parking spot close to the front door. I rang the bell and an excited Legs came to the door. She was wearing a robe saying, she's getting ready to take a shower. I was upset at first because I didn't have a lot of time to spend here. The alarms weren't on at the bar and Ruby might double back. I gave myself two hours tops, to play with the pussy before I turned back into a pumpkin.

I entered the house feeling different than I did on my birthday. This was more of an invite than a chance encounter. There would be expectations this time. This time would be the start of something more long lasting. I wanted my home back but it wasn't in the same shape that I left it. Legs had become very adventurous. She wasn't my prized possession but there was more love now than before. I could see from the looks of things that life had been hard without me. Things weren't in place like I kept it. Legs wasn't in place like I kept her. She had lost a lot of weight and her face was even thinner. She smiled a lot but I could sense some pain behind it. I had back my own tears and just visualized her as the Queen that I knew. She was so caught up in the drug scene. Her new best friend was a cocaine addict and saw nothing wrong with it. I didn't come here to judge or to try and fix anything. I wanted to get my freak on as the rest of the city worried about the next terrorist attack. I sat down at the dining room table as Legs went into the bathroom. I pulled out the drugs as Legs quickly returned with some weed. She instructed me on making some cocaine cigarettes and also to lace some joints with the blow. She once again disappeared into the bathroom as I started to hear the shower water run. What I had was top shelf. If she was going to do drugs, I made sure it was the best I could purchase. I sat there at the table going through the motions I went through for so many others. Now I found myself doing for my wife. I never figured our life together would ever come to this. Still here I was preparing the drugs and thinking about the pussy. My friend Ruby didn't want me talking about God or Jesus around him. That didn't stop me from keeping Jesus on my mind. I wanted to pull away from that table and just disappear. I wanted to plead a case to Legs so that we all could just start over. I never considered leaving New York or Brooklyn for that matter. My sisters and all the friends I knew were here. I wasn't rich yet. I didn't have enough money to give up on this town yet. I had left here so many times before broke and on the run. I made a commitment to myself not to ever leave again as a failure. I went back to rolling up the joints and crushing up the cocaine rocks that I had. I wanted to cook this up and really give her something to get high. I was thinking so deviously and wondered how much I still loved her. It was so pitiful seeing her as the cocaine lady. That's what she had become. I still had to know how deep she was into this. I was tempted to go into the bathroom but was too busy rigging up the drugs. I made some strong coke cigarettes and began smoking one before she emerged. Now the freak was beginning to come out of me with the cocaine taking its effect. Legs came out naked with nothing but a robe covering her up. Z Baby was sleep in the back. I made sure the doors were closed in case she awakens unexpected. Legs weren't close to the size I knew. She was so small my eyes watered when I stared at her. Sometimes I think she sensed how hurt I was seeing this. I knew it had to be painful for her too. I made it all easier for her now by joining in. My own sickness had been activated now so her pain stopped being an issue for me. I had brought along a special cocktail mix that she had at the party. This was going to be a night we both remember.

Legs sat down at the table with her bathrobe hanging loosely from her body. I passed the coke laced cigarette to her that I was smoking. "Whew this is strong" she said, as she inhaled deeply. She then got up from the table and went into the back. When she returned, she placed a bag of weed on the table and a bottle of lotion. Legs continued to the cigarette until nothing was left. She mashed the butt into the ash tray and began rubbing some lotion in hands. She motioned for me to roll a joint as she rose up from her seat. Legs loosen up the robe's belt and let the bathrobe fall from her body. Her skin was taunt but free of blemishes. Her belly was flat and her thighs had some small dimples. She still had her curves but the pussy wasn't as attractive as I remembered it. The lips looked swollen because of the weight she had lost. She tried to smile as she applied the lotion to her body. She was trying to entice me with her nakedness but I was repulsed. I hid my displeasure and began to encourage her on. "That's my Nubian Queen make that body glow for your King." I gave her some blow to sniff when she finished rubbing lotion between her thighs. She dipped her head down for me to feed it to her as she reached for the joint I had just rolled. I began to feel real sick inside about what I was doing. I couldn't stop though because a part of me wanted some revenge, for all those months I had to live out of my car. I choked back the tears and continued to role play. I was imitating the guy that didn't give a fuck about this person in front of me. I was acting like she never gave birth to my daughter. I gave a good performance of the man that would dog her tonight and not feel any pain. I watched as she wet her finger tips and dip them in the small mound of coke on the table. She rubbed the blow across her lips and went back to the lotion. I lit another cocaine cigarette and dipped my own fingers into the coke. I stuck it in my mouth and dropped to my knees. I handed Legs the cigarette and told her to stop with the lotion. She immediately obeyed and started smoking. My tongue was numb and so was my mind. I motioned for Legs to put one foot on the chair while she stood up. This position gave me easy access to those swollen lips. I began to suck on her as she begged me to stop. I loosen my pants as I continued to make her pussy wet. I was living dangerously now and didn't care. I began to feel like no matter what the circumstances we should always be together. If this was me strung out I wouldn't have an audience. But this wasn't me and I wanted her to be comfortable doing what she wanted to do. It didn't matter to me if it would kill us both as long as we were together. Loving her for ever was my pledge and that had not changed. I rose to my feet because the pain in my knee became unbearable. I had no cushion underneath them just a hard floor. I looked at the top of the table and began to push things to the side. Legs had become excited from my assault on her love boat. I wanted to take her to another level. I continued to clear off the table. It didn't take long because there was not a lot to move. She looked puzzled at my activity. She reached for the cocaine and took another hit before I lifted her into the air and planted her on top of the table. I began sucking her titties before she could react. I remove a cushion from the chairs around us and placed it under her head. I gently pulled her to the edge of the table as she lay across it. It was a perfect alignment as her legs stayed propped up in the air. I put both her feet on either side of my shoulders. Her pussy was still wet from my licking. She took one last sniff before putting the cocaine down next to her side. I wrapped my right hand around my cock with only the head of it exposed. I began to tease the pussy by rubbing my head along the outside of her lower lips. She lay back on the pillow and closed her eyes. I reached for another seat cushion and placed it under her at the edge of the table. I was ready now to start my attack. I began to force my cock inside her. Easy she cried as I continued to push forward. She was well lubricated and some juices began to flow down her butt cheeks. I was encouraged now as she lay helplessly before me. I started my thrusts and she remained silent. I picked up the pace as my member became rock hard. Emmm it felt so good being inside her right now. All the love I had for her began to return. I looked down upon her as my cock went in and out of her leaking boat. My belly moved like an ocean wave as I rocked back and forth to a melody of my own. Ooooo she hissed as I thought about good times gone badly. I wanted to be back in her life but I feared for my own. Drugs had devastated me and the people around me. It was bad enough that I was medicating myself again just to cope. Now I was poised to be a more regular user in order to be with my wife. Oh the pussy was still good even with the weight loss. I forgot about the job I should be returning to and just kept pounding the pussy. Legs just took everything I had to offer with clenched fists. She liked it as her body started its first wave of spasms. On and on I went as her eyes opened and she grimaced with delight. "Whose pussy is this?" I asked as I continued to touch bottom again and again. "Yours Honey . . ." "Whose?" "Yours Honey I saiddddd Ah ah ahhhhh." Legs began a new round of shaking as she experienced repeat orgasms back to back. I was tender but the cocaine in my system had me pushing forward. The pillow beneath her ass was wet with the juices of love. I held her thighs like the handle bars on

ZEKE SMITH

a bicycle trying to reach a climax of my own. "Talk to me Baby tell me how good my dick feels in you." I wanted to cum but it was stalling. I needed some help and hearing her talk nasty to me just might do it. I wanted her to be a whore right now, my whore. "Come on I said tell me how it feels." "Oh see your dick feels good inside me." She paused for a moment and began speaking again as my thrusts became faster and deeper. "Oh shit Zee keep, fucking me like that. Your dick feels so good. Come on Honey for me I'm getting sore. Ahhhhhh I'm gonna cumm again Zee. Plezz cum with me Honey?" Damn it felt crazy listening to her. I had to block out the pain from her obedience but I was ready to now. "Emmmmm OHHH Yeahhhh I'm gonna get it all out Baby." My body stiffened and jerked as I released all I had in me. I flooded her insides with my thick cream as her juices mixed with mine. I slowed my thrusts as I enjoyed the heat generated from our combined passion. It was a silky mix that began to ooze out when I pulled out of her boat. The pillow beneath her ass was soaked with cumm. The pillow under her head was wet from the sweat pouring from her body. The effect of the drugs had worn off. I took my hand and smeared the cumm all around her pussy and she squealed with joy. I was back in the house but for how long. It was apparent to me that there was a lot of neglect. Things were not taken care of as well since my absence. Legs enjoyed my presence but would she submit to my rule. I didn't recognize this woman lying in front of me. I couldn't stop loving her no matter what she had become. I knew if the drugs disappeared, the woman I knew would return. She stared at me as if wondering what I was thinking. I could never tell her what truly was on my mind. I would have to fake acceptance of her activities until I figured out how to stop them. This would not be easy because sending her to treatment was not an option. It was hard enough for her the first time around. Legs' pride and her embarrassment at failure would not allow her to reveal how bad things had become. I would hang in there but was just as concerned for my own recovery. My child would be the motivation for me. Would it also be enough for Legs?

I finish washing off quickly and returned to the bar. I made up a story to explain my prolonged absence. Ruby was not happy but he didn't press me for more than what I was giving him. It was a small crowd in the bar now and closing time was near. I gathered up the garbage and empty bottles. I had taught my boss the value of saving the beer bottles. He could gauge his sell volume and also use the money from the returns toward the next purchases. I made it my responsibility to dump the garbage. I would drive around until I found someone else's heap to put it with. This increased my value to the business and it gave me a chance to scout for whores. I returned to the bar with Ruby waiting. "Are you staying here tonight?" He asked to determine if the alarms had to be set. "Yes was my response because I couldn't afford to lose this source of income. I also needed my own place because I was not ready to trust Legs by moving in. This was the beginning of the weekend and busiest time for us. I needed some rest any way and time to detoxify from the pussy and the drugs. I watched as Ruby drove off wondering if he knew the mischief I had gotten into. I went inside and made my palette on top of the pool table. I had the couch in the back but still didn't trust sleeping there. It was a lot of rat activity here and the elevation of the pool table offered more protection. I slept well that night pondering the rapid changes that were taking place again in my life.

I awoke early and began planning my day. I had no intentions of seeing Legs. It was time to focus on my bills and hope the dice table would be good to me. It wasn't long before the bell rang and Saturday morning customers began coming for their fix. The business had increased with me living here. I could open earlier than Ruby did before which caused an increase in revenue. I knew my presence here wasn't charity because I was bringing in extra money. I made a difference during business hours and after hours. Everyone also enjoyed my dirty dancing and the jokes I told while partying. Sometimes I felt so dirty because of what I had to do. I also had to give false alibis whenever Ruby got caught up in his own activities. It was the best I could do right now so I put God on a shelf and made a living. I knew this wasn't something I would retire from with a pension. I also knew that nothing lasts forever. The Lord would have to understand and be patient with me. This kept me from engaging in activities much worse. There was some prestige involved with my current position. I was developing a new following.

The evening was fast approaching and Ruby was still a no show. I continued to clean and get the place ready to open. He had not returned any of my phone calls. I figured he was either sleep or playing cards somewhere. I had not heard from Legs since last night. I wasn't missing her but just wondered if she was okay. I couldn't let myself become so concerned that I forgot about my own survival. It was always easy for me to get lost in love. I made all kinds of excuses when my behavior would change. The truth is that being in love with someone always felt good to me. It didn't matter if they loved me or not. It never took a lot to satisfy me. I was considered very low maintenance. Ah I began hearing noises coming from the bar. The boss had arrived. Ruby walked in and immediately started taking inventory of the stock. He was running late so he had to play catch up. He quickly drew up a list for me to go pick up. I had moved way up on the ladder of trust. It was no simple task with Ruby being cautious and paranoid. I gathered up the returns and headed for the distributor. I drove the van because of the amount of supplies I had to pick up. I called in the order as I headed out. I swung by Legs faking a bathroom trip, to show the juice I had with my boss. I also wanted to check on her and the house. I found myself making more of these trips as time went on. I got back to the bar to find Ruby playing cards with a regular. This guy was his best friend that he beat so often, the guy should have moved in. I could never quite understand their relationship. Sometimes they would argue and fight like a married couple. They both were used to me being around and I made sure they weren't disturbed while playing. I would keep the change on store trips. Other than that my babysitting was included in my weekly pay.

The weekend came and went not much different than the last. In the middle of next week I learned of some issues Legs was dealing with that also concerned me. She received an eviction notice from a new landlord. It seems the old landlord lost the building in court due to a lien on the property. He ignored a contractor's bill and the court dates when he was subpoenaed. He lost the judgment and she had a court date for the new owners. Legs had already paid money that month to the old landlord. He no longer owned the building but was still trying to collect money. I returned to the scene and stopped all of that. I entered into dialogue with the new owners and negotiated a settlement that Legs was satisfied with. She thought she could get rich off this situation but it wasn't that type of case. The other problem was someone made a complaint against her for child abuse. The complaint was taken serious and a home visit was scheduled. I had to be present to help make that go away. We were becoming friends again with me doing all the giving. I continued to pop in and out during the late night hours. I would have Z Baby with me after school until Legs came home. She had lost her babysitter so I became likely replacement. Ruby gave me high marks for the attention I gave my daughter. He couldn't understand though the attention I gave her mother. He knew all the details of the break ups and the other evictions after the make ups. She was still my wife and my child loved her mother. I refused to let her fail in the eyes of Z Baby. I kept things in place without moving in. I began to drop off diet supplements to help Legs bring her weight up. She had lost so much weight that she stopped being attractive. I even hunted a guy down one night on her say so. She was mistaken for a crack head while she had Z Baby with her. Legs was devastated that night. Only pity had me searching for the person that had robbed her of some dignity. Things were great at the bar. I became more involved with my adult entertainment. There was more sex than I could handle. I put on shows after hours and the list grew long for people wanting to stay. I felt no shame with the sanity that was going on at home. Yes it was still home to me. My daughter was the difference that kept me from walking completely away. I had to stick it out regardless of the pain it was causing me. They were still making it to church most Sundays so there was hope. My daughter's birthday was coming up and a party at the house was planned. The birthday party would be the event to let me know how sick Legs had become.

Z Baby was so excited about her upcoming birthday party. She kept asking me if I would be there. I assured her that nothing would keep me away. Z Baby was still the center of my life. I hustled hard to keep money flowing to maintain us both. Even when things weren't good between her mother and me, I stayed faithful to Z Baby. I gave Legs some money for the preparations. I also delivered the cake to Z Baby's class for the school celebration. The actual party would take place on Saturday. I was being the man of the house more and more without having a key. I had help settle the complaint against her for BCW. Z Baby's school records didn't indicate any mal treatment at home. We had court dates scheduled to deal with the pending eviction. I was doing a lot of commuting between the bar and the house. I had also started picking Z Baby up from school so she wouldn't be home alone. Legs had been letting her stay by herself but I stopped that. It was also risky with the complaint still fresh in the system.

The day of the party was here and legs assured me that everything was in place. I don't recall what gift I bought but I did attend. When I came thru the door there was a lot of activity. Z Baby had let me in because the downstairs door was unlocked. I recognized some of the children from our church and the upstairs neighbor. I kept looking but still had not seen Legs. Z Baby pointed to the bedroom and I entered without knocking. I was in shock when I saw Legs and Tease smoking a blunt with incense burning. "Legs what is wrong with you?" I shouted. "Are you crazy or something with those children out front? Especially with Z Baby's friends from the church!" Legs had a look of indifference on her face and began to defend her actions. "I have the door closed Honey and we have incense burning." When she finished talking, her friend chimed in. "I smoke in front of my son and it doesn't bother him." I stared at both of these two assholes and wonder what else was going on here. I went back out front and took some pictures. I kept a smile on my face as I entertained the children with my antics. Legs finally entered the room looking dazed and stupid. I hooked my little girl and left. I don't recall saying good bye to anyone but the children. I was heated when I got back in my car and took off. How life take such a bad turn when everything seemed to be getting better. The situation was worse than I thought. I had to come up with a plan that would pull my marriage back together.

I called Legs later that night. She wanted to take Z Baby to the city the next day as a birthday gift. She was apologetic about her actions and said I was right to be outraged. I agreed to go with them and would also be driving. This would be our first venture into the city since "9/11". I made the extra effort to secure some funds and had my boss Ruby chip in to help. I didn't do any gambling that night but I did dance. I wasn't in the mood for after hour activities. I wanted a clean mind when I took my daughter out.

There was a chill in the air when I arrived at the house to pick up Legs and Z Baby. Legs couldn't look me in the eyes and didn't want to talk about the party. We planned to have dinner at Olive Garden after playing games at a large arcade. Z Baby was so excited. I made sure there was enough money for her to have fun. We had decided to split the expenses. It was no simple matter driving in the city. There were many areas that were barred to traffic. I had to park at a garage that was a great distance from our destination. We took a slow walk and posed for pictures with the many firefighters and police that were around. I told everyone I talked to, it was my daughter's birthday. Legs was moody the whole time but it didn't spoil our fun. Legs could never accept being wrong or humiliated. It didn't matter that she was the cause of it! I would always be accused of being self righteous if I brought something to her attention. I blocked out her behavior for the moment and continued to enjoy the outing. Z Baby kept a smile on her face the whole time while she played games until she was tired. We ate at Oliver Garden and had them sing "Happy Birthday "to Z Baby. Legs attitude changed a little to the better but not enough to satisfy me. I paid the bills with only a small donation from Legs. I didn't want her complaining later about money and I wanted to be the man. I took them back home and refused to spend the night. I wanted to be back in the comfort of my own home. The important thing was that Z Baby had a birthday to remember.

Monday morning came and I did what I normally do. Clean and sleep with some cable T.V. thrown in for variety. During the daylight hours usually in the afternoon, I was available as a taxi. I didn't discriminate as long as you weren't a total stranger. I became transportation for most of the local hustlers because I was dependable and trustworthy. Yes even in the underworld a man's character defined who he was. The days continued to come and go with one not much different than the other. I found myself struggling again with my addiction. Those playful evenings with my wife were taking their toll. The week nights at the bar were filled with adventure as I called for the ladies of the night. I was starting to become unglued but only I knew it. My boss began to question the change in my demeanor. I blamed it on the added stress of trying to save my wife. I had to trust him with the information of her drug use. I knew this was risky because my own behavior would also be suspect. Thursday night started our weekends off with karaoke. Business was good and my presentation had to be correct. I always liked to sing so Karaoke Night returned some normalcy to my life. On a good night I was able to have regular sex with a decent person. I started to check on Legs more regularly after the bar closed. I would arrange to make my garbage drops after the boss left. This gave me a better opportunity to swing by the house. Legs had given me a key after I got her an advance from the new landlords. We were able to live rent free for the rest of the year. We would then receive another $2,500 after we left in January of 2002. Legs had assured me that there would be no more separations as we tried hard to like each other again. Most nights I when I dropped by Legs would be caught up in the drugs. It was a pitiful sight to watch her fumble around trying to mask what she had been doing. I found myself scolding her like a child. I reminded her about the holidays coming up and our need to start packing. There were things we had to either throw away or give away. My daughter was unaware of her night time activities because she slept like a rock. One night I came in, I found Legs sitting on the bed reading a book with her glasses on. She had a short gown on with no panties. She was non responsive to my questions and the room smelled like pussy. This was it for me because her ass had never stunk before. Z Baby was sleep in her room and the rest of the house was a mess. When I came by the next morning she had a hang over and was going to be late for work. I took Z Baby to school and came back to take Legs to work. During the ride I began to counsel her and asked for an explanation. She was remorseful and full of shame. She told me she needed help but didn't want to go to a program. She was a shell of her former self. It became even more painful for me because I had issues with drugs too. We decided on a plan of action which involved me moving in for good. She feared losing

Z Baby if she didn't straighten up. I convinced her that I could be trusted but she would have to show some progress. I became a regular fixture in the house. I stopped spending nights at the bar which upset my boss. He was forced to put the alarm on and restricted my daytime access to the premises. This was the beginning of my end at the bar. I really didn't have a lot of concerns because my welfare job was trying to hire me for real. I was such an industrious and knowledgeable worker that I impressed all my superiors. They weren't used to having a W.E.P.worker so committed. I had taken all the physicals and was in the process of getting my hepatitis vaccines. I was doing regular hours at the bar. I began to lose interest in the after hours sex and entertainment. This behavior displeased my boss even more. I was a tough act to follow!

I took Z Baby trick or treating for Halloween. We went everywhere in the car. I had everyone I knew give her some money and the stores added the candy. I went to so many places that my little girl grew tired of riding around. She was too young to understand what it meant to me to be doing this. We had plenty of fun during the coming days and weeks eating the candy and playing games with it. Legs continued to struggle with her addiction. I had to drive her to work more and more. She had trouble waking up on time and getting ready. She went to work so tired one day that her boss sent her home. Legs was good at hiding the problem. She was always small so any weight loss wasn't that noticeable. We only had pleasant times together, when I indulged with her. I received a call from her one evening while I was working. She had discovered that my back massager made a great vibrator. She had a fantastic orgasm and couldn't wait to show me. I waited for closing hours and rushed over at the first opportunity. I had started bringing boxes over hoping she would pack on those nights she didn't sleep. I walked in to find her with a giant Kool-Aid smile on her face. She had slipped a baggie on the end of the back massager because the condoms had kept breaking. I couldn't hide my excitement, when she applied it to the front of her pussy. In no time at all she began to convulse and shake as streams of cumm shot out from inside her pussy. I stood motionless for a moment as I assessed the situation I was in.

I stood wondering if this new revelation was an attempt to distract me from her drug problems, or an out growth of her addiction. It was a very tempting moment that I couldn't resist. My fleshly desires began to take control and I wanted to be in the driver's seat. She laid there recovering from that massive orgasm. I watched her pussy pulsate as it tried to calm itself down. I began to massage my own member while it struggled for freedom inside my pants. I removed my jacket and loosened my shoe strings. Legs continued to smile while holding the massager. I kicked off my shoes and let my pants drop to the floor. I was deliberate in moving slowly to take off my clothes. I was savoring this moment that never occurred when we were happily married. We did many things together sexually but never this adventurous. Legs body took on new meaning as my pace to join her quickened. I took my clothes into the dining room and laid them neatly across the chair. I returned to Legs wearing nothing but a tee shirt. She extended the massager to me asking, "Do you want to do me this time?" There was no hesitation in my response. I took the apparatus from her and turned it on. I motioned for her to move closer to the wall so I could sit on the edge of the bed. The massager turned vibrator hummed loudly as I drew closer to her. I sat facing her as I applied the machine to the insides of her thighs. She settled back with her eyes closed as I began circular motions around her pubic area. I watched with excitement as she squirmed slightly. I adjusted the baggie over the front of the machine and applied it directly to her clit. She opened her eyes and rose up on the bed as the pussy came to life. The front of it began to leak fluids while she raised her knees in the air. Legs positioned her body like she was ready to give birth. She had the strangest look on her face as I continued to assault her with the machine. Inaudible sounds began to come from her mouth. My own dick was rock hard and standing straight up in the air. I placed the machine at the top of the pussy so I could view its opening better. I grabbed Legs right hand and placed it in my lap. I was still seated next to her and wanted to be included in the pending climax. I dripped some baby oil in her hand as she wrapped it around my extended pole. Oooooooo it felt so good as she slid her hand up and down the length of it. Her pussy had opened up wide now with a lot of movement inside. It was quite an event to watch and a first for me. I watched in awe as the pussy lips swelled and the inside puckered. Legs began to grimace and squeezed hard on my pole. She began to ejaculate streams of cumm as I too shot a load up into the air. It was a messy scene as cumm from two directions shot all over the room. I was shocked by the amount of pressure behind her cumm. The pussy just kept pumping out her love juice like it had an inexhaustible supply. What was happening was too new for me to comprehend. I dropped the machine and rolled over on top of her as she released her grip on my pole. I slid right in to that wide as her pussy walls collapsed around me. It felt like I had dove into hot pudding as I started my thrusts. She was so excited at this point that I feared we both might have a heart attack. She held onto my waist as I felt her pussy pulling me inside. Damn this was good! We both were experiencing something that we never shared before. She was wearing a long nightgown that had an additional slit up the side. I did that to expose both her legs whenever she stood in front of me. Once again I allowed myself to be manipulated by the pussy. Was I such a freak or just a man in love? I kept rocking it because the well lubricated pussy was extending the life of my erection. I was fucking her so well that she never questioned the lights being on. His was new for her. My previous requests for illumination during sex were always denied. There was no denying this time though. She pulled me down and slammed my body hard into her. "Fuck me Zee harder I'm gonna cumm again!" She demanded and I answered the call. I increased the pace and the penetration. I was tender at this point and only my desire to please kept me going. "Ahhhhhh! Ohhhhh!" She hollered loudly as I stiffened my body up against her. I pressed against her as I remained still. I could feel the movement inside her pussy. She had achieved her final orgasm for the night. I was done and could go no further. I stated sliding in and out of her slowly as the pussy calmed down. It was too messy to remain inside and rest. I pulled out gently while she tried to keep me close. I resisted and rose from the bed. I had to get back to work praying I still had a job. It took longer than usual for me to clean up. I returned to the room after getting dressed to find Legs still lying there. I ordered her out of the bed and then removed the sheets. "You need to go wash dat ass and get some sleep!" I blurted out, annoyed that I had stayed so long. I stuck my tongue down her as I kissed her good bye. I rushed back to the bar to find the crowd thinning out. Ruby thought I was in the back sleeping when I entered thru the side door. "You can start collecting the bottles and check the bathrooms." He ordered as I surveyed the surrounding to see who was left. He must have taken in a nice sum because he was too happy. I couldn't see nothing inside that might have been responsible.

In no time the place was empty. Ruby had beaten some guy playing cards while I was gone. That's why he was so happy and didn't notice me gone. We locked up the place and I decided to spend the night at the bar. I had enough of Legs for the night. I needed time away to assess what had just happened between us.

I didn't want to believe what the world was showing me. Legs had a drug problem again and I was being pulled into it. Somebody had to wake up form this nightmare and take charge. I decided to take a more forceful stance with Legs. She had asked for help and I had to change the type of help I was giving her. I called on her best friend to intervene after I told her the truth about both of us. She was in shock and dismayed but reluctant to intervene. I began to make surprise visits to the house at night. I started filling the place up with empty boxes to pack. Whenever I came in to find Legs in "La La Land" I would start packing boxes. In a few weeks the place looked like somebody was moving. We had a dismal Thanksgiving at a I can't remember. It was early December and time to plan for Christmas. It would be our last one at this address so we wanted it to be good. We focused on Z Baby having a joyful one. Since my absence the tree was not being put up or either not that well. Z Baby was overjoyed that I was home to fix the tree. We decided to make it a family project. When it came time to start Legs didn't want to participate and an argument ensued. Z Baby was indifferent to it all because this had become too common. I relented and just father and child decorated the Christmas tree. During the following days Legs went deeper into her addiction. It became a habit of mine to take her to work in the morning. My boss had given me a newer car recently so I drove with confidence. My other car was left parked in front of the bar. It only had to be moved when the street needed cleaning. It would disgust me that Legs couldn't get it together. I wondered how much of this Z Baby may be aware of. I never dropped her off in front of the job. I wanted to preserve her secret from her boss. I used to threaten her with disclosure but it didn't help change anything. We made a settlement with the new landlord and had to be out by the New Year. Legs found a place through a neighborhood realtor. The landlord agreed to make the final payment on the compensation once we left. In a desperate attempt to effect some change in her behavior, I called her sister living out of state. Her daughter had also moved there to escape all that was going on in New York. I was disappointed to hear her sister to reject my pleas for intervention. She in fact called back threatening to take Z Baby from her. This was not the results I wanted and Legs turned on me after that. She decided against me moving in to the new place. This I had to learn from Z Baby when we were discussing the sleeping arrangements in the new place. Legs later tried to convince me that I wanted it that way and not her. The tree was decorated well and there were gifts, but the holiday spirit was not at this house.

THE LIFE AND TIMES OF ZEKE & LEGS

LET'S START IN the beginning as the two lives began their change. Zeke and Legs both had problems with drug addiction. Miraculously they made the decision that would cause their paths to cross. "Legs" was raised in Red Hook Brooklyn. This is a community located near water, of mostly large hi-rise buildings known as projects. Zeke or Z was raised in Ocean Hill Brownsville Brooklyn.

In the 1980s crack cocaine came on the scene and a new day was borne in addiction. Crack cocaine defied all the traditional rules concerning illicit drug use. The user be-came not only a slave to the drug but their behavior was dramatically affected by the Craving for it. Sleep was never desired and no task was off limits for anyone craving

The drug. It does not matter what other drugs Zeke and Legs used. It was crack that broke them down. It was the escape from crack that eventually brought them together.

They both attended different drug rehabs, but they were among the top three in N.Y.C.

What they experienced in long term treatment, led them to seek careers as drug counselors.

Having defied the odds their first jobs were with the programs that saved them.

This alone would not have caused them to meet. Zeke quit the job and his recovery changed which would lead him to Legs.

It was no fun playing big Willie when all you had to show was a lighter bank account. Chasing women wasn't the same when now you are the good guy. Those were the thoughts going in Z's head as he took a look at his situation. "I didn't plan to be in this position with the money I had saved up. My money was disappearing faster than condoms in a whore house. I either had to start winning or stop gambling. To stop was no simple task so I had to become a winner. I was seeing an old young flame who was hustling crack. She wasn't as cute as she used to be, but she still had those D cup titties.

Girlfriend wanted to move because her landlord wanted her out. She needed me to help with the credit check. I needed her to move out of treatment. Moving out became a top priority for me. If I didn't act soon, I would not have enough money to be approved.

I was not in a comfortable position having to explain myself to someone about my business. Mr. Bonehead was trying to appear smart, but personal issues made Mr. Bonehead a rubber stamp. Mr. Bonehead was the Director of the Program and my primary counselor. I presented my move out plan to him and all he had to do was sign it. This would not be the first time, I knew more than those above me. I always relied on my intelligence for survival and overall success. Getting physical was always a last option for me. In fact then it would be someone else sacrificing their body for my benefit.

I started saying my goodbyes as I prepared to leave upscale Manhattan. I would soon be living in Queens with a girl I thought I knew.

It was not long before that crack money was put to use. What a situation! Promising drug counselor living with a promising female drug dealer. I put up with it before, but now I had some authority. I began making purchases to bring both luxury and comfort to the apartment. She was also receiving state money for a crack baby, and her sister's two other children. It was pretty amazing that we had this arrangement due to past conflicts.

When she was a young girl I had a serious crush on her. I had to rise up a little, because my brother was being played by her. I was a local businessman at that time. I gave her some credit that she used to impress an older female friend. I only gave "Big Boobs" the credit because of what I felt. She also said the older woman would pay it back. They both played this back and forth game that I got tired of. The woman finally told me that "big boobs" told her she didn't have to pay it back. I couldn't get physical with that fine young Big titty cutie. I would never have a chance to the bush if I did. I thought of a way to get gangster and not risk jail time or retribution. I bought three eggs and kept them with me. It was an egg for each dollar she owed me. I waited for her to be hanging out, with her crew in full view. Having a good throwing arm, my eggs were deadly accurate. One behind the other whoop, whoop, whoop and my first hit on a deadbeat was completed. I never had a problem with getting paid or played.

It was a good feeling having a family to care for. My own son was living in Virginia with his mother and the new husband. These were all needy children emotionally and having a teenage daughter was a challenge. My brother's love for this woman wasn't an issue, because he had passed six years earlier. I had moved in during the summer of 92. By the Fall of the same year problems started. Oh, by the way, that teenage daughter was pregnant by now. NO it wasn't my baby but a 12 year old giving birth was hard to accept. "Big boobs" had a Jamaican male friend who was a gross, piggish, overly friendly person. He was also made too comfortable in my house. I'll call him "Horse" because he looked like one and he was hung like one. Don't even go there some things are obvious. I came in one day early and "Horse" was there. When I asked why, she stumbled with an explanation. She finally admitted to feeling neglected and had engaged in sex with this person. Yes I'm not that soft, and started making plans to leave. I just didn't let her know yet because I had to work. I waited for Saturday morning to call my sister to come get me. Baby Sis rented a van and everything left in one trip. "Big boobs" didn't know I was leaving until the van showed up. This has always been the moment, when women want to tell me how much I mean. They either beg for me to stay or at least plead: don't take the furniture I bought.

There was a steady rain outside but that would not stop me. I began to take my things downstairs and she began to perform. It was just like in the movies as she began to grab me and my things to prevent us from leaving. The presence of my sister finally caused her to calm down and she began to help. The rain came down and I thought to myself," shit moving back to Brooklyn."

Wow, moving in with "Baby Sis" wasn't bad at all. It was no big secret that she was my favorite. My mother often told the story, of how I led my "lil sis" around, when we were little. I used to say "Tum on Ninette tum on", as I pulled her along. In spite of those early years, we became friends based on mutual respect. The rain was still coming down as we began to unload the van. I recall my nephew pitching in as I began to tire. I wasn't losing any strength, but the emotionality of the situation was draining. I fought back tears as we finished up on unloading the van. I could see from the corner of my eye, a big smile on my nephew's face. Well at least someone was happy about my misfortune. I was also looking forward to getting closer to him.

"Baby Sis" had space for me, but I wouldn't have my own room. My furniture was integrated into the apartment. I would be sleeping on the couch, which posed no problems for me. It would be much later in life, when such a feat would be impossible. Commuting to work offered its challenges, because the train was a long walk away. That was a minor inconvience for me because I loved being with family. Drew (my nephew) and my sister both seemed to welcome my presence. I added income to the household and some hot meals. It would take a "Halloween Party" to set in motion my next relocation. A relocation that would bring me to the greatest love of my life.

I had already been working at Legs' job since February of 1992. It was now October and we had developed a pretty close relationship. Being the new unmarried stud on the job probably set off some friendly competition. I could imagine the available betting on who would be the first to date me. Let's face it, I was young hung and full of cum. Not only that, I also dressed sharp and looked good wearing them. I had my eye on "Chunky Chocolate" and "Light n Tight" but my girl Legs made herself more available. Damn she looked tasty in anything that showed her legs. Chunky Chocolate was big boned and pleasing to watch. She had a little country accent, that made her even more appealing to me. The girl was thick with a broad smile. When she spoke to you, it felt like you were a part of her world. She had the ability to make me forget, the last woman I spoke with. Light and Tight was a real beauty, working on her Bachelor Degree. I was working on being a bachelor in her crib. She appeared genuinely interested, when I rapped to her. She wasn't trying to be the office whore (at least not in the open). Light and Tight had medium sized titties and a curly red afro that turned me on even more. She spoke like all she ever did, was attend college. I was pretty good at this counseling thing because I was so manipulative in the streets. Plus my language skills were always top notch. Legs was having trouble staying up to date with her paperwork. I began to tutor her on keeping it current. The clients (female) were just as attracted to me as some of the staff. The clients posed no threat because this money was too soft to get away. The male clients had a different attraction but it all worked to my favor. People were opening up about their issues and I was keeping some accurate records. I became "Z Man" and when I spoke people listened. The "Program Director" took me under his wing and promised to make me an efficient manager. On that declaration I made a personal pledge to stay with this program for five years. The director or "Big John" was known to frequent a local bar. He had lived near where he worked, so the situation was ideal for him. He used to complain a lot to me, about not being respected by his superiors. Big John took a liking to me. I was determined to extract from him all the information I could.

My two sisters "Baby Sis" and "The Doctor" were in a women's club that was having a Halloween Party. Naturally I was asked to sell some tickets. Even though I was so suave and all of that, I was a loser in the dating game. I was still kicking it with "Big Boobs" so she had brought three tickets with the understanding that I would take her. On the job sells were slow but "Legs" would go if I brought her ticket. Like I told her; "I'll buy the ticket but don't stand me up." You see, my last few dates were no shows. She assured me that she would cum, I mean come. Wow what a shot for my ego. I went from no dates to two dates. Legs and Big Boobs what a comparison in contrast. I began to feel like "The Man" and suddenly Halloween became my favorite holiday.

Halloween was close and I began to confirm all my dates. Big Boobs began to protest about paying for her ticket but I was not moved. She stated that some of her friends may not be going but she still gave up the money. I figured that since I was paying for this stranger's ticket, that maybe I should pay for hers. It was now time to check on the other date Legs to make sure she was still committed. After all Legs was the prize and it would be no party without her. I had turned the money in for the tickets, and managed to satisfy both sisters with the sales. Now there was a buzz in the office as Halloween drew nearer.

Party time was here and I began to telephone both dates with directions. Big Boobs was familiar with the train she had to take because she lived in the area before. Legs on the other hand were more complicated, so she decided to take a cab. The good thing about the party was that it was in Brooklyn. The house was empty because Baby Sis was gone and Drew was at the baby sitter. Eileen called to say she was on her way. Big Boobs called next to say that she was getting on the train. I didn't have to go far to meet the train, so I finished up on getting myself in a zone. The crazy thing was that both girls knew the other would be there. What they didn't know was how that situation would impact on their evening. One thing is certain, both of them wanted to be with the "Z Man" and didn't care who else would be there. I heard a horn blow, and realized that the first piece had arrived. I went downstairs to greet her and saw right away that she was wearing too much make-up. I suppressed my laughter and began to engage in small talk. I could feel an erection coming on because this was the closest I had been to pussy in a long time. She wore a dress that took all the attention away from her face. She moved around slowly and deliberately, as she watched me watch her. I could sense her nervousness, and made no attempt to hide the excitement I was feeling because of her presence. She began to question me about my place and complimented me on its neatness. I really wasn't trying to hear that shit. I just wanted to know how fast I could be between those fine legs of hers. I wanted to know what kind of sounds she made when she started to cum. I knew for me this would be a night to remember. The mood was quickly broken, as the phone rang. Big Boobs was in and needed me to meet her. I settled Legs down and made her take the oath, not to search around the house when I leave. I almost didn't make it out because I hugged her before I left. I trotted down the block to pick up piece number two. I thought about the fire in my lions, when I was hugging that other piece.

I don't know how the two felt when they met because I never asked. I know I felt like a "bad mother shut your mouth". When I walked up in that party and announced who I was, the music damn near stopped. My sisters and their friends had a" shit eating grin" on their faces, as they realized I had two on my arms. I planned to be an equal opportunity slut that night. I even hoped that having two would make me more desirable to the meat up in there.

The lights were the proper tone for me. Down low, but bright enough to see if you had a mutt or a French poodle. I went and found us a table. I wasn't interested in having a drink but the girls ordered. Big Boobs wanted hard liquor and Legs ordered wine. I had me an orange juice with cranberry. This would become my signature drink, whenever I wanted to mask that I wasn't drinking. The music was o.k. and the DJ was making an effort to get the party started. There is one thing I learned when I re-entered life after drugging for so long. Party goers needed their drugs or alcohol to take effect, before they could begin to dance. That was not my problem so I began to scan the place. I wanted to see what else was in stock. "You wanna dance" this soft voice purred in my ear. I looked around to see that Legs was making the first move. I got up from the table and all my attention shifted to Legs. My lions began to stir as I guided her to the dance floor. I put my arm around her to feel the small of her back. I felt her tense a little as I drew her close to me. "Damn this bitch is sexy", I thought to myself as I developed this massive erection. I let her feel the heat of my body before

ZEKE SMITH

I put some space between us. We made eye contact as we began gyrating hips and popping fingers to the beat of the music. The adrenalin in me had started flowing. The DJ was changing tunes but I was still on the floor. Here I was dancing with a vision that had me ready to cum. I pulled her close to me again. She could now feel how excited I was and did not back away. I started grinding my pelvis into hers as sweat dripped down my face. I became oblivious to the people around me. I just wanted to release and I was caught up in the frenzy of the moment. Reality began to set in and I began to fall back. I let her visually inspect where she had taken me and a smile engulfed her face. I motioned to her to help me hide this protrusion from my body. She moved in front on me as her butt cheeks swallowed me whole. Damn I almost came at that moment as our bodies became one. We two stepped back to the table and rejoined Big Boobs. I sat back down and asked Legs if she would order me a drink. I needed a wine now and I handed Legs some money. She refused to take it. I started giving Boobs some attention because I could see jealousy all over her face. When my drink made it back to the table, Boobs was now ready to dance.

Boobs weren't as graceful as Legs, but she was just as game. I got the sense that she was going to out do what she just witnessed on the floor. I didn't have to pull her to me. She started out pressing up against my lions. The fit wasn't as tight as Legs. Big Boobs had more belly than ass, so I couldn't get up in there like before. I now had to settle on an old technique of mine. I began to press my chest up against her breast, giving up one helluva massage. Now she was getting aroused, as all that liquor she had, began to take effect. It wasn't doing a whole lot for me, but others began to notice what it was doing to her. I noticed a look of interest on some of the women faces. They had that look of excitement that I saw before, in porn movies. I continued to put on my show and began to feel movement in my pants. I started to come alive like never before. I spun my dance partner around and started slow gyrations on her ass. I soon found my member positioned just between her crease. It was like I was splitting her ass in half. I began to gently massage her shoulders, slowly forcing her to bend over a little. My spectators began to blush as I leaned back and forth mimicking the movement of an ocean wave. This had to stop because Legs was not amused. I started to come back to my senses as Legs began to rise from her chair. The tempo of the music shifted and I was able to stop dancing.

I let Big Boobs walk back to the table alone. I did not want to lose this erection before I could grab Legs for another dance. We were more casual than before. My conversation shifted to showing my appreciation for her being here. She stated she was enjoying herself but would not be staying much longer. I could tell she was uncomfortable with the situation but happy with me. We danced to a slow jam and we were so close I could feel her heart beat. We had some more small talk before walking her out to get a cab. When I returned to the party alone, Big Boobs smiled and began drinking like a fish. The DJ began to play reggae music and I started my dancing alone.

This young girl came up on me and started some gyrations of her own. I couldn't believe my good fortune, as I turned to face my new dance partner. I began to squat like I was doing the limbo walk, and placed both hands on my knees. I started rolling my body in a rhythmic motion and duck walked until I was between her legs. She did not hesitate or flinch as our private parts began to make contact. Oooooo I purred, as I began to whisper how safe sex was on the dance floor. She giggled as she turned up the heat and began to force herself up against me. My member was now laid down alongside my right leg. We were now cheek to cheek and it felt like all eyes were on us. Damn this girl was into me like we had walked in here together. She was pumping and grinding her body up against me, like she wanted us to cum in here together. We were now on our third song and neither one of us hinted at wanting to stop. Sweat was pouring down both our bodies.

I could feel her breathing getting heavier. We now were holding each other by the waist. We pulled our bodies so close to each other, like we were trying to pass thru. We each took it up another notch, and didn't care at this point who was watching. She kicked off her shoes and motioned for her friend to pick them up. She made that move without skipping a beat. Oh my God it felt like we would both cum at any minute. We starting moving so slow, it looked like we were standing still. My knees began to buckle and I saw my dance partner's friend out of the corner of my eye. She was trying to show Ms Nasty something in the corner of the room. We both turned at the same time and saw Big Boobs shooting murder ones at Ms Nasty. She started to ease up her grip on me. I began to tighten mine.

She began to pull away feeling so limp. I did not want to see her go but I understood. Even after I told her that wasn't my girl, she thought it best that we stop. I stalled the break up as long as I could. My dick was so hard I didn't know what to do with it. I bent over as much as I could and rushed over to Big Boobs. I let her know that I didn't like what she did. I finally got my joint to relax enough to dance with a few of the other guests and my sisters. When the party started slowing up and the end was near, we left but the night was not over. A sleeping giant had awakened and I was not ready to put it back to rest.

We left there and I took her to one of my after hours spots. I came into the club feeling like the old Zeke. I had not hung out since damn near getting broke before I could move out of "treatment". It wasn't long before, I made my way past the bar and into the "crap room". Like always there was plenty of money floating around. I really wasn't interested in gambling. I surely was not using my money. Big Boobs started showing interest in what was going on. Before I knew it, she was peeling money out her bag. The only problem I had with that, she was being too independent. It didn't take but a few comments from the men around the table, for her to restore me to my proper position. She got open fast and the money went just as quick. We made a decision to head to Queens, and pick up some money from her house. I wasn't trying to take no cab, so it was a long ride on the train. I found plenty to talk about, as I laid down my best Mack game. Words were flowing like poetry and she became butter in my arms. Eventually we made it to the house, after a long walk from the train station. I kept her close to me like I was the only man she knew. The alcohol she drank was taking its toll. Big Boobs didn't want to leave the house. I still wanted that money to leave though. I started stroking her back and forced her to the bed. This had to be fast and good, because I did not want to spend a lot of time in Queens. I snatched off her top and released those double Ds. I swallowed one nipple whole and put the other one between my fingers. I began to make little circles around her nipples as her breathing became more labored. I started to fumble with the buttons on her pants, trying gain better access to her love boat. She easily could have been called "juicy fruit" by the way she responded to the right touch. I stayed focused on the time as I plunged my hand between her legs. She let out a gasp as I began to flick her clit. It was now my turn to give her something to play with. Big Boobs was behaving like a dog in heat. She grabbed my joint with such force that I almost came. Yeah that's right! it feels good when you get rough with mine. I kicked off my shoes and worked my pants to the edge of the bed. Lifting my body up with both hands, I ordered her to finish removing my pants. Ooooooo I purred out loud as she took me by surprise. Boobs began to beat my joint against the back of her throat. She cupped my nuts and like it was ice cream she was licking. I bit down hard on her nipple causing her to release me for a moment. I then grabbed what was mine and put it inside her. Using long steady strokes, she started to react to this new intrusion. I showed no mercy as I began to pound with more rapid thrusts. Big Boobs began to fight against my onslaught. I didn't let her escape as I pinned her down. She began to buck wildly as her juices flowed like a broken dam. Again and again I banged my hips into her as she came again and again. I did not want to hang around for thanks. I asked for some money and she just motioned to drawer. I peeled out ten twenty dollar bills. I tried not to put too big a dent in her bank roll. I grabbed up my clothes and made to the bathroom. I realized in my haste to move, I had left all my cosmetics. I did my just fucked wash by putting suds on "navel to knees". After putting my goods in a bag I went to say bye. The closer I got to the bedroom, the louder the snoring became. I gazed down at this ill shape body wondering "who was drunker me or her?"

The ride to Brooklyn seemed like it would last forever. That's usually how you feel when you got fresh money in your pocket. It was almost daybreak, so I knew I would be heading home. I wanted to get some rest because I was anxious to speak with Legs. I didn't know if she made it home, or was wandering the streets. One thing was for sure, I couldn't wait to have my arms around that small waist of hers.

Monday came quick. I blushed the first time I saw Legs, but she didn't crack a smile. It wasn't long before I found out why. Legs didn't think that double date was cute and neither did her friends. I was now this bad guy and some type of player. Light n Tight and Chunky Chocolate came at me like gangsters. They wanted to know how I could play their girl like that. I wasn't trying to discuss my business on the job. I didn't even appreciate Legs coming to work and talking about it. The day progressed on with not too much more fanfare. We kept regular contact throughout the week as we both, considered another date. I was really starting to like this girl. Shit! I would have liked any girl about now. My Italian friend that worked there convinced me, that Legs were a good catch. We had both decided on meeting up again on Sunday. I wanted Sunday so it wouldn't interfere with my gambling on Saturday.

Think God it was Friday and a pay week at that. After settling down for the evening I found myself feeling very lonely. I thought this would be a good time to call Legs, and plan our Sunday. I made the call and she quickly answered the phone. We started out laughing about our date. I explained why I had broken up with Big Boobs. She didn't think though, that bringing her was such a noble idea. She felt that I was still involved in some way. When I asked about her status, she said she wasn't in a relationship but had recently stopped seeing someone. I asked if that was the man that had gotten her pregnant. She was in shock that I knew. Legs also expressed dismay, when I told her I also knew about the recent miscarriage. The more we talked the more we wanted to be in the same place. The conversation was long but not boring. We moved our date up to Saturday as we found more pleasurable things to talk about. She wondered why I wasn't out hanging. "That's not me now, I like talking to you." I stated in my best Billy Dee Williams voice. "You don't have to stay on the phone, to talk to me." was her reply. Now things were really starting to heat up. We both were feeling the pressure of being alone. I made the first move and asked if I could come over now. She was overjoyed at first and then became very quiet. "I need some time to clean up the house a little." She said this in a voice that made my imagination run wild. I asked if I should pack some pajamas and she said yes. I hung up quickly and began to throw some things in a sports bag. I put a knot in my pocket, just in case I was able to make some bets. I had this fly short set that I would use as my pajamas. To be safe I also threw some condoms in the bag too. Legs lived downtown and a cab ride wouldn't cost that much. Yes with me, cost was always a factor. I just couldn't stop thinking about how good this woman felt in my arms. I was so anxious to be there I promised the cabby a big tip if he hurried.

There I was in front of the building, and before I could figure out what bell to ring, the door opened. She wasn't looking as I knew her at work. She was wearing this short one piece, which could have been a dress or a shirt. Those legs pf hers had a glow that begged for attention. She smelled like a bunch of fresh picked flowers. She walked ahead of me up the steep stairway to her apartment. She took slow deliberate steps, as she ascended the steps. Her slow pace gave me a prolonged look at the back of her thighs. I even had a good view of the bottom of her but cheeks. This view made me wonder if she wearing any panties. It was now time to go inside and I took a deep breath as I drew nearer to her body.

The apartment was cute but small. Located far and away from any temptations, I found the area ideal. I scan the place rapidly with my eyes. It wasn't lavish but it also didn't have a ghetto feel. I looked around for a place to set my bag down. I was feeling pretty darn comfortable, to be in another woman's apartment. Well she said she didn't have a man now, so what was there to worry about. I set my bag down and was offered something to drink. I wanted some soda or juice and she quickly brought me some juice. I sipped on my juice, as I continued to take inventory of the apartment. It was a studio with a small bathroom, located behind the front door. There was a kitchen just big enough for the essentials. There was absolutely no room space for any thing extra. There was a large black and white stripe sofa, with a matching love seat. In front of the sofa there was a large square shaped glass coffee table. This sat atop a bulky thick X shaped base, two and a half feet high, which weighed about fifty pounds. The walls were painted a bright white and blinds covered the windows. She had a decent sized television which had a VCR hooked up to it. Underneath the television on a separate shelf there was a small music system. All this was on a converted cart that was made to serve drinks or food. The place wasn't shabby, but it still cried out for my attention. She had a small table in her kitchen, whose placement I considered a marvel in space management. We both knew why I was here so I began to pay more attention to Legs. She looked good in any thing she wore. My girl had a petite body with enough wait not to be skinny. I walked over to her, which didn't take long. I stood over to her and pulled her up from the love seat. She had been sitting there since we came into the apartment. As she rose up her hair met my chin. I tilted my head so I could lean down into her neck. Eileen was wearing a fragrance that had me overwhelmed. Man she smelled so damn feminine. I lowered her arms as I still held her hands. I placed them behind her back just above her ass. I let go of her as I began to check the firmness of her ass. Mmmmm! I thought to myself, can this get any better. I began a gentle massage of her ass, as my own member began to stiffen. I started pulling her even closer to me, as my member continued to grow. I wedged my cock right between her legs and began a slow pumping action. Legs began to respond immediately and she gave out a soft moan as I felt her body shiver. Oh what a turn on. I didn't make a woman cum standing up since I was a teenager. Now I was excited and I began to back her up to the sofa, as my tongue started dancing across her lips. My cock was feeling so tender now but I was not ready to cum. I put a tight gripe on her ass and lifted her off the floor. I demonstrated my strength as I hovered for a moment, above the sofa, with her in midair. She put a firm grip on my neck and I lowered her to the sofa. I fell on top of her as we crash landed. I began to lift her right leg up, causing her dress to rise hi and expose her panties. With my dick laid alongside my right leg and her right leg now bent, I began to stroke her.

ZEKE SMITH

The pussy was so soft and cushy. I rubbed my dick up and down that pussy as I lifted my weight up off her. She began to meet my thrusts with thrusts of her own. We were in a rhythm now and had a new way of fucking. The pussy started getting real wet as I allowed my left hand to explore. I lowered myself down and rested on my right elbow. I leaned against the back of the sofa and started working my way beneath her. I forced her right leg between mine, which made her pussy press hard against my dick. Now I was starting to drip precum, which made its way to the surface. I began to grind my pelvis into hers and sweat began to pour down my face. Damn it was really getting good as she began to hold me even tighter. I felt her body begin to shudder as my own became to stiffen. We both started our journey to Climax. When I began to shake uncontrollably, Legs also began to shake. We arrived at our destinations at the same time. I couldn't stop my grinding and began to release another load. My dick was so tender, and it was so long since pussy was this good. I switched to a pumping motion and she responded like wise. We began our journey one more time before we collapsed into each others arms and wetness.

The nap we took didn't last long. I woke up wanting to play some more. I could tell she was enjoying me. She never pulled away when ever I grabbed her. I just couldn't get enough of her. I went in my bag and got my short set. Legs then me led to the bathroom, and I invited her to join me. She hesitated at first until I reached under her dress and began stroking her pussy again. The panties were extremely wet and I was anxious to wash my next meal. There was very little room in this bathroom. A large old fashion tub with a shower attachment, accompanied a small sink and toilet. The water was turned on and we began to remove our clothes. I kept my drawers on because I planned on washing them. She peeled off her panties, revealing a luscious mound that appeared manicured. I quickly sudsed up, being very careful as I moved about in the tub. I moved to the other and watched her begin to wash. I told her to take her time cleaning the pussy, because watching it was making me hungry. Legs wanted me to wash her back. I took her rag and made it nice and sudsy. She moved away from water coming down and I began to massage her back with the soapy rag. She had her back to me, so I reached underneath her, and began to wash her pussy. I let the rag soap up the insides of her thighs. Next I got down on my knees and began washing her ass and those sexy legs of hers. She turned around to face me putting that pretty pussy right in front of my face. I froze for a moment wandering what to do. I handed her the rag to rinse all the soap out. When she turned back around to do that, I began to rub my hands all over her, as the soap made a very smooth surface. Her stomach was incredibly flat, as if she spent a lot of time in the gym. The soap started to cascade down her body, as the streams of water started striking her again. Her pubic hair was once again in front of me, as she turned around to face me again. I knew what to do this time and began to clear away the remaining suds, from between her legs.

I began to lick the insides of her thighs, as the water ran down over my face. My knees were starting to hurt, so I sat on the edge of the tub, as I turned the water off. I placed both of my hands on her ass, as I pulled her closer to me. First making sure I had a firm grip on her ass, I stuck my tongue in between her legs and licked that pussy from top o bottom, over and over again. She wasn't enjoying it as much as I was. Good tasting pussy was the fountain of youth for me. I tried to swallow the lips as I held them between my lips. I was in a rhythm now and was forced to take this dripping wet body to the bed. She offered no resistance as I lifted her up, with my lips still planted firmly on her pussy. I cautioned her to duck as I squatted and stepped out of the tub. I plopped her down on the couch and continued my meal. She put her hands on the top of my head, as if to push me away. I eased up on sucking and began to apply soft gentle licks. She responded right away, so I knew this would be the motion to rock the ocean. Back and forth, side to side, up and down was the dance my tongue was doing, all in that pussy. I was pressing my own hard cock against the edge of the couch. I used my hands to part those pussy lips, and started to caress her clit. I stayed at the top now as she started to buck. I took a gamble and stuck my tongue, all the way into her love box. Honey is the only way to describe both the taste and texture. My onslaught was relentless as her juices began to flow down her butt cheeks. The pussy had received all the attention and it was time to involve, the other body parts. I inched up off the floor and placed my knees at her feet. I began to massage her bust that was more nipple than breast. My dick had been very patient in waiting his turn. He could no longer wait and began to grow in the direction of his destination. Her tittie was the size of small a plum, so I easily placed the whole thing in my mouth. She enjoyed this as much as I did. Legs knew what was coming and she tensed up, as I began to stroke her pussy with the tip of my dick. She cautioned me that it might be tight. She said it had been some time since she did anything. I let the dick slip into her fold, just a little as her juices continued to run. I tried to hold back, but the dick started to force itself inside. Ahhhhhhh! Ooooooooo Ahhhhh, Yesssssss, Emmmmm, Ah were all the sounds she made. Mmmmmm! Ohhhhh, Ahhhhhhh, yeahhhh that's it emm huh.

Oh the pussy was soft inside and she just kept purring like a kitten. My girth had filled her up inside and she began to move her body in rhythm with mine. OH easy, I said. I don t want this to end too fast. She understood and began to lie still as I took control of the beat. Yes that's it, I continued to say. Go ahead, right, hold it, yeah ah shit, move now, come on, bring it to me. Damn girl thissss puuucy is so good. I began to pump her hard now as she rocked from one orgasm after another. It got so good I started calling her Kitten, because she was purring and the pussy was just as soft. You like it she asked? She struggled to breathe as she spoke. Is it good, she questioned as I continued to dig deeper inside her. Yeah you know it is, I responded as my cock started to cry out for more freedom. I lifted my weight up off of her and she let out a sigh of relief. Now I began to make slower and longer stokes. I was now massaging my dick with this soft pussy. Slurp, slurp, slosh, slosh was the sounds coming from the pussy as I pounded my way home. Oh no Zeeee I'm coming again, Ooooooo ahhhhhhhh ohhhhhhhh that's it don't stop, yeah ooooo Zee. She dug into my back as I began busting my own nuts. Alright Kitten this is good Mmmmmm. My sperm started splashing inside the condom. I feared it might bust, but I couldn't stop. Down I went again and again until there was nothing left. Yes now I was tired, and collapsed on top of a piece of pussy, that belonged in the hall of fame.

WE BOTH HAD slept like babies. It was nice for us to have a warm body next to each other. It felt so amazing, how we clicked so fast. When I woke up next to Legs, it did not feel like the first time. I laid there in bed, thinking how wonderful last night had been. I wondered if any night after would be as satisfying. We gave each other so much attention. I thought to myself that, that was the best night of my life. I was in love but I was in love with the pussy.

I reached over and pulled my little kitten close to me. Yes! That's what she was to me, a little kitten. I snuggled my head into her neck as she slept soundly. I began to explore her naked body with my hands. I marveled at her softness. No bumps and no contusions, just inches and inches of smoothness. I couldn't help myself. I had to have her again, right now. Legs began to awaken, as I gently nudged her onto her back. She mumbled something but I didn't understand a word. I was too focused on finding my way, back to her love box. I started to engulf her nipples with my mouth. She started squirming in bed, as she shuffled her feet up and down. My hands were now on a massive search of her body. I explored every area being careful not to miss an inch. The morning after it was still good, and I wanted it even more. I slid my hands down from between her tiny nipples, over her taunt belly, to the top of her velvety smooth pubic hair. I began to massage it, drawing small circles on the top. I I used just the first two fingers of my right hand, as my left hand parted her legs.

She moaned softly, and displayed a smile with her eyes closed. She had this look of contentment on her face and I was feeling the same thing. Two people had found each other, at a time when they were in desperate need. Our lives had undergone some radical changes. We were now involved in a fight for survival, and couldn't afford to lose. We both had families that were demanding change. We did not want to slip back into old behavior patterns. We had to succeed at our jobs. Even more important, we had to succeed in our personal life. Drugging was not an option. Maybe just maybe, if we could make a love connection, this joy we felt would last forever. I was feeling very comfortable with this person, whose pussy was actually in the palm of my hand.

My mind refocused on the mission at hand. I wanted to cum with her this time. I didn't want her to reach any climaxes without me. I continued to part her legs even wider. She started to bend her right knee and raise it in the air. I slid my left hand down her right thigh and it landed atop her pussy. Now both of my hands were in the same area. They both started to apply pressure as if they were kneading dough. I felt the love box becoming slippery. I knew then if I didn't hurry and insert my penis, she would be coming without me. I reached down to my crotch, and hurriedly put on a condom. I rushed sliding it down, and the sensation of it made my penis begin to drip precum. I forced her right leg down and climbed on top of her. The lubricant on the condom with her box also dripping juices, allowed quick easy access to the inside of her chamber. The moment I touched bottom and without any upward stroke, I felt my kitten tense. I recognized this movement from last night and knew she was starting to cum. I started my pumping action as I lifted my weight into the air. She began to meet my thrusts with some banging of her own. She seemed determined to match all my strokes. I was determined to keep this awesome rhythm going until we both climaxed together. I dint have to wait long as she began to speak in tongues. My nuts were slapping the bottom of her ass, just where the crease ended. Slurp, slosh, slurp, slosh was all you heard as we raced to the finish line. Oooooooo, ahhhhhhhhh, emmmmmmm, yeahhhhhhh. We cooed in unison, as we reached our destination together. We rolled over onto our sides, in a tight embrace. Our bodies still joined as one. Our noses touched as we searched faces before us, with our tongues. I placed my lips over her mouth and my tongue dove deep as it flapped around inside. We continued to squeeze each other tight as if to extract juice from an orange. It felt good as we held on to each other, like we might fall, if we let go. I backed my face away from hers and looked into her eyes. They were watery as if preparing to cry. I was filled with so much emotion at that point. We didn't speak but our body language was shouting. Emm I love this, I love you, I love this, I love you emmm. That was the tune our organs were singing. We didn't dare interrupt or try to disagree. We knew what they were singing was true.

Saturday morning day two, of what was now my dream date. I started paying more attention to my surroundings. I paid attention to detail as I began to walk to the kitchen. I opened the fridge to see what I could make for breakfast. I was stunned by its contents. Nothing of substance, but sparse condiments and some old beer and wine. I looked next at the interior of it. It was in need of a thorough cleaning. Now there were two things on my agenda, that wouldn't include sex. We needed to buy some groceries and I needed to clean this house. I fixed my eyes on Legs as I exited the kitchen. "What's wrong, why you looking at me like that" she said in her imitation baby voice. "I like to eat" I responded. "Yeah I know" she shot back with a big grin on her face. "Lets get serious, I need food in this house, and it needs to be cleaned" I spoke with such authority, she rose immediately from the couch, and went to the bathroom. It wasn't long before I heard the shower running. "Yeah wash dat ass, I'm next." I started picking up clothes that was lying around. I wanted some order in this house. I wasn't going to wait for someone else to bring it. My "Kitten" was already submissive to me. It was like she had been waiting for the right man to come and dominate her. I was going to be that right man. The address and the pussy were both good. Just one night with her showed me how loving she could be. I stopped thinking long enough to finish picking up the clothes. I took the pillows off the couch to check underneath. To my surprise it was a sofa-bed. "Why didn't she mention this last night" I wondered to myself. Oh well, not a problem. We will have much more room to play with tonight. "Honey, I need a towel" a muffled voice shouted from the bathroom. I went and knocked on the bathroom door. "Where are they at "I asked. "Check around that corner in the tall closet" was her response. I grabbed a large fluffy towel and handed it to her. She hardly opened the door, as I squeezed the towel through the crack. "Damn what you hiding. I saw every thing last night. Is there something that I missed? Maybe it was too dark in here then." Legs did not think my line of questioning was funny. "What could you have missed? You almost ate the whole thing!" Now she had the jokes and I wasn't laughing. Yeah I loved eating the pussy but I didn't want to talk about it. That's how it was with most brothers. We might kill to protect that secret. "Do you go down on your woman?" was a question we often asked each other. "Nah man" was the usual response. You were not going to get a brother to cop to that in public. You may not even get him to cop to it in private. Even with his head buried between some thighs, he still would be denying it. What was all the fuss about any way? If you didn't have no strange growth coming out your face, how bad could it be. I went back to my cleaning, as my Kitten emerged from the bathroom.

The air filled with the most pleasant of scents. One thing I gave her high marks for, she always smelled good. I resisted putting my head between those legs again. I took the towel she was wearing, and she started to blush." Its o.k. baby, I'm the only one looking." She continued to smile as I walked away into the bathroom. I could still smell her scent as I turned on the shower. I looked around seeing all types of fragrances on the sink and atop the cabinet. This girl takes smelling good serious, I thought. I searched for a bar of soap, but had to settle for some shower gel. I stepped into the shower and began to lather up. I was so used to jerking off in the shower; I had to fight the urge, as my cock began to grow. "We don't have to that anymore." I said to my member. "We have some real pussy now, so stop staring at my hands" I started washing my body the same way I had since a little boy. First the head, face, and upper body. Rinse off and rinse your rag out. Now lather up your rag and start washing the 'you know' on down. You need lots of lather now, to cushion those strokes in a sensitive area. The task of washing was made more enjoyable, when you added masturbation to it. One thing I know, it wasn't just a male thing. Many women discovered the joys of having, a removable shower head. Even some just turned off the water and turned on that back massager. You know girls, whatever float your boat. I made it out the shower without cumming. That was a small feat but one I was proud of. I exited the bathroom to find Legs finishing where I left off. She was wearing some type of sweatpants that highlighted her curves. I came out the bathroom butt naked and Legs tried not to notice. Even with that object protruding from my body. I began to smear cologne over me, and applied my speed stick to my underarms. I began my Vaseline ritual and my body started to glow. I explained to Legs that I was raised on Vaseline, because my momma didn't believe in ash. I dressed quickly, putting on some sweats off my own. We were ready to leave now on our first shopping trip. We had variety since she was living downtown. When we got outside, we both smiled at the mild weather we encountered.

We started our walk down Atlantic Ave. I quickly noticed the difference in the neighborhood from what I was used too. Everyone outside had a purpose. I didn't see people at this time just hanging around. That was not the case on the other side of Brooklyn. A Saturday morning would be filled with more hustle and bustle. First thing to notice, would be the Friday night spill over. Those are the bodies still roaming around looking for a fix, or looking to be fixed. There was a time, when I could have fallen into either category. We continued our walk and before you knew it, we were holding hands. Legs began to point different things out to me, as if I really cared. She seemed so sincere in telling me about her neighborhood. It was like she was a real estate agent, trying to sell a house. I faked interest because I liked the sound of her voice. We finally reached our destination, about five long blocks, away from the house. Legs and I started walking up the aisles, and began searching the shelves, with our eyes. "Get that and pick up two of those. Don't forget we need some of that too. Remember you said you were going to cook." She was full of conversation, as she directed me to the shelves. "We need a cart because I aint going to carry all this stuff around. I still haven't picked up what I came for." My voice showed some frustration as I began to assert myself. Legs went and got a cart and began to take the items out of my arms. I then realized; Hey Zeke you never shopped for groceries before, with another woman you fucking." So this is the strain I must be feeling, I continued to think to myself. This is the beginning of my true domestication. When I was with Big Boobs she controlled everything. I didn't get too involved, because she was still juggling those drugs. I was just playing house because, I needed a place to stay. I wasn't even in love with Big Boobs or any thing she had. When I made love to her, it was out of duty. For the most part, it was like working in a factory. You hate the job, but you need the money. I used to close my eyes when I fucked her. I would think about all that other young pussy that came before her. I do mean came before, cause I put a lot of work in to make Boobs holler. I used to look back at her after I came, and wonder "What the fuck!" Legs were no joke and she was moving to close this deal. We got to the check-out counter and Legs wouldn't let me pay for anything. I went with the flow, but wondered if I was being set-up.

We left the store and started our trip back to the apartment. The walk back wasn't as romantic, because of the bags we had to carry. We finally got to the house. It seemed like coming back was longer than going. She pointed out to me, that the real estate office on the corner was her landlord. He was the largest realtor in Brooklyn. The building she lived in must have been a tax write off. It was a three story walk up, with a store at ground level. Right next door underneath, was a garage that housed a cabinet maker. He lived in the loft above the garage. There was a Deli across the street on the other corner. She had been living here for about a year. She was close to her upstairs neighbor. He was Gay and got a lot more action than she did. His apartment was also slightly bigger, which afforded extra luxuries.

We entered the building and started up the stairs. There would be no panty shots on this ascension. I still received a nice view of the movement of her butt cheeks. We got the groceries in the house and began unpacking.

We were constantly bumping into each other, as we maneuvered in her small ass kitchen. I was really hoping she would finish up and leave. "Man! this girl is such a distraction. I really have to learn some self control, when there's work to do around her. She has the perfect petite body that any sister could be blest with." My thoughts were so loud in my head, I felt like she could hear me. "Legs, you gotta get out the kitchen, so I can start breakfast." I sounded too much like a boss, to only be a visitor. I reached out and pulled her close to me. "I love having you in here, but I can't think with you up under me. Plus this kitchen isn't big enough for us. I need room to do my thing." I buried my face into her neck and began to grind on her. The sweats she was wearing, was so thin, she felt all of me. She tried to pull away but I kept a firm grip on her. I continued to grind as I positioned myself between her legs. She couldn't help but to start some movement of her own. I could feel her bottom lips pressed firmly against my member. It started throbbing as if it was trying to escape. It felt like the parting of the red sea, as my cock found the crease that split her pussy in half. I pulled her left leg up and leaned her against the sink. Oh no not now, I'm hungry and I don't want to eat any pussy. As much as I wanted to stop I couldn't. I looked in her face, only to find her eyes tightly shut. Well maybe in a few minutes, it will be all over. I felt Legs' fingers dig into my side. She began to tense, and I recognized right away, what was getting ready to happen. "Oooooooo Zeke what are you doing to me" was all she could say. I felt a warm sensation flow over my cock. I grabbed her ass and pressed hard into her. I didn't want to wet my pants so I practiced restraint, as her juices continued to flow. "Now can you please stay out of the kitchen?" I barked at her as I released my grip on her ass. I began to massage her butt, as she lowered her leg to the floor. "I'm gonna let you have my kitchen now." She stammered; as I stopped my massage, and she walked away.

It was almost lunch time, but I still had not eaten breakfast. I wasn't so motivated now. That little interlude had left me tired and sore. I took out three eggs and quickly beat them, as the pan on the stove started getting hot. I threw some butter in there and it started to crackle. I opened up the cheddar cheese we just bought, and cut up some pieces into the beaten eggs. I poured this mixture into the pan. I placed two slices of bread in the toaster, and slowly stirred my cooking eggs. I flipped the eggs over as the first batch of toast was ready. I turned my pan off, and let the remaining heat continue to cook the eggs. I put two more slices of bread in the toaster, and buttered the first two. I hollered for Legs to come and get her sandwich. I moved the pan off the heat and split the contents in half. I removed the next two slices of toast and finished making Legs sandwich. She was standing there all sassy. She wanted to say, "Why did I call her if the food wasn't ready?" But she kept her mouth shut. I continued on making my sandwich and motioned for Legs to pour me some juice too. She objected to me saying that because she was going to pour me some. We both grabbed our food and drinks and went into the room. Legs sat on the bed and I sat on the love seat. We ate quietly and all I thought about was taking a nap.

I did not want to lay in my clothes, so I put on my short set. Legs asked when I was going to start dinner. I said very early in the morning. We can eat some take-out today, after I take a nap. It wasn't long before Legs had cuddled up next to me. We both then dozed off.

The television blared in the background as daylight disappeared outside. It was almost five o'clock and I wanted to start Sunday's dinner. I had a sound sleep and was anxious to show this girl, what I could do in the kitchen. I began to rise off the bed. Legs stir a little, but she didn't get wake up. I went to the bathroom and wash my face and hands. I entered the kitchen and began searching closets, ovens, and drawers for tools. This being my first time here, I didn't know what I had to work with. Much to my surprise, she had a pretty well equipped kitchen. I turned the oven on to 425 degrees. I pulled the wrapping off the two hens we brought. I carefully washed the birds off and began my seasoning. I waited for the oven to heat up and put a pot of water to boil. I took out the open pack of cheddar along with the new one. Sharpe and mild cheddar, was the secret to my family's recipe. I opened up the bag of white potatoes and started picking some out. I was no joke when I started moving in a kitchen. Peel, slice, dice, peel, slice, dice, I repeated the process, until all my potatoes were done. I found a medium sized pot to put them in, and then placed it on the stove. I was flying and time was keeping up. I needed to boil some eggs, and soon found a pot to use. The oven was hot enough now, so I placed my birds inside. I looked at my watch to make sure, they didn't over cook. The water in the first pot was boiling now. I opened up the box of elbows and poured them inside. I took a green pepper out the refrigerator along with two onions. I peeled, washed, and chopped one onion for the potato salad. I put that in a cup and moved it to the side. I heard movement in the room. I turned around to see my Kitten was rising. I cautioned her not to come in the kitchen. I was on a roll and I didn't want anything slowing me down. The noodles, eggs, and potatoes were all waiting to boil. There was no room for error. Legs kept peering into the kitchen. I could tell she was impressed, because she didn't offer to help. The oven had that kitchen hot, but I was afraid of the draft, from an open window. I continued to work my magic as all the pots began to boil. I stepped out into the hallway for a minute to cool off. I figured that was safer than that cold November air. I put a spate of margarine in the noodles and turned off the fire. Next I checked the potatoes and decided they had enough heat. Grabbing two pot holders, I lifted the pot off the stove, and drained off the water. I put the whole batch in a large mixing bowl. I believed in mixing my salad hot, so the potatoes would absorb the flavor, from the other ingredients. I quickly chopped up some mixed pickles and with the chopped onions, added it all to the potatoes. I removed the eggs from the stove and put them under some cold water. The kitchen cooled off a little but not much. The other room in the house was starting to get hot. I already had on my short set, but Legs was still wearing her sweats. I watched as she started searching around the room. I imagine she was looking for something cooler to wear. Legs walked into the kitchen carrying what looked like fishnet pantyhose. She smiles and asked me how did I like it? "What is it?" I asked. She stretches it out, revealing a fishnet cat suit with the crotch missing by design. "Damn I love it. Are you ready to put it on?" I tried not to look too excited. "Sure, just hurry up and finish cooking.

I refocused my attention back to my meal. I started mixing the rest of the ingredients in the potato salad and placed it in the refrigerator. I began to cut up my cheeses and added them to the elbows. I poured some milk into the mixture and added margarine and two raw eggs. I grated the remaining cheese and sprinkled it over the macaroni. I removed the hens from the oven, and placed the macaroni inside. The hens had cooked up nice but there was still one more ingredient to add. I took out a one pound box of Carolina rice. I stuffed a half a box into each hen and added onions and green peppers. Using a large serving spoon, I saturated the inside of the hens with the hen drippings. I added a little more water and some seasonings and covered my pan with aluminum foil. I returned my two birds to the oven and noted the time. I needed thirty more minutes of cooking time, to finish my now stuffed birds. Emmmm the aroma of my meal filled the air. I think I out did myself this time? I began to hear my baked macaroni, crackling in the oven. I started washing up my dirty dishes and cleaning off the counters. It wasn't long before all evidence of a meal preparation was removed. It was now time to make the Kool-Aid. I searched the cabinets but came up empty. "Do you have any Kool-Aid?" I asked in an excited voice. "No" was Legs quick reply. "I have to run across the street, do you need anything else?" I asked in a more subdued tone. "No, just get your Kool-Aid and hurry back." Legs had impatience in her voice. She witnessed the creation of an extravagant meal, in record time. I hurried out and hurried back, as it was time to remove, the baked macaroni. When I pulled it from the oven, I also rotated my pan of hens. I then removed the foil, so the hens would get crispy. It was time to turn off the oven, and let the remaining heat finish cooking my birds.

I went into the next room to inspect the changes my Kitten had made to her outfit. The heat in the kitchen was nothing, compared to the heat in my pants. That fishnet cat suit was banging, as it was stretched tightly over her body. "Let me hear you say meow." I asked in a very demanding voice. You couldn't tell me anything now. I had spanked that ass good, and now I had this first class meal ready. I was ready to show off and show out. "Come here girl and let this dog, play with that cat." She started moving toward me in a menacing way. She was starting to look like an animal in heat. When is this sex going to stop? I wasn't complaining but damn, all we did was eat, fuck, and sleep. I took off my shirt, as she continued toward me. She was crawling across the bed like some Tiger, but without the growl. "Oh shit! Wait a minute, my hens." I stopped dead in my tracks and returned to the kitchen. I wasn't about to let scorched birds spoil this moment. I snatched open the oven and hastily removed the hens. Ahhhh! Perfection! The hens had a nice dark golden hue. I covered them back up with the foil, so the rice wouldn't dry out. "Woof, woof" I barked as I returned to my previous position. "Meow" she purred as we began to play out our new roles.

Legs were a lot of fun and I was really enjoying myself. We both were behaving like we just discovered, new best friends. Her tiny nipples were poking out from underneath the suit. She rose up in the bed, and stood straight up on her knees. Her legs was slightly parted, and the lips on box, hung down. I couldn't resist and immediately started sniffing, just like a dog. She took the hint and dropped down on both hands. Now we really were looking like two animals, and continued our wildlife game. I paced around her on my hands and knees. She leaned back dropping her head low, and stuck her ass in the air. When I crawled past her face, she bit into my shorts, and began to pull them down. Oh what a turn on. She continued tucking and with her right hand, she snatched them down to my knees. It was my time to stretch, so she could finish removing, the last impediment, to copulation. I grabbed the shorts with my teeth, and drop them over the edge of the bed. I flinched suddenly, as I felt a new sensation across my nuts. Legs had discovered a new area to place her tongue. Ooooo, Ohhhhhh, I cooed as she continued to lick my nuts. Before I could shout hallelujah, she had crawled to my side, and began engulfing my member. It sure was something different, to have my dick sucked sideways. Different or not, the intense pleasure I was feeling, was unforgettable. I couldn't take it no more, and just fell over onto my side. She continued to stroke me with her tongue. I continued to squirm, as waves of pleasure flowed through my body. It was either skill or courage, and maybe a combination of both that was urging her on. I didn't stop showing my approval, as she lavished lick after lick upon me. Next it was the suction that started my legs shaking. I wanted her to stop, but not for the reasons you might imagine. I was just as anxious to lick some pussy myself, but couldn't do it, with her head facing me. I reached down with my left hand, and grabbed her by her side. She winced a little, but understood what I wanted. Legs started side stepping over me, without lifting her mouth up. I moved my legs closer together, as she spun around, placing her ass directly over me. Now it was own, so let the games begin. We started going after each other, like it was some kind of competition. Up to this point we weren't using our hands, but things were about to change. I rubbed both her thighs with my hands, as I marveled at their smoothness. I moved my hands up over her ass, and continued to massage in a circular motion. She was beginning to tire, but it was alright, because it was my turn to astonish. She let my member go free of her mouth. I then instructed her to use her hands, as I began assaulting her pussy with my tongue. I pulled her down so we were belly to belly. I pulled her even closer until my mouth and her pussy, looked liked one body part. Ever so slightly with almost no contact, I began my soft strokes, with my tongue. My neck began to ache from this maneuver, so I reached over and placed two pillows underneath me. I placed them in a way, so my head and shoulders had some cushion and elevation. I held her with both hands on her side, just above her thighs. This gave me more control, if she tried to escape my onslaught. I began to probe the inside of her lips, as my own cock stood straight in the air. Emmm I never knew this forbidden fruit could taste so good. It felt like it was vitamin fortified to help the body build twelve different ways. Slurp, slurp, slurp, slosh, slosh, sliver, sliver she started to shiver. I held on tighter now because I could feel she was ready to run. "Ahhhhhhhh, ahhhhhhh, o.k, o.k, ahhhhhhh, Oooooooo, stop I can't breathe." She was crying out in both agony and ecstasy. I didn't let up, but it was a struggle to keep her still. I tongue dove into places, it had never gone before. I was taking her to new heights and was enjoying the ride. Yes, Yes, ah huh, ah huh, emmmm, yeahhhh, why are you doing this to me." I couldn't answer her now because my mouth was full. She began to shake like she was having a seizure. I was nervous for a moment until I had to duck streams of cum, that was jetting out her box. Damn did I break something? I never saw this happen before. I rolled her over and cum was still squirting up in the air. She laid there shivering and I began to massage her pussy. She couldn't speak and was still shaking. I just looked down with amazement. I pondered, what was this thing, I had just done. I just kept rubbing the pussy as I smeared her juices all over her box.

I couldn't move and I didn't want to play with the pussy right now. This was a new era for me. I had never brought a woman to such a climatic finish before. What did this mean? Was I a certified stud now? Should I consider a career in porn? I looked over at my Kitten, as she slept with an air of contentment and total satisfaction. "I'll never be able to get rid of her now. Would she stalk me, if I tried to cut it off? Maybe this was the norm for her. Maybe she always came this hard! I was in too much shock, to feel like a celebrity. She had curled up on her side as she slept facing me. My hand was still on the pussy, stuck underneath her. I eased my hand out as I began to lose sensation in it. Legs continued to sleep and I figured, it was time to join her.

End Chapter

A NORMAL SLEEP and it felt so good to lie next to her. That her was my new interest Legs. She actually made me feel so wanted and needed. I don't know how she was feeling, but it appeared she liked it too. I thought back on how so many women, had been taking advantage of my kindness. Sure I was expecting something in return, but I made that clear< before I started giving. I guess because I was considered soft, and didn't present a physical threat, they felt safe in manipulation and deceit. My mother didn't raise a fool, but I was still expected to give a woman the benefit of doubt. I was a grown man, but females were still able to tell my mother on me. Just out of respect for all her love and teachings, I always listened to Moms. Since I had returned from the undead and was being productive, I was not going to disappoint Moms again. She had suffered enough, when I was taking her money and possessions. Drugs had taken me to a place that was unknown. I found myself doing the unthinkable and not caring where. I was anybody's pawn, if they had some money or a hit. Yes a hit! That bit of "crack cocaine" THAT WOULD TAKE ME OUT OF MY REALITY. A reality that was too painful to face. Knowing the truth isn't bad, until you have to start applying it to your life. I was a late bloomer, when it came to sex. At a time when I should have been wrestling with the girls, I was chasing dollars. I was a part of the adult world, where games of chance ruled. What I learned about females, from the men I was around, couldn't be applied in my child's world. When I turned fourteen I was tired of jerking off. I thought it was time to start touching something besides me.

I found some comfort in kids my own age. I was much more advanced than the boys. The girls were different though. They weren't used to a kid handling money like I did. I could always buy the ice cream, whenever the truck came around. I had my favorites and beauty was not an after thought. I learned very early the power of money in one's life. I stopped thinking so much and brought my mind back to now. I continued to stay in the bed, but was no longer sleepy. I lifted myself up and went to the bathroom. I washed out the tub, and started to run me a bath. I found some beads for the water, after a brief search. This is not making enough bubbles but it smells good. I rushed to the kitchen and got some dish washing liquid. I squirted a little in the water and my bubbles started to come. I peeked out the door to see if Legs was up. Nope, she was still fast asleep. "that should be enough water." I said out loud. There were those times when I didn't mind talking to myself. My conversations were so deep sometimes. I was forced to take notes of what I was saying. Ahhhh, emmmm, the water was just right. Hot enough for a good soak, before it started to cool off. One thing being in "Treatment" taught me; a deeper appreciation for baths. You had to have special needs to use the tub, in those programs. I never qualified. This isn't a bad apartment. You had to be good friends to survive. There was no place to go, if you didn't want to be around your partner. I didn't see a problem with that. We were having an excellent weekend, but there was also an abnormal amount of sex. There were no two humans alive that could keep up this pace daily. I just did make it under the wire. The fucking was o.k. The dry fucking though was hard on my organ. I splashed around some more and started letting out the water. I stood straight up and watched the suds, slide down my body. "Damn, now what do you think you're doing?" I posed this question to my organ that was trying to reach new heights. "Didn't I explain to you that we were going to stop meeting this way?" The dick seemed upset that we wouldn't be playing alone for awhile. I started washing from head to toe, as the water continued to drain out the tub. When it was low enough, I pulled the shower curtains closed. I turned on the water and began rinsing the soap off. I never could take a bath, without showering afterwards. Mission complete, I stepped out the tub and continued to dry off, with my rag. The air felt good on my naked body. I didn't consider myself a nudist, but I did like the freedom. I went into the other room to see Legs still sleeping. I began my ritual of greasing up, and my body started to glow. I turned the television on, and started watching, an early morning news show. I really wasn't focused on it, because Legs had shifted her position. She was on her back with her mouth wide open. The covers had fell off her and I couldn't resist, as I started to play with myself. This was like watching live porn, as all her wonders, became clear to see. I applied more grease to my member, as it began to grow. "This shit is awesome, please don't wake up." I muttered to myself. She rocked to her side and lay flat on her back again. This caused the covers to drop completely off her body. Her legs were now parted, with a slight bend in her left knee. I looked around quickly for something to lie on the bed. I was almost ready to cum but I didn't want it shooting everywhere. "There the towel she used yesterday." I reasoned to myself, as I laid it out before me. Oh what a view. I felt like I was cheating, but still,

I was savoring this moment. I tried to stand still but my body started to buck. Oh, oh, huh, huh, I squeezed tight as the pressure was building up. I felt like the head of my dick would explode. I couldn't hold back any longer. I eased up on my grip, and the cum shot out before I could aim down. Whoooosh splashhhhh! The load exploded against the wall, like an out of control rocket. I forced the dick down, as it continued to empty itself. I began to apply more stroking motions as Legs started to squirm. Her movement had the pussy shifting around and I became more excited. My cock began to throb, as a wave of pleasure, swept over me. I was fixed on the pussy, because the more she moved, the more erotic it became. Oh, oh, oh, I was starting to release a fresh batch of semen. I applied more pressure, as my hand went the length of my throbbing member. That's it, the last drop oozed out onto my fingers. I grabbed the towel off the bed and raced into the bathroom. I washed quickly because I could hear Legs calling my name. "Honey where are you?" I almost broke out into an uncontrollable laugh. The worst thing about her asking that question; was that she was serious. I guess she wondered if I was in the bathroom or the kitchen. I continued to clean myself off. I stepped out the bathroom butt naked, with my dick in my hand. "What were you doing?" She asked, with her nude body still exposed. I wondered if she knew she was so exposed. "I just finished taking a bath. I wanted to clean it up before you came in." She looked at me puzzled, like I just finish speaking Martian. I walked over to the edge of the bed and took my hand off my cock. It started bobbing in the air like a diver's spring board. "I know you must be tired by now!" She said in a voice so sweet, I couldn't take her serious. I crawled toward her as she fell back in an inviting position. I really didn't think I had another one in me, but I was still going to try. My dick was still a little slick, so I tried to enter her, without foreplay. Easy she said as I positioned myself right in front of her. Legs wasn't joking. She allowed me to have my way with her. I couldn't stop thinking about how good it looked, when she was squirming around half asleep. I began to push and her box opened its doors wide, to let me in. Once inside I began to bounce off all walls. There was so much warmth, and I felt so secure, nestled up to her. Slow steady strokes, was my pace, as we decided to walk and not run, to our destination. We grabbed each others hand as we continued our stroll to ecstasy. We stretched our hands above our heads, as the fingers remained entwined. I rolled my hips as I pressed hard against her body. I didn't want any air between us. The feeling was so intense I began to explode. Semen splashed all around inside her. I forgot a condom, when her nakedness was lying before me.

Legs squeezed my fingers tight as spasms rocked her body. I continued my gyrations until the last drop of cum, had left my body. Strolled on my back and put my right hand over her box. "I think its time you went and soaked this kitten. We don't want nothing extra, growing inside." She continued to lie there, even after I told her to wash. It was either pleasure from the moment or fatigue. Whatever the reason, it was another two hours before she got up.

I had been dressed for some time, if you consider my shorts clothes. Legs had finally gotten up and wanted something from the store. I was tired and wasn't going any where. Evening had come again and it was time to have some real food. Legs loved her junk food, and wanted some chips in the house. "Just wash that ass before you go anywhere." I never had a problem keeping pussy around me clean. If you didn't want to feel embarrassed, you remembered to wash around me. She flashed a slight smile and went into the bathroom. After twenty minutes she emerged dripping wet with that cum stained towel around her waist. "Wait a minute use this" I cautioned as I handed her a clean towel, from the stack in her closet. When she bent down to pick it up, I gave the cumm stain on the wall a quick wipe. "Honey, dry my back please?" She made her request in that unintentional baby voice. I took my time drying her off and also patted the pussy dry. We both were so comfortable with each, and the weekend had been flawless. She put on her sweats as I began to clean up the room. I put the bed up, to give us more room to move around. I had not decided if I was going to spend the night again or not. We both had to work but I would be on a late shift. The place was tight in no time. I began to fix our plates as she left the house. "Please, not too much on my plate. I'm not a big eater." She yelled back at me as she went down the stairs. I watched from the window, as she sprinted across the street. It didn't take her long to enter and emerge from the store. She had a small bag in her hand, which accounted for the speed, in which she left the store. I left the window as she came back across the street. I returned to fixing our plates. I guess we'll be eating on the couch. I poured out some Kool-Aid, and had everything ready to go. I heard the door open and looked to see if it was Legs returning. "Come on baby, I'm starving, let's eat." I had to repeat this statement a second time, before she made it into the kitchen. "This food looks real good Honey. It smells like a professional chef made this." I didn't dare interrupt as she lavished praise, on the meal and the cook. "Thank you so much for the compliments, but can we please start eating!" We both entered the other room with our food and drinks. We sat as close as we could to each other, without being in each other's lap. Wait I said, let me say grace first, before we start. I recited a prayer my grandmother taught me. "Break not the bread of life as we fellowship around the table. May the food we've prepared, be translated into energy, that we may use, in service to thee. This is our prayer. Amen." That was beautiful, Legs responded. "Is your grandmother still alive?" Legs asked. No, but she is alive in my heart. I said with a solemn face. "You o.k. Honey?" she asked again. "I'm o.k. Kitten just let's eat. We can talk when we finish." I had to slow the questions down because my food was starting to get cold. I love talking to my Kitten, but sometimes her questioning, would last too long. I was attacking my food like it might get away. Legs were eating with much grace and poise. I just sat waiting, to see how she would handle that hen. She tried to eat it with a fork, so I was forced to intercede. "Girl, pick up that meat with your hand and stop looking so cute." I caught her completely off guard, and she started to laugh. I continued to devour my food and wondered why she wasn't commenting. Legs were unpredictable at this point in the relationship. Things I expected her to do, she didn't. What I thought she might disagree with she said yes. Maybe she was just being a woman. I finished eating my food and thought how great the day had been. I went into the kitchen and began cleaning up. Legs, was almost done eating, and reminded me about the glass I left behind. I continued to pack away the leftovers, and told Legs to hurry up. I had just begun to wash the dishes, when Legs came in with her plate. She placed it in the sink and went back for both glasses. "You can dry and put them away, when I finish washing." I told her. Sounds good, but do I have to do it right now." She said. "We can have a cigarette first, and I might want to lick on you for dessert." I couldn't help myself and she didn't like what I said. Oh well, nobody is perfect. I'm just happy to be here. My thoughts continued to focus on my blunder. Legs were not amused by sexual jokes. I guess in due time, I would find out why. We sat there smoking our cigarettes and eyeing each other down. We were both in our own worlds, as we recalled what got us to this moment. I was done smoking and it was time for me to vacation in the bathroom. I removed my top and slid on a pair of Legs slippers. I disappeared into the bathroom and tried to make some room, for the next meal. I sat there doing my business and thinking about that lady waiting outside the door. This had been such a glorious weekend. There was no bickering or disagreements. We actually made a connection, and I thought about the possibility of making it more everlasting. I rose from my seated position and started cleaning up. I washed my hands and as I was about to leave, I heard a commotion at the door.

"No you can't come in here. Get away from my door." I listened to Legs making this desperate plea, with panic in her voice. I emerged from the bathroom to see Legs braced against a partially opened door. "Hey what's going . . ." before I could finish my sentence, a 6ft.2in.brother bust thru the door. He looked at me with both anger and frustration on his face. "You! Out!" He commanded, as I tried to understand what was taking place here. I bolted down the stairs frighten and confused. I only had on my nylon shorts, which were wet from this drenching downpour. I raced to the corner realtor in Legs slippers. I told them there was an intruder upstairs, and would they call the police. They all looked at me and began to laugh. The place being open on Sunday was not my good fortune. I glanced across the street to see an ambulance parked there. They were parked directly across from the house. I hobbled over there and quickly told my story. They saw nothing to laugh at and gave me some paper towels to dry off. As I sat there you could hear Legs screams filling the night air. I attempted to leave but was stopped by the ambulance attendants. They put out a call on their radio and within minutes, police cars flooded the area. The rain was still coming down heavy. I told the police what was taking place and they ran upstairs. Again I was prevented from leaving until they brought the intruder downstairs. When I finally got upstairs, the place was in disarray and Legs was in a state of shock. I began putting on my sweat suit but didn't see my sneakers. I went to the wide open window and found my sneakers, sitting atop the bus shelter outside the window. I also saw that my money was missing off the dresser. I went and retrieved my sneakers and was going to ask this chump for my money. Again the police interceded and got the money from him. I told Legs to get her house keys and any thing else he took from her. The police got the rest of the property and began writing a report. All the beauty had left Legs. She was an emotional wreck and couldn't get herself together. She was too frightened and shook up to be angry. That didn't matter, because I was angry enough for both of us. Who I used to be possessed my mind. I went upstairs only to have the police flash me the intruder's address. They were as mad as I was, and didn't mind a little street justice being administered. I made note of the location and began to formulate a plan. First I would need more information on this character. I had to know, who he was to Legs and why did he have a key. Legs didn't want to press any charges and the police labeled it a domestic matter. There was nothing domestic about this matter to me and people better start talking. The police left and Legs' neighbor was downstairs, cussing Legs out. He was furious that Legs had put me at risk. "I forgot he had a key. He has somebody, so why cant I? Her friend Fabulous didn't want to here that bull, and continued to tear into her with words. I finally butted in and asked, "That's your man and you gave him a key to your house?" She sat there dumb founded with no response. "I'm sorry, I didn't mean for this to happen. We broke up weeks ago, but I didn't get my key back. I did forget he had a key. I haven't spoken to him in over a week." This story had more holes than Swiss cheese. I was going to give her the benefit of doubt, until I had more information. Fabulous continued his tirade until Legs grew tired. "Fabulous you can go now." She stated in a whimpering voice. While Fabulous headed upstairs, I told Legs to get dress. She continued to plead her "case of ignorance" but I was not listening. "How can you forget that somebody has a key to your house?" I refused to believe that anyone was that dumb. Someone could have died there. I would never have been there had the full truth been told. She didn't know me well enough to understand the beast she just released. The rain was still coming down hard. I didn't care about the rain, or who might get wet. I had retribution on my mind and nothing was going to change. "You have a rain coat? I suggest you put one on. I had become crazy without a rational thought process in place. I knew what I planned to do. I knew how I planned to do it. I didn't realize that getting the tools to accomplish my plan was flawed. We began to walk with my destination being, the other side of town. I didn't realize at the time, but walking saved two lives that night. The walk dampened my spirits and washed away my anger. We walked for more than an hour in the rain. I finally reached my destination. Columbia was surprised to see me at this hour on a Sunday. I just had one question, when he opened the door. "Give me a piece" "What's going on, why you want it? He asked in a voice filled with bewilderment. I told my story and he assured me it wasn't worth it. We talked for a minute and I introduced him to Legs. I never even stepped inside. We left and started our walk back home. My anger had subsided and Legs was tired of walking. I displayed some compassion and stopped the first cab we saw. We had walked for another half hour before that happened. I was feeling like the Alpha Male that I am when we stepped back into the house. She told the story of her relationship with the intruder. I still wasn't buying the whole story. I also wasn't going to give the intruder any room to get back in. My manhood and image was at stake. She then disclosed the problems she already had at work. Legs told how relationships continue to interfere with her employment. Legs begged me not to take any action, because the intruder worked on her job. I struggled with what to do in this situation.

The best thinking said walk away from this. I wasn't using the best thinking. I made a declaration to Legs that she was now mine. I asked her whose pussy was this, she said her'. I asked her again whose pussy was this, she said mine. I said whose, she said mines. That's right Kitten, this is my pussy and don't you ever forget it. I thought to myself if one day in the future, I would be the intruder.

I thought Monday morning would never get here. It was a long night and my body was still tired. I mustered up some strength and began to dress myself. We both had late shifts, so there was no hurry to leave the house. What needed to be done was a sit down to discuss, last nights events. My anger had subsided and now I just needed more facts. I began to tell Legs, how that incident tarnished the whole weekend. I wanted to know, how she could forget, who had keys to her house. She stared blankly into space, without responding to anything I was saying. "You need to grow up and stop ignoring me. Somebody could have been killed last night." My yelling made things worst, as she just began to cry. "I said I was sorry. I didn't expect him to come here again. I certainly didn't expect him to come this weekend. I enjoyed having you here and I want to be your woman." Legs were speaking from her heart and I couldn't resist believing her. She began to have that glow again as she continued to plea for me to stay. I stared at her for what seemed like hours, unable to say anything. This girl in a woman's body had won me over. There was only three years separating us, so she would be the oldest girlfriend I ever Time was moving slowly and I was becoming inpatient. I needed to go home and get some changing clothes. I feared leaving Legs alone. I didn't want the intruder getting back in, even without a key. Suddenly the silence was broken by the phone ringing. Legs picked it up and within seconds she was screaming into the receiver. The intruder was on the line. He was trying to negotiate a property pick up. Like most discarded lovers, he wanted everything back that he brought. She was repeating out loud the things he was asking for. Television, VCR, and even the phone she was talking on. "Give it to him, because he is not coming back here!" I said in a demanding voice. "No, he can't have anything. I earned that stuff and its not going anywhere." She responded with such anger and resolve, I dared not disagree. Legs let the intruder know, with me listening that it was over. She let him know about the tooth he chipped. She told him about the articles he broke, during his rage last night. Then I took the phone and emphasized everything Legs had said. I hung up without returning the phone to Legs. It was agreed, there would be no more communication with the intruder. On the job or off, this was the last conversation, she could have with him. It wasn't quite noon, so I left to get some clothes. I let Legs know, that I would be back before going to work. The good thing about Legs crib was the closeness of the subway. It didn't take long to get to my house. The trains were running good during that time of day. I went through the closet picking put a small variety of clothes. I grabbed a suit, some sweaters, a few shirts, couple of dress slacks, and a stack of underwear and tee shirts. I checked the time and only an hour had passed. I took myself a shower and dressed for work. I called Baby Sis and let her know, I would be staying out again. I headed back downtown to drop my clothes off. If the trains were still cooperative, Legs and I could leave for work together. The time was 1:15pm as I rang the bell for Legs. She stuck her head out the window and threw me a key. When I got upstairs, I could see Legs had been busy. The place was neat and she was almost dressed. "Hurry baby we can leave together." A smile crossed her face as I finished my statement. "O.K. Honey, I'm almost done." She responded as that smile remained on her face. This would be a challenge foe awhile. Legs were not allowed to fraternize with the staff, because she was still considered a client. It would not be until after graduation, that she would have control of her life back. That was just two weeks away, but a lot could happen in two weeks. Legs were having difficulty keeping her paperwork current. I was the best, but my system kept my supervisors, off my back. Legs were my girl now, so it was imperative that I kept her proficient at work. I gave her lessons in what kept me up to date. She caught on fast and in no time was better at her job. The one important key to the system was to bring some work home. There was a way to do this without risking a breach of confidentiality. The extra pressure at work disappeared but there was still one cloud hanging over her head. She feared disclosure of that tragic weekend. This was the one secret that Legs was able to keep. Legs knew disclosure would cost her the job. We continued to be the "dynamic dual" at work. Our co-workers didn't suspect that we were in a relationship. No one suspected that I was spending more time at her house than my own. I started to pick up some of the bills at Legs apartment. This led to the decision to move in. Legs were still a couple of days away from graduation, so it was a delicate matter. I had become this ultra honest person, who really avoided being deceitful. I always connected deceit with relapse. The one thing I feared the most was a return to drug abuse. I learned that the truth was much easier to keep track of. Even when people didn't believe you, the story never changed. The burden I felt from having this secret was great. I couldn't take advantage of the ride home, whenever

I worked the late shift. I had to be careful when I walked around downtown, because our boss lived in the area. I couldn't always speak to people when I saw them. There was also a vocational school in the area that our clients went to. Graduation Day was close and I couldn't wait. There was such a buzz this year for our Program. This would be the first time we were graduating our clients from the prison population. That's right the state became a savior for most of the Drug Programs in New York City. They learned from statistics, that most of the crimes were either drug related, or committed by drug users. There was both state and federal money available to fund these Programs. Crack cocaine had created an epidemic of drug addiction and the violence that went with it. Communities had been destroyed. Families had become fragmented. The birth of "crack babies" had become common place. Whole industries were created, specifically designed to address drug related issues. They couldn't train people fast enough to combat the problem. Former users became the noted professionals to heal the addicts. The prison population was over flowing due to harsh sentencing guidelines. These guidelines had been ushered in by the late Governor Rockefeller. Hence the term "Rockefeller Laws." I was not caught up in the politics. I was just grateful that it created an opportunity for employment. It also gave me a chance, to repair a world, that I took some responsibility for damaging. This would be my first attendance at the "Big Bird "ceremony. It was held in large cathedral, so the décor was elegant. I scanned the program I received to locate my graduating clients. I was also looking for my "Kitten's" name. The ceremony proceeded as planned. They made sure the staff was acknowledged for their dedication and hard work. In this business, we learned not to take credit for the success of a client. It was the individual that had to take credit for it. This was an important part of the recovery process. The client is responsible for his or her success or failure. I rose for the occasion and my eyes welled up with tears. The one thing being in treatment did to me, was make me more sensitive to the world. The drugs were out of my system and I had a different attitude towards life. I didn't have to be this tough rugged individual, to be accepted as a man. I could be emotional and express my feelings. This was so new to what I was used too. It always felt so good when I was able to cry. My tears were never just for that moment, but also the suppressed pain from years gone by. I released pain from a lost childhood. The pain from always being last or just forgotten. Those tears carried pain that came from rejection. Yes it felt good when I cried, and I never passed up an opportunity to do it. I

ZEKE SMITH

watched as my clients marched across the stage. I watched as my baby came up and received her certificate. It was a joyous moment for me. Next year this same ceremony would be repeated, as my Program held their graduation.

THE LIFE AND TIMES OF ZEKE AND LEGS

THAT WAS QUITE a ceremony. The Big Bird knows how to throw a party. Glamour, glitz, and good fellowship made the affair a huge success. I watched like a proud father, as all my clients received their papers. I stayed afterwards to take pictures with them and to share their glory. I looked on as I saw the beauty of recovery. Recovery was an individual, overcoming obstacles, and reclaiming his life back from drugs or other anti-social behavior. Yes, it was a nice ceremony and hard to believe, it was just two weeks ago. It seems like it was only yesterday. Now my baby was legal and could pursue any relationships she desired. The only one she should desire is me. Our secret was still safe and working together wasn't a problem yet. I never could take the free ride home on late nights. I would have them leave me at the train station. We continued to excel at our jobs. The clients were the recipients of good counseling because of our "perfect life". The world around us created no problems. WE were in love with each other. We had a nice social life outside the job and sex was fantastic. It's true about a woman that her attitude shows if she's getting some. It's not so easy to tell with a man. They're either always trying to fuck something or they're gay. Men can get sexually aroused or stimulated by what they see. They just need a quick trip to the bathroom, while the memory is fresh and "BANG". I know women hate men for this but hey they have their short-cuts too. A woman can rub that button anywhere without a lot of prep. She can also get a much more intense nut than a man can. Ladies start your engines. I began to plan for Christmas knowing that Legs would be hard to please. Legs were the ultimate material girl. I had to show up and show out. We had a grab bag at the job and did not want to pull each others name. We could only pray because it was no way to prevent it, without telling our secret. Money wasn't an issue with me. I had no contact with my only child. My friends had disappeared. I was working long enough to have bank along with a few credit cards. Legs had a daughter but her mother was taking care of her. Legs had become more involved. We had met and seemed to get along alright. I was cautious because my last girl had a daughter that saw me only as a money outlet. I had met her on the job but she didn't know I was seeing her mother. Legs had issue with her only child because of her past drug addiction. Legs mother had actually raised the girl because Legs disappeared once two many. Legs told me how devoted her father was to her. He often came to her house to buy groceries or to just give her money. She spoke of how hard it was for her family to watch her use drugs in the neighborhood. The shame that she also brought on herself finally forced her to flee the area. The details about baby's father were sketchy and I didn't force the issue. I do know that he was a hustler and might have been a user too. He was deceased when Legs and I began our romance. Legs was hanging out in the movie theaters on 42nd St. to get high. She told me she wasn't turning tricks and mostly talked men out of their money. This would not be the first lie she told me. When her father died her favorite uncle came there to get her. She was far gone at this point. Legs had finally reached a bottom that she wanted to escape from.

My story wasn't much different when it came to fathers. I had my so-called best friend living in my basement with me. I was already accustomed to running all types of errands for him. I was using heavy but didn't have the outward appearance of an addict. He was evicted from his latest baby momma he was living with. I gave him a place to stay with a reasonable charge for rent. The woman that evicted him worked up the block. We were friends because of my constant contact with her thru my friend. His name was Columbia and his ambition was to be a successful drug dealer. He tried hard but it wasn't in his destiny. Columbia had too many babies to take care of. He never ducked his responsibilities. There just wasn't enough money to go around. It was no help that all of his woman used drugs. He loved pussy more than me and couldn't pass any up. Well one day after his girl had left my house crying about him, I found some money. This money was hidden under a rug. I became nervous because if my company had found it, I would have taken the heat. I moved the money and waited for him to come home. He didn't come that night and I got high with some of it. I was able to put it back. He came in and claimed he was broke when I asked for the overdue rent. When he left I saw the money was still there. I used some to get high again. When that ran out the drugs told me that it wasn't his money. The drugs said his girl left that money there. The drugs said he owes you rent anyway. I started blasting and before you knew it, it was all gone. Now the paranoia set in. What would I do? I had no resources to get any money. I tested different hiding places until I couldn't handle being in doors. I left my house and roamed around until it got late and I got tired. I came into my basement and was blindsided with a bat. This bitch that lied about his money and owed me rent, was waiting to ambush me. "Where's my money. Where's my money." He demanded to know. He hit me from word go, without knowing if I even knew there was any money. This really pissed me off and I knew this was the beginning of the end. I got him to pause after he struck me several more times. He gave me time to find some money but I couldn't go far. My mother and sister Big Mama was upstairs. I asked them both for money but none could help. My mother suggested I call my father. I hid the truth from my mother, even though my ear was bleeding. I called my father and explained the urgency of the situation. He was reluctant because I was such a disappointment to him. He agreed to bring the $100.00 so I sat on the stoop and waited. I let Columbia know the money was on the way. More than an hour passed and there was no daddy to the rescue. I called him back and he said he was there, but did not see anyone out there threatening me. I assured him there was and let Columbia tell him. Now I had to go to his house to get the money. When I got there he only wanted to give me $50.00. I pleaded with him that it would not do. I then expressed a lot of anger for towards him for having me come this far. I said that he just have me a death sentence. His new woman came into the picture and gave me the rest of the money. When she left he told me he did not want to see me again. Columbia dropped me off at a hospital, and I never saw my father again. He was killed the first year I was in a drug rehab. He never saw me get my life together. I remember it was during the NBA finals when the counselors sent for me. I used to think my mother might pass but never my Dad. He took care of himself. Moms used to be more neglectful of her health. I was devastated because I was looking forward to Father's Day to show him my love. I had already done it for my mother. I went to his funeral and committed to be a better example for him. I did accomplish that. So yes this union between Legs and I was no accident. God has his hand in this.

"Come on Honey," Legs called out to me. Let's go get us a Christmas tree. December was leaving faster than a white boy in Brownsville. I didn't mind celebrating the holiday but it was not a cheerful time for me. There was something about this holiday that brought on depression. It could have been too few toys during my childhood. It might have been too much labor and not enough thanks, during my adulthood. Whatever the reason or the cause Christmas had become my darkest holiday. Sure I put on a cheerful face for the public. Underneath my smile was pain and anguish. I avoided spoiling the holiday for other people regardless of how I was

ZEKE SMITH

feeling. "How about that tree?" I reasoned, since it wasn't that tall. "Nah I think we better get something smaller than that." Legs responded as she continued her search. I thought about my last Christmas that was spent in a drug program. I recalled receiving a gift that didn't put a smile on my face. I couldn't hide my disappointment that time as the cameras were rolling. That video became a classic in the archives of the program. Come on Baby let's get something soon. I'm starting to feel this weather. I didn't want to upset her because this was her favorite holiday. Legs didn't mind going all out for Christmas. She had as much fun giving as she did receiving. Legs also believed in being on time with the gifts. "Are you serious?" I asked when she picked out a tree to sit on the table. This will be o.k. Legs stated, as she rushed her small decorated tree to the counter. The next stop was the supermarket to find some more trimmings. I wanted some nuts and Legs wanted some eggnog. It wasn't time for food shopping, just things to add a holiday atmosphere.

We got back to the house and started transforming everything to fit Christmas. During the week we continued to add gifts to the bottom of our tree. The table became more and more cluttered as the week went on.

There was just two weeks to go and "Old St. Nick" would be knocking at the door. I had my gifts purchased for my short list. Legs would be getting some clothes and jewelry. She loved them both so I couldn't go wrong. I got my mother some jewelry also along with cash money. My mother always said, don't get her anything, but no one was foolish enough to listen. Christmas came and went with no body feeling slighted. I was happy with anything because I kept my expectations low. We didn't even complain about our grab bag gifts. We both were just so glad to have each other without the drugs. We had been living together for over a month. Our secret was becoming harder to keep. We even felt some of our clients knew because of my smiles. I couldn't always hide my happiness whenever Legs was around.

I made it a point not to travel on New Years. I believed in playing it safe so only the next year might be on my tombstone. Legs wanted to hang out but I won the argument. We watched the ball drop on television and toasted the year with a drink. We didn't see a problem with it, since we were at home. I made some shrimp and fried potato wedges. Legs made a salad and we partied alone. The sex was fantastic that night. The only protection we used was a double locked door. It would be daybreak before we finally fell asleep. The life I found myself living was a dream come true. I was with a woman I adored who showed me a lot of attention. I had money in the bank and a good line of credit. I was paying my way in life and not complaining. I guess you could say I had grown up. I was finally functioning like a man. Legs and I were enjoying life the way we had never experienced before. What could possibly upset this balance in our lives? I had met her family and friends. She met some of the people closest to me. It would be later before she met my mother still Legs were no secret there. It would not be long before everything that gave us security would be shaken.

Valentines Day was on the way. "Damn having a real girlfriend can get expensive. I'm still paying for Christmas and I got to buy a gift again." I was talking out loud as I tried to get a grip on this relationship thing. This was a racket perpetrated by women and businessmen to rob a brother of his dough. Every time I looked there was some reason to buy a female a gift. Men didn't enjoy such a luxury. Then in between holidays and special occasions you had to buy flowers some times. I was starting to understand why broke men didn't have a woman. I also understood that love wasn't cheap. I need to stop this complaining and get out of bed. Legs was already up and was in the bathroom for quite awhile. Baby you took your shower? I hollered as I tried to know what she was doing in there so long. "No Honey, "she answered back. Legs came out the bathroom with a rag covering her face. "What's wrong," I asked as she slowly walked towards me. "I was throwing up and my period is a week late." I knew this information meant something but I couldn't understand it now. "Well what are you saying Baby." I countered with a look of concern and confusion. "I think I'm pregnant and right now I don't know what to do." This was only the second time I saw her look so helpless. The first time was the night of the intruder. I did not want to experience those feelings again so I responded quickly. "It's alright. Whatever you want to do I'm with you. Just understand that I don't believe in abortions. I lost enough babies to that procedure. I also don't plan on having any more children out of wedlock." Legs smiled but remained speechless. I began to think of what this all meant. I couldn't let her have this baby without being my wife. I was never married and I didn't expect to be married under these conditions. I had money but I wasn't prepared to share it like this. I liked this woman and everything about her but I wasn't in love. Yes, I loved the pussy but that's not the same as loving a person. I didn't mind her past because the "old timers" said they make the best wives. The relationship with my son wasn't good because his mother had taken him away. I wanted more protection from the courts so it couldn't happen again. I began to look at what role God was playing in this. Why was he presenting me with this and how would it affect my life. I continued to think about how this would impact on our employment. Who would leave and who would stay. They would never let us both work at the same location. Too much was going on in my head. I needed some help in making the right moral decision. I didn't know any preachers so I went to family.

I contacted my sister The Doctor. She prided herself on being able to give advice. I wanted her opinion on marrying without being in love. The Doctor stated that love was a learnt behavior and wasn't the most important ingredient in deciding to marry. She said compatibility and commitment to each other was higher on her scale. It sounded good to me. I figured any input from someone else would give God a chance to be heard. I wanted this child to be born no matter what. This was my seed and I felt strong about the Lord blessing me with a daughter. Now I had to make sure Legs would agree and support my decision.

"Come here Baby and let's talk about our family. I want you to understand that we have to get married. We also have to keep this pregnancy quiet as long as we can. If one of us have to leave the job, it should be you. Your resume looks better than mine." I rattled on to let Legs know the importance of what was happening and the changes that would take place. "O.K., I agree" Legs responded in a soft tone that I struggled to hear. "If you become pregnant again in the future, you will also have that child." I had to make this condition, so I didn't feel used in deciding to marry. "Sure Honey, if I'm blessed that way of course." Legs appeared to just be agreeing with everything without a lot of thought. I accepted her word and believed that we would have a successful union. Legs wanted to focus on the wedding right now but I wasn't prepared at this point. I suggested we wait and just get thru the rest of the week.

I came into work feeling a little strange. I went from a swinging bachelor with some nice money reserves, to a soon to be broke married dad. Infants were no joke and expensive. Life would not be the same for a long time. Sure we love having children around, for all the joy they bring. It's those times when you don't want them around that create a problem. I believe everyone at some point do not want their children anywhere near them. I went about my normal routine as I tended to my clients and responded to my other duties. I wanted to tell someone but knew that would be the wrong thing at this time. Legs appeared to be o.k. but I didn't trust her to keep quiet. I know she had to let someone know about her catch. It wasn't about the baby right now it was the husband. She could not contain her joy as she walked about doing her job. Why does she have to look so damn happy? I asked myself in silence. I know this shit is going to leak out and my job will be in jeopardy. The day couldn't end soon enough. I took my time walking to the train, to give Legs a chance to catch up. I was too inpatient to wait to get home. I had to hear about her day right away. I know she told someone, I just didn't know who. Legs still had the smile on her face that she was wearing all day. "Alright who did you tell" I asked as soon as she was close enough. "Why you ask me that. Didn't you say don't tell anyone?" I was listening but didn't hear a word she said. I knew she was stalling because she didn't answer my question. This was not the time or place to discuss this, so I shut-up and continued walking to the train. The ride home wasn't pleasant because I remained quiet the whole trip. I held her hands in her lap as she laid her head on my shoulders. There we were the perfect couple, going home after a day at work. I started thinking how different the home would be when baby arrives.

We arrived at our stop in a much better mood than when we first got on the train. We held hands tightly as if we didn't want to lose each other. I broke the silence by telling Legs, how much I loved her and the baby. She looked up at me with watery eyes and asked "Do I really?" I began to wonder if she knew. Did someone violate my trust and disclose what I was fighting with. I couldn't imagine Legs being that insightful. "What do you mean by that Baby" I asked in a non confrontational manner. "You say you love me and the baby but we are not making any plans." Legs were staring me in the face as we turned the corner to our block. She was waiting for a response but I couldn't think for a moment. Why was she pressing the issue so early on? We didn't even have a confirmation that a baby was actually coming. Sure it was probably true but a doctor had not signed off on it yet. This is the shit I was talking about, when you think nothing can go wrong. I was not going to go anywhere and we were going to be married. I just wanted some time to think. I wanted to believe that everything I did for now on was to benefit all of us. All of us included the baby. "I'm sorry Legs if I said or did something to hurt you. I want this to be the start of our family. I want you to understand that for me marriage is forever." I pulled Legs close to me as I finished my speech. I wanted her to feel safe and secure in my arms. Love or no love I was getting married to someone I wanted to be with forever.

Valentine Day was a week away and the period still hadn't showed up. It was pretty much a wrap but we needed a professional opinion. We had an appointment scheduled for the doctor to relieve everyone of their anxieties. I sat outside the office as Legs went inside for her exam. I had too many things on my mind to be distracted by baby talk. I flashed back to my first child and thought about how different it would be this time. I was not going to let the system rob me of the opportunity of raising my child. I felt strong about the Lord giving me what I wanted. It would be a girl this time and she too would be named after me. If there was a mistake and a boy showed up, he would be a junior. Legs emerged out of the office with a glee on her face. She could hardly contain herself as she walked towards me. Legs reached for my hands as we both started out the door. All this silence was killing me but I figured the news wasn't good. We made it to the outside and again Legs looked at me with those watery eyes. Just as I was about to ask a question she began to speak. I'm six weeks pregnant and the baby is due in October. How do you feel now Honey about the baby? I paused for a moment before answering. This was not the time to say the wrong thing and set off a chain reaction. I decided not to speak and just held her close. I was so happy I couldn't contain myself. I put my head on her shoulders and began to cry as the world moved on around us. This was a joyful moment for me. God had given me a chance at life again. I had a woman who truly demonstrated love for me. I found someone who I liked enough to spend my money on. I felt enough love for Legs that I stopped looking for another woman. I was so satisfied with her that we would be married. Now since the baby was real I had to make sure she stayed healthy. I stopped complaining about the house and took on all chores. She no longer had to do laundry or anything strenuous. The hardest job she had to perform was going to work. Oh no going to work! I would have to tell this now before someone else did. It would not be easy but the Mother Hen had to know. I thought I could trust her enough to give proper guidance. Tomorrow would be a critical day at work for me. I took my time choosing an outfit to wear. I wanted to look confident without being cocky. It was very important to be humble in situations like this. Knowing how to beg without a tin cup was an art. I relished in my ability to forecast human response to life's situations.

I rose earlier today to make sure I wasn't late to work. Legs had to work too so I got her up also. I reminded her of what we had decided on if someone had to be transferred. I didn't tell her my plans for the day because I didn't want any leaks. The ride to work was uneventful except for the occasional question about a wedding date. We arrived to work early enough to stop for coffee. I was a little nervous but I had to confront this as soon as possible. I didn't want to be going about my business one day, and be summoned to the Director's office. If I acted first I would have some leverage. I would also be demonstrating integrity. I also had recently learnt that legally they couldn't do anything to us. Our jobs were safe as long as no moral clauses were violated. I asked to speak with the Mother Hen. She was busy at the time but would still see me shortly. Mother Hen was a great lady. We had become close because I never hesitated to tell all my business. My own mother taught me that it took a second to lose your mind and a lifetime to get it back. "Hi Zeke, come on in. What can I do for you?" Mother Hen was all business. She went straight to the point whenever in her office. She had come through the ranks and took great pride in her work. You could also depend on her not to risk her job in carrying out her duties. I was always very comfortable talking to Mother Hen because of her nurturing qualities. "Hi Mother Hen, I need to tell you some good news about me." She stared straight at me, like I was the most important person in the world. "I found me a nice girl and we plan on getting married." I was taking my time with the information as her interest began to build. "She is pregnant and you know her. "I'm so happy for you Zeke. Please don't tell me she is a client." Mother Hen was not playing about hoping it wasn't a client. That was any program director worst nightmare. A staff member having a relationship with a client, was an unforgivable sin. "No Mother she isn't a client she's Legs." Mother Hen froze as if she was just hit with some death ray. I looked at her and she was expressionless. I never saw Mother Hen in a position where she couldn't speak. "Zeke you need to keep this to yourself before it creates a problem. Congratulation, you look so happy right now." Mother Hen had a look of genuine concern on her face. She didn't know that I had done my homework and was not concerned about negative reactions. "I am Ms. Hen" I started out the door after my last response. Legs had to be told that I officially broke the news. She had to be alerted, so she wouldn't be caught off guard. There she was with that damn smile on her face. I knew I did the right thing because it looked like she was still telling people herself. "Legs come here for a minute quick!" I whispered to her as loud as I could. "I just told Mother H en about the baby and the marriage. No I didn't tell her we were living together." Legs lost that smile as our reality began to set in. she knew it would be a very short time before she was called in. I knew there would be one person who would take the news hard. Just like Mother Hen liked me for her own special reasons. Legs had also been Big Papa's fantasy date. He had a crush on her that was evident to any open mind. I noticed it right away when I started working there. I taught Legs to use the information to her advantage. Now she would have to deal with his anger. Big Papa knew he couldn't bring any pressure on me without me pushing back. I didn't care about his authority. He was a man like me who overcame the same shit as me. If he wasn't careful I would pull his hold card and all hell would break loose. The news started to filter through the program community. I received a lot of respect because of the marriage proposal. Legs were viewed as a shark that ate a floundering fish. Big Papa had so much anger for me that Legs wasn't confronted that day. We both would have to speak with the regional director tomorrow. I had a brief run in with him, when he first got the position. He learnt then he had to bring his "A" game, when confronting me. The ride home that night was no quiet affair. We had so much to talk about as we compared notes on our day. We walked home feeling so close to each other because of what we went through. When we got upstairs, we were in a hurry to get out of our clothes. I took my shower first as I left the bathroom heated up for Legs. I took my time greasing up as my body on its familiar glow. Legs came out shimmering as the towel wasn't long enough to cover her ass. I began to get an erection by focusing on what I couldn't see. Legs let the towel drop to the floor as I began clearing off the bed. I couldn't wait to between her legs. I still didn't see any signs of a baby except for the tiny bulge in her flat belly. I knew my days of all night sex were limited, so I was going to take advantage tonight. The bed was ready now to get Legs ready. I grabbed my grease and put a generous amount in my hands. "Come here baby, I want you to look as slick as I feel" Legs was so obedient as she walked up and stood directly in front of me. She was beautiful with little water droplets sliding down her body. I watched intently as one drop bumped into another and formed small streams that continued to flow down her body. My greasy hands pulled her closer to me, as I began to lick some of the droplets off her belly. I continued to lick as I rubbed the grease into my hands behind her back. I stood briefly for a moment to apply some grease to her back. I massage gently as Legs raised her hands to embrace my neck. We began to kiss passionately as I started to massage some grease on her soft buttocks. I too was butt naked with an erect greasy pole yearning to be inserted. I reached down behind her to massage the back of her thighs. I stood straight again, and my pole slide right up, between her legs. She lowered her hands to the small of my back. Legs then began to dig her fingers into me, as I started to work my pole in and out between her legs. She moaned softly as my lubricated fingers, sought out an entrance from the back. Oh her ass felt so good in my hands. She was beginning to tire and I was becoming inpatient. We drew the same conclusion because as I lifted her, she began to pump her pelvis against me. I picked her up with my hands underneath her ass. I slowly lowered her onto the bed. Legs pulled me down on top of her as her ass splashed against the sheets. She had a firm grip on my neck and used it to pull me in tight. Legs stuck her tongue in my mouth and began to massage the insides of my cheeks. Her body began to display new love making positions, as I struggled to keep up with her pace. She became some new clawing animal as she reached down to grab me. Legs wanted me inside her and she wouldn't wait for my approval. "Come on stop playing and put that dick inside me" Legs demanded as if she had a gun on me. "I said stop playing nowwww6" I put that dick in her before she could finish her sentence. I put my hand on her back and lifted her up higher onto the bed. She wanted some dick and I was ready to give it to her. I began to pound that pussy like it had just slapped my momma. I was ramming dick in her like a driller searching for oil. The dick was so sick from all that grease that I had to keep pulling her tighter, so the dick would stay inside. Legs liked this ride because she wasn't trying to get off like she sometimes do. Legs was holding on tighter than me as she began to meet my thrusts, with thrusts of her own. "That's right baby fuck me, fuck me let me feel that pussy." I was yelling louder than her as the pussy began to transform me. I flipped over in the bed and had her on top now. This was her worst position but I didn't care now. I knew one day this pussy would not be this much fun. I was going to fuck my Baby often until the other baby came. Meanwhile I wanted this Baby to cumm. "Yes that's it keep your hands on my chest. Don't pump I'll move you. Yeah just like that. I'm not gonna drop you. Oooooo Baby that's it the pussy is so good. You so wet inside. I think I'm gonna cumm." I was giving orders like a sergeant in boot camp. I was fucking my Baby kike we were making a movie. "Ohhh Zeeeee don't stop, keep fucking me plezzzzz don't stop. Oh, oh, oh, yeah Zee let me go. I can do it by myself." I stopped pumping Legs like she was a set of weights. I listened to her commands and let her take over. I removed my hands from her waist and she took over like she promised. Legs put one hand at the base of my cock and the other hand on the bed beside me. She then dropped her head down, like she was on the starting line of a race. Legs then began to pump her ass in the air. She rode my cock like it was a championship race horse. She moaned and groaned as my cock slide in and out with ease. I reached up and began to play with those nipples. This freaked her out more as she began to quicken her pace. I ah, ah, ah, ah, she yelled, each time dick touched bottom. She was trying to speak but the words couldn't come out. "I ah, ah, ah, oh, oh, oh jus don't stop playing with my ooooooo, oohhhhh nipppples." Those nipples were so hard they didn't move when I plucked them. Legs were in control long enough and I felt like I was slapping the baby in the head. I pulled Legs down and rolled over on top of her. We stayed tight for a moment as I felt her heavy breathing against my chest. I raised myself up with both arms and took all my weight off of Legs. I began to slowly and ever so gently, massage the inside of her pussy with my cock. I touched the walls of her vagina so lightly that she shivered with each touch. I was not trying to punish her. I was in fact rewarding her for an early evening session of pure pleasure. I hovered above her with dick inside and watched as her eyes began to water. "I love you Zee. I love you so much." Legs spoke those words with such passion that my body weight became too much to bear. I eased myself down and continued to grind my pelvis into her. We both began to moan as we reached our destinations together. I looked straight into Legs eyes and muttered those words, that women love to hear but men hate to say. "I love you too Baby" It was not an easy journey for me to arrive at this stop. I've been reluctant to commit because of past letdowns. I couldn't go on living my life in the shadows of past failures. I couldn't hold what others did against the new relationships. This woman had demonstrated her love and commitment to me. What else should I expect of her? It sure felt good and I saw my life improving with her. Yes I was in love with her too, but maybe not for the same reasons. I reached over and pulled the comforter down on us. We remained in a tight embrace as our juices spilled out over us. We nestled in each others arms as we drifted off to sleep.

"Come on Baby time to get up. You know this is a day we can't afford to be late. We have to meet with the Bean Counter. They will use any legitimate excuse to get rid of us right now. You remember that news story about on the job romances. That couple sued their employer and won. People spend so much time on their jobs and develop relationships, that you can't penalize them for falling. The only thing the courts said was it can't be a compromising position. There also can not be a conflict of interests. Our situation passes all the legal tests. Just remember that one of us will have to be transferred. We could never work an overnight shift together. The size of the facility and that fact alone is enough to justify the transfer. So come on Baby let's step it up and not be late. This will not be easy but we have the law on our side. I'm wearing one of my power suits and a kool-aid smile." I didn't want to sound like I was giving a lecture, but my baby had to be reassured. If she didn't have enough confidence, she would fall apart under the confrontations.

The ride to work was pleasant and uneventful. We had said plenty before leaving the house, so I just wanted to relax and enjoy the ride. I was nervous but I couldn't show it. What kind of man would I be, if my woman wasn't certain of my strength? I was very old fashion in that regard. I believed in protecting the family and the household, even if it meant putting me in danger. I would never yield ground to any adversary that was threatening my family. My father was that type of man too. He didn't spend a lot of time teaching but he taught by example. He labored six days a week for his family. My dad then went out at night and hustled his numbers. On Sunday the one day of the week he was off, he would cook dinner. I enjoyed those Sundays when I was young, because we would watch sports on T.V. It seemed like my dad enjoyed the company and the questions I always asked. "What was that?" The train shook violently as it screeched to a halt. I looked over at Legs and asked the question again. "What was that" Legs looked at me with bewilderment as if she should know better than me. I had been day dreaming and for a moment didn't know if it was night or day. "I don't know honey. I hope we didn't run over anything?" Her response wasn't all that surprising when you consider the history of the subway system. I prayed that wasn't the case because we would definitely be late for work for sure. There was that familiar and welcomed jolt as the train started to move. "Well I guess we didn't run anybody over." I mumbled to myself as the train began to gain more speed. Legs our stop is next, so let's move closer to the doors. I reached down and helped Legs to her feet, as the train began to slow down. We both now stood in front of the doors and watched them open, as uncertainty lied ahead. "Legs guess what? We can walk into work together now. The truth has made us free." Legs smiled as I continued my jokes. She knew it felt good walking in there with her man. I know it felt good to me, walking in with my woman. I knew by now the whole facility knew what was going on. The residents probably knew before we did that love was on the horizon. "Good morning, good morning is the coffee ready?" I greeted all who was in sight as I made my way to my desk. I could tell by the looks on the faces of residents that the word was out. The people in my caseload smiled as I passed them. Some weren't happy as they realized I might be leaving. It was still early and the directors hadn't come in yet. I walked up to Legs and briefly held hand before settling down to my paperwork.

It was almost lunch time before I was called into the Director's office. The Bean Counter was there along with Big Papa. I sat down as instructed and before the conversations began Mother Hen also joined the group. Big Papa started out by blaming Legs and saying that I was a victim. He called my Baby a predator and pressed me for the exact time this relationship had started. The Bean Counter joined in with his rhetoric that didn't sound any better. Mother Hen remained quiet and I would not say anything to put her in jeopardy. This wasn't even about me, they wanted Legs. What did she do besides fall in love, to make them so angry at her? Was I considered such a valued employee that they would get rid of one of their own? She was a graduate. How could they devalue her so quickly? I got the same feelings when I dealt with gangsters in the street. I was living a new life but was seeing old attitudes in a corporate structure. I fought back and it just wasn't for my Baby's dignity. I fought back for who I was as a man. I couldn't accept being pictured as some weak individual susceptible to the advances of a woman. Big Papa acted like I couldn't think for myself. The Bean Counter thought he could say anything without being challenged. It was nauseating and it was time they found out who I really was. I denied any long term previous involvement with Legs. I made it known that this was no whim on our part. We had no plans of terminating our employment and would fight to keep our jobs. I stood up for my woman and myself but respected their authority. I talked about my fondness for the profession and the success I had working with my clients. The Bean Counter was impressed with my presentation but Big Papa couldn't let go. He continued to accuse Legs of violating policy as a resident and becoming involved with a staff member. There was no proof of that so the issue soon died. Mother Hen began to speak as she explained the conditions of our employment. We were not allowed to be alone in any office at any time. We could not work the overnight shift together. One of us would have to be transferred as soon as another facility was identified to accept us. I blurted out that; "We decided that Legs would leave because of my clients here." Big Papa seemed more annoyed with every word I said. I was dismissed without any response to my statement. I rose to my feet and adjusted my suit. I left feeling victorious and wanted to now put my woman at ease.

It wasn't hard to find Legs, she was lurking in the hallways until I finished. I walked over to her and began to tell what had just happened. "We need to be careful because Big Papa is mad at you. He really tried to get you fired and keep me. I told you he had a crush on you." Legs stood looking stunned, trying to figure out why this man hated her now. "I don't know what to say. I never led him on or had improper conversations with him." Legs were trying to make sense of this but there was none. You can't predict how you will impact on the people you meet. You sure can't control who decides to fall in love with you or develop a crush. We were not going to make someone else's problem our problem. Big Papa had to deal with himself and move on. I was not going to get involved because I still felt there was more to this story. I let legs know I revealed the agreement about her being transferred. She remained expressionless indicating I had something to worry about. The day moved slowly, as word of Legs pregnancy and romance, circulated in the facility. I had nothing to say other than it's about being a man. I took a moment to thank Mother Hen before I left for the day. She knew my silence about our conversation helped save her job. It was almost six o clock and time to go. I asked around about Legs whereabouts. We no longer had to hide. We both said our goodbyes together and made our way to the train. The ride home this night would be filled with joy. Legs was relieved that the worst was over. I was satisfied that we left with our dignity and jobs. I held my Baby's hand tight as we made our way down the subway steps. When Legs was with me, she would be the most protected woman in New York. It was way too early to know but I wanted a girl. A daughter would be a true gift from God, since woman had much of my respect. Legs was quiet the whole ride home. I was surprised she wasn't badgering me with a load of questions. She knew what happened in the office but I couldn't give a lot of details. We both just had to focus on doing our jobs and not cause any problems.

We finished out the week without any incidents than the news came. I was going to be transferred to a facility in the Bronx. The reason Legs wasn't moved was because of her pregnancy. It wouldn't be fair to ask another Director to accept her with that type of disability. That was nothing but double talk because Mother Hen never planned to move a strong female counselor like Legs. I also knew that Legs did not want to leave either. I was looking forward to a new location. The only handicap would be the distance to travel. I would also have to get used to a whole new borough. I decided it was time to get with the future and buy a beeper. This way Legs could stay in touch. I would also have to get one for her too, and hope she didn't abuse it. I found out quick how jealous Legs was when she left that Halloween Party. The party that started this romance! I made my rounds speaking to all the clients that became close to me. I took time out for a special gathering of my caseload. I received permission to have a pizza party, and stayed late to demonstrate my love for them. It was a sad occasion for me since I had grown so close to many of them. I also found time to express my sorrow to the staff and thanked those that had helped me. The move represented a new chapter in my career. They said they picked this facility because I worked so well with the mandated clients. Good, bad, or indifferent I was out and Monday meant change.

"Hey Baby I'm leaving. I don't want to be late coming on the first day. You know traveling to the Bronx, is like going to another state!" I said what I had to say but no response from Legs. I knocked on the bathroom door and went inside. Legs were sitting on the edge of the tub crying. "What's wrong Baby" I asked. "I don't know. I woke up feeling depressed." I'm no shrink but I think she was concerned about not being able to watch me. I had become her favorite hobby and losing it would not be easy for her. "O.K. Legs, I'm not that far away. You can always beep me if you miss me too much." She looked angrier as I spoke and then said something that explained everything. "You know they got a girl that works up there, and I don't trust her. Just don't forget whose man you are!" Legs spoke those words with a look on her face that I never saw. This woman was not joking. Now I couldn't wait to see what her concern was all about. Sure I loved women but I wasn't a whore. I never tried to have all that was available to me. There was plenty of pussy that I passed up and there would be plenty more. Legs seemed to have calmed down enough for me to leave.

I was anxious to see my new place of employment but I was not excited about the Bronx. I needed to take the four train saw I had to walk a little further than before. It also meant I would not be walking in the same direction as Legs. I took Fulton St. so I had a more scenic route. There was nothing more pleasing to my eye sight, than to watch hordes of women, hustling off to work. They were usually the freshest in the morning, but there are exceptions to every rule. I would have to make sure I left on time with plenty of time. I did want to hurry and miss any of the delights that awaited me. Girl watching was one of those hobbies that didn't require money. I finally made it to the station and so did another horde of women. I was in heaven and I could see now, my attendance would remain good. Who wants to miss a journey like this with so many pleasant and smiling faces? There were no empty seats and very little standing room. Normally I would complain but there were none this morning. My life seemed to be alright and it was time now to give God some thanks. I had a chance to start over at a new facility. My reputation as a drug counselor was developing and people were starting to notice. The hustler from Brooklyn now had a legitimate career. I was determined not to give my life back to those streets. I was not going to fail.

My new assignment was located in an old building. It was sometimes hard to tell what these places were used for before the Big Bird took over. There was a construction department that had miracle workers, when it came to conversion. I received a chilly welcome which wasn't uncommon. Recovery people sometimes displayed suspicion towards new arrivals. They were considered competition or spies. Either way the newly arrived had to prove themselves before being accepted. I walked thru the building making mental notes of its cleanliness and organization. I looked carefully at space for both the staff and the residents. This was a residential program, so that much didn't change from my last location. The current Director was a big man I called The Commissioner. The Commissioner had been around awhile and had the respect pf the top brass. That was not always the case in a business that relied on personal affiliations. I too was starting to acquire my personal affiliations to help further my own career. I was soon directed to the second floor office of the Director. "Good morning Commissioner" I said in a loud firm voice, as I entered the room. His response was cordial and he began questioning my background and abilities. My responses were quick and to the point with a lot of detail. He seemed impressed by my confidence and began to lower his guard. He began to ask me about people he knew and congratulated me on my pending marriage. I too relaxed and became less hostile and defensive. It looked like our first encounter was rough for both of us. The commissioner explained my job and his expectations. He informed me that I was recommended here because of my own personal background, and previously displayed insight. I left his office feeling needed and excited about what laid ahead. I went and introduced myself to the senior staff member, who would be responsible for pulling me into their system of doing things. I quickly learned that this was the person, my soon to be wife was concerned about. Baby Girl was the Senior Counselor and had come from the ranks of the Big Bird. She wasn't the neatest or most efficient but she knew enough to hold her position. I bonded quickly with the residents both male and female. I think it was more from their need for someone fresh, than my interpersonal skills. There was a lot here that could be done but wasn't being done. I always battled at staff meetings because I had so many ideas and others didn't want to be overwhelmed. I thought the whole purpose of our existence was to further the interests of the residents. To help them identify their weaknesses and formulate a plan to eliminate them. I never concerned myself with the effort that it required. I knew if

ZEKE SMITH

I could be rescued, they also could be changed. The recovery process was all about change, no matter what you were recovering from. You had to first learn how the drugs or behavior impacted on your life. You then had to accept the reality of this revelation. Most addicts or people with self destructive behaviors, operated in their world for quite some time. These things provided them with comfort and security. They would not be eager to give them up. This is when the effectiveness of the program and the skill of the counselor came in. The first thing on the agenda would be trust with integrity a close second.

I slowly became accepted by my fellow staff members. I was a sensation with the residents because of my personality. I had the gift of making the complicated simple and the difficult easy. I translated all they needed to know in easily understood terms. My theatrics held their attention during seminars and workshops that I conducted. My own recovery was a model example for them to follow, especially the males. I maintained solid boundaries so there was never any confusion about my role in their lives. Some residents received more of my attention than others. This was based on their needs and not personal favoritism. I continued to impress as my reputation grew. I could be depended upon. I maintained excellent attendance and punctuality. The commute to the job posed no problems. I had arrived in early March. Before I knew, it was May and the countdown was on, to our wedding.

Legs wanted a spring wedding so that her belly wouldn't be too big. I wanted a fall wedding to alleviate too many red letter dates in the same month. May had Mothers Day and my mother's birthday. I naturally gave in because I didn't want any complications with the pregnancy. My mother had showed me how a pregnant woman's disposition is transferred to an unborn child. I wanted a happy and healthy baby. I made sure that Legs' life was as care free as possible. I also did what ever to keep her happy and safe. We had decided on a civil marriage at Borough Hall. We figured to do it again in five years in a grander fashion. Even though Legs were pregnant she managed to keep her records up to date. She was still using the system I gave her and impressing her superiors. We had become the darlings of the organization. We constantly checked on each other at work. Life for us was good as we continued to move forward. We planned to wed on the week of Mothers Day. The only significance was the date had worked for us. We both had invited our close friends to attend. In addition my sister and Legs mother would also witness the event. It would be on a Thursday because we were leaving on our honeymoon the next morning.

The day had come and the sun was shining brightly. Legs had a bridle shower but there was no bachelor party for me. I think I hung out the night before, trying to win some money for the honeymoon. I must have done alright because we had plenty to spend. The Lord had blessed us with some beautiful spring weather. I wore a suit and Legs wore a dress made of kinte cloth. We had both bought these outfits for the occasion. It was so warm outside we didn't need any coats or jackets. We had our wedding party meet us downtown because we could walk from our house. "Legs come on Baby I don't want to be late for my own wedding. You better hurry up before I change my mind." Legs laugh out load as I made jokes. I was serious about hurrying up though. We had people meeting us and it wouldn't be fair to them. They were taking time off from their jobs to be there. "I'm almost done Honey just be patient. It's fashionable for the bride to be late for her wedding. She is supposed to be the last one there." I heard what she was saying but didn't agree. Legs were always late getting ready for things. "Look Baby I'm gonna straighten up some in case your mother wants to come by." I had to do something because this waiting was killing me. Legs continued to drag along as our planned wedding time approached. I couldn't sit because I didn't want to put any wrinkles in my suit. Just as I was about to yell Legs name again she emerged from the bathroom. "Damn you look good my Nubian Queen." Legs smile to my comment radiated joy throughout the apartment. My Baby was looking fantastic and I wanted her to know it. The dress accented her belly so well. The colors matched her complexion. The hairstyle she wore showed off her African ancestry. I was the proudest man on the planet at that moment. "You know you not supposed to see the bride before the wedding." She had a grin that caused a stir in my lions. "Yes I heard that one before. I want to do more than look at you right now. Let's go before I get that dress all wrinkled!" We left the apartment and proceeded down the stairs together. When we stepped outside and began walking down the street, heads turned and people took double takes. They knew this was a special day for this couple. They knew because our facial expressions said, "We'll love each other for ever."

We arrived at Borough Hall to a small crowd gathered outside. Aside from the normal activity that generated congestion, we were not the only couple there. There was even a man selling bridal floral arrangements. Everyone was present when we arrived. I told some clean jokes to break the tension. We received a lot of gazes as we posed for some pictures. "O.K. gang lets go in. My soon to be mother in law smiled as I drew closer to her.

We had several meetings previously so we weren't strangers. I found my mother in law to be a very likable person. She was soft spoken, polite and appeared to be very determined. The type of person that could accomplish anything they set their mind on. My oldest sister big Mama was their along with me and Legs best friends. My best man, who was my best friend, had brought his girlfriend along. Just as we started to enter the building a surprise guest showed up. It was a surprise because I couldn't recall ever hearing about him before. Legs favorite uncle, the one that brought her the news of her father's death had come. "Uncle Cee", we chimed in unison as he gave both me and Legs a hug. "Where you coming from?" mother in law asked him. This was her brother and they had a close relationship according to Legs. "I was home Sis, your daughter mentioned this wedding to me. I wasn't sure if I would be able to make it. Well here I am." He smiled and chuckled to himself as if he just told a joke. "Everybody lets get upstairs, I want to be married today." I spoke loud enough for all to hear and some. We finally entered the building and proceeded to the bank of elevators. Our destination was the clerk's office. I thought a Judge would perform the ceremony but that was just in the movies. It was no nonsense, brief, unscripted affair.

I had a camera which I passed on for someone to use. There was one other camera with maybe two exposures left. This was starting to look like the wedding that couldn't say I do straight. A city official with the power to perform these ceremonies would marry us. We did need the rings and the witnesses signed the papers right after I said I do. When we got back downstairs I announced, we all would be going to lunch. This would be our reception. In fact it was the only reception we ever had. My best man had to leave to do what he do. His girlfriend stayed to represent him. Uncle Cee put a hundred dollars in our hands. He then told us for the first five years, never argue about money. Uncle Cee also left so that left a party of six. Those were some manageable numbers, but I could have fed a whole lot more. I did well on the crap table. I guess the Lord saw fit to bless this day too. My gambling days were numbered, because my new wife was not about to be second. The lunch was a tragedy. People with no money made choices based on what was convent. We took a slow walk back to the house as our guests dropped off one by one. The only gift received that day was the hundred dollars. Most of that went to the lunch from hell. I guest the devil was getting his last licks in. It would be a long time before he would get another shot at me. We received congratulations all the way home from almost everyone who saw us. We stopped along the way to buy some luggage. I was not planning on taking a honeymoon with inferior baggage.

Wow! I'm married now. I began to talk to myself wondering, how much would my life change. I even wondered how much it had to change. I was use to having it my way. It felt good living with Legs, now I was legally responsible for her. Yeah I know she was just as responsible for me but I was the man. The law always had a different way of looking at things no matter how it was written. I wasn't going to focus or even think about that now. I was a married man with a new baby on the way. I was a married man getting ready to go on a honeymoon. Damn Zeke you came a long way.

We had a small toast before going to bed. This had to be the rarest moment because I didn't want to have any sex. This was a long day and we were both exhausted. We did manage to pack our bags before we went to sleep. We both tossed and turned all night. This was our milestone and we had so much gratitude for each other. We fell asleep in each others arms. It was probably the most peaceful sleep we ever had together.

Morning came fast and we were anxious to leave. Our bus was leaving from Port Authority for the Pocono. It was a good deal that we had. I made sure Legs packed a gown for every night we would be there. That meant bringing along at least four. I packed my own variety of night wear. We both made sure there was leisure and evening wear in our luggage. I had prepared some food for the ride upstate. I even packed a little beverage in case we became thirsty. This was an opportunity that would not be wasted. Four days and three nights! That was more than enough time for us to commiserate our marriage. We left the house and took that short walk to the train station. This was one time I didn't have to rush Legs out the house. In fact, she was dressed and ready before I was. We both were in good spirits. Change had not come easy for us. There were still skeptics in both our families. Only our mothers seemed to accept the fact that we were tired of using drugs. Everyone else seemed poised to witness our relapse or collapse. We stopped a stranger on the street to take our picture before we entered the subway. We were wearing the new outfits that I brought the day before. Legs were so happy and I was so pleased. She was happy that she had a man who loved her enough to marry her. I was pleased that I had a woman that loved everything that I did for her and didn't complain. We were both in top form. We were so high up that morning, that the only way to go afterwards was down. We made our way down the stairs and told everyone where we were going. We were like two kids discovering happiness. Yes, there was a lot of happiness between us. I couldn't stop

ZEKE SMITH

smiling and neither could Legs. Damn we were actually married and the Lord was smiling upon us now. We watched as the train roared into the station. We stepped back from the platform to avoid any mishaps. I had been practicing safety since the decision was made to have the baby. I was not going to let anything happen to my new family. Legs knew I was over protective but loved every minute of it. She was extremely jealous and didn't trust any woman around me. She didn't mind them looking but all was forbidden to touch. I lavished so much affection on Legs in such a short time that she never wanted to experience anything less. I didn't blame her. I understood what she was going through. I had jerked off so much in my life that I was in love with me too. Sometimes I had to fuck myself before I gave it to somebody else. We stepped on the train with our luggage and brightly colored outfits. People watched us intently while trying not to get caught. We were so flattered by all the attention we were receiving. We found some seats that allowed room for our bags. We kept looking at each other smiling. Every time someone made eye contact with me, I told them we were going on our honey moon. That statement had such a nice ring to it. Legs held me tight as I put a piece of gum in my mouth. My mouth had gotten dry from all the talking and smiling I was doing. I cautioned Legs not to lay her head on my shoulder. I didn't want my outfit to get any make-up on it. She understood and placed her hands in my lap as she sat up straight. It would not be long before our stop came. This was the express which meant only five stops. Legs kept moving her hands around in my lap. Her little small swollen belly was hardly visible. The more her hands squirmed the more excited I became. Legs looked in my eyes and started to smile. I leaned into her ear and whispered; "Please wait for the cabin before you start playing with the dick." Legs bust out laughing as I tried hard to conceal my growing erection. If she didn't control herself soon, we could be arrested for public lewdness. I heard the conductor announce the next stop that was our'. I rose slowly behind Legs as she continued to laugh. My bulging member was visible in the sweat suit I was wearing. I was happy to be leaving the train. Legs couldn't stop laughing. I started laughing myself as I left the train partly bent over.

We made our way thru the station to the bus terminal. I don't know if people were curious or just happy to see a couple getting away. Everyone we encountered seemed genuine and joyful at our departure. I had Legs stop and get some candy as I went ahead with the luggage. I had one more flight of stairs to conquer before reaching our final destination. "Honey I got you a Mr.Goodbar and some M&M." Legs voice could be heard all over the terminal as she drew nearer to me. "Thank you Baby, now let's get to that bus and find us a nice seat." Legs began to move as soon as I finished talking. I know she was anxious to leave. She told me a lot of things about her past and what she went through. She also shared the joyful moments that she experienced. In all those stories, I don't remember anything about a trip that took her out of the hood. She was such a beautiful young woman. Why did she stay trapped so long before being rescued? I know I stayed behind by choice. I never felt trapped because I made the decision to help others get out while I stayed behind. I don't think that Legs was a volunteer. She allowed herself to be placed in a hopeless situation with drugs becoming her only escape. I was determined for us both to rise to the top and reclaim a life that we so willing gave away. We arrived at the designated area for our bus. We were a few minutes early so it gave us time for some more chit chat. I began reminding Legs about our first date. I told her that when I was introduced to her all I thought about was those legs. She laughed and I continued to joke about our first date when I had two girls on my arm. She didn't want to talk about that. She got cocky and said I was hers now. We heard what sounded like a loud engine and realized that our bus was pulling in. We started gathering up our belongings as a line began to form towards the bus. There were only a handful of people waiting but we could see more already on the bus. We waited patiently for the driver to exit and begin boarding passengers. This bus would be making no stops in between. That was the main reason why we had this early bus. We could have gotten something later that would have given us more sleep this morning. I chose not to because I hate those busses that be making so many stops. It was finally our turn to enter. We handed the driver our tickets and went straight to a pair of empty seats in the back. I did not want to be close to the driver or anybody else. I might get frisky plus I had a little taste for the trip. I wasn't comfortable letting Legs drink but I didn't want to spoil the trip for her. There would be plenty of time to be sober and not hurt the baby. We snuggled up close to each still excited about tying the knot. I didn't care about Legs staining my clothes. We were on our way out of town. I celebrated the moment with a drink and some frisky fingers. Everyone on the bus seemed to be headed to la la land. The bus began its spiral turn out of the terminal. I started thinking about all the things I wanted to do in the Pocono. The brochure described a place filled with fun activities for adults. It also described some lavish rooms that catered to the tastes of honeymooners. We would have a private pool located in our room. Legs was terrified of water. I had assured her that I was an excellent swimmer. She had nothing to fear because her head never had to go under

ZEKE SMITH

the water. Legs had such confidence in me that I felt super whenever she was around. Man this woman really was something else. In the short time we've been together, she has demonstrated her love and happiness with me over and over again. I had already started making purchases for our new place. We didn't have anything picked out but we knew we had to move. There wasn't enough room for us and a baby. I told Legs how important it was for us to start saving money. She listened but saving was her weakness. She liked to spend money but not on the good stuff. I had paid off one of her charge cards. I was tired of the letters and the phone calls. I also didn't want her negative credit rating to pull mine down. That drink I took was starting to take effect. Legs was sleeping with her mouth partly opened. It was tempting but I did not play those kinds of games. I gave her a light kiss on her lips. I then inserted my tongue in the small opening between her lips. My tongue danced around in her mouth as she rose up and took hold of my member. She began to give me a massage causing my dick to throb uncontrollably. My lips continued to meet hers like two pillows on a bed. I raised the armrest between us forming one loveseat. I leaned over and faced the window as Legs turned her back to me. There wasn't anyone back there with us. Legs moved her body closer to me and my erect penis. I wasn't about to pull it out, so Legs put her ass right on top of it. That ass was so soft. I started to make gentle gyrations as my penis lay alongside the crack in her ass. I put my hands on her waist and continued to guide her back. Legs was so willing to please me. She also felt a sense of adventure as she raised a foot to give better entry. I began to pump now as the penis reached its maximum length. The bus was on the thruway now doing well over sixty. I too was on the thruway but I wasn't trying to reach those speeds. I was just coasting along as heat began to build between us. I was close to cumming and Legs had fallen asleep. I wasn't going to let that stop me. I placed a hand on her belly and one on her back. I continued to grind my dick up in ass crack. It was so soft and the silk track suit she wore made it feel even better. Yes the honeymoon had started. I wish this bus would hurry up and get there. Just as I uttered those thoughts I began to cumm. I didn't care how wet it made me. This dry fuck in public felt great and a little stain was not going to make me stop. I grind the last little dropout as Legs began to squirm from the pressure up against her butt. The alcohol and the energy I just used up had me feeling faint. I le my head fall against Legs' back as I too fell off to sleep.

We were both awakened by the sound of chatter and the opening and closing of doors. Feeling a bit disoriented I looked around to see passengers leaving. It appeared as if we slept through all the other stops and had reached our destination. We gathered our belongings and were among the last to leave the bus. The lodge was a short distant away but we still had to call for transportation. There was so much excitement between us. We had never stayed in a hotel together before. I was looking forward to having some room service. I had become the primary cleaner at the house so I welcomed this break. It wasn't long before the car from the resort arrived. I hustled my new wife into the car as I brought in our luggage. The driver immediately began to tell us about the features at the resort. He asked about our status and whether this was our first time here. He was very friendly but I just wanted to be in our room. This resort was unique in that it had structured activities for the guests. It was also none as a honey moon resort that catered to married couples and newly weds. It had been family owned and operated for a number of years. All this information came from the brochure. We were directed to a central meeting place in the lobby to receive our room assignments. It was refreshing to know that we were not the only newly weds in attendance. We did soon learn that we were married the shortest amount of time. We met our host and hostess and were given the keys to our room and its location. It was a short walk from the reception hall and we got a tour along the way. The pool was visible from our room but we had no intention of using it. We stepped inside and were taken aback by the opulence. I gave our guide and butler a generous tip and proceeded to unpack. We had a few hours before our scheduled orientation. We would also meet the other guests at that time. I headed straight for the shower after getting buck naked. Legs was in another world too. She walked around the suite surveying all the luxuries that were offered. I was happy to see her happy. We had achieved a milestone in our life. We not only had gotten married but we honeymooned the next day. The pool in our room was behind another glass enclosure. The décor was in mostly red and the pool area was generous in size. I watched as Legs tried to pick out a gown to wear. This was one of those times when she was going to please me with out being asked. I continued into the bathroom which featured glass shower doors. I could be watched and I also would be able to watch the bathing of my wife. This was some awesome stuff and I was enjoying every minute of it. I had traveled to seven different countries and other states during my time in the Navy. Still I had never experienced what I was going through now. "Honey I forget my cosmetics. Could you please bring me my little bag?" Legs was in another world still, but my yelling brought her back. "Alright Baby, just give me a minute." I began to wonder what Legs was out there doing. I know she was as exited as I was. I also had to be mindful that she was four months pregnant. She didn't look it but that didn't change the truth. Legs came I the bathroom just as I was building up the lather around my nuts. You could tell by the size of my member that I had been at it for awhile. "Damn maybe I should get in there with you?" Maybe you should I thought to myself as Legs placed the bag on the sink. Legs just stood there watching me lather as my head started to bulge. She seemed mesmerized by the attention I was giving my cock. "Stop looking and come help me." I told Legs in a demanding but playful voice. Legs let the robe she was wearing drop to the floor and entered this oversized shower, with her bra and panties on. She was either in a hurry to get wet or she wanted me to take them off. There were enough suds around my dick for both of us. I pulled her to me and began kissing her so passionately. Our large stomachs made it difficult for me to meet the pussy face to face. I continued to explore the insides of her mouth with my tongue. Legs breathing became heavier as our bellies touched. I placed both of my thumbs in her panties and began to slide the garments down. Once they passed over her ass and pussy, I began to massage her pubic hair that was covered with my suds. I forced my erect cock down until it fit between her legs. The suds made a lubricant that allowed my dick to slide smoothly between her legs. I had to crotch down a little to make it work. Legs became a little unsteady on her feet causing me to lean on the shower wall as she grabbed me around the waist. This was really starting to feel good. Legs was a bit nervous, fearing she might fall. I assured her that I had her and continued to massage her pussy with my dick. I stopped for a brief moment to pull the panties all the way down. Legs protested to my stopping but quickly calmed down when I resumed my stroke. She always told me how much she enjoyed dry fucking. This action was dry fucking with a twist. I let the water fall between us to rinse off the soap from our bodies. I was starting to hunger and food wouldn't satisfy this appetite. Once all the soap was gone, I lowered myself down to face the pussy. Legs didn't protest this time but instead grabbed my head with both hands, and forced it between her legs. The water was still falling between our bodies giving an effect of a waterfall. I started doing what I liked as I began to gently lick the outside lips of the pussy. I motioned for Legs to turn off the water as I began to engulf myself into this new activity. When the water stopped flowing, only droplets were left. This was almost like having the pussy covered with sauce. I don't know if it was the baby or the honeymoon, but the pussy had a much different taste to it. I started to slurp as my gentle licks became more aggressive. I could hear

Legs start to make some new sounds as I peeled the lips back and stuck my tongue inside. She was now leaning up against the shower wall with no fear of slipping. My knees were starting to hurt but I had no intention of stopping. I moved closer to the stall door as Legs followed not wanting to lose contact with my mouth. I slide the door open and reached fall the robe that lay crumbled on the floor. I pulled it inside and placed it under my knees. I was now comfortable and there was some room for Legs to also stand on it. I placed both of my hands on her butt cheeks. I pulled her so close it was like I had a hero sandwich in front of me. I continued to feast on the pussy as Legs began to make more strange noises. I went from licking the pussy to sucking on the clit. This move caused Legs to jerk violently as juices began to squirt against the bottom of my chin. I sucked the clit hard, while I flicked my tongue across it. Legs cried out; "Oh Yeah Oh Yeah." I rose to my feet as my dick slid up the length of the inside of her leg. She was still cumming when my dick slammed up against the bottom of her crotch. I held my stomach in as I grinded against her body. I was tired of this shower and began to lead Legs out by the hand. I picked up the robe as we left and threw it atop the chair outside. Looking ahead I saw Legs still had her gowns spread out. I walked ahead and placed them on the loveseat. I drew the covers back exposing real satin sheets. I wiped some of the water from my body and did the same for Legs. I wanted to lotion Legs, down but was too anxious to insert myself into her pussy. Her growing belly was no longer an obstruction. I spread her out like cold cuts on rye bread. I laid my dick between her legs like it was a piece of cheese. I started probing with my dick like it was a spoon filled with mustard. She just laid there so submissive to my will. I sucked on her tongue like it was an appetizer. Legs began to wiggle under me like meat sliding on a sandwich with too much mayo. Legs reached down and stuck the dick inside her. She was licked enough she was ready to be fucked now. I kept my weight in the air as I started to pump my cock in and out of the pussy. Slow at first then the speed increased, as she pulled me closer by my thighs. It felt so damn good to be inside her velvety pussy. The hair around the pussy was like silk. No doubt I was whooped and was enjoying every minute of it. I maintained a steady pace as the pussy started to snatch at my dick like it had teeth inside. Damn! This was some new shit. The pussy had never acted like this before. "Do that shit again Baby! Let me feel that pussy bite." I had to tell her because I wanted to feel that again. She flexed her muscles again and I could her pussy locking itself around my dick. I had heard about this before but I never experienced it. "Damn Legs you good. You feel like a virgin now with this new shit you doing with my pussy." Legs looked at me and just smiled and said: "I love you now more than any other tome we've been together." I could see the sincerity in her face when she spoke those words. I looked at her and without a smile on my face I said: "I love you much more than that." We both just kept staring into each others eyes as I continued my strokes. I slowed down a lot as I became more and more gentle as when I first started. My dick became so tender I knew what was getting ready to happen. My body stiffened as the juices began to leave me faster than a Negro at a Klan rally. I went limp as I lowered myself down next to Legs. We fell off to sleep, both hoping to awaken in time for our scheduled meal.

My eyes blinked as I began to realize that I was no longer dreaming. I rolled over and slowly climbed out of bed. Just as my feet hit the floor Legs started to stir from her own peaceful position. I stretched out my arms as Legs started to yearn. "What time is it Honey?" "Time for both our asses to be out of bed." I responded with a bit of annoyance in my voice. I did not want to be late for our first meal. This was also the time when we would meet the other guests. I felt satisfied and fulfilled but I still was anxious for the next event on the agenda. I didn't want legs to fall into that lazy mode that she was capable of. I told Legs to go shower and it might spark her up a bit. She obeyed without discussion which showed her willingness to be cooperative. This was so important, if we expected our honeymoon to be a success. I started to straighten up the bed as Legs showered. I declined her invitation to join her. I didn't want to slow her up anymore. I also didn't want to stir up my other man and never make it to dinner. I wasn't used to eating this early but the meal was welcomed. We lived through lunch without eating. Now to keep on living we both were ready for a meal. Legs came out the shower with water droplets cascading down her body. I wish I had brought the video camera. This moment would have been a wonderful shoot. My eyes stayed fixated on her as she walked slowly to the bed. I watched as she let the towel drop to the floor and began applying lotion to her body. Her swollen belly began to glow as the nipples on her now enlarged breasts stuck out. "Damn she was getting aroused putting on that lotion." I murmured under my breath. I suddenly became aware of the time and rushed into the bathroom. I was still naked from our nap together and just had to step into the shower. It took only a few minutes for me to finish because I just stuck to washing only. When I came out Legs had on her bra and panties. She then looked for an outfit to match. There was no delay in a selection for myself. I put on a short set after greasing up my body and applying some cologne. I finally had to help Legs make a selection because she was taking too long. We checked each other out before leaving the room. We made the short walk to the dining hall as smiles returned to both of our faces. When we walked inside it felt like all eyes were on us again.

We stepped into the dining room and found a suitable seat. Dinner was being served with and there were few choices. It was such a delight for us just to be here that food wasn't a priority. What they served was what we ate. I looked around and saw another Black couple here. Why do we do that as a routine? Whenever we as a race are in settings with new social contacts, we look for us. It's important that we take note of the number of our people there with us. I was looking over our brochure as it described the games and other activities that were planned. "This seems like it's going to be a lot of fun Baby!" Legs looked at as if to wonder, how much would her belly affect her fun? She then responded with a dry; "Yeah." The food was actually real good and the company was alright too. There were about ten other couples sitting in the room eating. It was a mixture of nationalities. Whenever someone made eye contact they would smile back at the other person. Legs was eating good. Two things had changed about Legs since the pregnancy. She was eating more and her tits were much bigger. I kept trying to get her to breast feed so the big tits would last longer. She would always say, enjoy them while they're here. Legs' fear was that the titties would start sagging if she breast fed. I think she saw some tiny sagging titties on somebody else and it scared her. The waiters started to clear off the tables as everyone finished their meals. It was already explained that, because of the scheduled events, meals had to start and finish on time. The tables were cleared and everyone's eyes began to roam the room. Now we all began to stare at each other wondering what our stories were. The freak in me started to wonder, which one of these couples were swingers?

The hostess came in and introduced herself as some of the guests began changing seats. I was satisfied where I was sitting and so was Legs. The hostess introduced her husband and began to give a history of the lodge. The story was entertaining but that's not what I was interested in. The room began to warm up as more of the guests began to engage the host and hostess with questions. This was an opportunity for anyone to find out more about the lodge if they wanted too. Most of us were still tired from the trip up here and just wanted to be in our rooms. The hostess recognized this and allowed everyone to leave. Our next gathering would be at lunch time tomorrow. Breakfast was served early buffet style. We were constantly smiling at everyone as we left the dining room. Legs seemed to liking what was going on. I sure was and couldn't wait for the morning.

It wasn't long before we were back in the room because it was located so close to everything. I picked out a long flowing gown for Legs to wear to bed. There was always something exceptional about a woman in a long night gown with no panties on. Looking at the nipples trying to poke holes thru the garment was exciting. Watching the butt cheeks taking turns rising and falling was even more of a turn-on. Legs was still the most gorgeous woman I knew even with that belly. Like last time I was the first one in the bathroom. I didn't need a shower but I wanted to just freshen up. We had the heat in the room blasting because Legs wanted to get in the pool. We had been told earlier when we checked in, what we could and could not put in the water. I rinse all the cosmetics from my body and slid into the water. Legs took a little longer than me because she insisted on taking a shower. The water was just over belly. Half way between my navel and chest nipples. The water was deep enough for me to swim across. There was a descending layer of steps that was wide enough to lie across. This design gave the pool a more enchanting feel. I continued to splash around as my Baby took her time getting ready. At last the princess had arrived and it was worth the wait. Legs looked like a real starlet in that gown. It clung to her body so perfectly. She walked slowly to the pool's edge as I moved thru the water to meet her. She reached the beginning of the steps, just as I started my ascent out of the pool. "Ooooo where's your swim suit Honey?" Legs looked amazed as she peered over my nakedness. "Baby this is our pool. I don't need a swim suit. I just need you to cover up this body." I emerged out of the deep part of the water to meet Legs. I watched as she patiently walked down the steps with her eyes fixed on my erection. It was quite a sight to see as this protruding thing raised itself from the water. Legs draped her arms around my neck and followed me back into the water. The deeper we went the closer she came to me. The water began to raise her gown up as it floated around her body. This was so much to behold as her naked body underneath made contact with my erection. The head of my dick floated beneath the water like some attack submarine looking for the enemy. There were no torpedoes for this sub to fire, so it would have to ram the enemy vessel. The sub went all ahead full as it found its mark within the folds of flesh before it. Dive! Dive! The supposed command as I sank my sub deep into the canyon. When the sub reached the bottom it tried to back out only to stop and go forward again. It repeated this maneuver over and over again until the canyon it was stuck in began to shake. The folds of flesh that encased the sub began to excrete a smooth silky substance that clouded the water. The sub began to go in and out at a much quicker pace as if time was running out. Pressure began to build and before anyone could sound an alarm the sub exploded. A burst of fluid shot from it and slammed against the walls of the canyon it was trapped in. This fluid when it ceased to flow caused the folds of flesh to loosen its grip on the submarine. The mountain shook one last time as the sub began to float away. The violent waves in the water disappeared and cal returned to the region. I held Legs close to me as the last bit of sperm escaped from me. The water made Legs so light that I had no trouble keeping her up. She kept a tight grip on my neck as I raised her horizontally in the water. I placed my left hand under her legs and my right hand under her ass. I began to massage her butt cheeks as she became more relaxed in the water. My erection began to return and I started to wonder if this ass was ripe enough for penetration? This was such a moment for both of us. Legs was so relaxed in the water that it was hard to imagine, she used to be afraid. I backed Legs up against me. We waded over to the edge of the pool so Legs would have something to lean on. I tilted her head forward just enough for her ass to stick out. I rubbed my penis between her butt cheeks. She began to moan gently as I tried to enter her. Legs ass opened wide but the water wasn't lubricating it enough. I allowed my penis to slide down and entered her pussy from the rear. She let out a gasp as I sunk deep inside her. I began to move in and out of her very gently. She started to wiggle her ass, as I plunged even deeper inside. My cock began to throb as my pumping action increased. The water around us began to swoosh and splash and I took a firmer grip of Legs' waist. This pussy was so good and inviting as my nuts slapped against her vulva. I was ready to cumm and it felt like Legs was ready too. I leaned back in the water as Legs moved her ass to meet my thrusts inside her pussy. My body began to convulse as Legs let out a scream. Ahhhhhh Zee keep going, plezzzz don't stop now. I'm almost ready to cummm oh no I'm cumming too. Oh baby yeah. Ah shit damn Oooooo emm huh ahhhhh. Legs entire body began to shake as I continued to empty my load. Water was splashing everywhere as we continued to race to the finish line. I arrived first on empty but Legs was right behind me. I let my dick stay inside for awhile as Legs continued to shake. I eased out slowly and spun Legs around. I sunk my tongue deep inside her mouth as I tried to touch her tonsils. She locked her lips around my mouth and our tongues flicked back and forth against each other. We were both satisfied as we struggled to leave the pool. I walked closely behind legs with my left hand resting comfortably on her ass. I continued to grasp it as she removed her wet gown. This was not the end of our session, but only the beginning. I left her ass for a moment to retrieve a rag from the bathroom. I wanted to wipe off that pussy so daddy could eat. She spread her legs wide as the warm rag found its mark. The pool left no evidence between her legs. I still had to be sure not to swallow anything we didn't bring in here with us. She started her moaning again as the rag in my hands became an instrument of pleasure.

Legs was anxious to finish what we started in the pool. Although she became used to the water, Legs was still a land lover. I applied soft touches to her skin as I wiped off the vulva and gently swiped her clit. She started squirming as if to encourage more swiping. I tossed the rag to the side and began to use my fingers. I moistened my fingers with saliva and began to attack her clit more vigorously. She appeared delighted with the way I was massaging her most sensitive part. I began to tell her how important she was to me. I nestled my face along side her neck as I continued massaging and whispering in her ear. A smile flashed across her face as I raised myself above her. I perched motionless in that position as a tear began to roll down her cheeks. I grabbed my now enlarged member and began to rub its head between her lower lips. She began to moan from the expectation of what was going to happen next. I slowly inserted the head into her well lubricated pussy. She arched her back as my member slid deeper inside her. I sunk deeper and deeper until I reached bottom. I paused for a moment as her silky warm lubricants engulfed me. I could feel her pussy vibrate and tighten around my cock. "I so love you baby and your pussy feels so good." Legs responded to my words by grinding her body against mine with both hands gripping my sides. I placed both of my hands on the bed along side her and began to raise and lower myself against her. She would raise her body up to meet my thrusts as we were now in a rhythm. "Yes Baby" I cried. "Good pussy, good pussy, keep moving like ya moving Baby." We went on like this for the next half and hour with sweat pouring down our bodies. There was no indication of either of us tiring so we went on for another twenty minutes before collapsing in a heap. We slept until dinner time and awoke well rested. We dressed in our matching sweat suits and headed for the dining room.

This time we found ourselves sitting at the table with the other black couple. We were surprised to learn that they were from Brooklyn. In fact they lived in a neighborhood that I was very familiar with. They were very pleasant and we invited them back to our rooms. Our conversations were cordial and we promised to stay in touch. They didn't stay long because we expressed a desire to go to bed early. I wanted to get involved in some of the activities here. We had been spending most of our time fucking and thinking about fucking. We decided that we would check out the rifle range and take some outdoor pictures. We already had enough pictures of us playing in the bed and the pool. We now wanted some pictures we could show to other people. Once again I picked out the night gown for my baby to sleep in. We had two more days to go and I wasn't going to waste any time. We showered together without arousing each other too much. Tomorrow would be different than the other days we had here. We exited the shower at the same time. I watched as Legs stepped out carefully. She was such a beautiful woman to me. The Lord had really blessed me with her presence. I too stepped outside the stall and immediately went to her side. I began to gently rub the towel over her body. The water droplets on her skin were glistening in the light. She placed her hand on top of mine and said thank you. I didn't know if she was thanking me for drying her off or for being there with her. I continued to remove the water from her swollen belly and placed the towel over her moist pubic hair. She let out a sigh as I began to rub the outside and penetrate slightly between her lower lips. I drop to my knees unable to resist the temptation to lick the opening that my child would be emerging from. Legs placed her hand atop my head and began to guide me deeper into her most private crevice. It was an unimaginable experience to be where I was right now. Legs stepped back against the wall to keep steady, as both hands had a firm grip on my head. I needed no encouragement as my licking picked up its pace. Legs moaned as my mouth engulfed her swollen clit. My knees began to hurt but I couldn't stop. It felt good and it tasted good to be between her legs right now. I placed my hands behind her thighs just below her ass. I held on tight as I dove deeper inside her with my tongue. She began to convulse slightly as juices slid down her thighs. In one brief moment she cried out Zeeee! I held on and sucked hard on her clit as her juices splashed against my neck and chest. I continued sucking and massaging her ass while her movements slowly calmed down. I rose up off my aching knees with my chin sticky from her flow. My swollen cock was now stuck between her as she resisted my kisses. I laughed out loud as I inserted my cock inside wet pussy. I wanted to cum just like she had and proceeded with gentle strokes. Legs urged me on as her pelvis rose to meet my thrusts. I feared slipping but took the risk as I raced home to my own glory. "Ooooooo my turn Baby I ready to burst." I said in a whisper. "Go ahead Honey don't hold back, I wanna feel your sperm inside me!" Ahhhhh, I yelled as cum splashed against her pussy walls. "It's so warm inside me." She responded as I continued to empty everything I had inside her. We finally both calmed down as our bodies stopped jerking. Legs also had cum again whole I was emptying my load inside her. We looked at each other with our heavy breathing and laughed. We had so much sweat and cum on our bodies that we had to shower again. This time we took separate showers to avoid being aroused once more. We had a very comfortable sleep that night anticipating the next day's events.

I rolled over as the morning's light shone through the window. My tee shirt felt damp as I kicked the covers off me. Legs was still asleep as I pulled over on top of me. We both slept with tops but no bottoms. I shifted her slightly so she wouldn't be resting on her stomach. Since we met it always felt so good and safe to be between her legs. I just laid there with my cock growing more and more and throbbing against her vulva. It was still early so I saw no need to wake her. I began to daydream about our future life together. I thought about the changes that would come with the birth of the baby. I was looking forward to being a fulltime dad raising a child. I was denied that opportunity with my firstborn. My son's mother broke up with me before he was born. I still didn't let that prevent me from being there for her prenatal or his birth. Legs pregnancy motivated me to marry her. I didn't need to be in love but I was getting closer to her as time went on.

Legs began to stir as she rolled off her side onto her back. I lifted up gown as I stared at the mirror above our bed. I rubbed her belly as she threw the covers off her to the side. She continued kicking until her body was fully exposed. "I see you sweating too Baby." I murmured sarcastically as she raised her right knee up. I kept looking in the ceiling mirror as I placed my right hand on her left thigh. I felt like I was watching a movie as I started to massage the top of her pussy. I didn't want to get too involved because my erection was feeling good just the way it was. Legs used her left hand to reach over and began to play with me. Now we were both looking in the mirror as the sunlight became even brighter in the room. This was not normal for Legs to play with me this way. I jumped up abruptly to return with a well greased pole. I had enough left on my hands to also lubricate her lower lips. We return to our previous positions and continued to give each other pleasure. I instructed Legs on what works best for me and she caught on fast. Her hands were almost as good as the pussy. The head of my cock became very tender as Legs' hands rose up and down the length of it. It was becoming hard to concentrate on her pussy as I felt brand new sensations. Legs looked pleased as I continued to respond to her touching. I pressed down hard with the palm of my hand against her vulva. I let my finger tips find the beginning of her ass as my sperm began to squirt all over the room. Legs seemed fascinated by what she was witnessing. She squeezed the head as sperm squirted between her fingers. She kept up her pace as I started to insert my fingers inside her pussy. I was determined to bring her where she had left me. Easy she cried as I massaged her clit with my greasy fingers. I rocked my hand back and forth as my middle finger rested inside her. She began to moan as my hand started to feel her pussy pulsate against my palm. She started to drip heavily as my hand rocked faster and faster. "Keep it up like that, I'm almost there." She stated in a barely audible voice. I could now feel her juices forcing their way between my fingers. Legs arched her back and her leg shook, as wave after wave of pleasure took over her body. I continued to apply pressure as another round of spasms engulfed her. We both finally rested satisfied at our accomplishments. "Time to wash and get dressed Baby." I instructed, as we both searched for the strength to rise.

We still had outfits didn't wear yet. I had brought some new sneakers just for this trip. I made sure I had some matching gear to go with them. I also made sure my Baby had new sneakers too. We both hurried to get dress after leaving the shower. Our outfits had us color coordinated with orange, black, and white. We arrived on time for breakfast and met up with the other couple from Brooklyn. They looked real cute as they wore identical outfits. I had to suppress those urges that didn't realize yet that I was a married man. I wasn't just a married man but one who was committed to success. The breakfast lasted as long as it was necessary. I was anxious to continue on our itinerary. We decided to go to the rifle range. This might be the only time I'll get to shoot without being shot back at. I also didn't have to worry about the police trying to make an arrest. We both looked so much younger than our years. We didn't try to correct anyone that guessed early thirties. Legs were thought to be even younger than that. The morning went fast as we lounged around outside taking pictures and playing games. We didn't stop for lunch as the area experienced record breaking high temperatures. The Lord continued to demonstrate his involvement with our lives. The Resort had some beautiful landscape and I convinced Legs to keep touring it with me. Legs was the city girl and I was the country boy. I loved the outdoors and knew a lot about nature. I impressed Legs with my knowledge of the insects we saw and some of the amphibians.

The sun was beginning its descent as we began to tire. I wanted to sleep outside but that wasn't possible. We walked slowly back to our suite as shared stories about the day. I made excuses for not being the great shooter that I thought I was. It was still warm out so I suggested a swim before we had dinner. I had trunks but Legs would have to swim in her gown. I didn't mind because when it got wet, I couldn't take my eyes off it. We spent so much time playing in the pool that we had to order from the room. I had always avoided this because of the extra charge. I made the exception tonight because we were having such a good time. We ordered seafood which seemed so appropriate. While we waited for the food to arrive, I swam a lap as Legs waded near the pool's edge. I started to emerge from the water keeping a close eye on Legs. Although she was now so comfortable in the water, I still had concerns about her safety. I stepped out the pool onto the carpet dripping wet. I dried myself off and motioned for Legs to join me. She hesitated a bit before making her slow ascent. I watched as her gown clung to her body showing off all her womanly curves. Her nipples were rigid as she began to lift up her gown and squeeze out some of the water. "Come here girl, let me do that." I called out as she walked seductively toward me. I gathered the bottom of the garment in my hands and raised it above her head. I carefully removed it exposing her naked body. It landed in a heap on the floor as it fell from my hands. "You are so dramatic!" She said, while I began to dry her off with my damp towel. I started removing my own trunks while she walked towards the bed. I had already placed a black negligee there for her to wear. She looked so peaceful going into the bathroom to wash off. I stared like a peeking tom at her spreading suds over her body. I removed my wet trunks and searched for wash cloth. Finding it nearby I wiped my body down and started to apply Vaseline all over. My body began to glow as the grease was spread over me. I pause for a moment to see if Legs was done. She was rinsing the suds off leaving small pools of bubbles at her feet. I watched intently she squatted slightly to wipe her feet. What a view to see as her love boat seemed to pop out from its base. I stayed focused and finished on some cologne and my underwear. Legs used a fresh towel to dry off. She wrapped it around her and came over to the bed. She began to splash on her perfume and rubbed lotion on her moist skin. Her body glistened in the light. I pulled the towel from around her and began finish putting the lotion on her. She smiled as my hands glided over her body. We were having so much fun caring for each other. I did not want this end but reality would soon set in. I wondered if the wealthy enjoyed their money as much as I was enjoying mine. I helped Legs put on her black negligee. She then went and sprawled on the bed while I began to straighten up the room. It wasn't long before room service was at the door. I retrieved our food and gave a generous tip. Legs protested at the size of it but that's who I was. I laid a clean towel on the bed and placed the food on top. We stretched out on either side and began to eat. We took turns putting food in each others mouth. We talked about what tomorrow would be like. It would be our last day and we didn't want this honey moon to end. The room grew silent as we both just thought about what our future lives would be like. I continued to eat while staring at Legs. She was unsure what to say and just kept smiling as I kept staring. The food was good and I was full. I fell back against the pillows while Legs finished eating the shrimps. I couldn't move and just dozed off to the smacking sound of Legs' lips.

I woke up in the middle of the night to find Legs fast asleep and the food tray still on the bed. I placed everything on the cart and left it outside our door. I returned to the bed and pulled Legs close to me as I the sheets over us. Legs stirred but didn't wake up. I fell back asleep while massaging Legs' ass.

I took a long yawn as the sun shined brightly through the windows. The shades were drawn but the sunshine found its way thru the cracks. I looked at Legs who was on her side with her back to me. It appeared she had done a lot of shifting during the night. The last thing I remembered was pushing the food cart outside the door. I drew closer to Legs and began to grind in circular motions against her plumb ass. The silk material of her gown made like a lubricant as I began to get a stiff erection. I closed my eyes and continued to grind as Legs began to awaken. "Oh Honey let me sleep please?" She beckoned as I continued my assault on her body. "Just relax Baby, this won't take long." I reasoned as my member continued to grow longer and harder. I found the soft cushion just under her ass while the gown still made like a lubricant. I switched from my circular motion to an up and down stroke, which was simulated penetration. Now the head of my cock was rubbing up against her pussy and she began to respond to this new sensation. She began to moan softly as my cock had reached its maximum length. It was now too long to be concealed by the gown and began to poke its head at the pussy opening. I had not planned on going inside but Legs began to push her ass backwards. The pussy was dripping wet and I could do nothing to stop Legs from forcing my little head inside her. Ahhhhh! She cried out as my dick disappeared between the lips of her wet pussy. Legs continued to push back and forth as she pumped her ass up against my pelvis. She drew her knees up and demanded that I start fucking her. She was my wife now so I had to get used to obeying. I gripped her waist firmly and began to do what she ordered. I raised the gown up to get a better view of the ass that I was pounding. I forgot about the baby as I went deeper and deeper inside. It was like dipping into thick pudding as I easily slid in and out. Legs was clutching the sheets as she kept urging me on. I know longer needed anymore encouragement as the pleasure sensors were being overwhelmed. "More, more it doesn't hurt." She cried as her juices began to flow more heavily. I was giving her all I had and it felt like the head of my dick would explode. I was beginning to welcome the end of the honeymoon as my ass started having spasms of its own. "Come on Zee I'm almost there. I love you so much Honey. Keep fucking me harder now harder." Legs was possessed. The words coming from her mouth were brand new. I continued to be obedient but the end was near. "I can't hold back any more!" I yelled. "That's alright Honey I'm getting ready to cummmmm!" Legs body began to shake and convulse violently. I became nervous wondering if she was having a seizure. "Ooooooo! Ohhhhh! Legs began to sing as I felt the insides of her pussy tighten around me. Then at the same moment I let out a sigh of relief, as my sperm exploded inside her. Gush after gush the thick streams collided and began to run out onto the sheets. The sensation felt so good that we both began to pump into each other again. In and out in and out I went until we both reached a climax that caused us to collapse. There we lay with me still mounted behind my Baby while her legs were sprawled wide open. It wasn't long before we were both dozing again. It would be two more hours before we awaken and begin our last day at the resort.

I was the first to get up. Legs continued sleeping as I rose and took my shower. I was fully dressed before I began to shake Legs telling her it was time to rise. I looked real neat in my new short set. The design was intended for a much younger man but that never stopped me before. Legs wasn't as excited as I was. I think she was feeling depressed because our honeymoon was coming to an end. I urged her to be more joyful because the end of the honeymoon was the beginning of our marriage. She smiled and tried to laugh but still her sadness showed. I escorted her to the bathroom and reassured her of the good things awaited us together. I reminded her of all the obstacles we had overcome to reach this point. She smiled again as I helped her step into the shower stall. I left the bathroom to retrieve her under garments as the water started cascading down her body. I was wearing gold colors so I picked out her money green short set to wear. It wasn't long before she was calling for her panties to start dressing while she was still in the bathroom. I thought to myself "She'll be alright!" Legs were a tough girl from the projects. Life had already improved for her since we had been together. Her mother showed more respect towards her and she was providing more for her daughter. She always appeared so helpless to me as I began unravel the affairs of her life. Marriage had me feeling more and more like a real man because of the responsibility that came with it. Although we weren't married in a church by a preacher, the union was still ordained by God. Legs emerged from the bathroom wearing her sexy panties and glowing from the lotion on her body. I beckoned her to the bedside where her clothes were laid out. She seemed more jubilant than she were before. Legs approved of her outfit and commented on how good I looked in mine. That's the one thing we did a lot, tell each other how good we looked.

We packed up our belongings before leaving the room. We made sure we stuffed a few of their towels in our bags. It was almost customary to take something with you that you didn't pay for. I don't think we were being ghetto because even the rich did it. We left the room holding hands to have our last meal in the Pocono. Everyone was already in the dining room eating when we came in. We sat with the couple from Brooklyn. I went to the buffet table for our lunch while Legs stayed behind talking. It appeared we had made some new friends as Legs happiness began to show. I returned to the table as Legs was exchanging phone numbers. We took our time eating as the conversation shifted to talk about family. This was the first time we gave any indication of how old we were. Our new friends were amazed because of our youthful appearance and energy. All the guests present began clearing off their tables as the Host and hostess began thanking everyone for their presence. A few of us committed to returning and were given coupons for discounts on meals and lodging. I planned on returning with a car to take advantage of the outlet mall nearby. We returned to our rooms for our luggage and went to the lobby to wait for our ride. The resort had free transportation to the bus station. The hostess came to us again expressing her gratitude. She spoke of how good we looked as a couple and gave us a parting gift. The drive to the bus station was brief and our bus had already arrived. The driver loaded our baggage and we settled into seats near the back. I couldn't stop smiling as I remembered all the things we were able to do. I t was Wednesday and we both had to work on Thursday. We didn't mind because it was a payday. The ride lasted about two hours and we weren't looking forward to riding that subway home. I definitely had to drive if I ever went back to the Pocono.

The bus grinded its way up the ramp inside the Port Authority. The city never looked better. I was returning with my new bride and a lot of responsibility. Once again we navigated our way through the station with luggage in tow. People watched with curiosity as rush hour had the trains full. Legs jacket hid her bulge so nobody rushed to give her a seat. Five quick stops and we were home so the discomfort didn't last long. This is one time I really appreciated having our apartment only a few blocks from the subway. We waved at two of our neighbors before making our way up the stairs. The apartment was stuffy because we left all the windows closed. We set the bags down and collapsed in a heap on the bed. I stripped down to my underwear as Legs followed suit. I wasn't ready to do any unpacking and neither was Legs. We stretched out on the bed and cuddled up next to each other. We kissed passionately as we began to doze off. My wife's warm body felt good next to mine. I planted myself firmly between her legs before she fell asleep. Her fragrance entertained my senses as I massaged her back. Home never felt as good as it did now. My lions stirred as I shifted Legs body to lie more on top than to the side. I throbbed as my erection gained momentum beneath her. My hands moved to her ass with circular motions. I continued this activity until I also fell asleep. I thought to myself as I drifted off to never land "Life is good!"

THURSDAY MORNING MEANT a new a day but it also meant a new time. I looked across the room at our bags leaning against the wall. Still unpacked and filled with more than our clothes. It held memories of an event that solidified our commitment to each other. It held memories of a time when our personal needs were addressed by each other. I looked across the room at all the occupied space and wondered, where could I place a crib? I had to stop day dreaming and begin to prepare for work. Legs was so tranquil in her fetal position as she continued to sleep. I wondered if she was as enthusiastic as I was about this new day. I went into the bathroom and rinsed out the tub and began running a bath. I started searching thru my drawers for some new underwear. I was always so dramatic when it came to identifying defining moments. I went into my closet to find a suit I hadn't wore in awhile. I walked over to the bed and planted a soft kiss on Legs' cheek. She didn't awake as I disappeared into the bathroom. I squirted some Joy under the rushing water and watched the bubbles form quickly. I removed my underwear and slid into the tub. The water felt good as I stretched out in the tub. Using my feet I turned off the water and began to relax. The hot water was soothing and comforting. My mind began to wonder again as I replayed the all the events that proceeded this moment. There were memories of turmoil and joy, triumphs and failures. I thought about the many introductions of new friends and farewells to some old ones. I reached for my rag and soap and began to lather up. I didn't want to be late the first day back. I also wanted Legs to be on time so I hurriedly began to wash. In no time I was looking liking a snowman with my body completely covered with suds. I unstopped the tub and stared down at my erection. Washing my member felt good and I wondered if trying to cumm would make me late. I took a chance and began a more gentle massage. I pulled the shower curtains shut as the water disappeared from the tub. Emmm it felt good as I closed my eyes about Legs' wildness during the honeymoon. Just as my cock was reaching its maximum length Legs knocked on the door. I turned on the shower and gave her permission to come in. "You almost finished Honey?" She asked as I tried to reach a climax. "Yess Baby I'm almost done." I replied in a voice barely audible. "You alright in there, it sounds like you're catching cold." Damn I wish she would stop asking so many questions, I thought to myself. I was so close and the sound of her peeing was helping me along. "Yeahhh Baby I'm alright." The toilet flushing made a loud noise as Legs pulled back the shower curtains. "What are you doing?" I shouted with my hard dick held tightly in my hand. "Damn you still horny with all the fucking we been doing?" I couldn't answer and Legs began to strip. With no invitation she entered the shower with me. I move to the side as water splashed on the floor. I grabbed my sudsy rag and washing her ass while she faced the running water. "We have to hurry Honey it's getting late." She said as I applied soap to her back. I turned her to face me as she moved away from the stream of water. She reached down and began to rub my cock while I rinsed the soap from the rag. Her hands felt good gliding over me. The more she rubbed the more excited I became. My body jerked as semen rushed from my cock and splashed against leg. "Emm get it all out Baby!" I squealed as she squeezed the head of it in her hands. She frowned with amazement as the last drops emptied into her hand. "You feel better now freak?" She asked seductively while turning her back to me. She fumbled behind herself with my cock still in her hand. "It's my turn now." She said as she began to lean over and insert my still erect cock into her pussy. "Ooooo she cooed as the head disappeared inside her pussy. She removed her hand and placed them against the wall in front of her. I began to pump rapidly inside her fearing that I might lose my erection. She rolled her pelvis and urged me on as she tried to climax. The more I pumped the harder I became. It was difficult to focus on the pussy because I didn't want either of us to fall. Legs was not having that problem as she increased the pace of her movements. Having gained some confidence I grabbed her waist and slammed deep inside her. "Ahhhhh!" She screamed as her body stiffened. I continued banging into her as she reached her goal. She began to relax as my thrusts became very gentle. It wanted to continue but I reminded the dick that we both had a job to go to. We turned the shower back on and wash off quickly before leaving the bathroom to get dressed. We left the house together but took separate trains to work.

I entered my job amid smiles and glances. I checked in with The Director and shared a brief story about my honeymoon. It was entertaining to him and it helped me to increase my influence with him. I began my day still foggy from the honeymoon. It didn't cause me to be lax but instead gave me a new energy. I went to my desk and started checking my client's folders. I wanted my work to reflect my attitude towards my job. It was no longer just me but a family now. I began to make the necessary entries and called my people in one by one. Some were at work because of their level in the program. The most important thing about what I did wasn't the talking but the documentations about the services I delivered. Week after week and month after month went by without incident. I became consistent in being up to date with my records and my professionalism. I started attracting the attention of my superiors outside my facility. Yes Zeke was making a name for himself in the business.

The summer was upon us and there were a lot of record breaking temperature days. I stayed in contact with my wife while at work. I catered to her while at home. She was experiencing a trouble free pregnancy as I focused on keeping her happy and healthy. I tried to get her to stop smoking but she could only slow down. My love for her soothed, any and all pains, I felt from so much responsibility. I didn't just have her and the upcoming baby to worry about, my mother was also very important to me. I found myself spending less and less time with momma, and that weighed heavy on my heart. We were still in our cramped apartment and I made it even more cramped. I started making purchases for our future place that remained packed in their boxes. The sex slowed down to a crawl as Legs grew larger and she became cranky. I endured the mood swings and stayed cheerful. When she found the time she would thank me and shower me with gifts. I was in the habit of buying her flowers and perfume. This kept us both from exploding on each other during some difficult moments. It was a struggle keeping up with the rent because we both wanted to move. Legs was due to give birth anywhere between late September and early October. I had her take it easy on the weekends that she didn't have to work. This was done to control the swelling in her feet. She had planned to work up to the last minute to conserve as much time as possible for maternity leave. Legs wanted the leave for after the baby arrived and not before. I was due to attend my graduation in October and Legs wanted to get a new dress to wear. She was such a procrastinator and still didn't have a bag packed for the hospital. It was the end of September and Legs was going to stop work on the last day of the month. The week went by without her doing any of the things I told her. That weekend I rented a car so I could be at her side if she went into labor while I was at work. It was Friday morning when I drove to work in my rental. Legs had planned to pack her bag after she went out and bought a dress for my graduation. This would be the start of her maternity leave but it wouldn't be official until the following Monday. I kissed her as usual and rubbed that big belly before leaving. I went to work believing that sometime during the next week the baby would arrive.

I came into my office sharp as a tack. I was known to dress GQ so my outfit didn't draw any unusual attention. I let all the staff no that I was on alert for the baby to come any day now. I told The Director about my rental outside and the reason I had it. I settled down and went about my normal activities not expecting this day to be any different than the last. Legs called me that morning to let me know she was leaving the house to shop. Our conversation was brief because I was in the middle of the checking the dorms for cleanliness while the clients was either at work or having breakfast. Less than thirty minutes after speaking to Legs, The Director was paging me to his office. Now what I thought to myself! I came in with a lot of joy in heart and didn't need my foundation shaken. I walked into the office as The Director displayed a worry look on his face. "I just got a call from the police department. Your wife went into labor while waiting on line for a store to open." What! Oh shit, is she alright?" I asked with both excitement and concern in my voice. "Go ahead and leave, they're waiting for an ambulance to take her to the hospital." My gears began to shift as he finished his sentence. I bolted down the stairs as the staff and residents I passed showed looks of confusion. I took my pager off vibrate as I exited the building. I hopped into the car and sped off to the Major Deegan Highway. I was not concerned with the speed limit as I headed down the highway. I figured if the police pulled me over they could provide an escort. The pager was beeping off the hook as I entered the F.D.R.Drive. I was coming across the Brooklyn Bridge and about to exit as sirens blared in the background. It was less than twenty minutes since I had left the job. It was hard to believe that I made the trip in such a short time. I pulled over as soon as I could to answer the pages. One number was my job and another one was unknown to me. I called the job to hear that Legs was on her way to the College Hospital. They were shocked when I told them that I was in Brooklyn. The hospital was close by so I was there in seconds. I went in and found her in the delivery section. She was in some distress but was laughing as she told me the story of her morning. "Honey my water broke this morning, but I didn't know that's what it was. I thought it would be more liquid than that." I laughed out loud at the implications of her statement. She continued on to explain what happened while she was trying to find a dress. "I was outside a store with a bunch of other women waiting for it to open. I was standing there and then this sharp pain hit me. I didn't think much about it because I had been standing there for awhile. Then it came again and I could hardly stand up. When I told the women helping me, that I had peed on myself this morning they called 911. They started laughing too and said I was going into labor." I couldn't stop laughing as she finished up her account of the events. The room was small and she was the only occupant. It was different than when my son was born. They were monitoring her contractions waiting for the cervix to dilate to ten centimeters. We continued to chat with me trying to distract her from the pain. There would be no drugs for comfort, this birth would be natural. She was not in a bed. It was some sort of chair in a reclining position. She also didn't have a doctor that would be doing the delivery. It was a nurse qualified in this area. I arrived way before 11:00 a.m. but the dinner hour was approving. Legs had me removed from the room a few times because of my jokes. They were funny to her but it hurt more when she laughed.

The nurse came outside and called me in. Legs was in a lot more pain and the baby was ready to come. I placed a gown on to cover my clothes. I was being allowed to stay but had to wash my hands first. I talked about how I was present for my son's birth. The next thing I saw left me amazed and concerned. I thought she would be wheeled to the delivery room but was told this is it. The nurse had Legs prop herself up as this chair transformed and Left legs almost suspended in the air. "What are you doing? Where is the baby going to go? What if you drop her? I was certain it would be a girl because that's what I wanted. I didn't even have a boy's name prepared. I stood alongside Legs head as she was told to push. It was after five and the wait for this moment had been a long one. I wasn't brave enough to watch the baby enter from that opening. I did not want to exchange my memories of that location for something less desirable. It didn't take but a minute for Baby Z to pop out once Legs started pushing. The time was 5:30p.m.and the weight was 5lbs.13oz and it was a girl. They wipe the baby off a little and handed her to me. She was a little something with short thick hair. She had a pretty chocolate coating. My eyes welled up with tears as I handed her to Legs. "We did it!" I said while Legs reached out and received her new daughter. Legs was hoping for a boy because they were scarce in her family. I wanted a girl because they were scarce in my family. God wanted a healthy child which made everyone happy. The birth of our child ended the care free attitude we had about our leisure. The focus for me was on the baby and staying together. We settled on a name that reflected mine. In this story she will always be none as Z Baby.

Times had really changed when it came to child birth. Rising health costs meant a shorter stay in the hospital. Once the baby passed urine and it came back free of illicit drugs it was cleared to go home. The next requirement was the method of transportation with the necessary car seat. My child came into the world Friday evening and was home Sunday morning. Legs was in excellent condition. There were very little effects on her body from child birth. We were given a crib from my sister. It was a challenge to find a place for it because of the size. It would be awhile before Legs returned to work. It would be even longer before she returned to her regular household chores. We were given a lot of the necessary baby items we needed from the baby shower. We received even more from Legs' mother who welcomed the birth of another grandchild. Z Baby was a happy baby that gave us little problems. She grew at a normal pace with no complications with her health. I was doing double duty with working the job, cleaning the house and waking up most nights to care for the baby. I never complained because this is what I wanted. Romance became a thing of the past as I waited out the six weeks recommended before sex could resume. Even when that time arrived I was still hesitant and waited even longer. I urged Legs to breast feed so those titties would remain large longer. She was not agreeable to that, so after a few months they returned to pre-baby size. We were fortunate to find a sitter on the block we lived. I had concerns about the pit bull she had. We soon learned that it wasn't nothing worry about. Life continued to get better for both of us as Legs returned to making a full pay check and I returned to gambling on the weekends. Money wasn't a problem for us but we still had our occasional arguments about it. The perfect babysitter became a nightmare and we had to find someone else fast. Once again God smiled upon us and Legs was able to get help form The Salvation Army. The location was in her old neighborhood which made travel easy. We would take turns dropping off Z Baby and picking her up.

The years went fast and so did empty space in the house, as we continued to buy more things. I applied for an apartment in a large Brooklyn development. It was a small down payment for a credit check. It would be based solely on my income. Legs credit wasn't good. I had paid off some of her debt and began to teach her how to make it better. Our place was starting to choke us because of the size. Z Baby was running around and needed more space. We went out a lot probably because it was more room outside. Z Baby was four when we suffered a set back. I had to withdraw my application at the rental office when Legs argued with a receptionist. It was a major compromise but it wouldn't be the only one in our marriage. I began to spend more time in the street chasing money as the pressure was on to move.

I came home thinking about the lack of romance in the marriage. We were arguing a lot and there was no where to go inside to get away. Legs called me to tell me about an apartment in Brooklyn. It was in a part of town known for its night life. I was very reluctant to consider it. I did not want to go back to that jungle where so many things could go wrong. Then I looked around at where I was at! I figured looking couldn't hurt and Legs had sounded so excited about it. Legs came in cheerful with Z baby in tow. She immediately began to tell me more about the place. She then told me about the Section 8 voucher she acquired. She made some phone calls and was able to set up a viewing time. In my depressed state we went and checked out the apartment. It was love at first sight. There was plenty of room for everybody. Z Baby would have her own room. The master bedroom was large enough to accommodate us, without feeling crowded. There were high ceilings and the landlord lived in the building. It was freshly painted and he was still replacing the rugs. I allowed him to keep the carpet on my daughter's floor. I would live to regret it. We went home that night with a burden lifted. I had also changed jobs that year. I was lured to accept a position in New Jersey for more money and opportunity. I had also brought an expensive hoopty that Legs had seen advertised. That car had taken a big chunk of the savings but receiving two checks for a couple of weeks helped to replace some of the money. I now had to scramble to find the money for the security and first month's rent. This was no simple task but I got the job done. The next step was securing a truck and some people to assist me. We also had to buy a lot of new furniture. Legs wanted to go to the bargain stores but I couldn't agree. My first place had to be a showcase with all the struggling I had been through. Since it was my money and credit cards, it was a rare moment that I had my way.

We filled up a large U Haul truck and my car with that studio apartment. We left owing a month's rent. That was pay back time for me when they laughed the first weekend I spent there. I had the new furniture delivered. Z Baby had her bed but I brought bedroom, living room, and new dining room sets. I had brand a new music system that never was unpacked along with a tape stand. I purchased a large area rug for the living room and the décor was now complete. I'm back Bed-Stuy but don't expect to see a lot of me!

It was June of "98" when we had relocated. I had been at my new job in Jersey for three months. I found myself in a neighborhood that was so familiar. I knew some of my neighbors from the past. The past that now I was being forced to remember. I recalled one morning when I was robbed of my winnings by a local thug. He was led to believe that I was a safe mark because he didn't know me. I was set up by the very people that were supposed to be protecting me. He quickly learned that I was a force to be reckoned with. After some careful negotiations he returned most of the money that was taken. We became close friends after that because I spared him a jail sentence. You see, I had no problem notifying New York's Finest on any thug that violated me unlawfully. I lived by two codes, the streets and the world. Right across the street lived an old gambling adversary that always had more than I could win. That's why it's important to maintain good relations because you never know who you'll see again.

God continued to smile upon us and show favor. The commute to work wasn't difficult even with the new address. I drove Legs and Z Baby to the sitter when my schedule permitted. I usually had time to take Legs to the nearby train station afterwards. I had the longest commute to work. I had to tackle the morning rush hour traffic going thru the Holland Tunnel. Life was being so good with such order that we couldn't imagine anything disturbing it. It would be near the end of the summer when good fortune disappeared.

Z Baby responded to her new surroundings with joy. She had plenty of space in her room to play. She had her own closet for both toys and clothing. I purchased a second hand dresser that soon filled with clothing from her mother and grandmother. On the days I couldn't drive them, they rode the bus to train station for their commute. It was a nice arrangement that worked perfectly for everyone. On one of my trips to work I had an accident that shook me up more than it injured me. I went to work late and was a nervous wreck throughout that day. A pot hole was the culprit but I wasn't informed enough to secure the proper evidence. I took the blame feeling relieved that no one was hurt. Afterwards I began having a lot of car trouble. I found myself being pushed thru the Holland Tunnel more and more. It happened so often that I developed the shakes whenever I approached the tunnel. I had the car worked on but the problem persisted. I finally found a honest mechanic. The problem was too expensive for me to fix. I left my car with him for $25.00 and a discount for repairs on my next automobile. I was now forced to commute by train and bus to work, which created new problems for me. I enjoyed the days I had to take Z Baby to the sitter. We would play games along the way that taught her how to read. I then would have to rush the rest of the way to get to work on time. I never had to pick her up after that. It was early August when this started so it did effect our summer.

Like so many other things in our lives we adjusted and began to rely on the mass transit system to ferry us to our destinations. We grew closer as a family and spent more time at home. My weekend routine was to awake early to fix breakfast while Legs slept. Z Baby was an active child that loved to play. She especially loved to play school and I enjoyed teaching her. On Sundays Legs and I shared the cooking duties for dinner but I still made the breakfast. We generally sat down together to eat. I wanted my child to grow up knowing the proper way families should behave. We both continued to advance in our careers. Z Baby was developing into a very bright child. She was more advanced than her peers. The Salvation Army Program used provider moms that were certified to teach preschool. Z Baby had the same Provider Mom until she started first grade at regular school. Her Provider Mom would remain though as her after school baby sitter. We used my mother in law address so she could be a back up sitter. It also gave her a chance to interact more with her grandchild. Our move to Bed-Stuy had also placed me closer to my mother. I was able to visit her more often and make her latter years comfortable. She was still my chief adviser and best friend. On some Sundays I would take her dinner and occasionally Legs and Z Baby joined me. The sexual escapades we enjoyed before the baby never returned. It was only a rare moment with much persuasion that we both had the desire after hours. Z Baby was still sleeping with us which created friction I the marriage. We stopped doing things as a couple unless it involved Legs' friends. I had accepted her social network but she rejected mine. Legs was such a jealous wife that most of my personal friends just disappeared. The only exceptions were two females and one male that weren't intimidated by her. She was then forced to accept my relationship with them, and include them into our social network.

The summer of "98" was grand with many accomplishments to our credit. We had money in the bank and a well furnished apartment. There was enough space in the house to separate when we needed time alone. I continue to press my case for Z Baby to sleep in her own room. Even when I put her to sleep in her own bed, I would wake up and find her lying next to her mom. I began to spend more time after hours gambling. I would sneak out the bed at night and often return a winner. I used this money to build up my personal bank account. Whenever I returned a winner and Legs would wake up, I was able to bribe her to have sex. When I came back a loser I used guilt to get it on. Sex in either situation wasn't as enjoyable when we both were in the mood. That didn't happen often enough so our arguments were usually about sex. I stopped making it an issue and found relief in the strip clubs. This became my introduction into the adult entertainment world and pornography. I began to purchase sex tapes at such a rapid pace that I soon had an impressive library. My late night viewing caused Legs to be more serious about moving Z baby to her own room at night. We also started planning more romantic evenings on weekend nights. We both started acting out our fantasies during those times. We didn't realize it but we were both setting ourselves up to relapse.

It was the middle of August when I received some disturbing news when I came home from work. My mother had suffered a heart attack while on the Dialysis Machine. She was pronounced dead but was revived after four hours of CPR. The staff at the hospital all rushed to help when they learned of her condition. My mother was the social butter fly. After thirteen years on dialysis at the same location, she had developed quite a following. We all left to go to the hospital but decided to leave Z Baby with our upstairs neighbor. I was devastated and in shock when I saw my mother's bloated body. The Lord had allowed her to live another day but I couldn't shake the vision of what I saw. We stayed as long as necessary. The ride home was dramatic as my heart was filled with sorrow. Nothing Legs said to me on that ride made me fill any better. It wasn't her fault but I couldn't see that then. I had $12.00 in my pocket. I made the decision then to get high, if given the opportunity to slip away. Legs gave me that opportunity when we arrived home. I told her to get Z Baby while I went to the store for a beer. While she walked upstairs to get our child, I walked across town to get me a hit.

It was a wet night but it didn't faze me. I thought about everything my mother meant to me as I walked. The air was cold and breezy but I pressed forward. I knew I had a timeline when Legs would be calling. When her own pain subsided, she would begin to focus on my absence. I had so little money to work with. I knew once I got started the ideas to get money would flow. I just wanted one hit to make the pain go away. Mama had kissed death and walked away from it. I was not ready to see her leave me. We accomplished a lot of the things I promised as a child. She had jewelry and a suede coat. We often traveled together in either rental cars or the ones I had purchased. I cooked for her and often surprised her with gifts and an extra clean house. I would stash my money there at her home. Sometimes when she needed some I would tell her where to look. The Bible was my favorite place. Mama was my whole world and we both envisioned her reaching "100". I kept walking as my destination became closer and closer. The rain keeps some people inside. I always used it to hide my unpopular activities. Whether it was drugs, stealing or cheating on a woman, the rain provided excellent cover. My ten minute trot seemed like hours but I was at my destination. One thing about an addict that was well known! They could always find another junkie to sympathize with them when there was sorrow. I knocked on the door praying for an answer. She was home and happy to see me. It had been a long time since I had knocked. She was used to me coming with plenty but that was not the case tonight. I told my sad story which got me an immediate hug. She wasn't the prettiest flower in the patch but her booty made up for it. I pressed my body tightly against her hoping that an erection would set the tone for during my visit. She offered me some of the drugs she already had. She was home alone with the kids fast asleep in the back room. I openly rubbed myself to maintain the hard-on she gave me. I took a pull off the stem in my hand and started to drift away into another world. I felt cheap as I pictured the concerned look on my wife's face. I fumbled in my pockets for the money I came with. I handed her the $12.00 and she quickly left the apartment. I sat very still as my horniness battled with my paranoia. There was a time when that didn't happen. If you do cocaine long enough, it catches up with you. I fought back the images that were materializing in my head. This was one of the safest places I could be doing what I was doing. The brain couldn't recognize the normal now. I began to talk to myself to stay focused on reality. I knew this could happen but I just hoped that it wouldn't. I began to see danger in my hostess leaving so soon. Long forgotten enemies seemed to be right outside the door. I began to play with myself believing that an erection would make the demons go away. Damn what was taking so long? I needed her ass now more than the drugs. I decided not to smoke anymore here. I had to use the drugs though ot extend my visit. I couldn't walk in this neighborhood feeling paranoid! I couldn't walk with that look on my face either that was so well known. Just as my libido picked up and my mind settled down, Big Booty walked in the door. She had another fresh pussy with her believing that I wanted to trick. I got the girl to massage me while big Booty took a hit. I was okay now and took full advantage of what I had. I was allowed to take Fresh Pussy into the other room. She gave me some head that caused me to forget all the pain I was feeling. I knew on a rainy night like this I could have my way but I left before temptation over powered me. I didn't have any money but I felt safe again. I still couldn't face Legs yet, so I headed for my mother's house. I always had my own key for emergencies and this was one. I started up the hill as the rain slowed down. This would be a longer walk than the first one. I didn't mind as my cell phone started to ring.

THE RELAPSE CONTINUES

MY PHONE KEPT ringing but I refused to answer. What was I going to say to a wife that cared? I did not want to listen to anyone that cared about me. I did not want to get off the road that I was on. I was determined to upset my life and all the benefits I had. Looking at my mother lie on top of that table was a vision I couldn't forget. The image was buried in my mind and caused so much pain and confusion. "Why Mama?" I kept asking myself. She was the jewel of the earth who gave much of herself to the world. I wanted to turn my phone off, but that would cause even more alarm. I had to prepare for an excuse if I made it back home. My daughter should be sleep now and I would soon be in safety at my mother's house.

I spoke to the security guard as I went in. I knew him well and let him know about Moms. It upset him to know but death was no stranger to this building. When you have seniors and the severely disabled living somewhere, you prepare yourself for death. My mother had outlived many of the friends she had made since moving here. I took the elevator upstairs to her fifth floor apartment and began to ponder my situation. I wasn't high now but the urge to get high was strong. I looked around the apartment for a picture or magazine that would stimulate me. I had to trick my brain into believing that I was getting high but without the drugs. That's one of the things I learned about crack addicts. The same feelings you get from crack could also be achieved from sex. That's why the girls always tried to get a trick to take a hit first because his urge to fuck was diminished. It's also why many girls were hurt by a trick, because they didn't want to do anything after the drugs had disappeared. Now the trick was ready to fuck because he had come down off the cocaine high. There I was playing doctor to cure me before I stayed out too long. I picked up the Bible and begin to flip thru the pages for a passage to rescue me. My body began to tremble and my mind started racing as I looked down at the money between the pages. This was not good and I remained motionless for a moment. I convinced myself if I found a trick just one twenty would do. I knew I was fooling myself but the mind couldn't tell the truth. I left the apartment with good intentions but in a bad situation. Finding a hooker or the drugs was not difficult. I didn't have to travel far because I knew enough places and people. It was 1:30 a.m. before I had the courage to answer my phone. I was broke, sprung and alone in Mom's house. My wife seemed compassionate and understanding as she encouraged me to come home. I spent some time in the mirror trying to get my face right. I then had to talk to myself out loud until I sounded okay and loud enough. Crack would distort your facial features and rob your voice. When I was ready to leave, I called and was told to take a cab. I had wanted to walk to give myself more time to be normal. Initially I lied and said I was gambling but the truth quickly came to light. I didn't want this to turn into another prolonged battle with drugs. Legs wanted more details than I wanted to give. It was almost as if she was being entertained by the story. I felt like she was upset that I was able to go taste the fruits again and return. She was acting more jealous than concerned. We began to argue and I was accused of shutting her out. I did not want to talk about what I did. Shit I still wanted to get high and she was pushing me out the door. I held on long enough for daybreak to come and rescue me. I stayed up in the living room that night and Legs took a day off from work. I called my job the following morning against Legs wishes and went on disability leave. I knew if I told without failing a drug test to be discovered, I would have job protection. This was because of the provisions of the Drug Free Workplace Act.

The day was difficult for both of us. I struggled with the guilt from what I did and Legs remained angry from a lack of details. Legs began to call around for me to get into a Detox Facility. I would be able to use her insurance but my stay would be short. Her plan was to get me into a long term program which I refused. I was not about to commit to a residential program because of a night of indiscretion. We argued for most of that day. She then confided in her boss to get some more direction. We began to grow apart from that moment because of her hard line stance. I decided to go to a hospital and convince them that my problem was severe. It would be a six day stay to allow me to get the drugs out of my system. There is no recognized detoxification for cocaine because there is no physical dependency. I was so guarded about my identity while in the hospital. It served its purpose because I left without the urges. The next step was to find an out patient program to finish my rehabilitation. The only option for me was the Veteran's Hospital. I gained admission readily and it was to my liking. I had to explain my absence to my mother during my stay at the Detox. She figured my emotional weakness to her condition was the cause. I didn't disagree with her so that it would be a resolved issue. She was beginning to do better but the hospital stay would be long. The money that I spent out of the Bible was for her insurance. This information only increased the amount of guilt I was feeling for my actions. I was at the hospital almost every day visiting Moms, while I continued going to my out patient program. I was able to release a lot of the pain and sorrow I felt. The other vets were very supportive. I received more support there than at home. There continued to be tension between me and my wife. She remained suspect of my activities when she was at work. She called often as if to track my every move. I was beginning to feel suffocated and unloved. The sex was already infrequent since Z Baby was born. Now sex was non existent as Legs began a new social life that didn't include me. She used the excuse of my relapse and secrecy about it to draw away from me. I pressed on rediscovering the strength that comes from the lord.

My oldest sister Big Mama was a regular fixture at the hospital. She tried to take control of our mother's life. She would dictate so many directions that Moms would sometime resent her presence. Big Mama even spent nights there against Mom's best wishes. I guess this was her way of dealing with the tragedy. The rest of the family made there rounds too but not to the extent as Big Mama. I generally came during afternoons and early evenings. I was not allowed out at night unless accompanied by my wife and or daughter. I enjoyed some of the most tender and informative moments with Moms while she was at the hospital. Her short term memory was gone unknowingly to me. She was viewing me in a different time period, but I didn't know at the time. My wife came a few times but not as much as I would have liked. Z Baby was too young but I snuck her in there any way. I brought my best female friend there once and Moms was confused about who the friend was. I drew closer to my mother again like when I was a child. My marriage had caused me to make fewer visits. She would always send me back home if I stayed too long. I didn't know how much I had missed Moms now. We laughed and cried together. We did more laughing than crying. There were times when she would talk about death. She began to prepare us for her journey back home. She talked about the visions she had when she touched heaven. She wanted to make sure we could carry on without her. My sisters were uncomfortable about these types of conversations. I welcomed them because it gave me more insight into her feelings and desires. I would entertain her with my own declarations about life without her. I would tell her I always tried to do as much as I could for her while she was living. I expressed how pleased I was in this area of our relationship. "When I cry at your funeral, it won't because of what I didn't get a chance to do with you. I'll just be crying because I miss you." Every time I told her those words she would smile. Sometimes when I came to visit, she would ask me to repeat it and start laughing. Yes, this was a very special time that The Lord blessed me with. I took full advantage of it. She would always say that she didn't want to die on the machine. She had been a dialysis patient for thirteen years and so many others passed on. Moms were in the hospital for thirty days before she was released. Her heart had become much weaker and she was advised not to take long walks. She actually needed an aid to assist in her mobility. I planned to secure a scooter and teach her how to use it. She was excited about the prospect of riding around in her neighborhood. It was a Saturday morning when she came home. Everyone possible was there. I stayed with my family at my side and just enjoyed her victory over death. My mother came up hard and her family helped change the direction of her life. She married a man that was devoted to her until his death. Even when he separated from her and lived in another household, he still responded to her needs. Moms was someone special that gave comfort, joy, and support to so many. There wasn't a child she didn't love. She didn't hesitate to make women respect themselves. Moms had her disabilities but they didn't stop her from continuing a life of service to others. She had been saved for many years now, trusting in the name of Jesus. The direction she took her life became an even greater inspiration for me. I sat there with my family listening to every word and marveling at her greatness. She continued to display courage in spite of her condition. She began to give comfort and guidance to all present. Moms started to give directions and wanted everyone to return to their homes. She wanted some privacy and rest in her own home. I was the last to leave with my family. I assured her that I would be returning the next day. We went home feeling relaxed and joyful that my mother was home now. I planned to cook her meal the next day and surprise her. There was less tension in the house as Legs displayed compassion for my personal ordeal. We were all feeling happy that Moms was home. Her presence broke the sorrow that had filled our home. I slept well that night with Legs at my side. I was back in the bedroom but not back in Legs. We rose early and prepared ourselves for church. We had a lot to give God thanks for. We arrived early enough for Bible Study. The class prayed for my mother's recovery as they did the previous Sundays. We left church full of love for each other. We stopped to get some items for the dinner I was going to cook. The weather was nice and Z Baby was allowed to play outside with the neighborhood children. There were some other girls next door her age. I thought about the crisis I survived to talk about. Relapse from drugs resulted in death for others. I

ZEKE SMITH

was blessed by God to survive. The job still was not allowing me back until I had completed my program.

I made the solo trip to Moms house with her dinner. It was early evening and the sun was still out. Traveling by bus gave me time to compose myself. I knocked before using my key. I stepped inside to find my mother cheerful and upbeat. She welcomed me with a smile and a joke. I laughed out loud and brought her the food. I sat watching the television as she ate. My mind wondered back to her hospital stay. She would always complain about the food not having any flavor. She had no such complaints today. I removed the plate when she finished and gave her some juice. We began to talk about death and its certainty. She became very philosophical as she retold events in her childhood. I listened to her personal history as it moved to her marriage and child birth. I wished I had a tape record as mother known and unknown things to me. She then talked about what she expected at her funeral. She didn't want anything big and even asked to be cremated. I told her Big Mama would never let that happen. I told her she wasn't going anywhere too soon. "You will live to be a hundred." I said with conviction in my voice. I didn't want to hear this stuff but I let her speak without interruption. She began to share personal feeling about her family and children. She didn't want it repeated. It was just for my ears she said. I couldn't understand why she stayed on this topic so long. I was asked to repeat my story about why I did so much for her. "I would not be crying at her funeral because of what I didn't get a chance to do in life." She had a big smile on her face as she listened. She told me to stay with my wife and love her. She then expressed how much she loved Legs and her ability to pick out the right outfits for her. Legs had brought her some gowns at the hospital. Legs had also took her shopping for a dress once before. I looked at this legend sitting here that was my mother. I knew God was preparing to take her home to glory. I knew my prayers couldn't stop it because she was ready to go. I just prayed for enough time to be strong for that day. Moms told me to leave now and go home to my wife. She said she would be okay and was ready to sleep. It was late now because my visit had lasted a long time. I gave her a hug and hid the sadness in my heart. I left feeling better than when I arrived. I felt that my mother wanted me to be prepared. She even expressed her desire for me to stay close to her best friend. A woman that knew all the trials I had been through. This woman that gave labor and love, when I needed it. I journeyed home with nothing but Mama on my mind. The house was quiet when I entered. Z Baby was sleep but Legs was wide awake. I showered before going to bed.

My wife was in bed with my favorite nightgown. I entered the room with nothing but a towel wrapped around me. I began to grease my body while standing in front of the mirror. I began to wipe on some deodorant and the tears just started rushing down my face. Legs didn't ask any questions. She stretched out her arms with the covers thrown to the side. I limped toward her bawling like a baby. The towel fell from my body as I crawled into the bed next to her. The smell of her perfume distracted me from the pain I was in. She had planned this moment while I was at Moms house. She pulled herself up close with her hands on my hips. I was still distraught from my conversation with Moms. In spite of her own weakness, she had the strength and courage to prepare me for her demise. I snuggled up close to my wife. I had been longing for her touch and it felt so soothing to be next to her. I buried my head in her neck as she reached down to feel my growing member. Legs hand was warm and her grip was gentle. I began to relax and stopped crying. My member was lubricated from the grease I had just applied to my body. I was rock hard now and Legs continued to massage me gently. I pulled the towel from underneath my body. I threw it to the side and began to insert myself inside Legs warm and wet pussy. We didn't talk as I started to grind against her body with my member deep inside her. She moaned softly as the pressure of my body stimulated her clit. She pushed me onto my back as she straddled me. She placed her knees alongside my hips as I remained inside her. "Hold still!" she demanded as her body began to rise and fall against me. This was unexpected because she hated this position. I felt as if she was going out of her way to please me. Her pussy was much lubricated causing me to slide in and out of her without any effort. I could feel the muscles inside of her tense whenever she rose up. She continued on with her movements as the pace began to quicken. I reached up and started pinching her nipples as she dropped her hands on either side of my head. Legs began to move against me like a professional dancer and I responded by meeting her thrusts with thrusts of my own. Whenever I slipped out of her she would quickly reinsert me. We continued on until we both climaxed. Legs body collapsed on top of me. I held her tight for a moment as her pussy continued to throb against my member. When her breathing returned to normal, I rolled her onto her back. We both laid there drained of all our energy. We fell off to sleep without saying a word.

The next morning there was a lot of cheerfulness in the house. We didn't speak about last night but our demeanor said it all. We were very helpful to each other in getting ready. I volunteered to take Z Baby to

ZEKE SMITH

school while Legs continued to get ready. It was an educational experience whenever we traveled together. Z Baby was learning to read, with the signs on the bus being her text books. We hugged and kissed before separating for the morning. I had plenty of time to get to my Day Program. It was a relief to have my wife back. It was so intolerable to be in the house with her and not talking. We always enjoyed sharing our day with each other. I kept thinking about all that passion last night as I traveled to my program. Things went as expected for the rest of the day. I returned home first so I began to start dinner. Legs would pick up Z Baby on her way home from work. I resisted visiting my mother in order to give her some relaxation at home. I knew my sisters would probably stop by and I didn't want to tire her out. She had to go to treatment the next day and that's when I planned to visit her. I did call to check on her before retiring that night.

We rose on time Tuesday morning and began our normal ritual. It was now my job to take Z Baby to school which even made it easier to get to my program. I arrived as usual and began group therapy with the other veterans. I never hesitated to speak because of all the turmoil I was going through. The counselor welcomed my openness because it helped to stimulate the group. This day would be different than the others after my gold chain came loose. I was sitting there listening to someone's disclosure and noticed a piece missing off my chain. It came loose but was still hanging on my neck. I looked around for it and checked the floors too. The piece was no where to be found. I asked the other vets but nobody knew anything. It changed my whole demeanor as I thought someone had found it. I asked the counselor if I could leave during our lunch break. I was given permission and started my journey home.

I was very upset as I left the hospital. We were all brothers up there with a common bond. Regardless of our personal conflicts, we are not supposed to victimize each other. My heart pendant was no where to be found. Somebody had to have picked it up. I continued on to the bus stop trying hard to get rid of my anger. I decided to take the bus all the way home. I wanted to give myself extra time to rekindle the joy I felt from last night. The trip was longer but I didn't wait long for the connecting busses. I was own my last bus when I received a beep from my wife. I couldn't respond because I was still on the bus. I kept riding and before long another beep came as 911. That was our code fore an emergency. I got off the bus to call maybe six stops from my house. My wife was excited and distraught when she answered the phone. In a frantic voice she said my mother had another heart attack at home and the ambulance was on the way. I immediately held a cab and went straight to my mother's house. I fought back tears and tried to maintain my composure. Arriving within minutes, I raced upstairs passing by startled residents sitting outside. The front door to the apartment was ajar. I stepped inside to find paramedics working to revive my mother as my oldest sister looked on. I looked down at my mother stretched out on the floor with her wig missing. I knew in my heart that this time she wouldn't be coming back. I went into the bathroom and started to pray. I recited "Hail Mary" and asked God to comfort her on her journey home. My face was wet with tears at this time. I left the bathroom and continued to view the heroic efforts of the paramedics. One in particular refused to accept defeat. She received a number of ejections to stimulate her heart. Finally a decision was made to transport her to the nearest hospital. I walked alongside the medics as they took her downstairs. The hallways felt like 100 degrees as we rushed to the elevator. I climbed into the back of the ambulance for my mother's final departure from her home. I knew she was at peace and I was at peace to see her go. Things were never the same for her when my baby brother died. Then her husband left to live with the other woman that she always knew about. It was said that they were married but Pops never admitted to that. He still came when she called no matter the reason. We got to the hospital and Moms was pronounced dead on arrival. I stayed in the treatment room where they took her. I pulled up a chair and sat beside her. It was almost as if I was guarding her departure to heaven. I stood on post to ensure no interference from the world. A nurse came and asked if I was alright. I said yes, as long as I was not asked to leave my mother's side. I was left alone as I continued to keep her company. I wanted to take the journey with her. She was the best friend I ever had. The tapes began to replay in my head about our struggles and triumphs. We both had overcome so much. My sister came in for a brief moment and left. I knew it would be difficult for her. I was happy for Moms but sad for myself. My chief adviser was gone and I was hard pressed to keep it together. I rose from my chair and said my last goodbye. I took my hand and crossed over her eyes to close them. They were wide open but motionless. I went to pull the sheet over her face but my sister rejected. I relented and left the room. By this time the rest of the family began to arrive. I pointed to the room she was in, unable to speak. I went outside to smoke a cigarette. I was being consumed by sorrow and overcome with grief. I didn't want to hear anything from anybody. I just wanted to feel relaxed in the memory of this great woman. My mother touched so many lives in her time. The dash between her date of birth and death could never tell the story that I knew. I looked up to see my wife and daughter entering area. Z Baby understood what was happening and came over to me. My wife wrapped her arms around me and began to sob openly. I soon joined in and our tears soaked the garments on our backs. I had no plans to get high. I would not let the passing of this giant destroy my life. I pledged to love and honor my wife and child. I would step up and be the man my mother raised me to be. Legs went inside to say her goodbyes to Moms and I kept Z Baby at my side. We went home that night and I was kept under guard. Everyone's attention and concern now turned to me. They all feared what this death would cause me to do.

The night was filled with tears. I cried uncontrollably at times and Legs would join in. Z Baby was too young to express any emotion or she just insulated herself from it. God has a way of protecting his people. I had back slide, but was still a part of The Kingdom. I awaken the next morning drained from my night of sorrow. I was constantly watched by my wife and grew annoyed from the attention. I realized she didn't want to lose me. The devotion I had to my mother was no secret. My father even expressed some jealousy at way I trusted Moms with my money. The funeral would be within a few days. There was no reason to delay it. We began contacting our out of town relatives. My sisters took control and were doing a fantastic job. The only thing I could handle was me and that's all they expected. I had to buy my own flowers and I made sure my mother's surviving brother would attend. My mother died on the 7th of September and her burial would be on the tenth. How tragic that she was laid to rest on my birthday. My mother wanted a small ceremony but she would not have her way. The event was a grand affair with people from all over and way back attending. Children she help to raise, who were mothers and fathers themselves were there. Childhood neighbors and long forgotten associates were there. The church was filled to the rafters. I wrote a poem that my sister read. This had become a habit of mine for close family relatives. The first was for my brother's funeral. My poems always put the programs in high demand. There was a seventeen car procession that went to the cemetery. She occupied a spot with her son leaving one more space. We all joked about who that would be. I could not stop crying and everyone was avoiding me because of it. I was so sadden but had to remain strong and recover from this. The days that followed were different. There was no will so we basically just reclaim the gifts we had each brought. Most of the jewelry went to me but I relinquished my share in the T.V. and VCR. My wife took some articles of clothing to my surprise. I continued with my day program for the next couple of months. I returned back to work but couldn't get my previous position. I was shunned by my superiors as they took my collapse personal. I found myself working and programming seven days a week. The strain caught up with me and I resigned in late November. The pressure was back on for me to go to a residential program. I was too weak from grief to argue. I relented against my better judgment and found myself back in treatment. The departure wasn't pretty because this time I was being forced out the door. This would count as eviction number one. There would be two more before reuniting for a final time.

The monster which was my addiction had returned with a vengeance. When I was working that late shift before I resigned, the urges had come back. I used to watch the hookers apply their trade right across the street from me. I used to imagine them servicing me many nights. I even let one use the bathroom. Now I found myself in a residential program forced by a wife that I was in love with. I tried to be as inconspicuous as possible. This place seemed to have some low standards with a staff whose skill was questionable. Still I was in no position to complain and quickly settled in to regain my self respect. My first few weeks were spent in their wayward building. There was a newer facility that took me some time to be relocated. My first bed assignment really tested my commitment. The abandon buildings I lived in at one time in my life were in better condition. The program consisted of mostly group programming with very little individual counseling. I was assigned to a young attractive woman who was still working towards her Bachelor Degree. I placed her in an uncomfortable position because of my knowledge of the field. I didn't create any problems. I actually made her job easy when it came to me. I just cooperated and followed her lead. When I got to the new building, I became more relaxed and focused. I showed up on time for all my meetings and shared regularly about my situation. I mainly talked about my mother's death and my relapse after so many years clean. I soon developed a following with other residents looking forward to me speaking. Time moved slowly for me because there were no visitors and money was scarce. I avoided the woman but one did get my attention. We met one day in the laundry room. She even knew my wife from a previous program. I watched this young woman make progress in her treatment and with me. I got her to give me a pair of her panties that kept me company at night. We used to entertain each other with dirty talk and plans of future liaisons. The first time my wife came to visit with my daughter, panties spent the whole time talking to Legs. Legs enjoyed that talk more than she did with me. This would be the start of my resentment towards my wife. I began to see her as an adversary that was hastening my demise. The program had a strong religious undertone and began to make my way back to Christ. During the week we attended service where our choir performed and testimonies were given. On Sundays you were free to choose the church you attended. The other option was to stay at the program and participate in what ever they had panned. I never knew what that was because I made sure I was out as early as possible. I began to accept my situation as divine intervention and started to feel the presence of god in my life. I evolved into a spirit filled person always preaching The Word. I participated in bible study during the week and also studied in my spare time. Events occurred, that showed God's favor in my life. My wife came up unexpected one day with some checks for me to sign. The money was coming in for my disability claim. I was already having my credit card bills paid with my insurance on those accounts. I was always pretty smart about money matters. I just threw a lot of it away on foolish things. The roommates I had began to look to me for leadership. There was a pain in my side from my wife's neighborhood. This pain glorified the thug life and took offence at me rejecting his friendship. I was not here to meet people and was already struggling with the amount of attention I as receiving. My wife only stayed long enough to discuss money. I was disappointed that Z Baby wasn't with her. I gave her more than she deserved and that wasn't enough. I kept two of the checks and deposited them where I was at. That was the last time Legs came to see me. In case you weren't counting that was visit number two.

I was getting my soul in order so I began to pay attention to the body. I had my feet taken care of while there. I even got all my business in order with the Veteran's Administration. I stopped thinking about Legs and just paid attention to Z Baby. It was evident to me that legs had another agenda and I wouldn't let it side tract me. I had petitioned Legs to let me leave early but she rejected it. "You have to graduate from the program or you can't come back here!" Those words stung like a thousand bees. The welfare money finally kicked and my account began to look impressive. I started looking good and feeling good. I didn't care who knew I was here. I was dealing with me and having some success at it. The pain didn't even matter when we passed in the hallways. It was difficult to travel after I had my foot surgery. I was on crutches and in a lot of pain. I still didn't let that stop me when I was able to get visits home or other social events. It was quite a sight to watch me hobbling along on that train. The trip was never worth the effort with the reception I received from Legs. God was working on something and someone, but I didn't know it at the time. My faith continued to grow as I trusted in the Lord more and more. I even gave my hand to Christ. I would always kneel at the alter for prayer on Sunday. I started to work out in the room and the bathroom. I became more fit with the help of the V.A. my social activities increased and I stopped those punishing visits home. Life was good again because Jesus was present. God now was ready to see if I truly believed in His Word. I was not prepared for what was getting ready to happen. Legs had a job prospect for me but I still couldn't come home. The job was available so her friend's job could be easier. I still couldn't come home. Now it was time for god to act.

I prepared myself for the upcoming job interview. It was at another program but I couldn't reveal my current status. Who would hire a drug counselor that was living at a drug program? I went on the first interview a little skeptical about my chances. I was given all the necessary information to be successful but I still had some doubt. The place was located in the Bronx which I had become familiar with. I entered the building feeling more confident because I had nothing to lose. The location offered services other than drug rehabilitation but it was of no interest to me. I approached the meeting hall to slight glances from staff and residents. I was not allowed to reveal my affiliation to the staff that I knew. The interview went well in part to my preparation. I was scheduled to have a second interview with a panel of three in a few days.

The second interview was more intense than the first and that was when I met a previous neighbor of mine. I had once considered renting an apartment from her and had even tried to work for her. The apartment was too small and over priced. I was told then that I didn't have enough experience to work for her. Wow times had sure changed. Now I was being courted for a position that would lead to management. My neighbor asked about my wife unaware of our current difficulties. I was pleasant and revealing without giving harmful information. I impressed the panel and was offered the job. I gave a start date to allow me time to work out the logistics. They understood that proper notification to any current employer was acceptable. I left there excited and began to imagine living alone in my own apartment. I went to my counselor with the news and she was as excited as I was. The job gave confirmation of the skills I said I possessed when we first met. She also understood that the job could not know about my living arrangements. The first week went alright with no complications. I had a cell phone to help me keep my secret. During my second week Legs became ill and she needed emergency surgery. When she was to be released someone had to bring her home. She would also be unable to care for Z Baby while she was recuperating. I had resolved myself to my situation and didn't want it disturbed. I planned on moving out on my own because of the lack of support I received from Legs. She didn't want me home and now I didn't want to go. My bank accounts at the program were healthy. I would soon be able to draw money from my welfare account. That was something I had been unable to do. It contained $500.00 which I couldn't touch for another week. Legs began to paint this rosy picture of the way things would be with me home again. Graduating from the program was no longer a requirement. The rules had changed like always to suit her needs. I went to the director for an emergency discharge from the program. I wanted to maintain my good standings and preserve my welfare money. I had met one of my old clients here whose sister worked at the new job I took. There was a lot at stake here. I did not want to tarnish my reputation with blatant deceit. I was turned down and Legs continued to apply the pressure. She knew family was important to me and she played her cards well. Too bad she didn't know how to play poker. I ultimately made the unselfish decision to leave. I trusted The Lord to be the judge of what was right or wrong. I went to the hospital to pick up Legs. I had to carry her up the stairs because she couldn't walk. She was in a lot of pain and had the medicine to prove it. She thanked me for being there but I didn't feel any gratitude from her tone. I was made to feel it was my job or role as her husband to do what I did. "Where was this philosophy when I hobbled home on crutches every week to visit a sleeping child? Where was this philosophy when I yearned for affection and understanding form my wife?" I accepted my role and began to rebuild my empire. I was back to working, cleaning, caring for Z Baby, and now also a bedridden wife. It would be weeks before Legs regained her strength. It would be months before she resumed her role as wife and mother. Once again I had some power and authority in the household. There wasn't anyone else available to step in and do what I did. Whatever plans she had, for life without Zeke had fallen apart. She allowed someone to use her for entertainment and then run when the goods were damaged. God in all his wisdom had prepared me for this moment. I was armed with The Word so I served The Lord and not man. I excelled at work and monthly raises became common. The summer was coming upon us. We had a car to use on the weekends if my mother in law didn't need it. I was a man in two households. We had even gotten our mothers together for dinner before mine had passed. I was given respect even when there was no love. I was seen as a man of strength and character, because I performed my role as defined in the scriptures. During that summer we lost our transportation after I had made an investment in car repairs. It seemed that my sister in law needed it more. I guess the few hundred I spent made it attractive and capable for the trip south. It didn't cause me any grief because I learned to expect the un-expected with this family. The summer of "99" was one of recovery and change. It also was a summer of growth as I matured after my mother's death. The Lord continued to smile upon us as we were blessed with a good used car. That joy didn't last as my mother in law's illness began to resurface. This was her last year of working as she prepared to retire. The cancer progressed quickly as she fought to survive. This was a solemn moment for us all because she was so well liked. The anniversary of my mother's funeral had not arrived before we were planning another one. I was able to be more support for Legs than she was for me. She had no experience but unfortunately I did. The death was a painful blow to Legs. Things were said and done that only increased her pain. I stood by her to the end until she began to function on her own. I was able to let people know what I really was made of. I took charge in advising Legs on her responsibilities. I made sure her devotion was demonstrated by the floral arrangements at the funeral. The attention turned to her daughter who was struggling raising her child. In time we all healed from this event. We all gathered strength from whatever source was available. We learned to live without the people we loved. We learned to survive on our own and began to trust God more.

I was attending church in our neighborhood and my family soon followed. I'm gonna flashback to Mother's Day of this year. We all went to the alter that day and accepted Christ as our savior. I chose that day to give honor to my own Moms. We had some faith to lean on as we moved on with our lives. The deaths of our mothers were a traumatic event but it also brought us closer together. We began to function as a close knit family. We worshipped together every Sunday and our child was introduced to Jesus. The most glorious moment during this time was our baptismal. We were all sprinkled with the holy water. Z Baby's godfather was there but her godmother was absent as usual. It perplexed me someone could accept that responsibility and never show up for the important events. The godmother had purchased a $50.00 savings bond at birth. Then her involvement grew less and less as time moved on. I often used Legs selection as a point of reference for incompetence.

The dream job I had that gave me steady raises became a nightmare. The person that ran the program couldn't accept responsibility for any of its failures. I was now the assistant director but without any real authority. I was a puppet with a banned staff member pulling the strings. I lasted as long as I could without causing a scene. I knew my days were numbered because my presence was no longer desired. I refused to quit but the strain was having an adverse effect on my health. I began to have restless nights and my day at work became unwelcome conversation. I used to come home nightly bickering about the bizarre behavior of my bosses. Yes there were a few and they took turns berating me. It all came to a head in October of that year. I was called into a meeting with no allies or representation present. They wanted me to acknowledge my incompetence and hand in my resignation. The heart of the matter was my residency at that Christian themed drug program. I wasn't concerned about how they knew. I was not wanted there and had no problem leaving. I was promised unemployment benefits if I left quietly. I gathered my belongings and left with an escort. That institution was so corrupt with their employees and had the pending lawsuits to prove it. When I applied for unemployment they said I just quit. I eventually won the argument on appeal and received my benefits. I learned then that you should get a separation when changing jobs and never resign under pressure. The money I received wasn't enough so I took to hustling again. We did save money on childcare since I could make my own hours. There was some tension at the house but not enough to cause a breakup. I didn't pass up any opportunities to make a buck. I found myself involved with the people I had left behind after marrying Legs. They welcomed my return but I dreaded the experience. I couldn't afford to be a loser at the crap tables so I always left early. I never stayed to chance the big wins. I began to lose some respect from the other players. There were even some rumors that I was using drugs. I used to have Legs beep me at prearranged times for my alibi to leave. This used to work good until she started to deviate from the script. She couldn't understand that loneliness or concern was not the reason to call. I was back out there in the streets trying to take care of my family until something better came along. I was still tithing regardless of where the money was coming from. I just prayed harder for forgiveness and hoped that the Lord would understand. My heart was in the right place but my mind was somewhere else. This continued on into the millennium before I had a break through. Z Baby's godfather had a position for me in New Jersey and I was guaranteed to be hired. It would be to my liking and it took me back off the streets. The world we live in is so small that you always run into familiar faces. The job was just what I needed because it had plenty of overtime. I was a per diem worker with the possibility of becoming full time with benefits. It was a type of rehab I wasn't accustomed to but rewarding just the same. I became educated in a new field and emotionally it suited me fine. I knew I would have to answer for some of my missteps with the Lord. I just didn't know how or when. It would not be long before my back sliding would cause me to fall. I put myself in a position to be tempted by the devil and not have enough Word in me to resist. I fell victim to lust and rapidly lost all that I had gained. I fought to stay afloat but the strain was too much. I even accepted the additional treachery of the adversary because I had invited it on myself. I had amassed a small fortune because of all the overtime I worked. It was used up in legal fees and bail money. I eventually found myself homeless and living out of my car. Baby Sis was the only one that assisted me during this time. I was fighting battles in family court and criminal court. I blame no one and immediately asked for forgiveness when the event happened. Only god knew the truth and I accepted all that He put me through to survive.

I began to tire of the life I was living. I was bitter at what I allowed myself to become. I had no family and friends were disappearing too. I went back to Legs after so much time away. I believed her when she said this time it would last. She moved on without me and started another life. The first time she was alone in the new place I thought we could talk. I had spent many nights watching her and Z baby from a distance. I even had a safe place to park and sleep, where I could watch them begins their day. I lost control one night when she ignored my phone calls. I thought she wasn't home so I waited for her arrival. I was in shock when a light came on hours later and a man exited her apartment. When he left she answered the phone explaining that he was gay and nothing happened. I made her feel so unsafe the next morning. Only the voice of my savior kept me from doing the unthinkable. Still she was frightened enough to fear me. I knew she was still using drugs at this point so I stayed away. It was the spring of 2001 and the police were still trying to get me to come in and talk to them. On this day I was tired and missing my daughter. I was baited to come to the school to pick her up. It hurt when the teacher told me I wasn't allowed to be there. I left angry cussing the world. I struck back at Legs letting her supervisors know she was using. I was blindsided with accusations from Legs. She had told them how fearful she was of me. She was in the office listening to the conversation as I spoke on the phone. I gave my car to a friend I was helping to sell books. I had her friend drive me to the precinct. I knew the promises the police had made to me were bogus. It didn't matter now. I was ready to be with Jesus.

RIKERS; GOD REVEALS HIS PLAN

I SAT THERE waiting for a promise to be kept. I didn't like the way my last meeting went with my daughter. I actually believed that I would see my child. I came in like I said, so why shouldn't they let me see Z Baby? I grew angry as time went by. My anger for my wife went away as it turned toward the police. They didn't have to lie, I was ready to come in. I wanted to make peace with the world and with God. I knew I needed a rest and jail would give it to me. I also wanted to be alone with Jesus and jail would give that to me too. "Mr. Smith your daughter doesn't want to see you. They have already left the building." The detective delivering the message seemed to take pleasure in giving it to me. "How long do I have to stay here?" I shot back. "You will be going to Central Booking tonight." He wasn't telling me anything I didn't already know. I wanted to know if I was going to make night court. I did some push ups and settled down for my long wait. It would be morning before I see a judge. I had been through this enough times to know what lied ahead. I just wanted to test the police honesty. I wanted to know if they were ready to be truthful. I had money and cigarettes in my pocket. All I wanted now was a jail cell of my own so I could finally get some sleep. More bodies were added before night fall came. They had people coming in that were caught up in drug sweeps. They were different ages but carried the same attitude. "I'm innocent! I wasn't doin nuttin!"

They piled us up into a police van and started the trip downtown. I gave a fast survival lesson when they started begging for cigarettes. "Yo! I aint got nuttin to give away. I'm gonna be gone for awhile, so these cigarettes are a dollar a piece." I was giving them a break because it would cost them two dollars once we got to Central Booking. "Yo Pops, I'll take two of dem cigs for me and my man." I passed the cigarettes after collecting my money. They lit up right there in the van as others began asking for the saves on them. Damn I was back in this twisted world that I knew so well. I hated this position but I knew deliverance was just around the corner as I continued to call upon Jesus. I knew enough about the Lord that even a silent prayer would reach him. I began to pay more attention to my fellow passengers. The young wanna be drug dealer caught with a few bags of crack. We all watched him dig in his ass for the other ten the police missed. The over the hill alcoholic, locked up for being too drunk to run. The homosexual who's every word turned my stomach to hear! Gang bangers, petty thieves, bullshit pimps and me, all together now like family. Jail didn't care about whom you were only what you were. "Yo easy driver!" we all shouted in unison as we rose in the air from a big bump in the road. "Are we there yet?" I laughed out loud as the rest of them seated just grinned. This was some bunch. I couldn't wait to be separated from them all. I still knew that the odds favored me seeing anyone of them again. I made sure that the memory of me wasn't as a sucker. The van began to slow down and go down a hill. We all knew that meant we had arrived. Now it was time to separate the men from the pretenders. Central Booking was like a bee hive of activity. Cages crowded with live bodies housing dead minds. Guards smart enough for the job but not smart enough to keep it simple. Jail was only as bad as the people watching you. If I could just do time with nothing but a pet for company I would. The addition of people with guards at the top of the list made it tough. We were unhooked from the bar in the van and led inside like chained slaves. Once inside we were uncuffed one by one and put in a cell. We had one of two choices to go into. "Yo Pops, come over here." That was one of the gang bangers hollering for my company. He either wanted a cigarette supply close by or he wanted to hear some more wisdom. It didn't matter to me but I didn't like the attention so early on. I never knew how the guards would interpret this. "Yo young blood, don't holler for me like that again. I don't need the extra attention." I could tell he didn't like what I said or how I said it. I could care less because he wasn't going to see me as something soft he could call upon. I found me a seat in the corner with my back against the wall. I could see everything and everything could see me. I felt safe and secure enough to dose off.

Sleep didn't last long as I heard my name being called. It was time for that bullshit interview where they find out who you supposed to be. This was the probation department that conducted these interviews for the judge. This was how they determined your ties to the community and your ability to make bail. This was also the only way you would get that phone call that you should have gotten at the precinct. They already knew that I had a warrant because I had walked off from probation. I was not about to report when I knew my wife had made that complaint against me. "Zee Hey Zee over here!" I looked around to see an O.G. from the neighborhood. "Man you still coming through the system? I asked rather sarcastically. "Man look at you." He shot back with a big grin on his face.

ZEKE SMITH

It appeared I brought him some comfort in being there. Most of the guys from our generation had stopped doing time. Jail was for the young bloods. There was no glory or fame in being locked down. It took more than one bid for some of us to realize it. Yes, we both found comfort in each other being there. I passed him a cigarette at no charge. We both knew the game and he would have to pay for that cigarette at a later date. It would soon be time for the strip search. I watched the nervousness on the faces of the youth as they began to stuff their drugs and money. It was time for me to focus on selling the rest of my cigarettes. I would not be allowed to keep an open pack. I also wanted the money in my account and not my pocket. It wasn't hard to get rid of the cigarettes. Only a few had any and no one else was trying to sell them. By the time my name was called, I had my business in order. This time I had my P.O.BOX as an address. I was married but separated. I always used Baby Sis as an emergency contact because she would take care of things properly. The other sisters were okay but they dropped the ball too much. They also would put their interests ahead of mine. I figured you had to learn to take a back seat when you're helping someone. You also had to keep any commitments you made. The world didn't always see it that way, so you had to pick your people carefully. During my interview I was reminded about the case hanging over my head. I would have to settle that issue with the legal aid that would be assigned to me. I returned back to the cell and waited to be searched. Damn! I was looking forward to the vacation from the streets but I hated who was handling the arrangements.

The most demeaning thing about this whole process was the strip search and my turn had come. I started to empty my pockets as I drew closer to the area. I put everything in the hat I was wearing to make the ordeal swift and organized. The officer quickly let me know that he didn't need the help. I guess he felt I was insulting his intelligence. I managed to put close to seventy-five dollars in my account. This money would go a long way in providing m with comfort and security. They refused to count the pennies I had so I kept those along with my driver's license. Time dragged on and tempers started to flair. I found a spot to take a nap and speed this waiting period up. I flash back thinking about my girl Vee. She put a lot of effort into helping me. She was angrier than me about the situation I was in. When I was out there selling those books for her, she would tell me that I should write one. I laughed off the idea because life was already complicated enough. Some new police came in with a fresh batch of cuffs. This meant it was time for some more movement for somebody. They opened up an empty cell and began calling off the names that would fill it. When I saw people from my precinct called I knew I would too. We were moved upstairs to the court house. Now the legal aids would be assigned to assess your situation. My case was simple enough. I would accept any plea deal less than ninety days to settle my probation case. I could have taken this in the beginning but my lawyer feared me being locked up. He tried to save a job that I lost anyway. They would have to send these new charges to a grand jury for an indictment. That's when my story telling would begin to minimize the damage to my reputation. It was day break now and the lawyers were starting to interview their clients. My city appointed came to me and our talk lasted five minutes. I didn't expect to have anyone out there and I would take a plea to get rid of my current case. She asked for ninety days and credit any time already served on this charge. I would enter a not guilty plea on anything else the D.A. was considering. I found myself being angry again at my failed marriage. Why couldn't I just have agreed to take care of the baby?

The courtroom was welled lit and full of people. Didn't they have something else to do? I was puzzled to see this many people on a Saturday morning. I received just what I asked for when I went before the judge. My lawyer said she would contact me at Brooklyn House. Riker's Island would have to wait a little longer before they see me. The time I spent at Brooklyn house was relaxing and I was able to add to my commissary account. I didn't waste any time in starting my exercise regiment. I knew I couldn't do all my time here. I wanted to be in shape whenever those transfer orders came. Those orders came a lot quicker than I wanted them to. I was able to receive my legal mail from the legal aid before I was shipped out. I watched guys bicker and beg when they received notice. It doesn't make any since to become so comfortable in jail that you fight to stay put. The Brothers didn't understand how damaged they had become by accepting their conditions. I didn't have anything to give away as I prepared for my morning transfer. They waited until the very last moment before they told you. This was for security reasons but others used this to beat you for money owed. I headed to Rikers Island a new man. I started my transformation the moment I decided to go to the precinct. It had been a very long time since I was there before. I knew things would be different but I didn't know how much. I didn't care because this time I was doing time with Jesus.

The ride out of the borough was long enough to be relaxing. We went over that last bridge headed into a new kind of civilization. Over the years many stories have been written and told about Rikers Island. I don't know what was true or what was false. I was about to start an extended stay, on the last place I would have chosen to take a vacation. I was taken to a permanent dorm because I had been sentenced. I would be here until my time was up. The majority of the inmates were under twenty one. Guys my age were like dinosaurs. The foolish ones even tried to act younger and always found themselves in trouble. I went right to work hustling groceries and cigarettes. I gave everyone credit and had some young enforcers to insure payment. I did this to survive because money was short and visits non existent. This also gave me company at chow time and partners to work out with. I also spent time trying to convert them to Jesus. They gave me respect and I would often help settle disputes in the dorm and at home. I wanted to make a difference in these guys' lives. Hey didn't have to go through any thing that I did to be considered a man. I became a father figure to them and developed a genuine concern for their well being. They repaid my kindness with love and admiration. It wasn't expressed in the normal way but I understood what I meant to them. I helped them get past the tough letters and the rejections from home. I tried even harder for them not to become institutionalized and immune to the pain of incarceration. I was having my own difficulties with home. I couldn't sleep at night. I was in love with my wife again and missing my daughter. My oldest sister was sending me tings but the promises she didn't keep hurt the most. I had her take my car but she wouldn't turn in the plates for me to get an insurance refund. I was in church every Sunday and sung on our choir. I saw a lot of people from the streets but only talked about God. I got a job in the commissary and my popularity really took off. I made the most of that job as I gained goods and services. I saw all the newly jailed from the streets. I didn't accept any shorts and people paid well for special treatment. I even had to use my communication skills on the police to keep the tip gates open. I was faster than the average person in all that I did in life. Now this energy along with my math skills was paying some good dividends. I received a lot of threats along the line but never backed down. I didn't disrespect anyone so I was going to be bullied. Eventually I had to move again when I was sentenced. I became an aid in the psycho dorm. These are the nut jobs or those pretending to be a nut job. It's easier to get SSI when you get out. I prospered while inside doing time. I never let a negative situation defeat me. What I didn't realize at the time was that God was preparing me for some greater things.

The new job I had was easy. It was like being a counselor again. The only problem was is that I wasn't supposed to care. The brother that helps me get the job was a psychopath. I just made sure I made sure I stayed awake or least didn't get caught sleeping. The mornings were cool because there was extra food to eat. I usually had enough to take back to my dorm. This was one of the better paying jobs so my account began to grow. I couldn't spend any money until my surcharges were paid off. Surcharges were another way for the system to make sure that crime doesn't pay. I began to develop some close bonds with the inmates in my housing unit. It gave life behind bars more meaning for me to try and save some lives while I was there. I didn't expect to see any of them later. I still dealt with honesty in case life did cause our paths to cross. It was always important to me to present a positive image of myself to new associations. I kept the same rule even behind bars. Working made the time go fast but I still wasn't getting any sleep. Legs stayed on my mind. I jerked off at daybreak many mornings just to relax. This wasn't working out and I didn't know what to do to make it better. I began to write letters to her since I wasn't able to talk. I began to take responsibility for all the mishaps in our relationships. I would use some of the younger brothers in jail with me as sounding boards. I stated to feel more at ease and the anger started to disappear. The letters were working and I began to fall asleep at normal hours. Here are some of the letters I wrote.

(Insert letters)

I began to feel normal and fit into my new environment. The job was a tremendous benefit to me both financially and emotionally. I was the unselected leader of the dorm. I made sure there were no conflicts that made anyone's time more difficult. We began to plan future meetings on the outside as brothers began to be released. My phone calls to Big Sis became important as I sought more guidance with my walk with God. I attended Sunday services regularly. I would also continue bible study when I returned back to my unit. The other inmates started seeing me as "The Holy Man". I didn't mind the title and tried to live up to what it implied. My jailhouse bank account grew and I would soon be able to pay off my surcharges. I would soon be finish with my sentence for the violation of probation. One morning I received a letter from my lawyer about a court date. They were trying to get an indictment from the grand jury for the incident with my wife. I was unsure of how to handle this. I had repented and accepted Jesus Christ as my savior. I could no longer be dishonest and I wanted my negative past to vanish. Once my sentence

ZEKE SMITH

was completed, I was held on the new charges. I was transferred out of the dorm and placed in a transitional unit. My bills were paid and I was able to shop. This still didn't satisfy me because I lost my job with the transfer. I would see my friends from the other unit on occasion at chow. I once again placed all my trust and faith in the Lord to make things right. I testified on my behalf at the grand jury. I masked the truth hoping to be released without getting indicted. I made a few more court trips without being seen. Something wasn't right but I couldn't figure out what. Finally on one court appearance my lawyer showed up. I was informed that the grand jury didn't indict me on any felony charges. The D.A. was now trying to get me on some misdemeanors. I was elated and felt this victory belonged to the Lord. I rejoiced back at my unit and had to decide if I wanted to continue fighting. I again turned to the Lord and received my answer. I was unable to make any beneficial contact with the outside. I didn't know what my wife's situation was and I didn't want to cause her any more harm. On my next court appearance I was the last one seen. I was awaken from a deep sleep and hustled into the court room. I had a two minute meeting with my attorney who convinced me to accept a plea. I would be sentenced to a year but time already served would count towards the new sentence. It sounded good because I be out of jail before Christmas. My niece would be coming to see me. I had learned from her earlier that Legs had moved to whereabouts unknown. I took the deal and was transferred back to my old unit. The Lord again let me know that I made the right decision, when he gave me a job in the commissary.

I was so excited when the officer came to tell me that I had a visit. The unit was even happier than me because I had never received a visit before. I came down expecting to see my sister but my niece was there with all smiles. It was such a joy to see her. We both shed some tears before beginning our conversation. "Hey cousin!" I said with such glee. It felt so great to have someone come and see me. There were so many questions I wanted to ask which couldn't get answered over the phone. "Hey Uncle Zekey!" She replied with just as much emotion as me. We had developed such affection for each other over the years. I always felt a sense of duty when it came to my family. I especially had to be the protector of the women. Her mother was always more like a sister than a cousin. I became an uncle because of that relationship. Just like her mother she provided food and shelter when I needed it. She also provided no holds barred advice when I needed it also. "So what's up cousin, have you seen my people? I'm hoping they don't press the issue so I can get out of here." "I went by the house uncle but she doesn't live there anymore. I spoke with a lady that lived upstairs." My joy quickly became sorrow as I realized she had taken off. There was no telling where she was at or with whom. I began to conjure images in my mind that didn't make me feel any better. I had to stop thinking so I could enjoy this time with my niece. "Thanks cousin I appreciate you going by there." I had to hide my disappointment as I responded to the information. "Well cousin I'm going to be here for my birthday but I'll be out for Christmas." My niece looked at me with sadness in her eyes. I knew she missed my presence and the driving lessons I was giving her. She looked around the visiting room and began asking me questions. "Do you know anybody down here? How much time do you have before they make you leave? I tried not to look upset but I was more interested in what was happening on those streets. "I know that brother in the corner. He came from my dorm. Did you speak with my sister about the sneakers?" "Sorry Zekey she didn't give them to me like she said she would." I reached across the table and held my niece's hand. My eyes began to water as my time was almost up. I hated being in here and was mad Legs had cut out on me with Z Baby. 'Its okay cousin, I'll be home soon enough and you can make me some ribs." My niece put a smile on her face but couldn't hold bake the tears. I squeezed her hand a little tighter and told her that I'd be alright. The guard came over and I hugged her from across the table before she left. She looked back one last time before she disappeared around the corner. It was my turn to cry but I held on until I reached the bathroom. I began to speak out loud to myself; thank you Jesus, thank you Jesus.

I had to go through the body cavity search all over again. When I returned to my dorm, I went straight to my bed. It was almost time for the count and we would be going to chow soon. The young brother I was closest to came over and asked about my visit. It was a strange situation for me to be responding to a younger man's concern for me. I was polite in my response and grateful that he had came over. "Yo my wife broke out and took my daughter with her. I don't know where she's at. I can't even inquire about her because I might wind up with another charge." Youngblood listen but didn't have much to say. "Just hold your head and keep trusting in God Like you tell me." The young brother spoke some true words of wisdom and I didn't have any problem following his advice. I lay back on my bed as he walked away. It was time for the count and time for my nap. I gave thanks to the Lord before I dozed off. After all if not for God where would I be?

I rose up in the bed not sure of where I was at. I looked around me dazed trying to figure out the last thing I did before falling asleep. This was not the first time I had awakened in this manner. I looked around at the nude pictures pasted on my walls. I began to focus on the one that looked most like my wife. I began to relax as the anxiety of the moment began to leave me. I lay back with my pillow slightly propped up. Day light was trying to sneak into the dorm unnoticed. I inched my drawers down past my knees. I began to imagine that the woman in bed with me was more than a picture on the wall. My member responded to the touch of my hand. I reached down for the bottle of lotion on the floor by my bed. I squeezed a generous portion of it into the palm of my right hand. I carefully screwed the top back on making sure not to spill any out of my hand. My member started to swell as if realizing what was about to take place. I checked the front of the dorm and the surrounding area making sure all were still asleep. I wanted no interruptions when I started to make love to this luscious woman. I did not want to stop my dreaming once I penetrated her in my mind. I began slow deliberate gyrations with my right hand around the head of my cock. I felt something in the pit of my stomach as a perfect picture formed in my mind. My cock grew even more as I began a slow descent down the length of my member." Mmmmmm "I murmured as shock waves canvassed my body. "Legs" I whispered as my hand rose back up to envelope the head again. I repeated this motion over and over again not caring about anything around me. "Mmmmmm, Oooooooo, Ahhhhhhh, was all I could say as my throbbing member began to eject its load. I wrapped my hand tightly around its head to capture all of the escaping thick fluid. The release was so gratifying that I just laid there for a moment as if in a private room. This drama would play a few times a week in order for my love to continue. I feared developing a deep hatred for Legs because of my circumstance. I had to use the one thing that always kept us connected in order for the love to survive. I was so involved with cumming that I didn't notice that daylight had boldly stepped into the room. I finished the trip my drawers had started and tossed them into the corner. I grabbed a large towel and wrapped it around my waist. I slung a pair of pants over my shoulder and headed for the showers with the rest of my supplies. The pussy was real good this morning. I wanted to finish off session with a shower alone with her. I had to hurry though because soon the rest of the hood would be waking up. When that happens there would be no more moments like the one I just had.

I came back to my bed with beads of water still running down my body. I like greasing up my body and I wasn't going to let jail stop me. I still knew it wasn't something I could do with other men watching me. When I got to my waist area, my member acted like I was coming to play with him. I would have loved to but this was not a good time. "Yo Pop you got some sugar?" I looked up to find Damien staring down at me. "Yeah, but step back while I put some drawers on." This young blood didn't understand how disrespectful that move he made was. I did not have the desire to teach it to him now. "Damien, here you go." "Thanks Pops you the man!" Damien had above average intelligence and was pretty good company. He thought highly of me and wouldn't hesitate to prove his loyalty. I had stopped being a gangster a long time ago but would fake it to survive in the streets. I wanted to convert Damien to Christ by example and honest testimonies. He felt that most of the ugly things about his life he couldn't change. He always saw himself as being at least a little involved in some type of illegal activity. That was the thought pattern of most of the young men that wanted to stay out of jail and live normal lives. They felt that low level crimes were part of the norm for them.

It would not be easy but I was committed to showing them love without any expectations. I wanted them to feel the love and concern that a stranger could have for them just because they were human beings. I knew that anything I did for them was to give God the glory. It was my acceptance of Jesus Christ that had changed my heart towards people. I wanted them to see it without me having to preach it. "Yo Damien, when you finish ya coffee lets do some push-ups before chow." "Sounds good Pops bring some cards." Damien then walks off with a big smile on his face.

I went to the bathroom and started to do stretches, to limber up my body. When you reach a certain age the mind is willing but the body is illing. After a few minutes I grew inpatient and called out for Damien. "Yo young blood come on. Let's get busy in here! "Take it easy Pops, I'm right here." "Damien, I don't want to spend all night doing push ups. I want to watch the movie tonight too." I was very humble in my response to him. These kids were so sensitive to feeing disrespected. I learned how to exert my influence and still let them feel in charge. Damien was a rare breed. He didn't belong in here or in criminal environment. He played the role because of peer pressure. He had a steady girl and a baby on the way. He needed more education but was still smart enough to get a general labor job. I was real stuck on Damien because he respected me and protected me like a favorite son. I kept him close to me as possible always trying to influence his behavior. "Shuffle the cards and let's get started." I demanded as he began to remove his tee shirt. "Pops, I hope you don't pull too many face cards. I don't want you to have a heart attack." Damien responded in an assertive tone, to let me know he didn't like orders. "Don't worry about my heart youngster. It's bigger than your chest and stronger than your muscles." I watched Damien do a half grin as he passed the cards for me to cut. I instead pulled the top card off the deck and dropped down to do my push-ups. Face cards were ten, aces were fifth teen, and the rest were whatever they indicated. I drew the Queen of Hearts. "One two three four . . . . nine and ten." That was light it wouldn't start getting tough until half the deck was gone. "Seven of Diamonds" Damien sounded off as he dropped down to do his. We went back and forth alternating between him getting high numbers and me getting low and vice a versa. I was the first to pull a ace with almost half of the deck finished. I started pumping out my push-ups like I had just started until I got to number six. "Seven e i g h t, nineee, ten, eleeveeen . . . . fourteeen ann fifthhhh teen." It was not an easy task pumping out those push-ups but I was not going to quit first. "Damn Pops! You okay?" Damien quickly asked as he held back his laughter. "Hell no but its your turn to pluck!" The kid's brashness was unnerving but I dealt with it. Each time we pulled a card completion became an arduous task. We both held our ground as the push-ups took longer no matter how low or high the number. I was near the breaking point as my turn was about to come up again. "LIGHTS OUT" The familiar phrase was music to my ears. "That's it kid I got to hustle into this shower before the Man comes through." "Do what you got to do Pops, I some clothes to wash myself." Damien's reply showed he was just as relieved because he offered no resistance to ending the work out session. I quickly took my shower as muscles ached from the intense session we just had. It was difficult to wash my back, as tight arm muscles made reaching around me painful if not impossible. My bed felt like a pasture thick dry grass as I lay back recalling the day I had. I fell off to sleep thinking about how fast time was moving with me working in the day and working out at night. The summer was coming to an end but not my jail time. I still had a few months to go and a birthday to celebrate.

I started early in trying to stash some goodies for my birthday. I never relied on anyone else making my special day special. Damien and Harlem (the other youngbood doing time with us), both planned on getting me gifts. I was dong a good job of keeping us united, well fed, and well respected. We didn't want for anything and people paid their tabs on time.

When it came time for my birthday they dropped the ball. Their visits didn't go right which didn't disappoint me. I was hesitant about getting high just to flaunt my superiority. I was with the lord, and had to guard against worldly desires. I cooked up a lot of food that night and even had dessert. What we had wasn't as important as the fact that we had it. I stopped spending money at this point and began to hoard all the valuables I could. I used food t buy cigarettes and cigarettes to buy street goods or cash. My surcharge was paid so now all my money would be leaving with me.

I sat thinking about my daughter on Halloween. I would take her trick a treating all over the neighborhood. We would have candy that lasted until the next Halloween. In the Kingdom there is no Halloween. It is a pagan holiday that denotes evil spirits and witchcraft. I had never let that prevent me from trick a treating. We just never did wear any costume or make-up. I was very emotional when Thanksgiving Holiday came. There was so much pain and joy associated with this one. My baby brother (who was deceased) and my niece both shared birthdays at this time. I had memories of both abundance and scarcity in my childhood and adult life. Thanksgiving always had me focusing on where my life was and what I was doing. Being incarcerated did not make for a joyful time. Being with Christ and trusting in the Lord for deliverance did! My sister was having a big dinner and I was able to speak with her before the holiday. We were twins born two years apart. I asked her to freeze me a dinner and I would eat it next month when I came home. I began to count the days down because now my time was real short. I could go to bed any night and wake up a free man. I started to get my paper work in order and made sure I got all the necessary documents to show where I was for the past year. I also wanted that shot in the arm from welfare while I qualified for a hand out. I utilized the jailhouse pastor to facilitate my transition. I even arranged to meet him for lunch upon my release. I didn't have a home to go to, but I had Jesus and no fear.

My phone calls to my sister Big Mama were focused on locating my possessions that were left behind. I didn't think about shelter because the cash I left behind, long with my car, would have to do. I had close to $200.00 in my commissary account. I didn't owe the jail anything so I was good. When the big day came there would still be disappointing moments. I processed out with everybody else but was held up from leaving. I had left my footlocker full of food to my young brothers that had my back. We exchanged numbers and promised to meet on the next Father's Day. That would have been an appropriate time because of our desire to become better men. The guards separated me from the rest of the people; I was supposed to leave with. They said that I had a warrant on me and would have to go to court first. I was more confused than upset because I felt this was some ploy my wife had instituted. Upon further investigation, the warrant had originated from the 81st Precinct. I was now convinced that this was the work of my wife. I had done all my time so what could they possibly have on me now. I sat around all that morning and most of the afternoon before they let me go. They never explained to me what really had happened or the cause of it all. Free at last and anxious to get back to the hood. I began to look for a shoe store to buy some fresh sneakers. I had a big enough bankroll to treat myself. Just as fast as that idea came, I remembered that my sister Big Mama was supposed to have a new pair of sneakers for me that she never sent up. I began to make my way home after picking up some White Castle hamburgers. I think the first thing everybody does after getting released from jail is to buy some food. I made my way to the train station and started that long trip to Brooklyn. I was filled with so much anxiety as the train made its way along the tracks. I began imagining this big reception with lots of smiling faces. I also wanted to find the number man that I left my money with. I wanted to know why he never sent what I asked for. I wanted to know why he deserted me when I needed him the most. I decided on finding friends before family because that's who had the most resources for me. It was early evening when I stepped off the train in Brooklyn. The #3 IRT brought me straight to area I wanted. I went to the liquor store to get a line on the number man where bouts. I was able to get some information after buying a bottle of Caskin Crème. I had just missed him but was told how and when I could find him. I had not returned to the streets just to forsake The Lord. I needed more than a scripture to take the edge off and get rid of my anxiety. I took the bus to Big Mama's house to what I thought would be a joyful reunion. I gazed out the window of the bus as I passed through neighborhoods that I did my dirt in. I began to tire as the bus brought me closer to my destination. I stood up and rang the bell as the bus crossed Thomas Boyland and Sumpter St. When the bus stopped at Marion St. I started my slow walk to begin a life filled with uncertainty. When I rang the bell to my sister's house, I felt no warmth when she answered. "Hey little brother, praise the Lord!" "God is good!" was my response. I was offered something to eat but wasn't hungry. I was more interested in going to sleep. I was told there was no room there but I could sleep on the floor that night. I asked about the sneakers and was told she never brought them. It felt so cold in there and there was something so different about my sister. She began to tell me about her friend Barry and how I could help him. Just that fast she was more focused on him than me. I listened as long as I could without showing a lack of concern. I asked about my car only to find out that it was parked on the church lot and never used by her. She had a jeep that I didn't know about and never needed my car. I became even more dissatisfied because of the wasted car insurance money. I had to get out of there before I exploded. I used the phone to call my other sister the Dr. on the Island. She was holding my Thanksgiving dinner, so that would be the premise for the visit. I politely said my goodbyes and gave her a hug. I thank her for her support and promised to return later. It would be much later before I made it back to Brooklyn.

I forced again to make another long journey using mass transit. I was hoping for a better ending than my last trip. When I left the Bronx, I had brought a N.Y.C.TRANSIT AUTHORITY FUN PASS. It cost $4.00 and allowed you to ride all in the system, up until 2:A.M.of the day it's first used. I had to go to Jamaica, Queens to get the bus for Long Island. I took the #7 bus and transferred to the #24, whose last stop would be in Jamaica, Queens. I would still have some walking to do to get to the Nassau County bus line for South Floral Park. It was well into the night when I finally reached my destination. I started the approximate seven block walk up the hill as night began to fall. Sparsely placed street lights created many shadows along my route. I was still a little disorientated from the short nap I had on the last bus ride. My breathing became labored as I drew closer and closer to the house. It really was a magnificent neighborhood with an abundance of well kept homes. My sister had a long history in the area and I had often come here to escape. I found both solitude and luxury. I was always a welcome guest because I required no maintenance. In fact I usually left the residence in better condition than I would find it. A devotion to my mother's comfort gave me definite skills in house keeping. There was usually space for me in the basement to lounge, relax, and watch T.V. or sleep. Selena came to the shortly after hearing me ring the bell. I received a much warmer reception from her than from Big Mama. She had already taken the dinner from the freezer when I had called her. I went to the bathroom to wash my hands. I had to wash them twice because after the first time the running water made me pee. "Hey sis" I cried out as I came back into the kitchen. "You ready to eat now?" my sister asked. "Yeah Selena nuke it!" was my quick response. The plate came out the micro wave piping hot. My sister stayed in the kitchen as I began to eat. One thing about Selena, she had no problem satisfying her curiosity. I knew she had questions she wanted to ask me. Plus she was the one that had access to my post office box. I gave her a key long before I was arrested because she worked in the area. I could count on her not to let the box get to full if I took awhile checking my mail. The arrangement really paid off when I was unexpectedly detained for such a long time. I prepared myself to respond as I ate, because it didn't look like she was going to wait for me to finish eating. "Where are you going to stay at tonight?" Selena asked in a caring manner. "I don't know sis. I asked Big Mama about staying there for the night and she offered me the floor." "You can stay here tonight but you have to speak with Harold to stay longer. What ever you do, don't mention anything about jail. He understands that you are having some problems with your wife. I never told him that you were locked. You know that's where his brother is at now." I remembered when his brother Danny got into trouble. I didn't know he was still locked up. I was actually expecting to see him. I used to stay in the basement with him and his other brother Tony. When I had first become homeless from my wife, I stayed for a few weeks to avoid the streets for my birthday. I asked Harold for permission. He gave but expressed early to stick to the time period. I managed to keep Danny out of trouble and committing any violent acts. He thought the world of my sister but felt Harold and her were stealing from him. Danny won settlements for two childhood accidents and was currently receiving SSI money.

Harold was my sister's husband. We got along alright but he was short on patience with people that had difficulties. It was after I left that last time that Harold regretted my departure. I didn't have any money then and was relying on my hustling and pending unemployment benefits. My baby sister Nina gave me a place to stay after that. My mother had blazed a trail of goodwill with all my sister's friends and in-laws. Mom's humor, cooking skills and organizational talents, gained her a large following. It was peaceful out here because it was far away from the gangster activity. I would start my stay with a thorough cleaning of the kitchen upstairs and the basement downstairs. I would even cook that meal for the first night of my stay. Just my cooking alone would get me extended visit privileges. This time it was critical because I had to think carefully of what my next move would be. I didn't have the luxury of using my old friends. I had left jail with Jesus and I was not about to tell Him, to get lost.

"Thanks sis tonight is fine right now. I'll be ready for bed as soon as I finish eating. Is Danny downstairs?" When I finished talking, a ghostly look appeared on my sister Selena's face. The words did not flow smoothly as they began to dribble out of her mouth. My grand better than the rest and smarter than the best sister, began to look humble as the words now cleared the air. "Danny was sentenced to seven to fifteen years in prison for robbery." I sat stunned at the news wondering what had gone wrong with such a simple case. Danny was no criminal land his diminished mental capacity was well documented. I really was in a hurry now to swallow the rest of this food. I couldn't help but think that Harold's non caring attitude had a lot to do with Danny's current state. I could finally rise from the table. "Wow thanks sis that food was worth the wait. I'll go downstairs now and speak with you tomorrow. I plan on going to the welfare department to get some assistance. Fresh out of jail is the best time to see them." Selena still with the ghostly look suggested I get a ride with Harold into Brooklyn. He left for work at a more reasonable time than my sister. She reminded me again about what not to talk about. "Good night sis, see you tomorrow." I turned my back and headed down the stairs to the basement, just as the word; tomorrow, left my lips.

I was downstairs in the basement surveying the situation. Things were not as I remembered them. There was total disorder and uncleanliness. I began to shift things around, just to clear space to sit and sleep. I was not about to get too involved in this now, because I was ready for bed. My sister came downstairs unexpected with some fresh linen. I told her I would be cleaning the place up, when I returned tomorrow. She also had a box with her that contained all my accumulated mail. "Wow" I said, that's a lot of mail. "I also have some more but I can't locate it right now." She responded. I watched as she went back upstairs. I looked at the box anxious to see the contents inside. I wanted to speak with my daughter and let her know where I was at. I began to sift through the papers to find my phone bills. I wanted the phone number of my sister in law. I knew she would know where my wife and child were. My face lit up when I saw a few AT&T envelopes. I opened one up and began to scan the listed phone numbers and their origin. "There, that's it!" I said out loud, when I saw Newport News, VA. I didn't want to disturb my sister, so I would contain myself until tomorrow. I went into the bathroom to shower and saw conditions worst than what was outside. I began to scrub here and wipe there with (probably unused) cleaning products. Dirt and grime began to disappear faster than a cat in a dog pound. The habits I developed in jail quickly returned as I washed my drawers, socks and tee shirt out. I poured bleach on the shower floor to protect my feet. I didn't have any shower slippers. My feet were in too good of a condition to risk infection again. I used the cosmetics I found to sooth my body. I found a clean tee shirt and sweat pants to sleep in. The clothes belonged to Danny and he wouldn't need them for a long time. I had a lot of trouble getting to sleep. I searched around for a men's magazine for any picture that would stimulate me without having to use my memory. I found a hip hop magazine with mini skirt and bikini clad girls inside. I got a quick response from my member as I began to apply some grease. "Mmmmmm "I moaned as it grew larger in my hands. Yes, I was using both hands this time because I felt like having an orgy. Smooth and slow, easy strokes brought me to a thundering climax. I rolled over with my joint wrapped up in a towel and went to sleep. "My first nut on the outside." I thought to myself as my eyes closed shut.

The morning came too fast as the voice of my brother in law woke me up. "Hey Zeke, I'm leaving in an hour!" "Alright Harold, I'll be ready." I rose from the couch that was my bed and stumbled into the bathroom. I then realized that the lump in my sweat pants was the towel I went to sleep with. It dropped down between my legs as I lowered the pants to take a leak. The urine left my body with a lot of force as I pondered my current situation. I stepped out of the pants and checked my hanging underwear. They were still damp in some places as I put them on. I smeared some toothpaste on my teeth and began to gargle. I washed my face and lathered up my joint. I couldn't resist as I began to masturbate some more. It felt too good in my hands to pass up an opportunity to cumm. "Ahhhhh yes!" I exclaimed while the thick fluid oozed down the sink walls. It was almost an hour when I had finished dressing. I went upstairs and sat in the kitchen. Harold was more ready than me when we both exited the house and got into the car.

I sat down and waited for Harold to enter the car. He didn't waste much time before the questions started. "So Zeke how is the family doing? It has been awhile since I saw you." Everybody is doing alright and I've just been trying to survive." I paused for a moment before changing the subject. "Where is Danny? Does he still hang out all night?" Harold's face became a little twisted as he started to reply. "Danny is locked up for a robbery. They offered him 3 ½ years but he decided to take it to trial. He was convicted and received 7 ½-15 years." I sat numb for a brief moment before shouting out. "How could you let that happen? Danny is not capable of making a decision like that on his own! Didn't he have a lawyer?" I was so angry right now at both him and my sister. I felt like they were happy he was out of the house. There was a tense silence in the car as I waited for an answer. Harold began to speak like he didn't want anyone outside the car to hear him. We were traveling on the Belt Parkway with the windows rolled up. Still I could barely hear him as the words slid out of his mouth. "He had a lawyer but he didn't want to admit to something that he said he didn't do. The lawyer tried to make him understand but Danny felt it was some type of conspiracy against him." "He should have been examined by a psychiatrist and declared mentally incompetent." My response was meaningless because nothing but a miracle could reverse what had happened to poor Danny. I began to share some of the blame for leaving him in such a vulnerable situation. Danny had more than his share of mishaps in his life. He was born to a crack addict mother. He was slow to learn and still suffered from the effects of the drugs in his system. He grew up around a lot of love but it lessened when his adoptive mom died. His rough play and inattentiveness caused many accidents. When I stayed with him he slowed down on his craziness. He liked to talk politics but not in the normal since like others. There was always some dark twist to his understanding of the world. Still he was very likable and funny without trying to be. "Harold when was the last time you visited him?" I asked. "I'm waiting now for him to settle down in a facility. He is still in transit and going through evaluations." Harold began to loosen up and the tension left the air. It seemed like this was something he wanted to talk about. I know it hurt him for his brother to be where he was at. Harold was too straight to understand the workings of the justice system. The most he may have had was a traffic ticket. He used to be a loud drunk at point in his life but now he had Jesus. "Zeke my turn is coming up. Where do you want me to drop you off at?" "You can leave me over by the movies. I can take one of those busses to the train station. I really appreciate this ride brother-in-law." "Its not a problem Zeke, I enjoyed the talk and the company." I started looking in the direction of the bus stop as he pulled into the movie parking lot. "This is good Harold. I can walk from here. Wish me luck on my job search. I'll probably see you again tonight." I saw a smile cross Harold's face as he replied. "That's good Zeke. You are welcome to stay since Danny won't be using his room. You may have to do some cleaning down there." "Okay later" I shuffled on off not wanting to hear any more conversation. I was too busy now thinking about my own circumstances. I needed an income and a place to stay. I needed to know where my family, car and pawn tickets were at. I needed to know all that soon in that order. I made my way to the bus stop full of gratitude for the metro card; my sister had given me last night. I had to pay attention when I used it, because she didn't know how much money was on it. There was a small group of people already standing there. It looked like a mixture of students and laborers. Females out numbered the men two to one. Freedom sure felt good and the females sure smelled good. I found me a window seat in the aisle. My neck did a constant swivel as I watched everything moving. I told Harold I was job hunting but my first stop would be to the welfare department. They had a new name for it but it was still the welfare department to me. I had to take advantage of this opportunity while my release was fresh. It would be much easier to answer all those questions since I spent my last year in jail. Well almost a year, but who's keeping track! The bus continued its journey thru East New York, as each new stop had more passengers than the last. Soon there were all types of bodies standing around me. I enjoyed the view that freedom had delivered to me. By the time the bus reached the train station, it was filled to the max. I rose slowly not wanting to brush up against any of the young fertile bodies that stood around me. I had already weathered one storm from being inappropriate and didn't want the suggestion of a reoccurrence to appear. I stumbled my way to the back exit door as the crowd began to thin. I disembarked quickly and raced up the stairs. There was a train waiting and I wanted to be on it. I chose an empty seat near a door on the end. I wanted to lessen my contact with the other passengers. The chance of just one undesirable sitting next to me would be enough. After a brief moment the doors closed and the train began its trip along the tracks. My view of the outside was obscured by the unfortunate ones without a seat. It really didn't matter because not that much had changed. The elevated train began its descent to the underground after only a few stops. The sunlight disappeared and was replaced by the bright glow of the overhead lighting. Stop after stop the train took on more passengers as if there were no limit to its capacity. I had no complaints but felt sympathy for the standing bodies caught in the crush. My mind began to drift as I thought about the many trips I had previously taken on this line. The late night trips I took early in my marriage, were fresh in my head. The times I fought to stay awake with pockets jammed with cash brought a smile to my face. I stopped daydreaming for a moment to see eyes fixated on me. The frequent smiles and muffled laughter coming from me had some people looking concerned. In this town you never knew when someone's reality would change dramatically and cause a violent outbreak. They didn't have to worry about that from me. I was very focused on prosperity that awaited me since I had chosen Jesus. I peered through the bodies and saw that my stop had come. I rose to my feet hunched over a bit from the crush of the bodies. I could see people eyeing the empty seat I left wondering if they would be the one to fill it. That was not my concern as I left the train when the doors opened. My eyes shifted up and down the platform to make sure I chose the right exit to leave. I made my way up the stairs as daylight began to greet me. I reached the top of the landing and exited the station to find the bright sunlight eager to meet me. I scanned the streets as the early morning rush was in full motion. It was still too early to enter the building so I found an empty banister to lean against. I watched as women young and old move about me. Everyone seemed to have a mission to complete and would let nothing interfere. I saw soft bodies and hard bodies all mixing and mingling, as they strutted with their stuff. I just enjoyed the visions they created as they went about. Once in awhile I would mumble a good morning or a "hello Sister". I began to pay more attention to the people standing closest to me. It was amazing how some would put on this act of acute poverty to gain an advantage with welfare workers. Then their were others that didn't care and looked better than the people paid to serve them. I guess I fell somewhere in between. I was just coming with the facts and how I looked shouldn't have a bearing on my situation. People started to move closer to the glass doors lined along the entrance way. The security guard inside, was making his way to the front, and unlocking doors as he went. Once those doors were opened there was a mad dash to the elevators. Some stop to ask questions to be sure of their destination. I was one of those people. The worst thing about waiting down here was waiting in the wrong place. Nobody had sympathy for you once you got it right. Many a fights had broken out in this place. People wanting to go to the front of lines for various reasons usually were the cause. I rode the packed elevator to my floor. I secured my spot on line and checked with two more people before I was comfortable with my selection. My turn came after twenty minutes of waiting on line. I was given a stack of papers and forms after showing my identification. The pleasant woman told me it would be an all day process. I had nothing else to do but wait and give thanks to God. I knew I would be getting some money today because of my "just released from jail "status. I went from room to room and person to person, as the system went to work to give me some cash. I had arrived at eight in the morning and it was now four thirty. The lady was honest about the time I would spend in here. I was given a voucher for carfare and a list of things had to bring the next day. "Damn! I thought I would at least get some food stamps." I whispered to myself. I left the office tired but not dejected. This was not the first time I had to do this. It was just the first time acceptance was a sure thing. I made my way cross town to my sister Big Mama house. I was ready to check on those sneakers she said she had brought me.

I waited in line to turn in my carfare voucher. There was a lot of tension on that floor as people vented their frustration with the system. I was a bit disappointed too, but being angry would only effect me. I handed in my slip and smiled as the older woman took it. In a very short time I was given enough $4.00 metro cards to cover travel for all the appointments I had received. I left happy with a sense of accomplishment for acting so fast in addressing my poverty. I made my way out the building and around the corner to the train station. It was a long walk down a wide corridor to the turnstiles. I picked up my pace as the loud noise of an approaching train flooded my ears. I swiped my card through the slot and raced downstairs, trying hard not to bump the ascending passengers. I took the last three steps with one leap and made my way inside. I paused for more than a moment to catch my breath. I quickly scanned the train car for an empty seat near a door. There were none in sight, so I settled in between a large man and a petite young woman. I was unable to settle back in my seat, because of the room they allotted me. I leaned forward with both elbows on my knees and started the journey cross town. The only good thing about this crowded train was that it was the express. It only took three stops for me to reach my destination. I made my way from the middle of the platform to the exit at the other end. I had this long walk to make because I didn't move to the front when I first got on. I took my time upstairs to the disapproval of those walking behind me. I didn't care because fatigue was starting to set in. I decided not to use the free bus transfer at this time. It would serve me better after I left Big Mama's house for the trip to Long Island. This was a familiar neighborhood but one that held many secrets. I blossomed as a criminal around here. I played the good guy and the bad guy at various times. The memories in my head were too much of a distraction to live as I now had planned. Jesus Christ would be my anchor in my life. The only might I would be relying on now would be the power of God. I finally reached Marion St. where my sister lived. It had only been a few days since the last time I was here. I saw her jeep parked outside, so I knew she would be there. I rang the downstairs bell and waited for a response. The outside door upstairs opened and my sister motioned for me to come up. "Zeke you know I don't live down there. I heard the bell because I was in the hallway." Sis continued to watch me as I walked slowly up the stairs. "Yo bro you look like you got some new muscles?" Big Mama asked with a wide grin on her face. I was glad to see her in a cheerful mood. On a bad day she could really be more than anyone wanted to bear. "Yeah I guess I did gain some weight during my city paid vacation." I said with the same grin she had shown me. I wasted know time in explaining my purpose. "I came for those sneakers you said you brought me." A look of disappointment flashed across her face. "I don't have those but see if you can fit these other shoes." She handed me a pair of Timberland boots that hadn't been broken in. I tried them on and accepted the gift. "I thought you would come back last Friday to sleep here? She asked sheepishly. "No. I stayed on Long Island with Selena. She offered me a bed to sleep in." I was wrong for being so sarcastic, but I wanted to display my anger at her previous offer. Why did she think that giving me a floor to sleep on was acceptable? There were too many rooms in this house that I could have slept in. I thanked her for the shoes and reminded her of the long trip ahead of me. "I'm going back to Selena's house so I better get going." She nodded I approval and gave me a hug. She put a twenty dollar bill in my hand and promised more when she got paid. I asked about my car that she was keeping. "Your car is in the church parking lot." She responded. "Thanks for everything Sis but I got to be going now. I made my way out the door with some new shoes and a twenty dollar bill. I guess the trip wasn't all that bad after all. I walked swiftly to Broadway to catch a bus that would take me to Queens. I would pay another fare in Queens to board the bus for Long Island. Bye Brooklyn! I came back sooner than I planned but next time it will be longer.

It wasn't long before the Q24 rolled up to the stop. I boarded quickly because I was the only one standing there. My face stayed plastered to the window as the bus moved along its route. My thoughts started to drift to my absent family. Not having them in Brooklyn or in New York for that matter, would take some getting used too. I was very hurt by what my wife did, but I still would imagine us being together again. I began to tire as the bus continued along its way. It slowly began to fill up as determined people made their way home. "Last stop no more passengers!" I awakened to the loud voice of the driver and an empty bus. "Whew that was fast!" I said to myself. I staggered out of my seat as my legs struggled to gain some momentum. I limped off the bus using the back exit. My legs were still fighting to gain their strength. I did a slow motion jog across the street as I headed toward the Jamaica Bus Depot. There was a lot of activity as people were busy with their Christmas shopping. I didn't feel anything but my thoughts were on my daughter. I began to feel a little sadness as reality set in. Money was short and my priority was on housing and employment. I

ZEKE SMITH

knew next year would be better because of my resolve. The lines waiting for the bus in Queens were much more organized than Brooklyn. You had to go to the back of the line and not just rush the front door when a bus pulled up. Acting civil was never a problem for me. I just refused to be the only one doing it in any given situation. I swiped my Metro Card when my turn came. I found me a seat facing the back exit. I knew this bus would have very little standing room in a short time. I watched with excitement as mostly females in all stages of development and stature continuously boarded at each stop. When the driver felt he had his maximum load, he stopped picking up passengers. The bus went express until its first stop in Long Island. This was great for the riders but you hated it when you were the one on the curb waiting to get on. I turned my head to see the Belmont Racetrack as the bus rode along the Hempstead Turnpike. This was also my cue to rise up and ring the bell to get off.

I made my way across the busy intersection and started that long walk to the house. I had made this trip many times before, but never with so much uncertainty. The challenge would be to get my sister and her husband to let me live in the basement until I could do better. They also had to agree to accept only what The Welfare Dept. would pay them. I felt good about what I had accomplished today. I was looking forward to a quiet weekend. I would take that time to go through my mail and secure some clothing. My things were scattered about. If I could relax enough and clear my head, I would remember where they were at. Ah, there it is. The house was in view and I couldn't wait to be inside. My sister was home before 3:p.m., so I knew I could get in. I walk up the short flight of stairs and rang the bell. It wasn't long before my almost twin sis opened the door. "Hey Zee, how was your day?" she beamed out as we made eye contact. I did okay but there is a lot I need to talk to you about. I'm going to be able to get Welfare but I need some documents from you guys. I will have some food stamps next week. I watched as a smiled slid across her face. One thing about this sister, if you pay you could play. "You have to talk to Harold about that. I'm sure he will let you stay here. He was disappointed the last time you left." My sister has a way of making all problems someone else's fault. "I wish someone had let me know that. I asked for a couple of weeks and that's what I received. I didn't hear anyone begging or even asking me to stay longer." My sister looked stunned as I finished my statement. She was in a very uncomfortable position now. Generally people ignored the truth when it was in opposition to what she was saying. Even when someone was being charitable to me, I labored hard enough around them to pay my way. It was like an undercover barter system. In fact I over paid them with the work I did. I could see sis wanted to say something so I changed the subject. "Selena could you give me that mail you told me about. I know you said you were still finding boxes with some mail." I flashed a big smile when I spoke. "Yeah Zee and I also have some fresh linen for you." "Wow sis thanks a bunch. What I've been using had a stale smell." Selena left the kitchen to get the box. I was anxious to go downstairs and shower. I still had my jailhouse routine in my head. I knew it wouldn't just stop like that. Selena returned in a short time with a small cardboard box. "Here you go Zee. This is all the rest of the mail. If I come across any more, I will give it to you." I began to wonder as she stood there if any food was around. I didn't have a chance yet to rummage through the fridge. "Okay thanks for everything sis. You did a good job of looking out for me." I was exaggerating but it made her feel better than before. "I'm going downstairs now. I'm used to going to bed early." I grabbed the linen and then I picked up the box and started down the stairs. I stopped abruptly and turned around. "Oh sis, will you let Harold know about the papers I need and we can talking the morning. I will probably be sleep when he comes home." "Sure Zee, I will tell him. Goodnight." "Goodnight sis." I walked slowly down the stairs because the lights were out. I wasn't all that used to the furniture arrangement yet. I rubbed my hands along the walls until I found the lamp. "Click! Let there be light." I spoke out loud enough for me to hear. I placed the box down on the floor next to the bed. I laid the linen on top of the bed. I looked for my bag with all clothes I brought from jail. I needed fresh underwear for my next appointment. This one would involve a physical. I stripped down naked and headed towards the bathroom while peering up the stairs. I only had a minimal amount of privacy because the laundry room was down here. Once in the bathroom I made sure the door was latched. The shower was fast because I didn't have time to play around. I applied my cosmetics and went straight to bed. I slept like a baby that night with no strange dreams to report. Daylight came in the form of Harold yelling downstairs, if I was up or not.

This was a new day and knelt down to pray as Harold's foot steps faded away. It wasn't hard to tell what room someone was in upstairs. The creaking of the floorboard or the sound of their voices, gave away their location. I began to thank God for another day and helping to make it this far. I asked for His forgiveness for my sins and for His protection. I began to include my wife and children and all the young brothers I left behind. I ended with a promise to never stop loving Jesus and gave thanks in His

ZEKE SMITH

name. Amen. I started to get dress and prepare myself for more questions from Harold. I believed my sister told him about my needs. I cleaned up the room and made it more organized. I did all I could do downstairs. It was now time to face Harold once again.

"Hey Zee, you want some oatmeal before we leave?" Harold asked in a friendly voice full of energy. This was the one food he could never get enough of. "Yeah that sounds good." I responded quickly. He then directed me to the pot on the stove. It looked like if I had said no, he would have been disappointed. There was a lot of oatmeal in that pot. "Harold, do you have a toaster here?" Yeah I still had those jailhouse eating habits too. I wanted to spread some jelly and butter on four slices of toast. This would hold me for the better part of the day. "Look in that bottom cabinet and it should be there." I bent down and pulled open the door. Once it left the locking mechanism it started to swing on one hinge. It seemed that the other hinge had lost its screws a long time ago. "Thanks I got it." I held the toaster over the sink and began to tap the sides to loosen any old crumbs that might be inside. I took the half of loaf of bread out of the bread box. I couldn't see the expiration date but I knew they didn't buy it yesterday. I dropped two slices in and began to search the fridge for the butter and jelly. All the while I was getting my meal together; Harold was sitting down eating his. I began to pick up my pace as the first two slices of toast popped out. I slid the next two in and bean to butter and jelly up the other two. Once done I moved quickly to place my oatmeal in a bowl just as the next two popped up out of the toaster. "Damn! I was getting hungrier just trying to fix this food. Harold tried not to pay attention to what I was doing. He didn't know where I had been for the past year. He thought I was home with my wife and had just broken up. Selena insisted that I keep this a secret. My food was finally ready to be eaten. I had less time to eat than I did preparing it. Harold began to rise from the table wit his empty bowl. "Don't rush Zee we got time. There isn't that much traffic on the belt right now." He was trying to show some kindness but I knew he didn't like his routine messed with. If driving me to Brooklyn in the morning affected him too much, he would be complaining to Selena. Then she would be preaching to me. Harold left the kitchen and went to the back. When he returned I was done eating and had started to wash the dishes. "Okay Zee you can get in the car when you finish." "Okay Harold" I responded as I put the last dish in the drain.

The ride to Brooklyn was quiet until Harold began questioning me about the Welfare. He agreed to give me the papers and I told him how much rent they would pay. He then explained that I could give any money to Selena. The ride to Brooklyn seemed faster than normal. I was relieved that housing had been taken care of. Now my focus would be on employment. Harold dropped me off at the usual spot. I took the same walk as the previous days. I rode the same route and arrived at the same train station. The ride to Downtown Brooklyn lasted no longer than before because there were no unexpected delays. I made my way up the stairs when the train reached my stop. I waited outside with the rest of the crowd until the doors were unlocked and dash to the elevators took place. I began to notice some of the same faces I saw when I first started my saga. It was not unusual to make friends because we all had something in common. We all reached a low point in our lives and needed a helping hand. I checked in at the appropriate desk on the appropriate floor. Everything seemed so systematic but mistakes were sometimes made. I was fortunate so far that no mistakes were made with me. This appointment was made to check and verify all the information I had to gather. I would also be issued an I.D. card that would be used to access all my benefits. They took my thumb print and a picture to help prevent any fraud. There were some people in the past that had welfare cases in numerous centers at the same time. There were kings and queens of welfare fraud but the women held the records. It was easy for them because they could claim children and the system were geared to be more empathic towards them. I made small talk with the caseworker that interviewed me. I never hesitated to tell my sad tell of rejection from my wife. This always seemed to get me an edge with the worker. It didn't matter the gender. I got a favorable response from either male or female. I next went downstairs with my carfare voucher. I had to walk a short distance to another building to receive my Medicaid card. I would need this card to receive food stamps, money, and medical benefits. I had to return to the center with a letter from Harold and an oil bill. They would only pay $215.00 a month for rent. I would also get $125.00 a month for food. They stopped issuing food stamps. You had to use the Medicaid card like it was Visa. I left Brooklyn as soon as my business was finished and made my way back to Long Island. I didn't have to ring the bell this time because they had given me a key.

I was real tired by the time I reached Long Island. I tested my cards by getting a hero sandwich along the way home. I used my new key to enter the house and went straight to the basement. My sister was home but conversation wasn't on my mind right now. I figured I'd wait for Harold to come home so I wouldn't have to repeat myself. I ate my sandwich as I watched the T.V. I was able to run some wire and activate the cable that was already downstairs. I looked around as I ate to figure out how to make it more neat and organized. Danny's possessions were all over the place. It would be at least seven years before he would get a chance to use them again. I sorted out everything that I could use now and the rest I put in bags and boxes. I figured that by the time he came home I could afford to take him shopping. I rose from my seat after eating and began to move things around. I started in the front and worked my way back to the kitchen. This was the most challenging room down here. Danny's other brother Tony shared the basement. He was no joy to live with. He had a nice personality and kept to himself. Tony just didn't have a clue as to how to keep his place clean. He didn't wash dishes or laundry on a regular basis. If he did laundry, he only took clothes out the dryer as he needed to wear them. If someone had to use the machine behind him, his clothes winded up tossed to the side. I believed that because his mother always did for him, he never learned or had the motivation to do for himself. I found myself cleaning the basement, kitchen included on a regular basis. I first had to do a massive cleaning just to get it to that point. Everyone marveled at my accomplishments and was very grateful, but no one paid me. Tony wasn't the only one making a mess downstairs. The so called accomplished ones upstairs also left things behind to clean up. The only difference, it didn't happen everyday.

I continued to make adjustments to my living quarters. I had a home visit from the welfare to verify my housing. I was implanted into this workfare program to get me job ready. It was no more than a required part of the system, to create the illusion of making you independent. I used it to develop my computer skills and enhance my social network. I also took advantage of all job leads and was very cooperative. My attendance or punctuality was never an issue. I believe my attitude about finding a job helped the counselors take a serious approach to finding me something. I also had an impressive resume with a variety of listed skills. It was not long before I started attending some job interviews. I felt strong about my chances. I just didn't feel as strong about the timing.

I continued to make my trips into Brooklyn for my Job Readiness Program. I wasn't pressured by the staff because they really couldn't find me any work. They were more accustomed to helping unskilled labor. It was easy for them to talk a person into one of the either security training or home health care. I made it through that winter by saving my check and hustling snow jobs. I even made some money with the New York Sanitation

Department by shoveling snow. I continued to sort through the mess that was the basement. I just washed and stacked, washed and stacked until all the extra junk had disappeared. I was also able to add to my wardrobe whenever I found some of Danny's clothes I could fit. I just figured he wouldn't be able to fit them and I would have the resources to buy him new ones. It was beginning to feel more and more like home. I labored hard and free to be accepted by my sister and her husband. I knew if I wasn't paying I wouldn't be here. It didn't matter that she had old unsettled debt from when I let her use my Sears card. My sister's memory always was selective about remembering when she was needy.

My Sundays were often spent worshipping with my sister at her church and then cooking the dinner at home. It was such a different routine than the one I was used too. I really didn't like being deceptive about where I came from. The deceit also took away from what I was accomplishing as my life got better. I was able to call my daughter on occasion but I didn't make it a habit. Even when there was an invitation, I would often refuse. I knew the climate I was living in, and I would have no future debts to disturb me.

It was a hard winter in 2003, so I welcomed the spring when it came. I was already spending time in Brooklyn because of my program. It was in walking distance of my old neighborhood. My collar and my pockets would be tight so I started visiting my old girlfriends' house. I was always close to the whole family with so many women around. I couldn't help the lust I had for them all, but I learned to control it. I always felt energized by a women's presence. In this household I was a superman with so much estrogen in the air. It was always something for a real man to do around here. The sons seemed to spend too time staying out of trouble to help anybody else. I became Mr. Belvedere once again to bring relief to a household in turmoil. There was a lot of love in that house for me. It was an important piece to my puzzle with my own family gone. My oldest sister was too caught up in a relationship to respond to any of my needs. In fact she was beginning to pressure me, to remove my car from her church parking lot. She wouldn't even let me remove the plates since the insurance had expired. No matter how many things came against me, (and there were a lot) I refused to give up. I just kept pressing forward with my faith in Jesus and a belief in The Word of God.

God answered some of my prayers with a let snowstorm in the spring. I was able to shovel for the Sanitation Dept., but this time they had applications for the next test. I wasted no time in applying and the filing

ZEKE SMITH

fee was waived, since I was receiving public assistance. I also began to focus on getting my car out of that parking lot too. I didn't want to but my best option would be to sell it. I was desperate for the money and also to get rid of the car. The spring had been so cold this year that people hesitated when the summer finally arrived. It made up for those cold temperatures during the spring. The heat would often be so unbearable. I was spending my days babysitting while my friend played bingo. The occasional hug I would get from her was worth it. I still had not gotten off with some real pussy. I was hanging around this house fantasizing about doing everybody. I got lucky once when some visitor felt sorry for me and gave me some head in an empty room. Whenever she came around I found a way to smuggle her into the back and bust a nut. I finally stopped when the Holy Spirit convicted me and I began another dramatic change.

I awoke one morning and felt the strong presence of My Lord in the midst. I fell on my knees and began to pray. I prayed for peace and reconciliation with my wife. I refused to find fault in what she had done in rejecting me. A profound love of Christ began to flourish through me. I begged for forgiveness because of all the wrong I had done. Tears began to pour down my face as I continued to call upon My Savior for deliverance. I wanted to be delivered from the pain and agony of my past. I wanted to be delivered from desire to hustle the streets. I wanted to view women with more respect and less desire. I needed to show and prove myself to God that my prayers were sincere. I called upon God to refresh my memory about the teachings from my ancestors. The guidance and good directions I received from my parents, uncles, and elder neighbors needed to become vivid in my mind. I started to tremble as I felt soothing warmth engulf my body. I began to relax as I felt my consciousness slipping away. I slipped off into a day dreaming state as visions my reunion with wife and child appeared before me. Oblivious to the amount of time that had passed; I rose from my prostrated position. I looked around the basement in a confused state, trying to understand what had just happened. Jesus, Jesus, and Jesus I chanted over and over again. I made my way to the bathroom as the name Jesus continued to echo in my ear. I felt a great joy and jubilation at this moment. I released the fluids that had built up inside me. I turned on the shower and began to remove my night clothes. It took a few minutes for me to adjust the water temperature. My thoughts were still cloudy by my encounter with The Holy Spirit. I began to wash my body with a new purpose. I wanted to remove all the dirt and grime from my past. I wanted to rinse away all the bad memories. I wanted the aroma of the new man to fill the air. I spent only the necessary time on my genitals to remove the dirt. I was not seeking to be aroused. I knew celibacy would be a must for me to grow closer to My Lord. I began to read the scriptures more than before. I returned to my two favorites. The 27th Psalm for deliverance and redemption and the 34th Psalm for gratitude and thanksgiving. I started to feel strengthened and confident that things would get better. My little stash was steadily growing and so was my affection for The Lord. I continued attending my job search program. When I left there I would stay in Brooklyn for babysitting and house keeping for my friends. The summer was moving fast and it was one of the hotter ones for the record.

One day in July the heat index was over 100 degrees. It was 2003 and the unthinkable happened. The power failed and the city came to a slow down. This time it wasn't like 1977 when Con Edison was the culprit along with high temperatures. No this time it was something much broader and a system few knew about became public knowledge. This power failure, affected the east coast and parts of Canada. There was a problem in the power grid that supplied this area. It was a domino affect as system after system went down. In my neighborhood like so many others like it, we began to barbeque when no end was in sight. Everybody seemed to be helping each other make it through the night. People were sharing flashlights and stores were giving away their ice cream. I spent the night in Brooklyn and helped to protect my old area. This was much different than 1977 when I was leading looting parties through the borough. I received a hard week in jail that time while I waited to see a judge. I was hailed a hero this time for the way I stayed up during the night. In the morning was when the grills started to pop out. I was a known grill master so it was some good eating that day. It was also the day that I established a new relationship with my favorite newspaper. I had been reading the New York Daily News before I had even started school. It was the reason that my reading level was always so high. I had encountered their reporter on Broadway when I went there to buy some supplies for our instant cook-out. She was doing some comparisons with the last blackout that we had. She had a computer print-out of every business that was located all along Broadway in 1977. Broadway was the hardest hit area in the city that day. They even destroyed my cleaners where I winded up getting arrested. I knew better than most what was left. There was the sneaker store and our barber shop. I gave so much details to her that she became impressed and was very grateful. I then asked her if she wanted to hear my blackout story and she agreed. She was in awe of the amount of information that I had. She then left to see if her editor would approve of the story. I returned to my grill and finished cooking. It was just like a block party as others began to break out their grills. Sure enough the reporter returned with an okay from her editor and a need for some more detailed information. I reminded her that I didn't need my jail time mentioned with so much of the other negative stuff. I was trying to get a new start in life again and was looking for a job. In her own words; "You are not that person anymore and look at the way you are helping your neighbors." I felt some apprehension but she had made a good point. I trusted my God and gave my approval for the story. The photographer came and took my picture for the paper. I even spoke with her editor before she left. Wow, what an impact that story had. The picture they took was also just as dramatic. I began to hear from people that I had lost contact with. I was being applauded by some for my honesty and called a fool by others. Broke but not disgusted I was now a local celebrity. I was still nervous about my new notoriety but things would change in a couple of months.

I was acting more like a counselor than a client at my program. I had become very comfortable there and began to receive some computer training. I had even loaned some personal resource materials to one of the staff members there. The problems started when he refused to return them and act like he never received them. I made a lot of noise with several complaints to the director and the complaint number located in their pamphlet. I got my materials back within a week and a transfer to another job search program. I now had to commute to Downtown Brooklyn which I didn't have a problem with. I was in this program for less than a month before a female counselor found me a possibility on Long Island. The job I was able to get at this major New York grocery retailer was a turning point in my life. I had to work at least 25 hours to satisfy The Welfare Department. The asst. manager that screened me was able to accommodate. I was hired onto their maintenance team and no chore was beneath me. I excelled at the job and it was a short bus ride away from the house. I bonded with the customers and I bonded with the other workers. Some took longer than others. I prided myself on knowing where everything was located in the store. I hustled extra hours whenever I could. The first year went fast. One month after getting hired that year, the good Lord blessed me again. I got me a cell phone from Sprint during one of their promotions in Brooklyn. I didn't need any money but a hundred and fifty dollar deposit to secure a line. I would also be limited to a two hundred line of credit on the bill. I was empowered now to communicate freely with my daughter. I was even able to send her money some time. The pastor at my sister's church started focusing too much on people that attended his church often without joining. It was unsettling to me, which caused me begin worshipping in Queens. I was not going to let man come between me and my God. I would get the word elsewhere. I found a suitable location where I switched to get my bus to Brooklyn. It was a large church and there didn't seem to be a lot of attention paid to new worshippers. This was excellent for me because I did not want to be bothered. I just wanted God and Christ in my life not people. I sat in the back where I could hear the word and still reflect on my life. I shed a lot of tears in that place whenever I prayed. I gave offerings based on my financial situation at the time. I felt the lord understood and would not pressure me to do more. Time began to flow more smoothly as I settled into a new routine. The new job continued to bless me as friendships began to develop. I still gyrated towards the younger workers as I tried to gain more understanding about my own daughter's development. Whenever Z Baby and I had difficult conversations, I found direction from some of the teenage girls on the job. They began to look up to me more as they admired the attention I gave my child. There were so many fatherless homes that a dutiful male parent was greatly admired.

I passed another re-certification process with the welfare and was given anther six months of assistance. My medical assistance would be continued for another three months after that period. I began to do some serious financial planning to establish some resources. I had started to send my daughter an allowance. She would wait with great expectation whenever it was mailed. I started out with postal money orders and switched to concealed cash, because Kitten took too long getting it cashed. This created a greater bond because we began to have secrets. I never stopped loving my wife but she would periodically exhibit jealous behavior, during my phone conversations with Z Baby. The spring of 2004 marked the time of a great blessing from God. The event increased my income and developed my skills. It also marked the beginning of a relationship that remains today. To God Be the Glory!

JESUS IS IN THE HOUSE

THE SPRING OF 2004 ushered in not only warm weather but a new perspective on life. I began to get noticed on the island. I demonstrated my work ethic by keeping snow off the property during a harsh winter. I showed my resolve by diligently seeking and securing employment. I showed my faithfulness by praising God for the good and bad in my life. The most important difference was my renewed commitment to influence my daughter's life and be a role model parent. We kept in constant contact with the phone I sent her. There were even times when I spoke with my wife. I was able to get a sense of our Legs was maintaining the household. The harsh winter had revealed some flaws in the structure of the house I was living in. A decision was made to make the necessary repairs. A close friend of the family that was related by marriage to Selena's sister in law was chosen to do the work. Mr.C. was a skilled craftsman with much work to his credit. When he began to do the work on the roof with his eldest son Johnny, I was recommended by my sister to help. I was hired and so began the process of me overcoming my fear of heights. I was a quick learner and soon was left on the job to complete assignments set up by Mr.C. I soon learned that one of Mr.C's weaknesses, were that he took on too many jobs at once. He also worked too cheap that added to his frustration. I would be paid $80.00 a day with one meal free.

I took to Mr.C. right away. He liked the energy I brought to the job and my punctuality. The only thing that limited the time I spent working for him was my other job. He made a point of only using me when I didn't have to work for Pathmark. We often found ourselves talking about family and relationships. I could be honest with him about who I was and the trials I had been through. The roof was a real challenge for me. The height wasn't the only problem. It also had a peak that tested my faith in not sliding off of it. I made pretty good time in completing the job. Mr.C. liked the way I worked and began to take me on his other jobs. I was immediately moved into a higher income bracket and started providing more for my daughter Z Baby. Jesus was truly working in my life and my devotion to Him was unchallenged. I spent more time on the island and less time in Brooklyn. My cash reserves began to build and I started opening up new bank accounts. The increase in my income didn't go unnoticed by my wife. The money and clothes I was sending to Z Baby caused my wife to start talking child support. I didn't mind because I saw an opportunity for us to improve our relationship. I also received notification from the Sanitation Department that I scored high on their test and placed #23 on the hiring list. I began to negotiate a figure with my wife over a dollar amount for child support. I really believed that my wife would eventually be receptive to us trying to make the marriage work. I had already forgiven her but she still struggled with the concept. Finally during the same time I started the hiring process with the Sanitation Department we agreed on a figure. I would pay $300.00 a month and all my child's medical expenses. I told her to send me a letter stating her agreement to those terms. I was caught completely off guard by what happened next. The negotiations had taken months and Christmas was just around the corner. I had to relive my ugly past as the Sanitation Department required dispositions of all my encounters with the law. I was working now on three fronts when you added the time spent on securing this documentation. I was so elated and filled with joy at the prospect of having a city job. It was vindication for the one other opportunity I lost with the health Department. It was around Thanksgiving that that I received the long awaited letter from Legs. When I opened it to read, the contents blew my mind.

Legs had constructed a legal type document with all these instructions. It was nothing like the type of letter I had asked for or what she had agreed too. I became very disturbed and annoyed. "What new ploy was this? Who had assisted her with this?" I spoke out loud to myself. It was a two page document that listed both of ours responsibilities, as it related to the agreement. What she agreed too was listed on the first page and mine were on the second page. This is where it got interesting! Each page of the document had a separate heading. The only place for both of ours signature, were located on the copy of what I agreed to pay. The documents didn't acknowledge the existence of the other one. If I was to sign this, she could tear up her copy. Once again she would be able to escape accountability for what she had said. I was too angry at the moment to try and communicate with her. "She had to have help with this." I thought out loud. "Why can't she have some integrity and stop being so manipulative?" Every time I allowed myself to be in love with her again she would do something to harden my heart. "Oh God what do you expect of me? How much pain do I have to endure?" When I spoke to My God, I didn't care who heard me. I spent the rest of the day in a sunken mood. I slept uneasy that night and made several trips to the bathroom. It seems when I found myself too depressed, the thought of pussy would relax my mind. I would need a fresh jar of Vaseline, if I had too many more nights like this. It wasn't Legs' pussy that I was thinking about.

I had been practicing celibacy for some time now. It wasn't as much a religious experience as it was my reality. Whatever the reason it yielded the same results. I wasn't getting any! The money continued t roll in with my new construction work. I remained consistent at my job with Pathmark. I even began to develop some close relationships with the young women I worked with. Those relationships were helpful in understanding my daughter's needs better. My world was definitely becoming a great place to be in. Mr.C was adamant about his work being perfect. This caused a lot of jobs to last longer than necessary. I couldn't complain because I was just a student and benefited financially from the delays. I didn't benefit though from his harsh attitude towards the people that sometimes developed. We began to start another major job as we wrapped up work on the roof. I didn't know at the time but he also had the contract to make major renovations, where we were at now. We started to commute between the two locations.

When work began on one, it slowed down the work on the other. He began to juggle the two budgets which resulted in even more confusion. He was not a book keeping wizard. The records he should have maintained to keep track of things were nonexistent. He relied too much on his memory or mine. When funds began to dry up and the work got more difficult my hours were cut to half days. I even had to except delayed payments because my labor was surely needed. I had a hefty amount saved up; it just wasn't in my name. I was very comfortable with my living arrangements. I started to contemplate making some purchases to make it even more elaborate. I awoke one morning in late May to some startling news. My sister would be retiring from her job and her husband would soon follow. Their plans weren't a secret which explained why renovations had become so important. My sister and her husband wanted some buy-out money for Harold's stake in the house. I really had trouble understanding why they expected some money for leaving when they had spent so much time living in the house. They were even collecting rents and did a poor job of maintaining the property. Their plans caused some tension in the family and the household. I became more aware of their selfish attitude as time went on. It would take some major work to make the property marketable and sound. Harold's other siblings would have to take out a mortgage on the house to meet their demands. He was also demanding an unreasonable amount to leave.

This is what happens when you incur debt to compensate your lack of budgeting skills. It was revealed during this time that Harold's basketball buddy had a sweetheart deal on his rent. He was paying hundreds of dollars below the market rate to occupy the two bedroom apartment upstairs. When Mr.C and I inspected the apartment to assess the needed repairs, we were appalled at the deteriorated condition of the dwellings. We nearly had to replace almost ¾ of the wall structure that was near collapse.

I had finally reached a level of understanding to forgive my sister and her husband for move they had made. I realized that their actions were consistent with the attitude they displayed toward me. What I didn't know, was that my rent payments to them were their secret. They had the rest of the family believing that I was a charity case living rent free. They promoted themselves as these good people helping me to get on my feet. Now I too was being forced to move when they leave because I had no agreement in writing. When Harold's sister found out it was nothing she could do because another older brother had already made the decision. The new mortgage was in his name and all non relatives except the upstairs tenant had to move. I also learned that my past history had become common knowledge revealed by my sister. If I said I was angry, it would be a gross misstatement. I carried on as if I knew nothing. I was deeply hurt by the betrayal and lies. I did not want to leave Long Island so I began searching for an affordable place in the area.

The search was filled with many disappointments. My current landlord which actually was no longer my sister was sympathetic, but could not over-ride the decision that was made. My sister was unaware of the truth that I knew and was still trying to collect rent. I just ignored their requests and then God stepped in. They made a trip out of town that eclipsed two collection dates. When they returned and requested some money, I politely let them know that any money I had, would go towards my new place. I had an open invitation from the home owners where my oldest sister Big Mama was staying. I just had to wait for a troublesome tenant to move out. When finally the apartment became available, big Mama tried to use her influence to block the deal. Serena was already filled with guilt at the prospect of me being evicted with no place to go. She knew the only reason why I had to move, was because they hid the fact about me paying rent. My two sisters got into a heated discussion about my situation. Serena let Big Mama know what a great and responsible tenant I was with them. She then almost ordered Big Mama to stop being an impediment to me moving in. I assumed authority over the place in September that year. It would be a slow process for me to move in because of the work being done on Long Island. I renovated the new place myself for the first month's rent. That alone made the landlord love me for being there. I then took a monthly discount for my labor, which remained up until the day I moved out. I utilized some of my young fans at Pathmark to accompany me. I still wasn't comfortable with being back in Brooklyn. I certainly didn't like being in an area which I helped to corrupt.

I was very consistent during this time with sending Z Baby money. I still hadn't reached an agreement with my wife about child support. It no longer mattered because Virginia child support was coming after. There were a series of court appearances in New York Family Court to address this matter. By the end of the summer my wife and I were in a heated battle over this money. I stalled their efforts as long as I could. I tried to make my wife understand that their involvement in our affairs were unnecessary. Their main motivation was the 3% they would collect from the payments. This was a truth that many dads and moms were unaware of. Sometime after Thanksgiving I was subpoenaed to appear in New York Family Court that following spring. I was not going to let this interfere with what I had planned for my daughter's Christmas. I sent money and some big ticket gifts that she wanted. I even purchased some things for a few of the women that I was trying to get close with. Christmas 2004 marked two years of freedom of my rebirth with Christ. I felt I did well because I had not returned to the streets. I had not returned to loose sexual escapades. I had not returned to deceit and deception as a way of life. I had instead returned to Jesus Christ and trusted him to communicate to The Father on my behalf. I had returned to a peace of mind that was based only on my faith in the Lord. "Hallelujah! To God be the glory." I would need all the strength that my faith in Christ could provide. I could no longer prolong my departure from The Island. It was now time to resume my residency back in Brooklyn. I celebrated the New Year in my new place. Dick Clark was doing the countdown on television. When he got to midnight as the ball touched bottom, you could hear nothing but the sound of gunfire fill the air around me. I just whispered softly to myself as I lay down on the floor; "Yeah I'm back in Brooklyn."

I rose the next morning apprehensive but relieved to be settled down in my new home. I looked around at my apartment and felt great comfort in the environment I had created. There were new linoleums on the kitchen and bedroom/living room floors. The bathroom in the outer hallway had been scrubbed clean. It also boasted a fresh coat of paint, which covered my expert spackling job. There was peeling paint on the ceiling and walls of the hallway but it wasn't my concern at this time. I would tackle the problem only with a contractual agreement to do the work. The stove was different but not new from the one present when I first inspected the place. I was adamant about replacing it because of my love of cooking. There was also a small table with four chairs around it that fit neatly in the kitchen. A door separated the kitchen from the rest of the living quarters, which appeared to add more depth to the space. The other door in the kitchen which led to the outer hallway was sealed shut. I hung curtains above the doorway to conceal that fact. I was able to divide up my space in the larger room by the placement of my furniture. I was able to create a sleeping area and a lounging area that appeared separate and distinct. I adorned my walls with masculine art objects which further divided up the space. A large wall unit which was opposite the two windows, cut off the apartment from the rest of the house. I was still receiving rent payments from Social Services in addition to food stamps and utility money. I would get this for at least the next six months until my case was reviewed again. "Don't laugh!" The one thing the government guaranteed for a honorable discharge from the military was Welfare. I had all the modern technological gadgets to add to my comfort. The plants I brought with would have to do for now. I hoped that my green thumb would encourage their rapid growth. There was a clothing closet created in the corner of the room with enclosed shelves built above it. It only took an opaque colored pair of curtains to make it blend in with the rest of the place. The clothes wardrobe I brought with me fit nicely against an adjacent wall near the kitchen door. The color and size of it made it even more attractive. It wasn't long before I started to imagine myself entertaining the ladies. Now it was time to evaluate my environment with security in mind. I not only had to protect my possessions from walking, but my money as well. I couldn't be concerned with getting robbed when I had some young pussy in here getting all my attention. I also knew that I had to identify places and spots secretive enough, to hide from visitors, which I could also find myself later. There were enough things in storage which would serve my purpose. The two windows had blinds, so I chose thin nylon curtains to let in the sunlight. I brought my large area rug with me that almost covered the entire floor. I had an attractive sofa that was placed between the two windows. My daybed was alongside the adjacent wall to the right in the middle of the room. I was content with the arrangement because it reflected my personality and sense of style. My music system was in the same wall unit as my television. I had remote controls for all my electronic devices, so I could operate them from a sitting or laying down position. It also gave a bit more elegance to the environment.

I went into the kitchen and began to make me some breakfast. One of the advantages of working at Pathmark was always being able to buy groceries. I made it a point to keep plenty of food in the house. I enjoyed eating but even more I enjoyed cooking for others. I used to share my meals with the elderly landlady until they complained that she was gaining too much weight. The first couple of months were uneventful as I focused on getting used to my new surroundings. Most of the younger men in the neighborhood were just young boys when I had left the area. When I got married I moved downtown and rarely returned. They all knew me because I was known for giving them candy and soda money. They showed a tremendous amount of respect for me and were still good listeners. I grew up being receptive to the advice of my elders and now gave it freely to others. The boys had now become men with children of their own. Some had acquired marketable skills and were making a good living. Still others seemed stuck in a time warp using those old hustling skills in a more dangerous age. The lives they saw destroyed from that behavior didn't register with them. They thought they could reinvent the game and be successful. It didn't work and the life they were living proved it. The one thing in the area that was hard to ignore, were the amount of drug dealing that was taking place. I could recall my own nephew being out there hustling. I always remember the few times I had to intervene to settle territorial disputes. I stayed away from those that I identified as dealers. I didn't need those types of ties in my life now. I had only my trust and faith in Christ keeping me clean. I knew enough about my addiction not to take chances. The more people began to notice me the more stories began to circulate about my past. Some of the more daring ones even came looking for my advice on how to be better hustlers. The only thing I would tell them was to get a job and embrace Jesus Christ.

It didn't take long for me to realize how difficult it was for me to commute to Long Island to work. Mr.C gave me less and less work because of the time it took me to get to him. I managed to get evening hours at Pathmark and did mornings with Mr.C. My pay was cut in half with the arrears still hanging out there. I was owed some hundreds of dollars with no mention of a near settlement. The knowledge I gained from him was invaluable but I couldn't mail that to my daughter or he mother. I was starting to receive more correspondence from Virginia Child Support. I was getting more pressure and the N.Y. Sanitation Department had called me. Travel time to work was four hours round trip and without notice Mr.C stopped calling. It was time to work closer to home so I began the process to transfer to Ozone Park. Travel time would be reduced by 75%. The new location would still be along the same route I used to travel to Long Island. I had developed relationships with a few of the bus drivers because they would have to wake me up when my stop came. I first used a contact at the new store that my sister Big Mama had given me. She frequently shopped there and knew the night shift manager. She was also well known by the pharmacist because of the medications she was purchasing there. I contacted my union to learn the necessary steps to complete the deal. I was beginning to have some problems at my store anyway because of the change in management. They had severely cut my hours at a time when I relied solely on them to pay my bills. I couldn't even get favorable time slots to ease the burden of my long travel time. The union told me my request should be honored because of the move to Brooklyn. They said I only needed permission to be accepted by the new store I wanted. It was easy getting their okay but my store was blocking the move. They even gave me a poor reference to the other manager to make me undesirable. I took these new revelations to the union and after several meetings and private conversations the transfer took place. The difficulty I encountered in transferring prepared me the initial hostility I faced at the new location.

It was a long and difficult process but ultimately I prevailed after meeting with the store's general manager. This was one of the most successful stores in the New York chain. It was large and vibrant in a location that offered a cross section of the population. I was eager to start after speaking with the manager. I later met with the night shift manager who was about my age. We made a connection when I told him who my sister was. My hours would not lengthen but I did move to the day shift for a moment. They had a huge back area which took some getting used too. A young brother who had been there awhile made it his job to get me acclimated. It was the summer months now and I found myself with more time to socialize in the evening. I began to attend my sister's church whose history I was familiar with. It had a large congregation and was politically active. I knew the Pastor of the church from a news story I viewed while incarcerated in 2002. There was a big local drug bust of heroin dealers that involved some close friends of mine. The Pastor was on the news commenting on the need to eradicate this type of activity from the neighborhood. I admired his courage at that time never believing we would develop a close relationship.

ZEKE SMITH

I came in one day from work to find some new neighbors moving in next door. Once in the past I had did some yard work for the landlord. I paid close attention to the young women that were moving bags and boxes onto the second floor of the house. One was small and very petite. She appeared to be the older one and in charge. The next one was much larger with well balanced portions. She looked as old as the other women but was quieter. Then there was one more that was young with a medium build. She was very pretty with a smile that lit up her face. She had a nice plump ass with ample breasts. My eyes were fixated on her as she moved up the stairs with her cargo. I said hello and she responded in a soft Jamaican accent with hi. I continued to watch her ascend the stairs as her butt cheeks took turns rising and falling. She glided up the stairs as if a soft melody was playing in her ear. "Ummmmm" I muttered to myself as she finally disappeared into the house. I stopped staring long enough to finish climbing my own stairs and also disappeared into my house. The vision of that young woman climbing those stairs was burned into my memory. I could still hear that "hi" vibrating in my ear. I cooked me a meal that I don't remember but knew it was good. I turned on the window fan and settled down in front of the TV and began to eat. Yes, I was going to like living here. The key to my happiness would be in that young pussy I watched climbing those stairs. I could not help how comfortable I was when around young pretty women. The energy that I felt escape from them gave me power and strength. It was a great motivator to succeed. The scent of their bodies ignited my creativity. The moment I felt their flesh beneath my touched made me invincible. I had an undeniable thirst for younger women. I believed it stemmed from me being a late bloomer when it came to sex. My first orgasm occurred on the dance floor when I was just 15. The record Stay in my Corner was playing. Then halfway through the song, someone restarted the record. The girl I was dancing with was cute but thin. We began to cling to each other as the rhythm of our created some intense feelings. I felt my member slide up and down the crevice between her legs. Then as if on queue our bodies locked and stiffened against each other. I was firmly planted between her legs as we both began circular motions to the beat of the music. It was almost pitch black and sweat was pouring down both our faces. I could feel her finger tips digging into my back as she tried to maintain her balance. I buried my face in her neck and blocked out all the people around me. I began to feel both our bodies vibrate as new warmth cascaded down my thighs. We continued our dance as the juices kept flowing. I didn't want the music to stop, but it was coming to an end. My member continued to throb against her lions as semen continued to be ejected from me. I was uneasy on my feet when the record stopped. I didn't want to let her go. I wanted another dance plus my pants were wet. I watched as she left my embrace without looking back. It was then that I noticed the audience we had. I rushed to the bathroom with a small entourage in pursuit. "Yo man what happened? We saw the way you and Vicky were dancing." Their curiosity couldn't be contained and I was hesitant about answering. They continued to mill around asking questions that I wasn't about to answer. We finally grew tired of playing that game and exited the bathroom. The most curious one Nathan rushed out to get the next dance with Vicky. I believe that single event had the most profound effect on my sexual development.

I went up the stairs and entered my apartment anxious for the next encounter with my girl next door. I slept good that night after eating and watching some T.V. This remained my routine for the next couple of weeks as I plotted a means of extending my conversation with my girl next door. I got my chance one afternoon when I returned home from work to find them painting their stairs. The job they were doing was well enough to get by but I added my expertise to prolong my conversation. I learned during that time that my girl's name was Candice, which I pronounced Candy. The older young women who appeared to be in charge were her cousin Tina. The other woman was just a friend that was visiting. They all were from the island of Jamaica but had made America their home. The apartment belonged to Tina and the landlord was her aunt. Candice had just moved up from Georgia and was pregnant. The baby's father was an older man whom she hoped to rejoin later. Candy was only twenty two with a supple skin tone that ignited my fantasies. I became determined to develop a closer relationship with her and replace the guy she had. It was a goo9d feeling to know that she was experienced enough to be involved with older men. The days ahead became more enjoyable as I was blessed with more opportunities to speak privately with her. The weeks grew into months as her stomach continued to enlarge. There were times when I was allowed to feel the movement of the baby. Laying my hands on her belly allowed me to feel the softness of her skin. When I leaned over to touch her I could smell the sweet fragrance emanating from her body. Sometimes her legs would rest against mine and instantly my member would become erect. On those days I would rush upstairs after our encounter and masturbate. When I came, I would remain erect which demonstrated how strong my physical attraction to her was. When I would return home from work, she

ZEKE SMITH

often would be sitting on the stoop. It appeared that she was anticipating my arrival. We started to spend endless nights sitting and chatting between the fences that separated our homes. Then one day I came home to learn from Tina that the big event had arrived. She had gone into to labor and gave birth to a healthy baby girl.

Candice was very excited about the birth of her daughter. I was just as excited but for different reasons. I knew that in six weeks, she would have a brand new pussy ready for attention. The pregnant women that I met in my life never understood the real interest in the age of their babies. I would count down the days more closely than them. I also tracked the type of relationships they had with their babies' fathers. I waited for the right moment of vulnerability to claim my prize. There were some times when I was able to claim the pussy before the baby came. It would be a few weeks before I saw Candice and the new baby.

"Hey new mom!" I shouted with joy as I approached my house. Candice had her baby out on the stoop. I climbed her stairs to get a closer look at the baby. Candice was wearing her usual skimpy outfit but I avoided looking at the crevice between her legs. "Hi Zeke, want to look at me new baby?" She asked in her sultry Jamaican accent. I drew near to her and began to pay more attention to her swollen breasts. They were trying to escape from the confines of her blouse. The first three top buttons were loose and the fourth was very close to popping off. I sat on the stoop next to her and peered over at the life cradled in her arms. I had to look past her heaving breasts that were held together by an undersized bra. I reached across her to pull back the blanket, in order to get a look at the face beneath it. The back of my right hand made contact with her breasts as it went by. "Oh what a beautiful baby you have!" I sat motionless watching the baby curl around as my elbow and forearm lay on Candice's chest. I was watching the titties more than the baby and my member began to respond. It took on a life of its own and attempted to see the outside world. I used my left hand to reposition my cock so it wouldn't stab Candice in the face as I rose. I reached in my pocket and took out a twenty and five dollar bill. I gave them to Candice to start the baby a bank. This practice became a habit whenever I got close enough to Candice to be aroused. The only thing that varied was the amount she received. I continued to nurture this relationship for the weeks to come. I learned that the baby's daddy was slow to send money but Candice had faith in the relationship. I began to express the benefits of my friendship while she continued to believe in this guy in Georgia.

I now had a need beyond my current expenses to increase my income. It seems that throughout my life I was drawn to penniless women. They not only had little resources but also a man that did little to change their circumstances. "Was this my gifting from God?" I used to ask myself. "Were I to be the caretaker for the world's disenfranchised women?" "Was I allowing the sexual stimulation that I received in their presence to be enough of a reward?" I went into therapy before to break this cycle and still the condition exited. I couldn't worry about that now. This pussy was craving my attention and I needed more resources to take care of it. I would be given some hope for relief when the Sanitation Department called me for assignment.

I was so honored by God when the Sanitation Department made their call. I had a lot of running around to do as my criminal past needed documentation. I trusted God as I answered all questions on their application. My past would be no hindrance as long as I revealed it. They needed medical information that was harder to get than past depositions. I remained faithful and obedient to God's Word as I moved through this process. I had scored very high on the initial test and with my added military points; I was in a very favorable position. It took some time to gather everything they wanted. Once all paperwork was in, I was placed on the active list. I just had to wait now for a class to start, for the CDL training. It would be provided by the city as long as you had the CDL permit. I did so I just waited for them to call me. It was near the end of the summer and I was anxious to better my position. I had my child to worry about and a brand new girl that I was going to make love me. My faithfulness was increased as I strayed away from the street elements and clung to my brothers and sisters in the church. It was during this time that I joined my sister's church and recommitted myself publically to Christ.

I remember like yesterday when I made the decision to join a church and recommit myself to Jesus Christ. I was floundering in my worship and praise of him. I allowed too many other things to take precedence over my life. I needed a host of fellow believers to keep me grounded in the Word. My sister the minister was caught off guard when she looked out and saw me sitting in the pews. I wasn't there to honor her but to honor God. I needed for Jesus to know how serious my love for Him was. I came early enough to be in the devotional service. I was humbled by the presence of God and began to feel so much remorse for the lie I had been living. My face was buried in my hands as tears streamed down. I couldn't stop when I wanted to so I just began to say thank you. I began to thank God for keeping me. I thank Him for having the patience to wait on me all these years. I thank Him for giving me life by resurrecting me from the ashes of a failed marriage. I rose to my feet with my face still wet with tears and began to shout "HALLELUJAH HALLELUJAH HALLELUJAH!" I slowly began to calm down as the devotional team started to lead us in song. It was a moving experience for me. It left me feeling cleansed and with a renewed spirit. There is a part in the service when the congregation is asked to rise and greet their neighbors. I went and greeted the Pastor telling him that; "I came to get right with God."

The sermon that day seemed to be directed at me. I was amazed at how on point his words were concerning my present condition. I was in a state of sorrow because of all the uncertainty about my life and future. I needed better direction and assistance in remaining focus. I was in the right place this afternoon and God confirmed it by the words I was hearing come from the pulpit. I came to Christ that day as a lost saved soul. I came to Christ as a sheep that had wandered off from the flock. I came to Christ that day as a man wanting to be a part of God's Kingdom. Yes I joined the church that day and immediately uplifted the spirit of my sister the minister. "Let the church say amen!"

I became some type of celebrity to the congregation because of my sister's status. I was often referred to as Minister Ealey's brother. My sister was overjoyed because a member of her family was now with her in Christ. I would imagine I connected with people a little faster than the norm because of this. I still had to follow the regular procedures before I could become involved in certain activities. The greatest benefit for me though, was the personal relationship; I was able to develop with the Pastor. He was also able to guide me in some aspects with Sanitation, because he had retired from there. I now faced other challenges with my new revived walk with God. I had to distance myself from the gatherings of my peers in the streets. I had to develop a different taste in women if I were to succeed. I continued to focus on my paperwork for Sanitation. I completed things soon enough to be placed in a class for that August.

I rose that morning with a lot of anxiety about the CDL training I was going to receive. My baby sister drove me that first day because I didn't want to be late. It would be a five day course that cumulated with the taking of the driving test with DMV. There was a bus that drove to a location just outside the airfield, where the training facility was located. I was never late and paid close attention to the instructors. I felt a lot of pride just by reflecting on the journey I had taken to get here. I became emotional at times when I spoke about the many hardships I had faced and the way God just kept delivering me out of them. My instructor was a young worker from the Bronx. He informed me of all the benefits that awaited me. He told me about the known and unknown benefits of being a sanitation worker. This was the only city agency still getting weekly pay checks. They also received large clothing allowances at the end of the year that amounted to a Christmas bonus. They say when it snows in N.Y. its green. The Sanitation Department gets a hefty summer check for any snow removal duty. Yes, when you're hired by Sanitation, you've just hit lotto. It was no struggle for me to handle the big dump trucks we used for training. It was an incredible feeling to have that much power under me. The end of the training drew near and my instructor began to give me some review. He didn't appear as confident as I was. I still went home that night ready for a test the next morning that would reshape my future.

I awaken that morning well rested and excited. I felt that I had all the information and training that I needed. I ate my hearty breakfast of oatmeal and jellied toast. I showered the night before and saw no need to repeat the process. It was quite an ordeal whenever I used my tub. It was shared by the landlord who saw no need to clean it, after he used it. The bathmat he let stay in the tub, had to be removed with forceps before I used the tub. The bathroom walls illuminated any area he spent at. I had painted everything when I moved in, but his body stains made it hard to believe. It was more than a year but it still shouldn't have been that worn out. My oatmeal seemed to have extra flavor that morning. I thought about how much more I could do for my daughter with a job like this. My son was a grown man now but he too would reap a reward from my employment. It was still dark outside when I left to catch my first bus. I had to start early if I expected to get there on time. Anxieties began to kick in as I started my walk. I lit a cigarette to accompany me on the first leg of my journey. By the time I reached my last stop near the air base the sun was trying to make its presence known. I stood patiently in the dim light as other cars began to drop off their cargo. Some cars left but others stayed to await the return of their cargo for the trip back home. Private vehicles were not allowed on the base but there was ample parking in a designated area. We all piled on to the bus and took the short trip to the training grounds. They had some coffee available but no donuts. I just went to the vending machine and got me some gum. This would be helpful in calming my nerves. The sun now had full command of the sky. It shone its light brightly revealing everything that the night had concealed. Everyone gathered in the same room as they began to take attendance and confirm the matchups for the driving test. We had to go to the Bronx for the road test. We were driven in a van while an instructor drove the dump truck that we would use. I continue to pray asking steadily for God's will to prevail over my life. One by one, applicants came and went with great success. The DMV examiner was known by the instructors. It was said that he was fair and quick. The pretrip inspection would not be lengthy or detailed. The young woman before me came back smiling and excited. She had passed with only twenty points being deducted. She said I was next as she entered the van.

I took my walk across the street and met the instructor. He asked for my license, confirmed my name, and then instructed me to start the pre-trip inspection. I moved around the large vehicle making notes of all the points I were trained to do. He stopped me at some points to skip all the details. We then entered the vehicle and I continued with the preliminaries by identifying the instrument and all the light switches. I started my break inspection and upon completion I started the engine and pulled away from the curb. It felt good driving and there were no nervousness on my part. I had adjusted the seat and the mirrors before I left, so I felt very comfortable. As I came up to the corner and made my first left turn, I heard sirens blaring in the distance. I looked up to see a fire engine blazing fast towards me in the lane I was supposed to occupy. This was quite a dilemma for me because I had not quite completed my turn. I pulled the vehicle over and stopped immediately leaving me in an awkward position in the street. I glanced over to see that the instructor had already starting writing notes. Now my confidence was shook for the rest of the ride. One unique situation after another continued to plaque me throughout the test. I had to call out my hazards and one narrow two-way street had a line of double parked cars. Then a car entered in front of me, when I finally had clear space ahead. During the time on the highway, I was doing high speed lane changes. A driver quite a distance behind came barreling up on my left and swerved in front of me as he gave me the finger. He then exited to my left. He apparently thought I was taunting him with my frequent lane changes. I was completely rattled at this point as the guy next to me continued to write his notes. I made a short right turn and a wide left turn before I started to be tested on backing up. The one thing I thought I couldn't mess up on also was a disaster. I did everything right but forgot what to do to ensure that the truck was lined up right. When my test was over I received fifty points which put me over the top. I failed put could try again later. I would have too pay myself and find a school to accomplish this. I didn't so I returned back to my normal life as a maintenance worker and part-time home renovator.

I couldn't tell my daughter about this set back. There was no sense in two people feeling miserable. I put all my paperwork together in one place until I figure out how God would intervene on my behalf. I still had that favorable spot on the hiring list. I just needed that CDL to qualify. I returned back to my regular routine with the regular people. I was a bit shaken and discouraged. I was able to get through that first week after my disappointing performance. The second week was a different story. I needed some stimulation that would make me feel great again and take away the pain of failure. I fell back into some negative immoral behavior. Sitting on the stoop at night became more than just a cigarette and fresh air. I began to pay more attention to the female customers of the local dealers. I watched with heighten interest as they came and went. I noticed how some came more than others. I started to question the dealers, whom were no strangers to me about some likely candidates for my entertainment. I made a mental note of all the information I received and decided a Friday night would be the best time to make a selection. The next two days were the easiest that I had in awhile. I went to work and then came home and slept to build my strength up for Friday night. I would definitely be breaking day with whatever woman was chosen that night. I knew what I was planning was wrong. I knew certain risks were involved. I knew I was placing my future in jeopardy but I couldn't change my decision. I wanted some sex in the worst way. I wanted a lot and I wanted it cheap. I would still be patient enough to choose the cream of the crop. I would wait on some virgin weekend freak that had as much guilt about her drug use as I had about using her.

I had no work to do this morning. It was Friday and all I could think about was some pussy. I focused on getting my laundry done and cleaning the house. I rearranged some things to make it more appealing for what I had planned. I made sure home security was in place and had both the kitchen and bedroom rigged to receive a stranger. I still had my night job to go to. I just didn't want to have anything to do but play with some pussy when I came home. I watched some daytime television before deciding on watching a DVD instead. I put myself in a comfortable position as the tape played on.

I began to stir as a familiar tune played in the background. I continued to listen as the melody stimulated my ears. I slowly opened my eyes as the light from the windows appeared to be dimming. The melody stopped playing and I soon realized it was my phone alarm. I jumped up from the couch groggy from my long nap. I tried to gain my composure and comprehend the time and the day. "Now I remember! I was watching a tape before I fell asleep. It's time to leave for work." It was just after six in the evening and I had less than one hour to get to work on time. I rushed out the door to the bathroom and released myself. The urine rushed from my penis as if to celebrate its freedom. I flushed the toilet and stepped up to the sink. The water in the commode began to refill as I soaked my washcloth with cold water. I applied it to my face and wiped vigorously. My head began to clear some more and I started to focus. It was Friday and my big night was about to arrive. I quickly exited the bathroom and returned to my room. I reached for the Vaseline on my night table and applied a liberal portion to my face, head, and hands. I looked for my jeans and a comfortable tee shirt. It didn't take me long to get dressed. When my outfit was complete, I placed my keys, wallet, and cell phone in my pockets. I rushed down the stairs after ensuring myself that I had locked my door. I stepped quickly down the stairs saying hello to the landlady, whom door were partially opened. I stepped outside and felt the warm late summer air cascade against my face. I took no chances and ran to the corner in case a bus was near. I was right to run because a bus was there waiting for the light to change. I was a little out of breath when I reached the bus-stop. "Whew" I said to myself. "God is good." I found a seat near the front after swiping my metro card. I sat firmly and erect in my seat. I could not afford to fall asleep before reaching my destination. The light outside continued to dim as the sun tried to escape from the sky. It took only twenty minutes for the bus to reach my job. "Thank you Jesus!" I murmured under my breath. I look at the time on my cell phone. It indicated that I had three minutes to punch in before I was considered late. I entered the store and was greeted by a few hellos. I remained polite and considerate as I pushed past customers and fellow employees to reach that time clock. I entered the appropriate numbers to identify myself. Ding went the clock when I was complete. I had made it just in time. Now it was time to go to my locker and get my smock. I needed to become visible on the floor before someone started looking for me. I liked the job I had. I always enjoyed working around people. I also enjoyed working in such a large retail outlet because of all the female shoppers. There was always such a variety of women of all ages and sizes. I grabbed a shopping cart to make my rounds collecting the empty cardboard boxes from the floor. This was the best way to view all the delights that the environment had to offer and still look busy. There were a couple of younger guys working with me. They weren't as careful to look busy while they did their girl watching. They even took it a step further by trying to collect phone numbers during their long idle chats with pretty customers. My shift only lasted four hours. The busier I kept myself, the faster the time went. The night shift manager, who was a large robust man, came over to ask me to make a bail. I happily agreed as if I had a choice. I didn't mind working. My mother had instilled a work ethic in me that surpassed most employers' expectations. The thing that I found disturbing was how they ignored the slackers and called on me. I found an empty aisle to park my cart while I went to the back of the store.

The machine that made the cardboard bails was large and threatening looking. It wasn't a delicate or complicated operation. What I found difficult at this location was the cramped space I had to work in. That cramped space made it very uninviting for anyone to make bails. This caused the machine to be over filled most times, making it difficult to insert the cables that held the cardboard together. I finished making the bail in about thirty minutes. I figured to stretch it to an hour by also cleaning up the back. The supervisors didn't like you spending too much time in the back. They wanted you visible in the front working on the floor. The nightshift manager, whom I called Big Bill, was about my age. This was a second career for him because the first one became obsolete. He was also the one that knew my sister and gave me a lot of respect because of my work ethic. When I left the back, it was almost 9:00 p.m. Time was moving fast with only two more hours to go. I continue to do all my assigned chores and anything else that I felt needed to be taken care of. Some of the supervision on my job liked the way I took initiative. The few other people felt undermined when I worked without their instruction. I refused to look at the clock as I worked. I knew my phone alarm would go off in time to alert me. The modern technology of the cell phones, were a definite plus to me. I relied on my phone alarms to remind me of everything from wake ups to important dates and appointments. "Oh there goes my favorite tune!" I shouted to myself. I made my way to the back where the lockers were locked. I put my freshly laundered smock inside along with the matching blue hat. I checked my urine before washing my hands. I never knew when the trip home would take longer than usual. I did not want to have an accident on myself because I couldn't hold my water. I went out to the front and punched out. I had a broad smile on my face as I exited the store. I know most people felt the smile was my relief that the shift was over. That was not the case this time. The smile I had was for the night of sin that I planned to relieve me of some stress. The smile was for the semen that I would be releasing time and time again this evening with some willing female partner. Yes, this smile was for me and the creativity that I would employ, when I began to entertain myself this evening. I stepped outside and walked at a quick pace to the corner. I looked down Atlantic Ave. to see my bus at the previous stop. I began to run across the street between the gaps in the traffic. There wasn't anyone waiting at my bus-stop, so I had to get there before the bus. It looked like he would make the light, so I brazenly continued to dart through the traffic until I reached my destination. When I stepped on the bus, the driver gave me a puzzled look and said; "Man the ride can't be that important to risk your life like that?" I said; "If you knew what I had planned for this evening, you would understand." We then looked at each other and started to laugh. I found me a seat where I knew I would be alone for at least most of the ride. I continued to review my plans for the night in my head. I switched from one scenario to another as the bus made its way along the street. "Calm down boy!" I said to my member that had grown to its maximum extension. I was so busy with my day dreaming about the night, that I didn't realize the excitement in my pants. Oh great, I'm almost there! I checked the seat next to me to make sure nothing was left behind. I hung on tightly to the bag that I left the store with. I had brought some snacks to have with the beer I planned on drinking. I rose to my feet as the bus drew nearer to my stop. I took a deep breath as the bus started to slow down in anticipation of stopping. I was feeling like a small child waiting for Christmas morning. I stepped off the bus not noticing the bodies around me. I took a slow determined walk to my house. I scanned the streets as I moved along. I wanted to get a sense of the atmosphere to gauge the activity of the late nighters. It felt right to me because of small crowds that were milling about. My young sexy neighbor was sitting on the stoop. I stopped briefly to make small talk, as the short skirt she was wearing, tried to reveal the crevice between her legs. This was an unexpected addition to plans. I couldn't resist the feelings she was creating in me. It felt good as my member pressed hard against my pants. It was as if, it would gain freedom by tearing its way through the material. Every word that came out of her mouth in that Jamaican accent caused my dick to throb a little more. She tried to act as if she didn't see the huge bulge in my pants. I refused to hide it from her hoping by some miracle she would reach up and grab it. I just stood frozen in front of her looking up. I was a few steps below her on the stairs. The light from the street lights gave some illumination to what had my attention.

I stopped caring if she knew what I was looking at. I had spent enough money on her and with her to justify my gaze into her dark secret place. "Do you have some beer in the house?" I asked timidly as my words struggled to be heard. "Corona Z do you want one?" Yes was my response to her question as she began to rise. She spread her legs a little, as she placed her right hand on the ground. Her body swerved slightly to the left as she started to rise. My eyes remained focused on the darkness between her legs. When she swerved, it was as if a flash light had lit up that area, because the lights from the street found its way directly on the spot. I moved quickly to steady her when she wobbled a bit after rising. I could only reach her thighs because I was too low to hold anything else. She didn't protest as I stepped up to a higher level as my hands remained planted on her sides. I caused he skirt to rise a little more because of my grip. The sensation was fantastic as I felt the outline of her panties through the garment. I was now at eye level with her breasts as I continued to step up to be closer to her. She now started to step back some more to give me some space in front. This action caused me to gently dig my fingers in the bottom of her waist to maintain my balance. She smiled slightly as my hot breath sent a breeze through her blouse. We now occupied the same ground, as we both wondered what to do next. My hands were resting atop the swell of her hips. I knew my erection before her would not be allowed to escape. I gently pushed her away from me towards her front door. "Ah Zee Mon, yah mustn't act so afraid." She turned away from me and walked into her house. I watched intently as her ass swayed with each step she took. She was such a tease and I enjoyed every minute of it. I always found myself digging in my pockets with regrets. It was hard for me not to reward a woman that had made me feel good. It always seemed so natural until they had left. Most men received far more than me for less money. Even when I was a teen-ager, they called me trick. Candice soon returned with the beers. I reached out for mine but she hesitated to release it. "Ooo Zee I forgot to open dem!" I stuck my hand in my pocket and pulled out a small coin. I worked it around the bottle cap until enough of it was lifted up. I then used my strong jaw muscles to free the cap from the bottle. "Damn Zee!" She exclaimed as I handed her the beer. I repeated the same process with the next bottle of beer. I couldn't resist her being this close to me without testing the boundaries. I watched as she raised her bottle in the air to take a sip. Her breasts lifted up and so did my member. I took a big gulp of my beer and drew even closer to her. The swell in my pants were now rested up between her thighs. She looked at me with a grin I never saw before. She began to gyrate her hips ever so slightly as my member continued to respond to her presence. I placed one hand on the top of the banister to keep my balance. It was late but people were still moving about around us. I wasn't concerned about who was watching. This felt too good. She used her free hand to grab my waist. She continued to drink her beer as she worked her pelvis into mine. Candice started humming a Jamaican while she did a belly roll against my crotch. It was almost as if she was in some trance as I continued to be entertained. I began to work my body against her pussy. The skirt she wore rose a bit as I forced her against the door. I knew in this position we wouldn't be so noticeable from the street. I reached around her to place my hand on her back. "Ah Zee Mon, yaw liking dis?" I didn't respond as the words flowed from her lips like a new melody. I was near my maximum extension and could feel the tenderness developing in my pants. I moved my hand down her back to cup her ass instead. I continued to push her against the door as my hand found the rim of her panties. The back of her thighs were moist to the touch as I worked my two lead fingers under her panties. I froze as I felt my pulse quicken and her movement slow down. I dug my fingers into the bottom of her cheeks as my member throbbed violently. I think she sensed what was about to happen and tried to pull away. I was too close to victory to let her retreat. It was my turn to gyrate as the juices in my body began to escape through the opening on my penis. "Oooo Zee Mon wha yaw doing?" The more she squirmed to be free of my grip the more the juices flowed. During our struggle my member had found its way directly under her pussy. She had changed the position of her legs so that she was actually sitting atop my leg. While my semen splashed against my leg spreading warmth to her body. She began to release some juice of her own as her body began to jerk ever so slightly. The skirt she wore rose so high that I could see the entire pair of panties she wore. She began to calm down as I massaged her ass. Her panties were soaked with sweat and cumm. My pants had a giant wet spot too as I lowered my leg and she slid down. "You ah bad Mon Zee." She spoke much softer this time as the words struggled to come out. I was elated about what had just taken place. We both felt awkward as we began to notice the activity in the neighborhood. I was sweating profusely. She placed her hand on my face and wiped away the sweat that was dripping down. She didn't speak as she dried her hands against the swell in my pants. She continued to dry her hands against me as my member started to search for an escape route. It seemed to fascinate her as my member started to throb. She rubbed up and down the length of my cock through my pants. She squeezed the head through the fabric as it started to jerk. "Oooo Candy Ahhhhh shit girl!" I began to release once more and the semen found its way through the fabric. She smeared it all over my pants as she reached underneath me to rub my nuts. She pulled her skirt down as she stepped away from me. She leaned over and planted a kiss on my cheek. I could see moisture on her legs, as the dim street lights made her thighs and calves glisten. I reached for the bottle still in her hands and she released it. I stuck my tongue in its opening and raise it high to drain whatever fluid was left inside. While she was part-way in the down I continued to use my tongue to play with the bottle's opening. She smiled and disappeared into the darkness of her hallway. I heard the lock click know now that my young pussy was safely inside. I hopped over the banister to my stoop. I put my key in the door to gain entry. While I limped slowly up the stairs, I wondered to myself if I needed anymore activity tonight? I stopped in the bathroom before entering my apartment. I cleaned the tub out and started to run me a bath. My legs were in no shape to stand for a shower. My back also suffered from standing so long with one leg propped higher than the other. It was time to take it down. I will let my body decide if I had enough. I went inside and found myself an outfit I could sleep in or sit on the stoop. The laid the clothes out on my bed and stripped down naked. My kitchen light was turned on but all the others were out. The only light in my other room came from the blinds that were tilted open. The lights that were generated by the moon, stars, and distant illuminated windows, gave my place a night club looks. It always felt good when I was nude in the dark. I enjoyed the freedom of my exposed body without being looked at. I put on my bathrobe while I made my way to the bathroom. Ii reached under the bathroom sink for the dish washing liquid. I squirted a generous amount under the running water. The tub quickly filled with bubbles before I turned the water off. The tub was halfway full so I would be able to submerge my whole body. The water was hot but that didn't stop me sinking deeper into the water. "Ahhh, this fills good. Too bad my girl isn't with me." I was speaking out loud to myself as the soothing hot water began to relax me some more. I began to rub my entire body with my rag as the water became a little darker and the bubbles began disappearing. It wasn't long before my member started to stiffen as it too received some attention. I rolled my body around in the water a few times before I started to let it out. I rose to my feet with my dick sticking straight out like a horizontal flag pole. I watched the water in the tub get low enough to pull the shower curtains. I lather up my rag and turned on the shower. I adjusted the temperature of the water until it was warm. I gave myself a good scrubbing paying more attention to my penis than any other part of my body. It looks like I didn't have enough so my plans for the rest of the night remained the same. I left the bathroom a little damp. I climbed into bed with my robe still on. I figured after a short nap, I would be dry and the pussy would be strolling.

The light seemed strange coming through the window. "What time is it?" I asked myself. I rose to my feet and peered out my backyard windows. I checked my cell phone for the time. "Wow 5:00a.m. I better hurry before day break beats me outside. Now where are those clothes I picked out?" I was having a long conversation with me to clear my head and give myself some direction. I wanted to catch me something pretty and new to the streets that weren't ready to call it quits. I knew I had to sneak a freak in now before the rest of the house started waking up. I finally located my clothes and quickly put them on. I put my small wallet in my pocket with a few big bills stuffed inside. I grabbed my keys and cigarettes off the dresser and tip toed down the stairs. I picked up the old newspaper before stepping outside. I took the lock off the front door before planting myself atop the newspaper that I had dropped down on the stoop. I was not going to fumble with any keys if I had to get back inside quickly. I lit a cigarette while I began to scan the area. I had a good vantage point from where my house was located. The trees growing all around, even offered some concealment, to anyone sitting here at night. Day break continued to make its way out of hiding. I felt sharp enough to leave my stoop. I marched across the street and joined the small posse gathered there. I had just finished my hellos when some fresh pussy came over. I wasted no time in luring her upstairs after getting the necessary goodies to keep her happy and still. The birds had already started singing in the dim early morning light. I signaled for her to walk softly up the stairs while I locked the door. She had a cute face with a short thick body. It would be a lie if I called her fat. The skirt she wore flared out when she walked up the stairs. The ass underneath that skirt looked bare because the panties on it were so small. I reached the top of the stairs and with both my hands on her hips, led her through my door. I never locked this when I hunted pussy. This way I could avoid the noise of the keys and the lock when I arrived with company. Once inside I began to peel off my clothes. I had her take off the blouse and expose her firm breasts before leading her to the kitchen. She sat down and started getting her tools ready. I also sat down in front of her and pulled my chair up real close. I threw to two little plastic bags on the table. A wide smile appeared on her face and I began to work her panties off from our seated positions. The seat of her panties was very clean and a sweet aroma was in the air. "Emm it smells and looks good down there girl!" She smiled slightly and remained focused on getting one of the little bags opened. I hung her panties on the back of the chair she was sitting on. I reached between her legs with my right hand and started stroking her pubic hair with my knuckles. "The hair on your pussy is so soft and silky baby. How do you keep it looking so good down there?" She began to speak this time while she tapped a small rock from the bag into the glass tube she held in her hand. "I guess it's natural because I don't do anything special to it except wash and grease it. You just keep rubbing it while I take this hit Honey." She balanced the tube in one hand while she held a lighter to it with the other hand. She sucked gently on the tube as the flame disappeared into for a moment. There was a crackling sound coming from the glass tube as the white rocks inside fizzled and melted. She moved the tube from her lips and paused a moment before exhaling some thin white smoke from her mouth and nostrils. I watched her ample breasts rise and fall with every breath she took. She raised the tube to her lips again and repeated the ritual with the lighter. This time she laid the lighter in the ash tray on the table. She reached for neck with her now free hand and pulled me to her. She placed her lips on mine and exhaled the smoke from her lungs into mine. I was caught completely of guard but didn't resist. The softness of her lips felt good but the deadly smoke it delivered had me nervous. I felt lightheaded and my erect penis began to retract. "How was that Honey?" She said with a smile. I tried to speak but the words wouldn't come out. "You alright Honey?" She asked with a feeling of deep concern for me. The words now left my lips but it was a struggle. "I'm good Baby. It has just been awhile since I took a hit. I wasn't planning on smoking. I just want to play with the pussy and the drugs are for you." "I'm sorry Baby, I didn't know." I could sense the sympathy she had for me because of what she had done. She put the lighter down on the table next to the ash tray. She reached down between my legs and began to bring new life to my member. She used her other hand to try and free my ever enlarging penis from the confines of my drawers. "Ooooo Honey, little man is getting big real quick." She seemed real happy about her accomplishment and dropped down to her knees before me. She began to flick her tongue around the rim of my enlarged head. She held my nuts gently in her hands and let the head of my cock disappear between her lips. "Ooooo Baby, please don't stop what you're doing to me." This young woman seemed to have a talent for what she was doing to me. I continued to encourage her with compliments and sounds of delight. This seemed to spur her on as she gave my dick her full attention. I had to rise from my seat to give her better access to the jewels she was cleaning. She was being very thorough in removing everything from the inside and outside. I smiled with delight as I massaged her head while she also massaged my other head. I could feel the juices in me building up for their release. "Baby I'm getting ready to cumm." I warned her of my impending release but it didn't change or alter her momentum. She took firm hold of my penis with just the head in her mouth. I couldn't hold back any longer as she held on tight. The warm tick liquid rushed from my penis and into her mouth. She kept holding on as the juice filled her mouth to capacity. She removed the dick from her mouth and spit into the garbage next to her. Semen splashed against her bosom when she first removed me from her mouth. She returned the dick to her mouth, when she finished spitting out, what she didn't swallow. "Yes Baby, get it all out." I instructed as she continued to apply some gentle suction. She switched to a pumping action as if dissatisfied that the flow of juices had decreased. She began a gentle massage of my nuts as the throbbing of my cock began to cease. "How you feel now Honey? I hope that hit I gave you didn't upset you too much. I liked how your dick felt in my mouth." This girl was different. I thought to myself. She was in no hurry to finish off the drugs. She was in no hurry to leave. I got up to turn on the window fan to clear the smoke from the room. I shared a bottle of beer with her when she asked for something to drink. I went over to the sink and stripped down to wash. "I want to do the same thing Honey when you finish." "Sure thing Baby, I'll get you a fresh washcloth." I continued to clean up while she prepared to finish off what was left in the bag she had opened. I lit a cigarette while I rinsed off the soap from my body. The floor had gotten pretty wet while I washed. I dried my body and watched how careful Baby was about getting high. I used the mop in the corner of my kitchen to dry off the floor. I put my drawers back on and finished smoking my cigarette. I poured a little oil in my urn and lit a candle up under it. I could see that my company didn't want to leave. I believed I could trust her enough to move into the other room. The fan did a good job of clearing out the smoke. I turned it off though when the oil in my urn heated up. A sweet smelling fragrance filled the air. I went and a got a rag for my luscious company. I then prepared my couch for what I hoped would part two of my evening. I didn't even know her name but she answered to Baby. I didn't tell her mine either but I answered to Honey. I wish all my relationships could be this simple and uncomplicated. I left the door to the kitchen open and went to lie on the couch. I could see all the activity from this position, as long as it wasn't in front of the window.

Baby rose from the table and cleaned it off. She began to move about the kitchen and continued putting things back in order. She would often bend down to pick up things and flash her naked bottom my way. She was so sexy in that skirt with no panties underneath. When she bent down exposing that naked ass, her pussy would poke itself out as if competing for attention. She finally finished her cleaning and stood in front of the sink. She turned on the hot water to run slowly while she began to remove the few items she wore. I watched from my horizontal position on the couch as she prepared to wash her plump ass and luscious pussy. "Put plenty of soap on that rag!" I hollered as she began to place the rag under the running water. "That's right; I wanna see a lot of lather on that rag." She was very obedient to my instructions as I continued to guide her in bathing. There was so much lather on the rag when she finished, that it resembled a stuffed animal. I watched closely as she worked the rag over her entire body. Her body began to glow as her smooth tan skin peeked from beneath the billowy mounds of foam. She placed the rag back under the running water in a tireless effort to rinse out the soap. I quickly interrupted when she began to squeeze the water from the rag. "Leave some water in the rag and don't make it too dry." She paid close attention to everything I told her. She took the wet rag and began to remove the soap from her body, which was starting to dry. She repeated this process a number of times before I could see more of her and less of the soap. "Just use cool water now to rinse the rag out. This will help the soap disappear faster." I felt like a father teaching his child to bath for the first time alone. The soap was now gone but the floor was a mess. She now began to dry herself off with a soap free damp rag. I jumped up from the couch and went quickly to the bathroom outside to get the mop. I hurried back inside not wanting to leave her alone too long. I motioned for her to step back when I entered the kitchen. I used the dry mop to wipe up all the water from the floor. It was now much cleaner than when she first began to bath. I gave her a small jar of Vaseline to rub over her body. I also placed some roll on deodorant and perfume on the table. I let the mop stay in the kitchen and returned to my spot on the couch. I body began to glisten as she applied the Vaseline to her skin. I never so a freshly washed female that didn't look good. Her pubic hair was soft and silky looking. Her breasts were round and firm without sagging. They appeared to be a 34 B cup size. Her nipples were like dark pencil erasers sticking out from her mounds. She combed back her hair after smearing some deodorant under her arms and spraying on the perfume. She than began to walk slowly toward me. "Turn out the light before you come here." I said in a voice quiet enough to be a whisper. She paused slightly and reached for the wall switch. Her out stretched arm revealed the firmness of her body and breasts. She proceeded towards me as her arm dropped down to her side. My eyes stayed fixated on the glistening bush between her legs. The night light peering thru the window blinds made her body glow. "Oh what a wonderful sight!" I thought to myself. I began to feel activity in my lions, as she was now close enough to smell. "Emmm you smell as sweet as you look. Come lay next to me so I can tastes you." I raise my hand to guide her down to a position along side me on the couch. She was warm to the touch and her youthful scent filled my nostrils. My member protruded outward as it poked her sides. She giggled slightly at the comical sight of my erect penis. It was standing up at attention as if in a military formation. She reached down to stroke its sides as I inhaled deeply. "Oooo your hands are so soft." I said in a whisper. "Your dick is so hard." She quickly responded. She bean to slowly slide off the couch and knelt down on her knees. I rolled over on my back as she continued to explore the texture of my member. She seemed fascinated by its length and smoothness. She lowered her mouth down upon it and began to lick its head. Her right breast was positioned just above my left hand, which was at my side. I reached up awkwardly to do some exploring of my own. The taunt nipple rested between my fingers as I felt the smoothness of her skin. She was such a young beauty that I couldn't imagine the circumstances that placed her hear with me. I fought back the urge to rescue her from this dilemma and just enjoy the moment. Sadness fell upon me briefly as felt the power of Christ engulf me. I knew what I was doing was wrong but the good feeling of sin had over taken me. I started massaging the breast as its nipple tickled the palm of my hand. She continued to feast on my member as remained erect and in her control. She was now riding my dick with her mouth acting like an elevator inside its shaft. Up and down she went as her saliva provided plenty of lubrication. I was brought to the brink a few times as I struggled to contained myself. I refused to soil this young beauty's mouth with my semen. She didn't seem to care and acted more determined to make me cum in her mouth. The only thing safe about this sex was that the front door had two locks on it and we were alone. I pushed hard against her breast causing her to rise up off me. She looked at me, and appeared puzzled by my action. "It feels good baby but I want to be inside you now." A wide smile appeared on her face and she started a gentle massage of my member. I pointed to the desk in the corner and told her to get a condom from it. She crawled the short distance to the desk and reached up for the condoms. What a sight she was as her thighs spread apart revealing the plum lips of her pussy. I good see the wetness around it from the dim light in the room. She crawled back towards me as her firm breasts and taunt nipples made a stimulating sight. My dick had lost none of its hardness and she began to free the condom from its wrapper. She skillfully placed it atop my bulging head and lowered it the length of my cock. She raised herself up off the floor as one hand kept a grip on my cock. I remained on my back in the middle of the couch. She balanced herself with one hand as she placed her left knee alongside me. She continued smiling as she guided me inside her. She kept her right foot on the floor while she lowered herself down. I could feel her heat engulf the head of my cock as I slowly disappeared inside her. She looked up to the ceiling as she let out a sigh. "Ahhhh Oooo Yeahhhh! She placed both her hands on my chest and began to paddle me with her ass, while my cock remained inside her. She was good at what she did to be so young. The Devil was now in control and I began to meet her downward thrusts with upwards thrusts of my own. We rocked in unison as if listening to the same melody. The pussy she had me in became well lubricated. The soft hands pressed hard against my chest kept me excited. I stared in her face as she fucked me with both eyes closed. I wondered if she was just concentrating or thinking about someone else. It really didn't matter at this point. This young, warm, and wet pussy was creating dreams of its own. I rubbed her titties with the back of my hands. I played with the nipples with my fingers and she just rocked on. I could not distract her form whatever mission she was on. My lions took a beating as she pounded her body against mine. The juices flowing from her pussy had saturated the sheet spread beneath us. I watched as she clenched her fists on my chest and bit down on her lips. I felt the inside of her pussy tighten against my member. It began to feel like teeth were inside her trying to hold on. I felt a fire building up around my cock. She increased the speed of her rocking as I fought hard against my impulse to release my load. "Ahhhh, Ahhh, Ahhhh!" She began to cry out while my body stiffened. I felt a rush of fluid pulsate down on me as my sperm began to feel the insides of the condom. We were coming in unison like a couple of trained dancers. She pounded me harder and faster like she was trying to drain herself of any liquid inside. The head of my dick was tender but I continued to keep up. I didn't want to be out done by this young pussy that seemed possessed by some unknown force. She started to slow down and soon collapsed on tp of me, with her head resting on my chest. Her ass was sticking up in the air with the cheeks spread far apart. I began to rub it feeling a mixture of sweat and cum. My limp dick had fallen from its previous home and lay between my legs. I pressed down on her ass until it rested on top of me. He sweat from her naked body left my tee shirt soaking wet. Both our scents were filling the air. Her breathing was still labored and the silence in the room gave a chilling effect. The stillness of our bodies showed no evidence of what had just taken place. The sex was gentle and fierce leaving both participants exhausted. I fumbled for the second sheet that I had placed on the couch before her arrival. I fanned it out until both our bodies were covered. She was so peaceful lying on top of me. I began to stroke her hair and the back of her neck. I couldn't remember if I knew her name. I could remember how good the pussy was as we both fell off to sleep.

The sunlight was strong coming thru the blinds. The blinding light filled the room. I wondered what time it was as a cramp tried to claim my right leg. I heard snoring in my ear while my dick started to come to life again. Young pussy was still asleep on top of me. I didn't want to move but I feared this cramp would claim my leg. I rolled her to the side and let her rest against the back of the couch. I slide myself off the couch on to the floor. I watched as my young pussy laid face first back on the couch. I wondered how long she had been up. She slept so hard that I had to check her pulse to make sure she was alive. I raise the sheet to look at her naked body. "She was still beautiful, even the morning after." I couldn't say that about everybody that found their way here. I couldn't say that about everybody that lasted until the morning. I stared awhile longer before realizing that today was Halloween. I went into the kitchen to release myself in the sink. I let the cold water run as the streaming yellow liquid made its way down the drain. I looked again at my young beauty as I shook myself off. "Emmm Halloween and I already had both my trick and treat. Ha, ha, ha now that's funny!" I went back and lay down on the couch to enjoy a moment I didn't want to end.

I was wakening with a cramp in my right leg. I shook the nude body that lay next to me. She rolled over on her back as the sheet covering her fell to the floor. The smell of sex was still in the air. It was too late for me to have company. I had to figure a way for my overnight guest to leave without being seen. I didn't want to rush her out like I had no more use for her, but that was the truth. "Hey Baby we need to get cleaned up. We can both wash at the same time in the kitchen." The naked beauty started to come to life as her body stretched and squirmed. The cramp in my leg started to leave and I didn't want it to change its mind. "I need to pee." She replied as I quickly changed my mind about touching her pussy. I rolled over her and landed on the floor. The cramp was gone so I felt save in rising to my feet. I stumbled into the kitchen and took the empty bucket from under the table. This was my guest toilet when too much daylight had arrived. I ran a little water in it and handed her some tissue. She rose from the couch and I couldn't stop staring at her. She looked even better in the daylight. "Damn Baby I can't remember your name?" I asked timidly with a sheepish grin on my face. She flashed a puzzled look on her face and said; "Damn after all that fucking, you don't know my name? Ha, ha, ha just call me Sugar." Sugar walked to the kitchen with steady legs. I set the bucket down next to the sink on top of some old newspaper. I watched as she squatted down with her ass in the air facing me. She reached up and held on to the sink to balance her. I watched her butt hole clench as a steady stream of piss gushed from her orifice. When sugar had wiped her pussy dry, I pointed to the garbage in front of her. I had removed my tee shirt, so we both stood there naked. I pulled sugar close to me and just hugged her. The warmness of her body was arousing me. I moved her to the side and began to run the water. I gave her the rag she used last night and I had a fresh one from my closet. We began to lather our rags in unison and hurriedly washed our bodies. There was some crack on the table from last night and I was eager to have a little taste for myself. I finished first and quickly put on a fresh pair of drawers. I asked for her stem while she continued to wash between her legs. "Take it out my bag and save some for me." It always felt good to me, when I smoked this shit with some pussy in front of me. I knew it would be awhile before I traveled down this road again so I might as well make it last. I knew if she got buzzed up again she would have to delay her departure. I could use that time bullshitting her about more drugs coming and have her play with my dick a little more.

I pulled the plastic apart and let the small crystals fall to the table. I made three small piles and placed one of them in the glass tube I held in my hand. I balanced the glass in the air as I flicked the Bic lighter and began to suck the little flame inside the glass. The smoke I sucked in thru the tube began to fill my lungs. I held my breath as the effects of the drug began to influence me. I closed my eyes as I started to release the smoke I held captive. The thick white smoke filled the air and my head felt a little lighter. I repeated the process with the lighter and began to inhale the remaining drug from the glass tube. I watched this time as the clear liquid inside made its way down the tube. I removed the lighter and continued to draw the smoke out. I sat the lighter down on the table as strange feelings engulfed me. I laid the tube on a cloth on the table so that it would cool off. I peered over at my young bathing beauty as she finished up her bathing. I kept gazing at her but felt no sexual arousal. I began to feel paranoid and wanted her to leave. I concealed what I felt from her but the look on my face was telling on me. "Hey Honey are you alright?" She asked in a concerned manner. I tried to respond and felt the words struggling to escape, but my lips could not move. I continued to formulate some speech in my mind but the words could not get past my lips. I just sat there and stared at her until the effects of the drugs had diminished. She walked over to me damp and naked and stood between my legs. I grabbed her waist and pulled her as close to me that the chair I was in would allow. I started to lick the moisture form her belly. I drank the water from her navel that was captured inside. I wanted to lick her pussy but couldn't reach it from this position. She reached down and picked up the glass tube and placed the two remaining piles of crystals inside. My head had started to clear and sounds began to come out of my mouth. "Yeah Sugar I'm good, you go ahead and finish it." She looked down at me and smiled as she balanced the tube in the air while reaching for the lighter. I began to rub her body from the back of her knees to her firm round ass. She seemed delighted to my touch but her focus was on the drugs. She flicked the lighter and applied some heat to the tube. She allowed the crystals to melt some before drawing on the tube. She arched her back with the tube high in the air. I pulled the towel from the sink and dropped it on the floor in front of me. She began to inhale the smoke that was escaping from the tube. I slid out the chair and knelt down on the towel in front of her. I was eye to eye with the pussy now and could smell the freshness of it. While she puffed on the tube and took a journey to euphoria, I licked the folds of her pussy and journeyed myself to ecstasy. We had separate destinations but we continued to ride together. The drugs in me had the pussy tasting good and feeling wonderful. She swayed her hips when she exhaled, forcing her body closer to me. She stood firm and rigid when she inhaled and I forced my face into her. We were like a dance couple performing to the sound of our own music. I wrapped my tongue around her clit and worked it like a bow to a violin. She took another hit from the glass tube and sat it down on the table. She still had her fist clenched around the lighter, as she steadied herself with one hand on the table. I had both my hands spread out on the back off her ass. I kept a tight grip to hold her pussy in place. She let the smoke escape thru her lips as her body stiffened and jerked. I could feel the warmth and stickiness of the juices that started to flow from her body. I waited for the jerking to stop before I rose to my feet. It was no simple task for me to get up. I had an enormous erection as I stood between her legs. I took a condom off the table and quickly put it on. I then moved all the objects on the table to one side and lifted her up. She offered no resistance when I entered inside her. The pussy was still throbbing as I began my thrusts. It was so loose and juicy that I couldn't go slowly if I wanted to. Sugar wrapped her arms around my neck as I griped her ass. It only took a few minutes with many strokes, for us to arrive at our destination at the same time. I wanted her to stay longer but common sense prevailed. It was time for her to leave and I rushed her out like she was a shoplifter. I walked her to the front door after we both had dressed. It was so late in the day that the neighbors couldn't tell when she came in. I watched her walked down those steps and work that plumb ass for me. I came back inside and noticed my mail had been placed on the table in the hallway. I grabbed it and disappeared back into my apartment. I had a lot of cleaning up to do and did not want to prolong the job. I didn't pay much attention to the mail at this time. I just wanted to clean my house and get some rest alone.

It felt like I was asleep for years when I finally awaken. There were some cramping in my back and legs but nothing a hot bath could cure. I stepped out to the bathroom and began to run the water. I went back inside to check the mail that I had tossed to the side. A great smile took over my face when I saw the letter from the Sanitation Department. It stated that some positions had opened up but I would need to call and set up a date for my urine test. I knew I had to act fast if I wanted to be considered for one of those slots. "Damn!" I said out loud to myself. "Why did I have to get so weak and take that hit yesterday?" I was upset with myself but I began to calculate the time it would take the drugs to pass through my body. I knew I would need at least 72 hours, which would make Tuesday the earliest. I would have to wait until Monday to make the call. I reasoned that they would probably schedule a day later in the week. "Oh, my bath water is running over!" I rushed out to the bathroom and stop the water just in time. There was more water in the tub then what I needed. It didn't matter though as long as I didn't splash around. I stripped down and climbed into the tub. The hot water felt soothing to my body. I did some stretching to relieve the pain and tension in my limbs. I began to lather up after lying in the water for at least ten minutes. I removed the stopper before standing up to wash. "Emmm, suds always felt good against my skin." I thought to myself. My body began to look like a work of art with lather covering me from head to toe. The tub was almost empty so I turned on the shower to rinse off the soap. I couldn't resist the temptation to masturbate as I began washing beneath my balls. My member responded immediately to my gentle rubbing. I continued to use circular motions with my rag as my cock kept growing. I closed my eyes and thought about most of the pussy I ever had. I began to see faces that were long forgotten. It felt even better as the head of my cock became tender. I let the warm water from the shower cascade down my body. I turned to look away from the water as I began to release my load. My body jerked as the thick liquid hit the bottom of the tub. I moved to the side to prevent semen from coming in contact with my feet. I kept squeezing my throbbing head to free every bit of fluid that wanted to leave. I took time to wash my rag and clean out the tub before I dried off. I returned to the apartment and searched for some church clothes. The daylight had broken thru the blinds indicating how I had been in the bathroom. I was going to give god some praise today, after I had asked for some forgiveness. I needed that job, not just for me but for my child.

I looked down at my nude body lying on the couch. "I must have dozed off." I rose from my slumber and searched the room for a clock. "Wow, its 8:a.m. and I don't know what I'm gonna wear." I started greasing up my body as I thought about a suit I could wear without a coat. I put on my under clothes and socks and decided my black and white plaid suit would fit the bill. I wore a black shirt with a grey and blue tie to match. It was 8:45 now, giving me enough time to slow walk the two blocks to church. I left the house with Bible in hand and enough money to satisfy all the offerings. I would arrive in time for Sunday school which I enjoyed the most. I even had enough time when I got there to help one of the trustees sweep the front and the parking lot before I went upstairs. There were a few early arrivals when I entered the large room. It was filled with seven large round tables that were encircled by chairs. I chose my usual seat along the borders but in the center of the formation. The class began to fill up as I shared greetings and hugs with the others as they arrived. The lesson was on stewardship and how we should manage the resources that God had blessed us with. People didn't always understand that God's blessings always weren't in the form of money. We also had to recognize that talents and good health were both important resources. The lesson was a good one that had almost everyone sharing their comments. I left that class feeling some shame because I had squandered my resources over the weekend. I was well known to the members of this church because of the many years my sister was here. She was now one of the Ministers and I felt so blessed to be here with her. We left the room to go to a small fellowship area for coffee and breakfast snacks. I continued my greetings as I moved about the church waiting for devotional service to start. That was led by an energetic and devoted young man to Christ. Deacon Brown had an uplifting spirit and never hesitated to engage you in conversation about Jesus Christ and the gift of salvation.

The service that day was like a revival meeting with the chorus getting me in touch with so many emotions. The sermon talked about carnal Christians. Those are the believers that still hold on to some of their worldly activities while still being active church members. They become selective about what they choose to give up for Christ. They commit their sins in the dark believing that it's okay as long as they are not public. The sermon hit me hard because I was still sheltering drug dealers and fornicating with the young women that were hooked on drugs. I was even gambling and selling drugs myself at times. I rationalized that my prayers for forgiveness and my generous and faithful offerings would keep me under the Blood. I left church service that day being more committed than ever to repent and pray for deliverance from my afflictions. I knew that I had to face God's judgment for my actions. I could only pray that I had acted soon enough to allow him to show mercy.

I walked home with the streets filled with activity. It was in stark contrast with its appearance when I came to church. My looks with Bible in hand generated smiles and some hellos from everyone I passed. There were those that I knew and others were total strangers, but they all smiled just the same. It was a good feeling when people looked upon you with admiration. It was even a greater feeling if you deserved it. I felt shame today. Although I had journeyed far in my walk with The Lord, I still had a long way to go.

It was Monday morning now and all I thought about was my phone call. The earliest I could call was 8:30 a.m. so I washed up and made breakfast. The time seemed to have gone fast because it was 9:00 a.m. as I finished washing up the dishes. I grabbed my cell phone with dried hands and began to punch in the numbers. I was feeling some anxiety as I waited for someone to answer. The woman on the other end asked for some identifying information after I told her the purpose of my call. She was very professional and courteous in her responses to me. I began to relax and was soon instructed to report to Manhattan for my urinalysis. It was the very next morning that I had to be there. This was the worst possible date. I rolled the dice in my excitement to be hired and lost. I would be cutting it real close but I couldn't change the date. I should have told them that I was out of town and wouldn't be back until the end of the week. Too late now! I just had to start drinking water and pray that the piss would clear up in time. Tuesday morning would be right at the border for my urine to be clean. I never thought they would give a date so close after my call. My whole day was filled with nervousness and high anxiety as I asked friend after friend their method of cleaning up their urine. This was the world I lived in where people used drugs. Times had so changed on jobs because of the drug epidemic. Everyone was checking your piss for some of the most menial positions. "Damn I'm such a fool for sabotaging my chances of success." I made my way downtown to make a purchase based on the best advice I thought I received. I went to a herbal store and got some one shot. It cost $35.00 and you was supposed to drink ht e last of it one hour before you pissed in the bottle. He could have come with me and gave me some hot piss for that much money. I wasn't the only drug addict at the mercy of these concoctions. I returned home and spent the rest of the day indoors. I didn't want to see anyone and I sure didn't want to be tempted.

I woke up Tuesday morning eager to piss for these people. I felt sure that I could give clean urine. I was confident even though I knew I was cutting it real close. I was so certain of myself that I didn't even piss at home first. I had to be there at 8:00 a.m. and felt I could hold my water until then. I arrived downtown a little early just in case I had trouble finding the place. When I stepped inside I found a cop and a transit worker already waiting. It seems that this place only existed to collect urine samples of city workers. It was a no nonsense woman in charge of collecting the samples. She handed me a chain of custody bag along with a bottle and some strict rules to follow. There was no chance of falsifying this sample even though you pissed with no monitor standing over you. If a foreign substance was detected in the urine or the temperature was not consistent with fresh piss, it would be considered a positive result. When I had first entered this place I had to sign in downstairs before coming upstairs to this floor. I had to piss real bad but decided against it so that I wouldn't be accused of stalling. The act would later prove to be my undoing at beating the system. I had no problem pissing and the water gushed out like the raging rapids. I was not even allowed to flush the toilet after I had finished. I place my bottle in the chain of custody bag, sealed it and then exited the bathroom and turned it in. I had to sign the necessary documents proving that the bag was sealed when I turned it in. his was done so that there could be no chance of it being tampered with before it got to the testing lab. I left the place faithful but not confident that my test would come back negative. I should not have given them my first piss for that day. I went home and began to gather my paperwork and necessary depositions of prior criminal cases. I wanted no further delays in being hired. I wanted to beat the deadline to receive that healthy uniform allowance around Christmas time.

It was Friday November the 6th when the mailman delivered the news I had waited all week for. I held my breath as I tore open the letter. There was a lengthy paragraph about the appeal process before I was able to read the results. My urine analysis had come back positive for cocaine. My heart sunk like a piece of iron tossed in a lake. I was destroyed and could not think of any course of action that could change what had just taken place. There were no excuses I could give that would make any sense but I still tried. I immediately filed for a review of the results. It would cost me $75.00 to have them retest my urine. I had to send the money with the paperwork and I had to send it fast. There was a narrow time period in which the papers had to be received by the city. The one thing any drug addict has plenty of is denial. The addict's denial surfaces in every aspect of his life. My denial of the truth had me spending money I couldn't afford to hear the truth one more time. My denial had me believing that I was crafty enough to evade detection. My denial made me believe that I could engage in negative behavior and not suffer any consequences.

It was a week later when I received the news a second time that my urine was dirty. My next inclination was to concoct a story to cover me not being hired by the Sanitation Department. I took a vacation from my obedience to The Lord and began to lie. I blamed it on my wife's zeal to garnish my wages for child support as my reason for turning down the position. A few accepted that lie, because I would not be the first to take action like that, to lessen payments to an estranged spouse. I went about my business for the next couple of months faking happiness. If I was caught in a depressed state, I blamed it on the holiday season. The devil was working his way back into my life, but I was too busy faking to see him coming. My efforts weren't a total loss because at least I had a CDL license. I was able to send my daughter some things for Christmas. I began to search the want ads for a driving position. I knew I couldn't survive on my supermarket salary since Child Support was taking some of that. I really had to stop the bullshit and leave those drugs alone. There was no position available that didn't require clean urine and involve random tests there after. The state and federal government took the CDL very serious. I began to move the dealers further away from my house and minimized my contact with them. I made sure I had what I needed in the house before it got dark. I stopped smoking cigarettes to avoid coming out and sitting on my stoop. I made sure I got to church early on Sunday and made my ministry meetings on Saturday when called. I began to preach about salvation to my friends around me to strengthen my relationship with The Lord. I accepted this job loss as God's will to wake me up and bring me closer to Him. One Sunday after the sermon was done I recommitted myself to Christ after confessing some of my short comings. I began to focus on developing better relationships with members that seemed to have a firm foundation in The Word. My sister the minister bought me a new study Bible that had my name engraved on it. I began to watch what I ate and started exercising in the house. I wasn't losing any weight but the activities kept my mind off the drugs. I began to study the scriptures more for guidance and understanding. I became entrenched in activities that increased my knowledge about Jesus and His ministry. I started waking up early in the morning just to pray. The dreams I started having, were also bringing me some enlightenment. In late January of 2006, I applied for a position at a transportation company. On February 6, I was hired after passing their physical. They were having problems of their own at getting quality drivers. The pay was low and benefits were non existent. The union representing the workers was a sham, but I didn't know it at the time. I stipulated at the time of my hire, the hours I couldn't work beyond. My evening job at Pathmark was not going to be interfered with. The union at Pathmark was no sham and provided some benefits. This was the first time I legitimately drove for a living. The route I eventually was assigned mainly had pick ups in Queens. This was a problem at first until I became accustomed to the borough. I used to call my baby sister at work to help me get to my destinations. This second job made it impossible for me to do any home repair. The other advantage though was that my two jobs were in walking distant of each other. My new income made life a little easier. I also cherished my first job more because it helped me to stay in shape. I was away from home the entire day whenever I had to work at the supermarket. I had to get to bed early because my first job started at 6:30 a.m. The garnish on my Pathmark wages became more tolerable. I also had another court judgment that was taking another 10% from my wages. This stemmed from the credit cards that my wife and I had before splitting up. This didn't seem to bother her when she decided to take action that involved the state in our affairs. Hallelujah, if not for the grace of God,

I could not have survived. If not for the Mercy of God, I would not have wanted to. My job driving a van had me taking seniors and some mentally challenged people to adult daycare programs. This was an unknown system to me but it further developed my relationship with god.

"Thank you Jesus!" I shouted out loud, after one week on the job. The people that I transported were so grateful to have me as their driver. They told some horror stories of past drivers. They spoke about the inconsistencies with having so many different drivers. I was just as appreciative of them. They added extra purpose to my life. They gave me the means of giving something back to the world, at a time when I had taken so much. Their presence and my responsibility to them kept me grounded in The Lord. We spoke about The Word during our trips. We played gospel music in the mornings. Everyone began to treat each other with such respect that new relationships were formed. I picked people up at the best time they would be ready so others didn't have to wait for the slow movers. They began to make an extra effort at preparing themselves. They even began to develop a more positive attitude towards their Day Programs. I felt a true calling from God because of my interaction with them. The director of the program and the administrative assistant even looked favorably towards me and was thankful for what I was doing. Still not everyone was overjoyed at my assignment. The lone security guard developed a harsh attitude towards my presence after only a few weeks. The driver I replaced was a woman and a close friend of hers. The woman provided her transportation to work using the van. I was not the one to continue that practice. The fact that I was so successful at my job in such a short time only added to her resentment towards. This was because there was no chance of her friend returning. The other driver also was not as professional as I was and didn't maintain the proper boundaries with the clients. There were some with severe handicaps that received special services when it was time to cash their checks. I was uncomfortable in keeping many of the practices that other drivers had started. I dropped people off at their homes and didn't loan or borrow money. I was someone new to get used and they all finally cooperated. The spring months went by fast after the winter had left. The summer months were a good time for us all but it brought with it my own personal demons. Drug use was rampant in the neighborhoods during this time. I had to really struggle not to fall in the trap of the enemy. Sometimes my loneliness would overtake me. I found myself up late at night tricking with the whores that frequented my area. I got pleasure but paid a price when I had to work the next day. It was only by God's grace and mercy that I didn't fall asleep at the wheel. The Day Program also had a new director, whom was more qualified than the one she replaced. She ran a tight ship and was pro client. She was Hispanic which made it possible the other Hispanic clients to communicate and receive culturally enriching services. I had to translate for some of my clients before she came onboard. This woman was also effective in getting the transportation company to recognize some of their deficiencies that impacted on her program. I was living a life now that was pleasing to God. I only hoped and prayed that I was doing enough. I even went on a religious retreat with the men's ministry at my church which further developed my relationship with God and His people.

I had money now and was able to treat my daughter well. I received an assessment from her about what her needs were for school. I would not be sending any money this time. I did the shopping myself to ensure that the type and styles she wore were my choosing. I spent over $500.00 on her and hid some cash money in one of the boxes I sent. The postage with the added expense of insurance and delivery confirmation came to almost another $50.00. I even had a wonderful birthday celebration as I continue to reclaim a stature that was lost with my imprisonment. I trusted and believed God but I don't think I was praising Him enough. I began to make plans for Christmas even before Thanksgiving had got here. Yes I was jumping for joy at my resurrection but I don't think I was praising God enough. I was supporting my church and blessing young woman that had children to raise. I found ways to cope with my loneliness and received hope from the woman I wished for. I still don't think I was praising God enough. No matter how good, no matter how bad, you have to keep praising God or he will help you remember. I was about to see how God will make you remember to give Him the glory and praise. It would be a lesson that I would never forget.

The prosperity I was enjoying brought with it some unexpected challenges. I had money that wasn't there before. I had friends that weren't there before. I also had demons that weren't there before. It was easy to suppress the urges that had crippled my life before, when my money was short. Now that I had extra funds I began to take risks to bring more enjoyment into my life. My wife was hounding me about money. My daughter was telling me things about my wife that I didn't need to hear. I was a lonely man wanting some pussy lying next to me every night. It was just a matter of time before all these things came together, to start my slow decline back into the abyss of despair. I was up early as usual one morning getting ready for work. I decided that it would be a good idea to make Thanksgiving dinner and have my children present. I began to make some phone calls to arrange it. I was anxious to see my daughter. The last time we were together was when I visited to be at her middle school graduation. She had grown so much and her mother had rejected my attempts at reconciliation. I had given her a key to my hotel room that she never used. I brought her some gifts that she never received. I ended up giving them to the flame of the month for a birthday present. My wife agreed to bring my daughter and son but she had no money to travel. I contacted my son's mother to make sure she would be able to bring him to wife's house. We decided the fastest and cheapest way to travel would be the train. I financed the whole affair and waited with great anticipation for the arrival date to come. My daughter Z Baby and I counted down the days together whenever we spoke on the phone. I was also anxious to see how well my wife Legs was taking care of herself. She had lost a lot of weight the last time I saw her at the graduation. We rode together that time in her car. We even ate dinner together afterwards with some of Z Baby's schoolmates. Still we didn't address any of the issues that needed to be talked about. I put all those things behind me and focused on being happy on Thanksgiving Day.

I had just two weeks to go before my kids would be here. I was talking with Z Baby everyday and getting high every night. Sometimes I would be so high that I couldn't even speak on the phone. A few times she called just after I had taken a hit of crack. Guilt would overcome me but not enough to make me stop. I was still making it to church and bible study. I would start getting high as soon as I came home from work. On the days I just drove the van I would start my drug use early while it was still daybreak sometimes. Those moments would offer some great challenges in trying to cope my drugs while the streets were so active. One thing about an addict; no situation is so insurmountable that it can't be conquered. I devised all types of codes and signals to alert my dealers when making purchases. The neighborhood had become so hot that I would often have to walk a distant to avoid detection. Three days before my kids' arrival I stopped cold and began the process of cleaning up the house. I had to make sure that there was no contraband lying around or any evidence of me smoking anything. It took the entire three days for me to completely transform my apartment to a family friendly environment. I delivered a holiday basket to one of my client's daughter, which I received from my church. I gave her an additional $25.00 to cover the extras. She was a chocolate stunner and almost thirty. I felt something for her the first time I saw her. My dream was that, if I hit on her she would say yes. I tried to arrive at her house to get her mother before she left for work. It was the type of stimulation I needed to get my away from the hookers. It was a long time before I gave up on that dream.

I had taken care of my holiday missionary work. I was now just waiting for my children to arrive. I would let this visit be the foundation of my rehabilitation.

The day before Thanksgiving was here and it would be a busy one for me. I got up early to do my last minute shopping. I would do most of my cooking today and save the turkey for last. My son Shawn and daughter Z Baby would arrive with my wife sometime this afternoon. My wife Legs had arranged for her best friend Donna to pick her up. I didn't have room for everyone to stay with me so Legs would spend the holiday with her friend. Shawn would sleep at his nearby grandmother's house. Z Baby would be the only one staying with me. It would give us a lot of time to talk without interruption. It would also give me a chance to see what type of personality she had developed. I prepared a nice menu of baked macaroni, potato salad, steamed carrots, collard greens, rice, and boiled egg gravy. The gravy was a family recipe started by my mother. I had sweet potato pudding and some banana pudding to serve as sweets. I had brought apple cider and eggnog to drink. I wanted to make sure there was plenty of food because they would be here until Saturday. I went to work late that day and came home early. The center had prepared a dinner for the clients but they too would be closing early. I didn't have to work at the store again until Sunday. I came home at about 2:00 p.m. and immediately started getting my food ready. It was close to 3:00 p.m. when my daughter called to say they were in Brooklyn and would be there soon. I had to give directions to Donna before she hung up. I stopped what I was doing for a minute and went and sat on my stoop to wait for them to arrive. My little girl next door was sitting outside smoking a cigarette. It had been a while since we had hung out or even spoke. I was ducking her because of my drug use. I could never let her know that I had started smoking crack. That would have definitely ended our relationship. We chatted about holiday plans as I stared down her blouse at her supple breasts. Soon after a jeep pulled into the block driving very slow. I came down from the stoop to see if I knew the occupants. "Daddy" someone shouted from the vehicle. I walked to the curb and waited for the jeep to stop. At about the same time Candy got up from her stoop and went back into the house. "Hey Z Baby, is that you?" I ran up to the car as she started getting out. My son was also sitting in the back. We hugged each other as I looked over at my wife sitting in the front. "Hi Legs. Hi Donna, thanks for brining my kids to me. I didn't know you could drive!" Legs forced a smile on her face as if she was in pain. I figured she still had a grudge. I would learn later from Z Baby that she was in bad health. She had overcome pneumonia but couldn't get rid of the cough. I carried as many bags as I could from the car leaving only a small one for Shawn to carry. I let Legs know that they would be ready early Saturday to return back to Virginia. I always thought it a strange twist of fate that both my kids' mothers would relocate to the same state. It was even stranger that didn't live too far from one another. I marched my newly arrived entourage upstairs to continue cooking my meal. It felt good having my children with me. It also felt good seeing my wife again. Once I got upstairs, I called Shawn's grandmother and let her know that he had arrived. I also let her know that I would walk him around there later. We all hung out for a couple of hours watching movies as I went back and forth to the kitchen. Yes it was a great feeling to have both my kids here with me. We all left together when it was time for Shawn to leave. It was a short walk to take but the suitcase I carried made it seem longer. I told Shawn what time to come back. He was already familiar with the area from his previous visits. On the other hand it was a strange neighborhood to Z Baby. I would not let her go anywhere by herself. She was just Thirteen years old but looked a bit older. I noticed when we walked back home how the wrong people were paying too much attention to her. I would make sure I spent some time putting the right things in her head. I would also take the time to remind her of the expectations I had of her. We were both up let talking and cooking. I slept in the bed and she slept on the couch we both fell asleep as the television played on.

It was about 3:00 a.m. when I first awaken. It took a moment for me to get my bearings because so much light was flooding my little apartment. The TV was playing and the lamp was on. My daughter couldn't sleep in the dark and I didn't like sleeping in the light. I turned the TV off and went into the bathroom. The urges that I was so used to at this time of morning had engulfed me. I wanted to get high. It had been more than a week since my last escapade. I knew that I couldn't but it didn't stop me from wanting to. I started to run me a bath, hoping that the hot water would quell my lust for some drugs. I left the bathroom to get some loungewear and fresh underwear. I would have to get dressed in the bathroom for the first time since moving here. I also brought some Joy with me to squirt in the water. This would be a Hollywood bath, a term I coined when I lived with my

ZEKE SMITH

daughter. This was a bath with lots of suds and it lasted a long time. It was a bath that was meant to relax you or create a party atmosphere in the tub. My daughter would laugh at me whenever I took a Hollywood bath. I never did ask her what she found so funny. The tub was half full when I turned off the water. I stripped down naked and slid into the hot water. Oooo chills went over my body, as the rapid temperature change took an effect on me. I began to reflect on the journey that brought me to this moment. I thought about the agonizing separation from my family. I thought about my lapse in judgment that led to it. I thought about the many different places I was forced to live in or at. I glanced back at the female relationships that I encountered in trying to sustain myself. I remembered my success at the crap tables and some of the failures. I continue to daydream in that tub about the glory I thought I had received from so much freedom. My thoughts and feelings soon became gloomy as I remembered the lies and the arguments that took over my marriage. I then started thinking about my daughter, who was the most precious person in my life. I thought about the plans I had for her life. I didn't want her to fall into the trap that other women in my family had entered. I stressed no boyfriends until she had graduated from High School. No children without a husband. No husband until she had a college degree and a career intact. I would repeat this to her often when we shared the same household. I reminded her of it once during our separation, only to have my wife go into a rage because of the content of our conversation. I felt that you didn't wait for the dam to break before you had a plan to stop the water. The water wasn't as hot anymore and my hands started to crinkle. It was time to stop the daydreaming and start washing. I pulled the rag from the drain before I rose up in the tub. The suds went rushing down my body as I stood erect. I grabbed my wash cloth as the suds moved towards the open drain like little islands in the ocean. I lathered my rag well and began the circular motions all over my body with it. My daydreaming had relieved me of lust for sex and drugs. The hot bath had taken away the aches and pains caused by my thirst for some drugs. My vision now was all about my future with my children and the focus was on rejoining my family. I finished washing as only suds were left standing idle in the tub. I turned on the shower to rinse off and to clean the tub. I converted my large washcloth into a towel and began drying myself as I stepped out of the tub. My feet landed on my discarded tee shirt as it lay on the floor. I applied some deodorant first after I had dried myself. I greased my entire body until it glistened like a lake illuminated by the sunset. I gathered my belongings when I finished dressing and went back into the apartment. It was still dark outside but you could see daylight threatening to break through. I stuffed my clothes into my hamper and returned all my cosmetics back to their positions. I fluffed the covers on my bed and climbed back inside. I wanted a cigarette but decided against it. I did not want to alarm my daughter by going outside. I did not want to do anything to change the image that she had of me. If my mind could stay focused on her future and the respect she had for me, I could stop practicing risky behavior. I laid down hoping to fall asleep quickly. I had a turkey to roast and some greens to cook. I needed some rest before Shawn arrived. I turned the TV back on and turned off the lamp. It wasn't long before someone probably heard me snoring.

I rose from my slumber with sunlight shining brightly in my face. I looked across the room and found Z Baby missing from the couch. I staggered to my feet and began to wonder, what it was that I should be doing. I searched my memory to gain some ideas. I knew it was Thanksgiving. I knew I was cooking dinner. What I didn't know was I should be doing right now. My daughter was in the bathroom and I had to piss very badly. I went into the kitchen and slid the cover over the sink to expose the tub side. This was very old fashion plumbing as was most everything else in this house. It even appeared that the original paint was still on the walls. I turned on the cold water and squirted some Joy into the tub. I watched some suds appeared and immediately whipped out my cock and began to piss. I rushed the fluid out of my body as fast as I could. The sink's edge was cold against my nuts. I had to raise myself up on my toes to clear it but my nuts still rested against its edge. Emmm that first piss after the wake up always felt good. I shook myself off, being careful that no droplets escaped the confines of the tub. I squirted some Joy into my hands and began to wash them. I splashed handfuls of water against the sides of the tub to insure its cleanliness. When you are raised in a household with three sisters, you quickly learn how to piss in the kitchen sink if nobody is looking. Standing in the kitchen started jolting my memory about what I should be doing. I turned on the oven to heat up at 425 degrees. I slid the cover back over the tub to expose the sink again. I walked the turkey over to it and began to rinse it off. I had a nice large roasting pan that would be home to this bird for the next 31/2 hrs. I pulled the bag of giblets from its cavity and rinse them off too. I started the seasoning process as my daughter returned from the bathroom. She entered the apartment fully dressed in some tight fitting jeans and a flimsy blouse. "You dressed like its spring!" I said in a joking manner. "Well father this is how I dress. It doesn't get that cold in Virginia and this is my style." She looked like she didn't appreciate my humor. I really did not care. She was dressed out of season even for Virginia. I let the conversation die down and finished preparing the turkey. I added some water and margarine to my pan before I cover the whole thing with aluminum foil. My foil had to be Reynolds Wrap for its toughness. I split up the giblets between the roasting pan and a small pot. They would be some of the basic ingredients for my boil egg gravy. I cut up an onion and some green bell peppers and added them both to the small pot with the giblets. I next filled the pot with water after adding my seasoning to it. I would also use this stock when I made my stuffing. I placed it on the stove under a medium light while the oven was still heating up. The stove was old like everything else in the house. The only thing new and modern was what either I or my sister had brought. Z Baby had found some comfort in the other room, as she channel surfed for the Thanksgiving Day parade. She had forgotten the channel line up in New York so it was taking her some time. I remained focused on getting this dinner ready. I started missing up my batter for the whole cake cornbread. I peeled and cut up a small bunch of white potatoes and put a half a dozen eggs on the stove to boil. I would use two eggs for my gravy and the rest for the potato salad. I wasn't trying to cook for the neighborhood. I had not invited anyone else to eat but my children. The kitchen was starting to get real hot now. It was time to put the turkey in the oven. I checked the clock for the time, to make sure my bird didn't overcook. It was 9:00 which meant the turkey would be finished by 1:p.m. I had one unoccupied eye left on the stove. I used that for the collared greens after placing the bird in the oven. The meal was slowly coming to life. I marveled at my ability to put it all together without any help. I always felt comfortable in the kitchen. I peeled my first onion at about four years old. I made my first pot of rice a year later. I loved being around my mama listening to the stories of her past. My sisters didn't hang around the kitchen as much as I did. You could also tell that from the way they cook or either managed their kitchens. I put the window fan back in the window. I didn't need this much heat in the house. I left the kitchen to go chat with Z Baby. I wanted to make sure she wasn't still upset from my comments about her outfit.

"Hey Z Baby, are you ready for this food? Shawn should be on his way over by now." Z Baby flashed a slight smile on her face and appeared ready to be defensive. "Yeah daddy it's only food!" I began to search my mind for a response. I started thinking that maybe this was not a good idea. "How are things with school and your social life?" "What do you mean by social life daddy?" Now she was trying to turn the tables on me with her question. I was being forced to be more pacific about the information I wanted. I didn't want to upset the peaceful mood we all seemed to be in. I began to hear some conversation in the hallway and realized that Shawn had arrived. I sent Z Baby to let him in while I returned to the kitchen. I turned off the fire to the potatoes, giblets and eggs, leaving only the collar greens cooking. I took the mixed pickles and onions out and began to chop them both up and place them in a large bowl. I took out the seasonings that I was going to add while my children started talking in the next room. I poured off the water from the potatoes to let them cool off. I fished my giblets out of the pot and began to strip off the meat from the turkey neck and chop up the rest. I grabbed my large black skillet from the closet to cook my whole cake cornbread in. I was moving at a fast pace like a professional cook as I rushed to meet my own deadline for having the dinner ready. I heard some laughter from the next room as the children continued chatting. They were comparing notes about their father and the past experiences they had. Shawn had the most to talk about as Z Baby laughter grew louder. I stuck my head in the room briefly and asked; "What's so funny gang?" They both turned their heads and responded in unison like a duet; "You!" and then burst out laughing again. I returned to my chores in the kitchen and finished making the gravy, potato salad and collar greens. I started clearing off the table and began arranging all the prepared dishes. The carrots, baked macaroni, and banana pudding were all made yesterday before I fell asleep. I opened up a can of cranberry sauce and after placing it in a saucer, added it to the display on the table. "Dinner is ready so go wash your hands." I was feeling good now because it was four o'clock and the food was done. There was no room in the kitchen to eat at the table so as I fixed the plates Z Baby rearranged the furniture in the larger room to accommodate our dining. Shawn came into the kitchen just as I was fixing his plate. "This is your plate I'm fixing son." He looked at me with a grin on his face and said; "Dad I don't eat carrots." I quickly shot back; "You need to eat some for the nutrition it has." He looked at me again but this time he was laughing and said; "Dad I don't eat carrots!" I responded with Z Baby watching this whole drama unfold and said; "Could you just eat a little to make me happy?" He put a serious look on his face and said; "Dad I'm a grown man now not a little boy. I don't have to eat no carrots if I don't want to, so please don't put any on my face." I looked at Z Baby who was now laughing out loud. I could feel the anger starting to build up inside me. My son had taken a stand against me while his younger sister watched. He

ZEKE SMITH

was not going to please me no matter what I said. I was caught completely off guard and didn't know how to react. The mood had changed from one of happiness and joy to frustration and despair. "Okay son I'll remember that the next time you ask me for some money." He looked at me as that grin returned to his face and said; "Don't get mad daddy I because I won't eat the carrots." I continued making the plate and gave it to him. He was right in what he said and did. Shawn was grown and I shouldn't get mad at him for asserting his independence. "I'm fixing your plate now Z Baby and putting carrots on your plate. You aren't grown yet so I can still tell you what to do." We then both bust out laughing. I had broken the tension that Shawn's defiance had created. I fixed my plate and we all went and sat down in the room. "Wait Shawn stop eating, I want to say grace for us all." I knew I had to avoid any situations that would give my son cause to assert his manhood again. I also had to let the anger in me subside. This was one of those times when I would rely on the Holy Spirit to walk me through. We started eating after grace was said and joy slowly returned to the house. I noticed before and after all the drama had started that Shawn was moving about slowly. There was one time when Z Baby had called my attention to his trembling. Now I noticed again how his hands were shaking while he ate. He appeared over medicated, so I made a mental note to question him later. The rest of the day went well. We talked, laughed and I told stories about their individual early childhoods. We watched two movies together before we all dozed off.

When I awaken, the light coming through the windows was dull and gloomy. I must have been sleep for a few hours because nightfall was coming. I searched around the room to find Z Baby sleep on the couch and Shawn sitting up in the chair staring at the TV. I rose from my slumber and instructed Shawn to get ready to leave. I went into the bathroom to relieve myself. Z Baby had started stirring when I returned. "Z Baby I'm getting ready to walk Shawn home. Do you want to come with us? She nodded her head saying no as Shawn began to rise to his feet. "I won't be long." I said to Z Baby as she returned to sleep. I left the apartment with Shawn close behind me. I put both locks on the door and we descended the stairs together. The stair steps creaked loudly from our combined weights. It felt like we both could go crashing through them before we reached the bottom. There was no sunlight when we stepped outside, only the gloom of the early night. We didn't talk much as we made the short walk around the corner and down the block. I waited for someone to open the door before I left. I was still groggy from my sleep and cursed silently to myself for not bringing a cigarette. I walked slowly back home watching intently around the neighborhood I was going through. This was generally the quietest time but I never understood why. The night of Thanksgiving was not one filled with activity. There maybe be an occasional burst of laughter or a car door slamming but that was it. This was a time when visitors were returning home and addicts were crashing from their binges. My home was now a short distant away and I increased my speed to get there sooner. I climbed the stairs with my head swinging from left to right, as I took in the last sights before disappearing behind the heavy glass and wrought iron door. I had a major job ahead as it was time to put away the food. I stepped into the apartment to find my child still sleeping. I knew from our phone conversations that she enjoyed sleeping. It was just like her mother who could stay in bed all day if she didn't have to work. She wouldn't even get up to wash her ass if I didn't say anything. I wasn't going to disturb until I had finished cleaning the kitchen and putting away the food.

I began to patiently arrange the dirty pots and dishes in the large kitchen tub. I ran hot water in there with some Joy. The suds developed quickly as I searched for the proper storage bowls to put the food in. I took out a fresh Brillo pad and turned the water off. I thought about my son as he stood his ground against me. I was no longer angry about it and just started to laugh. I remembered the look on my daughter's face as she watched the drama unfold. She sure got entertained as she saw her father lose an argument. That had to be the highlight of her day. "I had a few phone calls today but no visitors." I talked out loud to myself. I don't know why that seemed so strange to me now. The only company I usually had was what I brought home with me. I was making good progress but a lot of time had elapsed. It made me notice how it took longer to do the same things than before. Is this what happens when you start approaching those golden years. People in the past always wondered if I would ever slow down. Well they should see me now. The more I thought about it the more I slowed up and my body started to ache. Two hours had passed from the time I first started running the water. I was tired but didn't want t go to bed. This was the time that I would do my cruising, especially with this much food cooked. I could always find me a hungry tired crack head that appreciated some food and a warm bed. I would need no money or drugs to accomplish this. I noticed that we had not eaten any of the banana pudding. I found a small dish to put some in and then put the rest in the refrigerator. I sat down in the kitchen and looked at the neatness I had just labored to create. There was such order as even the different shapes seemed to blend in with each

ZEKE SMITH

other. I didn't always receive acknowledgement for my creative genius, so I gave it to myself sometimes. I recall the boxer and statesman Muhammad Ali once saying; "It's not bragging if you can do it." The banana pudding was good. I refilled the dish when I finished and ate some more. I drank a little eggnog to wash it all down. It was after 11:00 p.m. and time for me to go to bed. I had to wake up Z Baby so she could put on her pajamas. I offered her the bed to sleep in but she was still happy with the couch. In her on way she would show me how much she cared for me. I never remember her just walking up to me and saying; "I love you Daddy." I guess I wasn't the only father that felt that. I waited for Z Baby to come out the bathroom dressed for bed before I got in mine. I left the TV on but turned the volume down. I didn't need any background noises to have me dreaming some crazy adventure. That was often the case when I fell asleep with the TV playing. I stretched out on the bed with a sheet over me as my daughter arranged her covers. She over at me and said, "goodnight Daddy." I looked at her and said, "Goodnight Daughter." We both smiled and started laughing as we began to doze off.

"Z Baby, what's that noise?" There was some type of commotion in the hallway. I thought for a moment if I were dreaming or awake. The room was illuminated with bright sunlight. I could see my child looking very uncomfortable as she struggled to wake up. I searched my memory to understand what day and what time it was. I disrupted my child's sleep the way the noise outside had disrupted mine. "I don't know Daddy but it sounds like someone is outside the door. Now my adrenalin had started to race through my body. My muscles tensed up and I leaped to my feet. I causally approached the door, hoping that my movement would not alarm Z Baby. Then I heard a knock and a timid voice could be heard saying; "Dad." I angrily flung open the door and in a voice loud enough for my neighbors to hear I said; "Boy what are you doing here so early." My son had arrived and with him came commotion. He was first down stairs knocking on windows and doors trying to get in. The bell wasn't enough for him because no one was answering it. He had freshness about him that the rest of us didn't have a time to achieve. "Good morning Dad, you said to come back in the morning." He was absolutely right about that. I did say come back in the morning but 8:a.m. was just too early for all of us here. "Okay Shawn, come on in. You can sit in the kitchen and watch the TV until we get up." I had calmed down a lot from when I first opened the door. Shawn was used to my yelling and didn't seem phased by it. "Can I have some banana pudding Dad?" Shawn's request made me understand now, why he had came here so damn early. He wanted that dessert that he didn't get last night. I wonder how long he stayed up when he realized he didn't eat any. "Sure Son, go wash your hands and I'll get you some." I stepped up to the kitchen sink while Shawn went out to the bathroom. I washed my hands and got a nice size bowl for his banana pudding. I was going to give him enough to keep him from asking for any more. I wanted to sleep a little longer and it looked like Z Baby did too. I put the pudding on the table and turned the TV on. I put the remote control in front of his bowl and crawled back into bed. My kitchen was small but no space was wasted. I had a small portable television on top of my refrigerator, which had a VCR hooked up to it. I used to go in there to watch my porn and get high with most company. The kitchen set-up kept me from entertaining my company in my more private quarters. It also seemed to add a little elegance to my surroundings. I had placed a lock on the other side of the door, to contain my guests if I had to leave them alone for a minute. Yes my ghetto apartment resembled a Manhattan penthouse with my added extras. The other thing that kept it looking elegant was its cleanliness. I spent as much time in my kitchen as the rest of the house. I just wasn't always in there cooking. It even was able to turn into a lab or an office when I had business matters to take care of. I settled down in my bed and stopped thinking so much. I began to relax myself with clean thoughts of my relationship with God. I began to focus on the promises of God if I remained obedient and faithful. I thought of the gift of salvation I received when I accepted Jesus Christ into my life as my savior. I knew my walk with Him wouldn't be perfect. I knew mistakes and missteps would be made. I knew I would stumble and sometimes even fall. The one thing that kept me committed was that, as long as was able to ask for forgiveness and keep getting up, My God would not desert me. I loved Jesus and trusted God. Sleep began to fall upon me and my eyelids started to tighten. My mind drifted off with thoughts of joy and happiness as I felt the Spirit of The Lord engulf me.

I heard water running and dishes clapping. The voices in my head grew louder and louder. My eyes opened to an unfocused view of the world around me. I lifted up my body and sat erect in the bed. Z Baby was up and the couch was fixed back up. I continued to hear voices coming from the kitchen. "Oh yeah, I thought to myself Shawn was here." I rose to my feet and stepped into the kitchen. They appeared to be having a lot of fun eating left-overs and watching TV. "Good morning my children or should I say good afternoon?" "Yeah Dad you should say good afternoon because it's two o'clock." Shawn seemed amused as he agreed with my correction. Z Baby just smiled and continued to eat. This would be our last full day together so I wanted to do something special with them. I would take them with me to pick up my check from Pathmark. This way Z Baby could see for herself the things we talked about over the phone. I would leave the rest of the day up to them. I would be open to do whatever they suggested. "I'm going to shower and get dressed. We are going to my job at the store and maybe to a movie or just window shopping." Nobody responded with any remarks but both their faces lit up. I went and gathered up my clothes and cosmetics and headed to the bathroom. I didn't plan on being a lot of time getting ready. I couldn't believe I had slept so long without waking up. The day would be disappearing fast and riding buses everywhere would make it go even faster. I kept my word in the bathroom and took a quick shower and got dressed in less than half an hour. I was generous with my cologne so I left the bathroom smelling as good as I was. The children were just finishing up their meals. I was glad they had eaten so I wouldn't have to buy tem anything while we traveled. They placed their dishes in the sink but Z Baby was washing off the table. I told Shawn to wash the dishes while his sister cleaned the rest of the kitchen. I put my wallet in my pocket and looked for my metro card. I had a spare one that the kids could use. We could make two trips on one fare if we rode the train first to the job. Then we would have a transfer on the card to use on the bus. I would often plan my travel this way to get the most from this new technology of the transit system. It was now 3:15 p.m. and everybody was ready to go. We all headed out the door with me making sure both locks were left on. We stopped for a minute to chat with the landlady who kept her room door open most times. That brief stop took time away from our trip but it was for a good cause. She had lived a long and fruitful life but her health was rapidly declining. She wasn't near death but her mobility had been reduced. We had a long relationship and she knew both my children from birth. She even witnessed my own decline and recuperation from immoral living.

We had now left the house to start our journey. We didn't walk as fast as I wanted to get the train. My children were much younger than me but they still didn't have my energy. We passed my church as we approached the train station. The streets were busy with activity and I acted like I didn't notice anything around me. We headed up the stairs to the elevated tracks to get the train. The ride to the store should only take about fifteen minutes. The walk to the store afterwards would also be just as long. We had to make our transfer to the bus within two hours of using the metro card. It then gave you an extra fifteen minute grace period. It would be no problem for us because I wasn't staying in the store longer than it took to get my check. The train pulled into the station and we all made our way downstairs. I reminded my children about the time schedule in hopes they would try to keep up with me. We were making good time as we walked down the long blocks along Queens Blvd. I entered the store and went straight to the payroll room. I found it closed and had to go to the manager's office for my check. It would not be a lot of money with all the deductions I had. The first ten percent went to a court judgment against me from a credit card. It didn't matter that my wife was also on the account. They were satisfied with the one they could find. The next priority was for child support which was a flat fifty dollars every week. Now it was time for me to put something away. I had twenty five dollars going to my credit union. The credit union for me was safer than a bank and yielded greater benefits. I made it to the office while my children waited in the front of the store. There were some curious looks on the faces of some co-workers. I didn't have the time to introduce them so I know they were wondering who they were. The manager gave me my check and I quickly open the envelope to ensure there were no mistakes. "Emmm very good;" I mumbled to myself. I had a little less than a hundred dollars which was more than usual. I had a lot of hours because of the busy holiday season. Thanksgiving was the biggest grocery time next to Easter Sunday. I left the store feeling elated that I not spent too much time in there. We only had to walk a few steps around the corner after leaving the store. The bus stop was right there and I could see a bus was already approaching in the distance. I pulled out my metro card and instructed my daughter to have hers ready too. We were half the distance to our stop in Jamaica, Queens from my house. It would be a short ride, if there were no accidents along Atlantic Ave. I asked my kids what they thought of the store where I worked. It was an irreverent question but I was just making some conversation. They responded in unison with; "It's alright." We rode for more than twenty minutes before we reached the last stop. The weather was nice for a fall day. There was still plenty of sunshine and there was a lot of activity on the streets. People were taking advantage of the many sales going on, for the first shopping day of the Christmas season. I was sticking to my plan of just window shopping to get an idea of what I should get them both for Christmas. It was extremely crowded as I fought to keep us from getting separated. My daughter's focus was on clothes and especially the jeans.

My son didn't seem too interested but talked about how expensive his clothes were because of his size. He wasn't tall but his girth required him to buy triple x clothing size. We walked around for hours looking at the styles and prices of fading summer fashions and the new fall lines. The sun had started to fade and the pain in my feet were making a come back. I suggested we start looking for a bus stop to get us back home. My daughter had a disappointed look on her face because I didn't buy anything. "Daddy what was the point of coming way down here, if you wasn't going to buy anybody anything?" Z Baby asked the question to get some understanding of my actions. She was always questioning things even as a little girl. It was cute than but I felt challenged now. "My child;" I responded. "It was good to get out of the house and just spend time with you guys in a different atmosphere. I wanted to get an idea of what you might need and what you may have wanted. Did I answer your question Z Baby?" "Yes Daddy, I understand now. "Are we making any more stops before we go home Daddy?" She was in need of information to make sure there would be no more surprises. "My child, we are going straight home." There was a crowd at the bus stop when we finally got there. Our bus was not the only one that stopped there, but you still needed to shove your way to the front, to keep from getting left behind. When the bus arrived we were able to get the three single seats along the driver side. We didn't have any bags to carry so we sat more comfortably than most of the other passengers. It was close to dark when arrived back in the neighborhood. We rode two extra stops in order to walk Shawn to his grandmother's house. I reminded him how early he needed to be at my house in the morning. "Shawn pack your bags tonight and just leave out the clothes you're going to wear in the morning." "Okay Dad, I was going to do that any way." We continued walking till we arrived at Shawn's grandmother's house. I waited for someone to answer the door after we rung the bell. I looked up to the window just as Shawn's grandmother started looking down to see who was ringing the bell. I told her how early Shawn had to be at my house in the morning. I knew she would make sure that he was there on time. We stared our walk back to the house as Shawn waved good bye. It was completely dark now and I was anxious to get to bed. It was a long day for me and my feet was still hurting. I didn't do as much as I wanted to but I did enough. I was glad there was nothing to clean up at the house. I had enjoyed the time with my children and had learned some new things about their personalities. I walked down my block and was surprised that there was no activity. It was still deserted like last night. Z Baby and I made our way upstairs. We then started walking up the creaky steps to the apartment. I noticed a light coming from the room of the landlord that stayed on my floor. His place was in sharp contrast to the neat and clean environment that I maintained. You could smell a strange odor emanating from his room whenever that door was open. I unlocked my door stepping inside just happy to be back at home. Z Baby used the bathroom before coming inside. I took off my sneakers and collapsed on the bed. I fell asleep watching Z Baby gathering her things for the trip back home tomorrow.

It was Saturday morning two days after Thanksgiving Day. I was wide awake and alert as I climbed out of bed. I could see my child's suitcase sitting in the corner partially opened as she slept nearby. I rose out of bed fully dressed as if I was prepared to leave the house. "Now I remember, I fell asleep before Z Baby." I was thinking out loud as I went into my closet to find an outfit for the day. I could hear Z Baby snoring softly as the first hint of daylight entered the room. I went into the bathroom with my clothes in tow. I turned on the shower to heat up the bathroom while I arranged my clothes neatly on the toilet seat. I stripped naked and viewed my out of shape body in the mirror. "Man I need to start exercising." I thought to myself. I stepped into the shower and let the hot water batter my body. "Oooo too hot;" I reached for the faucet and began to adjust the water until it was warm and not hot. "That's better so much better." I began my ritual of soaping up my rag until it looked liked a billowy cloud in my hand. I worked the suds all over my body as I dodged the water coming at me. I cupped my balls with the rag and applied enough soap to give it a mustache. My member also responded and began to stretch as I went up and down the length of the shaft. I swung the rag over my back and with one hand high and the other low, I worked the rag up and down until I felt the back was clean. I reached down to wash my feet as the water now beat down on my back. The water was now rinsing all the foam from me as I probed between my toes. My member had calmed down a lot since I left its area and I was close to being finished. I started rinsing all the soap from my rag I scanned the tub for any dirt that might have lingered around. I adjusted the water more until it was cool. I began the process of cooling off my body to close up the pores. This was something I had learned in Jr. High School when I was forced to use their showers. The shower system was a walk thru, with the water going from cool to hot to cool as you reached the end. I turned off the water and dried my body with my rag before reaching for a towel to finish the job. I cracked the bathroom door to let some of the heat to escape. It was hard to stay dry as I sweated profusely. My underwear

ZEKE SMITH

was sticking to me right after I put them on. I shook some powder down there to help alleviate that problem. I greased up the rest of me and finished getting dressed. The bathroom door was now fully opened as I stuck the deodorant stick under both my arms. I sprayed some cologne on my bare chest before putting on my tee shirt. I gathered up my clothes, went back into the room and woke up Z Baby. "Come on girl it's that time again. Go into the bathroom while some heat is in there." She began to stretch her body before rising out of the bed. My little girl was not a morning person and took a minute to focus before going to the bathroom. She returned in a few minutes and gathered the clothes; she had laid out the night before. I stuffed my dirty clothes in the hamper along with the bedding Z Baby had used. I began cleaning the room up and putting things back in there normal order. I went into the kitchen and began to pack some leftovers for her and Shawn. I made sure they both had enough banana pudding. I put some more to the side for my baby sister who loved it as much as I did. I began to worry about Shawn being on time so I made a phone call to make sure he was getting ready. Legs were supposed to be here at 8:00 a.m. and I wanted everyone ready when she came. Z Baby was still in the bathroom when I heard the bell ringing downstairs. I rushed down the creaky stairs to find Shawn at the door with his large suitcase. I left his bag in the vestibule and ushered him upstairs. "Hey son good morning, how do you feel?" "Good morning Dad, I'm okay." He was slow in his response and seemed a bit fidgety. I knew once he left, I would have to talk with his mother, to find out what was going on. Z Baby was finally finished in the bathroom and re-entered the room. "Hey Shawn what's up? She was all perky addressing her brother. I guess that shower did a good job of waking her up. "I'm alright Z Baby. I just want some of that banana pudding." I heard their conversation clearly because there was little distance between us no matter where you stood in my house. "I knew you would be hungry Shawn. I packed food for both of you. You have to wait and eat it on the road. Legs is on her way now and should be here any minute. Come on we can go downstairs as soon as Z Baby finish packing the rest of her clothes." It wasn't long before we all were headed down the creaky stairs together. The landlord and landlady both had their doors closed so the kids couldn't tell them bye. I grabbed Shawn's bag when we reached the bottom because he was carrying Z Baby's luggage. Z Baby was carrying the bags of food I packed for their ride home. By the time we made it to the sidewalk their transportation was pulling up. I went up to the car and saw gaunt looking Legs, trying to force a smile. "Good morning Baby." I said with a smile.

"Good morning Zeke." She replied in like manner." "I put enough food in Z Baby's bag in case you wanted some of the dinner I made." Legs looked at me with a glow that wasn't present when she first pulled up. She had a smile like the one I knew whenever we were in each other's arms. The smile took me so far back in our relationship that I almost said; "I love you baby." My insides began to heat up as I felt her trying to express regret and remorse about our separation. I began to wonder what would I do, if she asked me right then to come back home. I wanted to reach out and hug her where she sat but feared rejection. I wanted to stick my head in the car window and kiss her cheek but feared her anger. The seconds that went by felt like hours as my world was moving in slow motion. "Okay Daddy I'll call you when I get home. Bye Dad thanks for the food." The sound of my children saying goodbye brought me back to reality and speeded up the time. I stepped back from the car and went to my children. I began hugging them both as one by one they entered the car. I watched them drive away feeling good about the time I had with them. Then sadness and grief overcame me, as I thought about the struggles my wife was enduring without me. I made my way upstairs watching as the car disappeared down the block. My eyes were watering when I reached the top of the stairs. By the time I reached my front door and stepped inside, I was bawling like a newborn baby. I was feeling the pain of our separation like never before. I remembered the dream I had earlier that year, a dream that saw us together again and in love. The dream was so real and compelling, that I awoke that day and wrote a song. It was as if God was giving me a vision of what was to be. I never planned on returning to my wife because of the last betrayal. She left me so broken and disillusioned that I came close to losing respect for all women. I started a journey that had me see sawing between admirations for females to utter disgust. It became easy to entertain other men with my sexual escapades with willing victims. Yes victims, because even though they were being paid and enjoying what I was doing to them, I knew it was manipulation of their weaknesses. There were times when I turned into the counselor and tried to get them to repent from their ways. This was always done in secret because it would have angered my benefactors. I was glad to be free of that environment but it left me confused about what I was now feeling for my wife. I laid down on my couch and balled up into a fetal position. I stayed that way until I fell asleep.

It was 4:00 a.m. when a disturbing dream awakened me. In fact it was more like a nightmare. I had to struggle to break my sleep fearing that death was close at hand. I t was sweating profusely when I rose up and went to the bathroom. I pissed long and hard before applying a cold rag to my face. I looked in the mirror at myself realizing I had time to get high before daybreak. This was not a normal routine for me because it was Sunday morning. It didn't matter though because I wanted a hit and I wanted it now. I was still dressed from the day before. I had spent the rest of the previous day sleeping off and after my children left. I stepped out into the cool morning air and searched the dark corners of the block for one of the dealers. When I got someone's attention I nodded and made my way downstairs. I flashed two fingers to indicate how many I wanted. We met at half the distant from our locations and made the exchange. I looked up at the windows of my landlord to see if anyone was peeking between the blinds. I made my way back upstairs to begin the transformation with the drugs I had. I went into my kitchen and pulled out my tools. I lit a candle and turned on the window fan. I put in one of my porn tapes and turned on the TV. I drew my shades down and placed a towel over the area that I thought someone from the outside could look thru. I took off my sneakers and my pants, and before I sat down, I brought my jar of Vaseline and placed it on the table. I started my tape and began to shake out the little rock that would send me on a mission. I tilted my glass stem in the air and applied the flame. When it started to snap, crackle, and pop I slowly inhaled. The fumes filling my lungs began to take effect. I became horny and light headed as I exhaled before drawing on the stem again. Emmm it felt good as I looked up at the young women parading themselves butt naked in front of the camera. I loved pussy so much that it didn't have to be live for me to enjoy it. I took one more hit before setting the stem down to cool. The only light in the kitchen came from the TV. I stuck a finger in my jar of Vaseline and began to massage my penis. The drugs made my dick reluctant to respond right away. I continue to induce it with my gentle touches. My focus was on the tape as the camera began to reveal a close up of the pussy in front of me. My member now started to stretch and I couldn't have been happier. I wanted the two dimes I brought to last until daybreak. I didn't want getting high to affect my desire to go to church. I couldn't help my weakness or control the lust that was in me. I still knew that I needed to fellowship in order not to lose control. I didn't want to return to the pit I came from. This was a constant battle for me with all the distractions and temptations around me. I leaned back in my chair and stretched my legs out. I grabbed my balls and pulled them thru the opening in my underwear. I took another finger of grease from the jar and went back to work on the dick. There was steady stream of fresh pussy walking across the screen as my member struggled to achieve its maximum length. I enclosed my fingers around the shaft of my dick and began an up and down motion with my hand. This was the classical masturbation maneuver that most men practiced. The head of my dick became real tender as I continue this stimulating exercise. I squeezed tight as I could feel the pressure building up inside. "Ahhh Oooo" I cried out loud repeatedly. "OH come on; let me get this one Lord." I couldn't control the things I was saying. It was a natural response to an unnatural moment. My toes stuck straight out as my heels rested on the floor. I placed my left hand on the edge of the chair as my member started to bulge. I forced my dick down and aimed for the floor as my body bucked and fluid raced out of the small opening in my penis. "Emmm Ahhh Ohhh" Streams of the fluid splashed on the floor. I squeezed hard on the base of my cock and move my fist forward to its head. I wanted to empty the basin that stored this sperm. I enclosed the head of my cock with my fist as the last drops left the reservoir. I repeated this activity while the tape continued to play, until all the drugs were gone. I changed the tape as I began to clean up my mess. I stood up when it was over and masturbated one last time to bring myself down from my high. I did make it to church filled with guilt. I clapped and cried throughout the service constantly asking God to deliver me from this madness, which was my life.

"THE WRATH OF GOD"

T HE WEEK WAS proceeding so good that I began to feel nothing could go wrong. I made plans to pay my rent early. I started to make my list of all the people I would bless this Christmas. I assured myself that this would be the best ending to a year of mine, since the problems in my marriage. I even considered trying once again to reach my wife with passionate overtures. I saw myself as this great conqueror of adversity. You could not tell me that I wasn't "The Man." The one thing that I missed which just wasn't on my mind was God. I was giving my own efforts more glory than God's grace and mercy. I saw my own rise from the depths of despair as a personal accomplishment. I forgot to include God in the equation. I gave no credit to the power of Jesus Christ in my life. I would soon learn what a grave mistake that was.

I got up early Friday morning happy that the end of the week had finally arrived. I had some crumbs left from the day before and quickly disposed of them to start my day. It was just enough to get me started on preparing myself for work. I had to be there by 6:00 a.m. because of my pick up in Queens. I knew the bus schedule so timing was everything. I dressed hurriedly after first washing my ass. I lavished cologne all over me hoping that my Brooklyn passenger's daughter would help her mother to the van. I had a serious crush on her even though the relationship could go no where. What a woman may feel for me never stopped me from falling in love. Sometimes just the thought of her wanting me or the smile she might have when I said hello, would be enough to sustain my desire to have her. I made my way out to the chilly early morning air. I waved at the night crew gathered in front of the all night store. I had no time to shake hands or give high fives. My bus was barreling down the street headed to my stop. If I wasn't there when it arrived, it would keep on going. I was still sweating from my shower and the little hit I took when I woke up. My paper towels were damp including the one stuck in the rim of my hat. I stepped on the bus and swiped my metro card as I surveyed the area for a window seat. The bus was pretty packed as usual but most would be getting off at the stop near the train station. It would be at that time that I would find a seat better suited for my condition. The bus made its stop at Broadway Junction and like clockwork the bus was almost empty before the next crowd started to enter. I moved my seat where I could avoid eye contact with the driver. I always felt suspicious of people's glare, when I was under the influence of some substance. I knew by the time I reached the job I would be okay. It was the time in between that was the hardest to survive. I had to keep patting my face to keep the sweat from dripping in my eyes. It took twenty minutes for the bus to get me to my destination and I was happy to be there. I had plenty of time not to be late so I took my time as I walked to my job. The cold air was soothing to my face as the adrenalin rushing through my body began to slow down. I stepped inside of the office of the dispatcher. I swiped my time clock and received my route sheet from him. He assured me there were no changes I had to be aware of and I then proceeded out the door. The Brother that pumped the gas and made sure the vehicles were road ready was outside now. I called him Cool Breeze because he was a throw back to an era that I came from. We were about the same age and even lived in the same borough but I had moved on from the activities that he was involved in. We both still had a lot in common. We were both trapped in a job that we didn't like because of the pay. We both had passed up on earlier opportunities to do better when younger. We still had to do other tings to supplement the income that we received from these unappreciative employers. We were both smart enough not to quit without a guarantee of something better replacing it. We chatted for a minute about nothing important. I respected where he came from but he had trouble recognizing the depth of my intelligence. He often entertained himself by giving me advice that I either couldn't use or didn't need. I started up my vehicle and began my rounds. My first stop was close by and it was a young Hispanic girl that spoke little English. Her parents were very glad to have me as her driver because of my concern for her and my ability to communicate with her. When I spoke Spanish people thought that I was Cuban, Dominican, or Panamanian. I would often agree depending on who I was speaking with. My next pick up was the longest trip and the most important. I had to keep this elderly woman in my sights at all times and had to physically walk her to my van. It was daybreak when I left her house and headed to Brooklyn. I would have to make three more stops before dropping off my passengers at the Daycare Program before heading back out for my next group of clients. I went to my stop in East New York Brooklyn and one of the two people there weren't ready. I informed her that I would be back for her in ten minutes. She was generally ready and headed waiting for people that weren't, but God has a way of showing us the flaws in our character. I went to my favorite stop where that young woman lived, which I had the crush on. Her mother was always late but had improved a lot since I had started picking her up. I made her last and would call to wake her up before I got there. I still had to wait but I didn't mind because I was able to see my baby. She had a nice cinnamon complexion with good curves and an inviting smile. Her body was well proportioned for her size with ample breasts. If I arrived at the right time she would still be wearing her night clothes. She didn't mind me seeing her that way and a few times I got a good view as she trotted back upstairs. "Good morning Mr.Z"; she said in a soft voice. I looked at her in that bathrobe and stood frozen for a moment. I wanted her to see me admiring her body. I wanted to stare long enough for that vision to be implanted in my mind. "I said good morning Mr.Z" She had to repeat herself because I had not yet responded to her first greeting. "Oh good morning Dee, please let me take that from you." She was carrying her mother's walker downstairs as her robe flapped around her thighs. The belt for the robe hung at her sides at the short night gown underneath exposed her supple soft looking skin. She was quite the Goddess in my eyes and my member began to grow as she came closer. "My mother will be down in a second." I took the walker and began to turn away as I noticed a bag of garbage at the top of the stairs. "Okay Dee and why don't you hand me that garbage after I set this walker in the yard." She turned to walk back upstairs and as she reached for the bag I looked up to see the bottom of her butt cheeks. I almost stumbled with the walker as I rushed to place it in the front yard. I came back in the stairwell to see her body fully exposed as she carried the bag of garbage in front of her. "Thanks Mr.Z, you are so nice." The sound of her voice was like listening to a love song. I could not hide the bulge in my pants and didn't want to. I was hoping she saw it to understand how she affected me. I reached for the bag and began to speak in a voice so soft that I hardly heard it myself. "Thank you Dee and I think you're nice too. Can I take you out shopping one day and buy you a couple of outfits? I think it's a treat thing that you do for your mother." She stood there in front of me with one leg a step lower than the other. The hem of her gown had risen so high that I could see the vee where her panties were. When she leaned forward slightly to hand me the bag, gravity forced her breasts to swing towards me. My eyes kept shifting from her breasts to her panties as I continued to prolong her presence with small talk. The only thing that broke up our conversation was the arrival of her mother in the stairwell. "Come on Dee I can't get down the stairs with you standing there." Mrs. Jones was a little forceful in her voice. I stepped back and kept the bag in front of me to hide my erection. Her mother was no joke and very street smart. "Okay Ma, good bye Mr.Z." I watched as she turned around to go up the stairs. The robe swung wildly when she spun around. I got my last views of her luscious body as she walked away. I stood frozen until she disappeared into the house. I still had the bag of garbage in my hands when I asked Mrs. Jones if she needed any help. "No sugar I'm alright. You go ahead and take the garbage outside." She seemed very happy this morning. I think she approved of the extra time I spent talking to her daughter. She had once played match maker because she didn't like her grandchildren's father. She would often share information about her daughter when we all spoke in the van. My passengers were like one big family and we all had concern for each other. I finally got Mrs. Jones in the van and headed back to pick up Mrs. Brown who wasn't ready before. My front seat passenger who lived in Mrs. Brown building was disturbed about the amount of time I spent waiting for Mrs. Jones. He wore diapers and wanted to get to the center before he wet on himself. It took only a few minutes to go back. I double parked in front of the building and rung the bell to let Mrs. Brown know that I was downstairs.

I went and sat back in the van. We listened to the Steve Harvey Show on the radio as we waited for Mrs. Brown to come downstairs. There was a light rain falling and the ground was still wet from the heavy overnight rainfall. Everyone was in an upbeat mood as the radio broadcast entertained us. We were all wearing our seat belts and sitting quietly at this point. Mr. Smithfield started to complain about the long wait. "Come on Mr. Z, I need to use the bathroom. You should have taken us to the center before you came back here." He was right but it was too late to change now. Just as I was about to respond, I noticed Mrs. Brown exiting her building. I unfastened my seat belt to leave the van to assist Mrs. Brown getting in. It was policy not to let the passengers enter the van without assistance. I always followed the rule with no exceptions. It also gave the clients more dignity with that type of personal attention. We were one family and I used any instance to make that point. I checked my rearview mirror for any oncoming traffic as I held on to the door handle with the door partly ajar. I was parked about seven car lengths from the corner in front of the building. The misty rain was still falling when I saw a big Lincoln turning the corner behind me. There was a four way stop sign at that intersection and no other cars were waiting. The Lincoln barely slowed down as he made the turn. He never came to a stop and began to fish tail as he made the right turn. I froze in my place and seconds seemed like minutes as the

ZEKE SMITH

huge car came swerving down the street. My body was still twisted with my eyes glued to the rearview mirror when the car hit the van. I had no time to warn anyone before the impact. I had no time to straighten out my own body or to close the door tight. I didn't realize the car was going to hit us until it happened. The whole scene was like watching a movie in slow motion. We all jerked forward and then were flung back in our seats from the impact. The collision was severe and we were all in shock. My passengers didn't know what had happened but I did. I tried to gather my thoughts as the adrenalin began to race through my body. "Is everybody alright?" I asked in disbelief of what had just happened. I started to try to exit the van to check on the passenger of the other car. I figured he was either sick or drunk to have been driving the way he was. What made him think that he could make that turn at that speed on a wet pavement? I started to hear a grinding noise like metal against metal when I realized the big Lincoln was backing up. I closed my door and watched from the mirror as he began to maneuver the car around me. I looked out my window as he drove passed. The car was literally crawling as it passed. His air bag had engaged so I couldn't see his face, but I knew it was a large Hispanic man from his hands and clothing. "I began to recite his license plate in my head. "7578XYM" The front end of his car was completely smashed in. It was a miracle that he could still drive. The front right corner of his bumper was embedded in his tire. I could smell rubber burning as he passed. "7578XYM! Somebody give me a pen and remember that number." I shouted to my passengers more concerned for them than myself. They all said they were alright except for Mr. Smithfield. He had wet on himself during the commotion. I finally was able to open my door, still checking for oncoming traffic. I stumbled out into the cool dismal air. The light mist had stopped falling but the heavy overcast made the scene even more eerie. Mrs. Brown was still standing in front of her building in disbelief of what had just happened. "Are you alright?" She asked as I walked towards her. "I think so Mrs. Brown. Do you have a pen and piece of paper in your bag?" She began to rummage through her bag until she came up with the items I had asked for. "Here you go Mr. Z, that jerk didn't even stop." Mrs. Brown was a member of my church and a good Christian. She looked poised to say some ungodly things about the man that had just hit us. I began to write down the license plate number and the time of the accident. "The time was 7:30 a.m. License plate number 7578XYM, LARGE DARK COLORED Lincoln Continental." I was still writing down information when someone approached me. I put the paper and pen in my pocket and started dialing 911. In all the excitement and concern for the passengers, I still had not alerted the police. The middle age woman that had just approached me began to speak. "The car that hit you is parked around the corner. It's my neighbor." She had not seen the accident but putting two and two together she realized what had taken place. She was out walking her dog, when her neighbor parked his damaged vehicle and ran in the house. "Thank you Miss I appreciate your help." I was grateful for her help and the information she gave. I began to speak with the 911 operator and gave her all the info that I had. She asked about injuries and I stated that the passengers were elderly and I was shook up. She informed me that she would send the police and an ambulance. I started to walk around the van to assess the damage. The operator wanted to know if the vehicle could move and was it blocking traffic. When I got to the back of the van I saw that the back bumper was completely crushed in. The force of the crash had caved in the back door preventing it from opening. The rear bumper had also wedged itself against the back door too. I went and helped Mrs. Brown into the van to shield her from the cold air. It was now time to wait for the Calvary as pain began to arrive in my body.

The more I moved the more I hurt. The drugs I had that morning had wore off. I began to realize that was the reason I didn't initially feel anything. I was still puzzled about someone driving that recklessly in this weather. The big car never had a chance once the driver committed to making that turn without stopping. One of the gawkers standing around began to inform me about the company I worked for. He said he had been in an accident with them and they tried hard to avoid any responsibility. He said that he was still fighting his case and that I should be careful. I was not concerned about that now. I wanted to know if I was hurt or just sore from the impact. I started hearing sirens as an ambulance and a fire company arrived at the same time. I called the dispatcher to inform him of the accident and the condition of the passengers. He was more concerned about me finishing the run than about anybody's health. "Are you listening to me?" I shouted in the phone. "The van can't move and the fire department and ambulance is here now. You have to send another van and a driver because I'm going to the hospital." I didn't think my pain was enough for a hospital trip. I started thinking about what the gawker had said and figured better safe than sorry. I thought about when a car ran over my wife's foot and she didn't think anything was wrong. The next morning she woke up, the foot was as big as a cantaloupe. The ambulance attendant came over to me and asked if I was hurt. I said I think so but to please check on my passengers first. She was reluctant at first until I explained that most were elderly with previous medical conditions. She led me over to the back of the ambulance and had me sit down. The police had returned to tell me that they located the car that struck us. They even said that they tried to switch drivers but a neighbor came forward and identified the right one. The fireman came up to me to ask if the company was sending anyone out. There were some fluids all over the street that they had started to hose down. My head started to throb and my back had sharp pains. My right wrist was sore and I began to feel a little dizzy. My heart started racing again as I began to feel some high anxiety. The female attendant had finished checking the passengers and returned to me. She said everybody was alright and how was I feeling. Time was moving fast but I was going in slow motion. I would try to respond to one person and then another would pop up with more questions. My head started spinning and before I knew it someone was waking me up. I had been sitting in that ambulance for almost an hour before someone finally showed up from the job. I was tired of the firemen and the police pressuring me. I now had to furnish paperwork for the vehicle which was no simple task. I had to furnish my own license and credentials to prove that I was legal. There was just too much going on at once, while the medical technicians wanted to get me to the hospital. "Damn this was payday! I did not want to be out of work for Christmas." I was thinking so loud it felt like everybody could hear me. They took my blood pressure and found it to be high. They were also concerned because I had fainted too. I got permission from the technicians to check on my passengers and let them know I was going to the hospital. I also had to give the police a list of there names and addresses, which I got before I left them. The dispatcher had come himself with another driver. I left them in charge and proceeded to focus on me. We left the scene and went directly to the hospital. When we arrived there it didn't matter that an ambulance had brought me. It was still a wait before anyone attended to me. The first thing they wanted to know was did I have health insurance. I completed that process and was soon tended to by a doctor. My wrist was wrapped up and I received some pain killers and muscle relaxers. I had to get the prescriptions filled on my own, but I was given enough for my first two dosages, before I left. The strangest thing happened while I was waiting for the doctor to see me. The receptionist called me over to the phone to speak with someone. There already was an attorney trying to make contact. Now I understood why insurance was so high. People in New York couldn't wait to sue and the lawyers were standing in line to help. I declined their services still puzzled about the legalities of that phone call. It was 2:00 p.m. when I finally left the hospital. I had chosen this hospital when given the option earlier because it was along my route to the job and home. I went by my job to pick up my check. The accident was already being talked about when I got there. The dispatcher gave me my check and asked if I would be coming back to work. He then asked if I had a lawyer. I looked at him in disgust and disbelief because he never asked me if I was okay. He never offered any type of assistance concerning my health. "Yeah you won't be back. I guess you're going to be suing us next?" The words came from his lips cold and dry with little emotion. He appeared more upset than me about the accident I had. What did I do wrong? I was parked when someone hit me but to them it didn't matter. I left there wondering what next. I guess I did need a lawyer. I guess the gawker was right about them. It wouldn't be long before poverty would overtake me, when everything seemed to be going so well. It wouldn't be long before my body would start to fall apart. I would soon be broke, broken, and bother by a situation that I thought I not caused. God would reveal after months of lawyers, doctors, and therapy, why He did what He did.

My weekend was not what I had planned, just a few days ago. Here it was Saturday morning and I was still in the bed. I didn't have the energy or the motivation to rise. In such a short time my whole world had changed and I was still trying to figure out what to do with it. I still had all the money from my check. I was supposed to work at my other job today but would have to call in. "Damn, what should I do? Is this a curse or a blessing?" The conversation I was having in my head went on for almost an hour. I sat up in my bed and looked around the room. I noticed all the things that I had accumulated the past few years. I thought about how depressed I was when I left that jail in 2002. In fact it was almost the same time of the year. "Damn Z, that makes it four years!" My mind began to clear and I realized that I did need some rest. I would leave it to the medical professionals to tell me what to do. My rent had been paid already so I canceled Christmas until some new money arrived. I called the store to let them know I was in an accident and would be out for awhile. They were cooperative and I didn't think they would miss me. I began to blame myself for my situation. I was so ready to show my friends and family how grateful I was for our relationship. I wanted to give gifts to the people that had given me support through all the turmoil I experienced. My wife leaving with my daughter after having me locked up left me bitter and cold. It took the associations of others to heal me and get me living again. I wanted everyone to know the journey I took to arrive where I was at. The drugs had provided me some comfort after I was forced back into an area I would have never chosen on my own. The drugs were as available as the people that sold them. The women young and hold that hung around them was another reason to indulge. Pussy was always a weakness since the time I knew what it was. I had allowed the enemy to enter back into my life with an engraved invitation. The space between me and God slowly widen until the gap was too large to reach Him. I had to deal with the consequences now and it was painful.

It was time to get up out of this bed. I had never slept until 10:00 a.m. even when I came in late. I got dressed and rode downtown to the bank. I didn't need this much money around the house. I had to go back to the doctor on Monday for the results of the x-rays they took at the hospital. It seemed as if this accident was going to be dominating my time for awhile so I thought it best to call a lawyer. I checked the back of the emergency room receipt for the phone number I had wrote for the attorneys. I had to place the paper under the bright sunlight from the window, in order to read it. I made the call but got their answering machine. I left my information without specifying the reason for the call. If they were a legit outfit they would know who I was. I stayed in for the rest of the day, still shocked from the events of Friday. I had no desire to get high and instead focused on changing my life once again. I was never so foolish to ignore when God was dealing with me. It seemed at times that my relationship with Him was complicated because of all the trials I went through. I never gave up on the idea that one day soon God would deliver me from all my burdens and afflictions. When the sun went down, I showered and got ready for bed. I was eager for this day to be over and looked forward to being, in church worshipping The Lord. All around me you could see evidence of the approaching holiday. I was not feeling the cheer or glad tidings that were expected. I should have felt blest for having my life. I should have felt blest for still having a roof over my head and food in the house. No, it wasn't enough for me right now. I felt cursed and betrayed by God for having my plans dramatically altered by an act that God orchestrated.

I rose from my sleep early Sunday morning ready to confront The Lord on His home turf. I knew He would be present at church. Our devotional service always brought God in the house with the many testimonies of His Mercy and Grace. I pulled out my favorite power suit for its fit and color. It was a black and white, wide patterned plaid, and double breasted. It hung snug on my body and I always felt good wearing it. I matched it up with a solid black cotton shirt and a powder blue and gray tie. My shoes were black and I shined them enough to look like glass. I was still carrying my beige bible that I kept from my wife. This was the only thing that I left with from her that she didn't try to take back. I always felt connected to the household that I was evicted from whenever I used it. I had sweat real bad during the night so I found myself taking another shower to kill time and funk. It looked like it would be another bright and sunny day but the air would still be cold. I would be wearing a double set of underwear on this day. I put on a pair of briefs to hold me in with a wife beater tee underneath my thermal. My second pair of drawers was the bottom half of the thermals with the legs cut off. I wore my best black socks that I didn't have to stretch to fit my legs. I didn't have any fancy head gear to compliment my outfit. I wore an ill fitting black cap with a stocking cap underneath. I passed on breakfast this morning. I didn't want my stomach getting any larger than what it was. I drunk a large glass of juice to wash down the pain pill I took. I left my house at 8:30 a.m. to take the slow walk around the corner to my church. I walked down the stairs and pass my sister's apartment. I could see she was up and getting ready herself. I began to recall how she approached me one Sunday evening and asked me to make sure she was up. She was upset one time when she had over slept so bad that she missed service. If I didn't hear her inspirational morning prayer from my bathroom, I knew she was still asleep and would make the call. Yes, I had to call because any noise would spook her and she usually didn't hear a knock. I continued on out the door down the steep brownstone steps that led to the sidewalk. I saw the small group of dealers gathered across the street with their loud chatter about sports. It was football season and that scene would be repeated until the Super Bowl was played. I would not be crossing the street on this morning. I would not be flashing any signals to indicate that I wanted to make a purchase. I just waved with my right hand as I clutched my Bible in the left. I had a noticeable limp now because of the injury to my right knee. My right hand grip was also weak from the twisting motion that occurred when the car struck my van. I continued my strut as I crossed the street at the corner. I looked across Broadway and observed the other regular group gathered every morning about this time. This was a mixture of dealers, wanna bees, and local residents either looking for company or a favor. I waved again at this bunch but added some vocals with the hand gesture. "Alright yawl"; I hollered as I walked past them on the other side of the street. I began to pick up my paste a little and had a new rhythm to my walk. I began to approach the long dormant train station that only served as a free pass to board for those brave enough to risk it. You had to have the climbing skills of a mountain goat to be successful. I looked at the front door of the house my family used to occupy before the Italian butcher gave up on it. It was now owned by an old school dealer that couldn't escape the world that brought him some luxuries. I just nodded at this group although some beckoned for more recognition. I had blazed the trail for all these guys' activities, so why should I be mad. It wasn't their activities that bother only the fact that I was back to witness them. I now approached the corner bar that was no longer a bar. This bar provided me much entertainment and notoriety during its heyday. It had stopped being operational decades ago but it still remained empty. There was no one willing to risk time or money to rehab the building. The only ones with comfort were the rats that frolicked freely inside. I continued along with my new hobble step and crossed the wide intersection. When I reached the other side I stood at the corner edge of a large structure that used to house a Loews Theater. It was now the Wayside Baptist Church. I had watched it grow through the years. I always admired its resiliency and the ability to grow when everything else around it was shrinking away. This was now my church home and I was proud to be a part of it. I had forged some solid relationships with the members. I had a connection with the Pastor who took pleasure in responding to my need for guidance and understanding. I wanted to be a Christian operating in faith as much as I had wanted to be a gangster operating in secrecy. The structure was almost the length of the block. There was a parking lot in between it and the other building next to it that once held a large supermarket. The supermarket became available sometime after the Blackout of 1977. This area was one that was hardest hit in New York and many businesses just disappeared. It took up until now for the area to make a real comeback. The church refurbished that structure and created additional space for dining and bible study. I saw that one of the trustees had already started sweeping the front. This was something that I looked forward to doing also. It was my means of making a real investment in the church with my labor. It also gave some opportunities to spread the gospel to passer byes. "Good morning Brother Taylor. Where's the other broom at?" He turned to look towards me and offered some comforting words before handing me the broom he was using. "Brother Zeke, you can use this one. I have some more things to do inside. Thank you." "No Brother Taylor, thank you." I always felt good about serving God and His people. I could never do enough for The Lord because of all the grace and mercy He extended to me. I died more than once and escaped being maimed just as many times. I knew there was a God even before I knew about Jesus. I removed every hint of any activity that was left on the ground from the night before. I made sure that even the cigarette butts didn't survive my sweeps. I scooped up as much dust as I could bunch up. I learned before that I usually had to rebuff my shoes when I finished my chore. I completed cleaning up in time enough to be an early arrival to my Sunday school class. I was not alone when I arrived upstairs where classes were held. Mrs. Garfield was there and we began the task of setting up the chairs and tables in their proper order. I always enjoyed Mrs. Garfield's company because she seemed so committed to Bible study. I also felt that a relationship with her would better my chances of success in God's kingdom. I once asked her if she would like to assist me in my study of the word. I tried to express my true feelings to her but was rejected. She suggested that I find a male in the church to mentor me. I needed more than a mentor. I needed female companionship that I respected enough not to try and seduce. She was that type but I couldn't tell her that. She was a much more mature woman and a snappy dresser. She appeared to have only a teenage son who seemed devoted to her. His relationship with her reminded me of the one I had with my mother. She had almost an entire head of gray hair that was always styled nice. In spite of her age she looked good and smelled even better. I did not attend church hoping to find a mate but I wouldn't reject any choice that God sent to me. I remained hopeful and continued to enjoy her company whenever she was around me. She would always flash an inviting smile that covered her whole face. She even blushed the time when I asked to study with her. We were almost done when other members began to enter the room. Our teacher usually arrived within minutes of the time for the class to start. Our Sunday school teacher was a committed Christian woman with strong moral character. I had developed a close relationship with her because she was attentive t my spiritual needs. She had suffered a lot of tragedy in her family including the death of her husband and sister. My hand was always raised in response to questions asked by her during our classes. I was also able to call her no matter the time of day if I needed some counseling or direction. "There she is now." I thought almost out loud as she entered the room. She began to set front of the room up in preparation for the start of class. The class always began with us joining hands in prayer which was followed by the reading of a scripture. We then sung our class song "Blessed Assurance" before the lesson began. Everything went as usual with no outstanding events to mention. I fully participated in the lesson even though my

ZEKE SMITH

thoughts were on my failure to be more obedient to God's Word. My sister was in attendance on this day and gave a lot of input on the content of the lesson. We then ended our session with prayer requests in which I quickly asked for prayers for my own commitment to the Lord. We left class afterwards and some of us joined others in the main building in our snack room, while others went straight to the sanctuary. I always had snacks, not just for the food but also for the opportunity for additional fellowshipping with other saints. I made sure that I found my seat in the sanctuary before devotional service started. I bowed my head down while seated and began to pray. I first asked for God's forgiveness of my sins and transgressions. I then acknowledged His greatness and thanked Him for the grace and mercy that He extended to all of us. I expressed my gratitude for His gift of salvation that came with the sacrifice of His Son. I began to cry as I began to thank Him, for His patience in waiting for me, to come to Him and accept His Son as my Savior. The tears began to fall to the floor as humility engulfed me. I thought of the journey I took to reach this point. I thought about the many set-backs I encountered in my walk with The Lord. I started feeling remorse and shame for my misdeeds with my family, fiends and strangers. I asked again for forgiveness as my crying became uncontrollable. The devotional service had started and was in full bloom as I continued my praying. There was something so different about this day. I began to feel God's presence all around me. I felt The Holy Spirit envelope me in warmth. I began to feel a comfort that I had not experienced before. I felt as if a heavy burden had been lifted as I began to recite details of my past wrongs. I started accepting responsibility for my current situation. There was some shouting going on in the background but I continued to listen to The Lord as remembered the promises he made. "I will never leave you or forsake you." I lifted my head up and rose to my feet as the tears continued to flow down my cheeks. The sanctuary was rapidly filling up as others began to occupy the empty spaces in my row. It was the regular people that generally sat around me. I always tried to seat in the center of the middle section. I liked making eye contact with who ever was delivering the sermon. I started clapping my hands and shouted; Hallelujah, Hallelujah, Hallelujah, thank you Jesus, yes thank you Jesus. I reached for the handkerchief in my pocket and patted my cheeks dry. I returned to my seat drained of all my energy. I was now ready to receive the message from God that would be delivered from the Pastor. The choir began to sing a rendition of the song "I cried my last tear yesterday" by Mary, Mary. The lead singer began to belt out the song as my emotional level started to rise again. I again started to think about all that I had overcome to get to this point. I raised my hand a few times to signal the presence of the Lord. The Pastor rose to the altar as the choir was finishing up the song. The song was a lead in to the sermon he had prepared. He preached about regrets that we sometimes have about past behaviors and situations. He talked about the difficulty of letting go of those things that imprisoned us. I knew I was struggling myself and felt his words were meant for me. He reminded us of the joy and glory that comes when we fully trust God to care for our needs. He reminded us that letting go sometimes refer to the people that we associated with. He said those people are sometimes close friends and relatives. He preached about the necessity of being like Job, who held on to his faith in spite of the difficulties he was facing. We have to keep trusting God in the good times and during the trials. He referred to different scriptures to support the word he was preaching. I was attentive and spiritually connected to everything he was saying. The church began to respond to the words flowing from his lips with shouts of amen and hallelujah. I was no different as I too began to shout as I rose to my feet. I was not alone standing as the Pastor began his walk from the pulpit preaching and shouting. I was mesmerized by his ability to capture the congregation with the different pitches of his voice. He ended his sermon by asking; "Who wants to trust Jesus? Who wants to forget the past and trust Jesus to change their future?" The deacons began to come to the front and ring the altar. The entire church rose to their feet as the Pastor opened the doors to the church and invited anyone to come forward and accept Christ as their savior. A young woman came forward carrying her baby. She was soon followed by a young man wearing jeans and sneakers walked down the aisle with tears rolling down his face. My eyes began to water as I felt compassion for what they both must have been feeling. The congregation clapped and the Pastor continued with his invitations as he asked if anyone wanted to recommit themselves to Christ. He begged for anyone fearful to take that walk to just trust God and come forward. There would be no one else on this day. The young woman with the baby and the young man wearing sneakers and blue jeans were ushered to the back by some deacons and deaconess. He now asked for anyone in need of prayer to come and stand before the altar. My sister the minister flanked him along with two other associate ministers. One third of the congregation and me walked down the aisle as the front quickly filled up. Most of us were left standing in the aisles facing each other and holding hands. My sister would be the one delivering the prayer today. The words flowed from her mouth like music as she called upon the Lord to intercede on behalf of his people, in the name of Jesus. She asked for a healing of the sick and faith and hope for the lost and misguided. She prayed for God to comfort the bereaved and show compassion towards those incarcerated. She asked for an uplifting of everyone's spirit in spite of their circumstances. She called again in the name of Jesus that all present would receive the message preached today and apply it to their lives. She then asked for the gory of God to continue to fill this place and hearts of us all. She ended by asking God to protect the church and all its officers and members. She ended with three amen, and each was louder than the one before. The new saints were brought back out and stood before the congregation. The two of them were candidates for baptism. It was unanimous when it was asked if all present were in agreement with them being accepted into the body of Christ. This was a normal formality before they became official members of our church. They would have to go through a four week course of new member classes first. The congregation had returned to their seats by now and was just waiting to be dismissed. The Pastor gave the benediction right after the new members were welcome to the church. I hugged and shook hands with those around me as I searched for a clear lane to the door. I hobbled my way through the crowd until I reached the outside. I was filling good now and just wanted to be home. I had a Monday morning appointment with the lawyers and didn't want to be late. I was determined not to let the message I received today to go unused.

I was awakened Monday morning by the bright sunlight coming through my windows. It had to be late in the morning for the sunlight to be so bright. I rose from the bed well rested but stiff. My back was hurting and my right knee could hardly bend. The lawyers wanted me at their office at 11:00 a.m. I had enough time to get ready because it was just 9:30 now. I put two eggs on the stove to boil while I went into the bathroom to take a shower. It would be all business while I was in there because time was too short to be playing around. It felt good to have the hot water beating down on my back. The soreness began to leave some but my knees continued to hurt. I didn't give a lot of thought to my situation now. I knew God was in charge and all things would happen in His time. I trusted God enough to care for me through my current ordeal. I gathered up my belongings and left the bathroom after rinsing out the tub. I was always tempted to leave it dirty because that's the way the landlord always left it. He was such a pig but I had no choice but to live with him right now. I never imagined that a sane man could live this way and not be affected by it. I did my usual ritual of applying grease, deodorant, and cologne to my naked body, while watching one of my favorite porn tapes. I then got dressed but not before I had came at least once. I slicked the patch of hair back on my head with some bee's wax. I then applied a little hair grease to give it some luster. I had been growing my back on my head since my daughter had left on Thanksgiving. I wanted her to see what I looked like. I also wanted to know how long it would take to get enough up there to comb. I turned off my eggs before all the water disappeared from the pot. I ran some cold water over them before I began to peel them. I loved my boiled eggs, especially between two slices of buttered toast. I washed everything down with some juice before leaving the house. It was a long train ride to Coney Island where the lawyer's office was located. I arrived there a few minutes early and given a lot of forms to fill out. It was no simple task to complete the paperwork because I was still stiff from the train ride. The attorney finally came out and spent a few minutes explaining the process to me. I was given a clinic to go to for my physical therapy. I was then given a referral to a Workman's Compensation attorney to fill another claim. My case was in two parts requiring separate lawyers to handle it. It didn't make since to me but that was the law. This lawyer firm which was called Reuben and Reuben could only handle the no fault case against the driver of the car. The workman's compensation attorney would represent me against my job since I was hurt while working. I became suspicious right after leaving the office because I spent more time with the secretary than the lawyer. I had to go straight to the doctor's office for my therapy. I had two locations to choose from. I picked the one closest to my home that was easy to get to.

It took me more than an hour to get to this place. I stood outside their store front office wondering if this was actually the right place. The address matched but the place looked a bit shoddy. I hobbled inside and identified myself. Once again I was given a bunch of forms to fill out. I was then seen briefly by a doctor who listed all my injuries and complaints. The office manager was the next person to interview me and gather the information concerning my legal representation. He then explained that my bills would be paid by the workman's compensation claim and not No Fault Insurance. I was shown the sign in sheet and allowed to begin therapy that day. The most I could come was five days a week but no less than three. I moved with caution even though I had a legitimate claim. I was victimized once before along with my insurance. They didn't respond to my concerns and eventually paid the claim without my approval. The therapy session left me feeling good. I was looking forward to the next one. I was not eligible for any money because I was a workman compensation case. I would have to file a claim for any expenses I incurred with my attorneys. I only had to walk across the street and maybe an additional yard to catch the bus that would take me home. The bus ride lasted about twenty minutes if there were no traffic jams. I arrived back in the hood tired and sore. I stopped briefly in the supermarket before going upstairs. I wanted to get something for dinner that didn't need thawing. I gripped the right side of the banister and pulled myself up the stairs. It was such a relief to be back in my house. I would have to repeat this process again tomorrow but at least I knew what to expect.

Week after week I continued my therapy sessions with some days being better than others. The major advantage for me was that I had a doctor that could write the prescriptions for me. I was able to even get a stronger drug because what the hospital gave me wasn't working. My new drug was the strongest I could get. I was concerned about taking a codeine based pain killer because of my addiction. I still didn't let that stop me and besides it became a high I could get without roaming the streets. I began to withdraw from my neighbors and also my associates at the church. The drugs made it easy because I felt nothing emotionally about my actions. I spent the entire month of December in the house, leaving only to get groceries, go to therapy or to play a number. Yes, I had started to gamble again even playing dice when a game was available. I found myself ducking church members because of my guilt and ungodly behavior. I didn't even come out for Christmas. I sent my daughter some things and the rest of the world didn't matter. One of the deacons from my church lived nearby and did a lot of jogging in the area. I was at the bus stop one afternoon on my way to therapy. The jogging deacon came out the store behind me and I couldn't avoid speaking with him. He was concerned about my absence from church and asked what was wrong. "I've been in a lot of pain lately from my accident. I've wanted to come but my medication makes me sleepy. I don't want to be there and keep nodding off." I kept a straight face as one lie after another fell from my lips. Once I got started it was hard to stop. He was an attentive listener and when I finished speaking he responded. "Well Bro. Zeke I didn't know about your accident I will be praying for you. I know how you feel about falling asleep but that can happen to anyone. I hope you can make it for the midnight service on New Years and trust God to keep you alert." He stood silent as I quickly glanced up the street to see if my bus was coming. I turned to him feeling so much shame for my and actions and responded to his suggestion. "Thank you so much Deacon for caring. I guess I will skip a dosage that night because I will be there. Thanks again Deacon." I spread my arms out and embraced him for a hug. I felt no shame whenever I sought some love from one of my Christian brothers. He raised his arms and hugged me too saying; "It's going to be alright Bro. Zeke, just pray and trust God." We loosened our grip on each other and stepped back. He began to cross the street and I glanced up the block again and saw a bus making its way towards me. When it got close enough I saw that it was the one I was waiting for. I boarded the bus thinking only of my conversation with the deacon and the way God had just moved in my life.

I walked into the doctor's office hoping that I would be able to get a prescription for my pain killers. I thought therapy would get me some back massages but that was not the case. I was spread out on a table that vibrated. They would then apply these hot towels to the areas that I complained about. I was not getting any treatment for my wrist or my knee. It lasted about one hour and always left me feeling rejuvenated. Christmas was right around the corner now and depression was right at my door. I mailed off my daughter's package and was certain she would receive it way in advance. It was almost time for my session to end. The therapist came into the room and drew back the curtains. She carefully began to remove the tabs and hot towels from my body. I smiled at her and she smiled back. I told her I wanted to ride the stationary bike before I left. I knew I had to start doing something to help this knee because walking was becoming more and more difficult. I went straight home when I finished my session. I was given the holiday schedule and signed myself out. I wished everybody a happy holiday and told them I would see them all next year. I got a kick out of saying that during this time of the year. The office would be closed for a week and reopen after New Year Day. The rest of the week was uneventful and went by very quick. I received a call from my daughter thanking me for the gifts and money I sent. My son also called and wished me a merry Christmas and then apologized for not sending me anything. This had to be one of the saddest Christmases I had since being an adult. I had so much hope this year but God saw otherwise. I continued to fight my depression with the memories of past times when I felt more joy. It was near the end of the week and New Year's Eve was Thursday. I would be in church on that night repenting and asking God for some forgiveness.

It was really no fun being in the house all day, but my focus was on being here in the year 2007. It had been a practice since I could remember not to die so close to the New Year. I don't know what made me start this but I had no problem with it. My mother would also encourage me to be home when the New Year arrived. She never wanted a woman to cross her threshold before a man. I could remember rushing over there some mornings when she was alive to accommodate her. I wanted to dress comfortable for church services but I also didn't want to look like I was hanging out. I decided on some dress slacks with a nice dress shirt with a collar. I shined my shoes real good and wore a leather jacket that was light enough to keep on in church. It was way past 10:00 p.m. and I figured I should start out since I had all my clothes on. I took my time making the short walk to the church. There was plenty of activity on the streets but I avoided eye contact with most of the ones that I past. I was not going to start the New Year the way I ended the old one. I would be letting go of some old friendships and relationships and reinforcing the new ones I had. My congregation would have to be the foundation on which I would build a future on. There were some real good people there besides my sister that I had grown close to. I had established my own identity with those that didn't know me previously. When I walked into the sanctuary there were only a few inside. The service was not scheduled to begin until 11:00 p.m. I found my usual spot in the center of the middle section empty. I quickly went and sat down and began to pray. "Dear Father God, in the name of Jesus, I ask that you first forgive me for my sins and transgressions and I thank you Father for delivering me safely to this place. I think you Father for keeping me thus far and protecting my home and family. You have been so good to me Father this year by providing me with employment and a good church home. I just pray Father that you continue to protect me and keep me in the company of your Angels. In the name of Jesus Father please keep the path of righteousness brightly lit before me. In the name of Jesus keep me empowered by the Holy Spirit. I will continue to rely on you for my sustenance and guidance. I recommit myself to service unto you and will be a willing vessel to deliver blessing to your people. Protect my neighborhood and my neighbors and I pray that they all come to know you as I do. Watch over my wife and daughter, for they are out of reach from my protection. I await the day father that you will deliver me from my loneliness and reunite me with my wife. I ask all these things in the name of Jesus. Amen!" I began shedding tears as the service began to start. I felt the pain in my body and heart, begin to subside. I felt a wave of warmth pass through me. The tears stopped flowing and I rose to my feet as I felt the presence of God all around me. My hand clapping and shouting took over as I began to praise the Almighty for giving me this day and this moment. "Thank you Jesus, thank you Jesus, I repeated over and over again. I sat down still excited as the devotional service ended and the sermon began.

The sermon was a timely message for me because of all the uncertainty I had about the New Year. It caused me to reflect further about my situation and take responsibility for it. I knew this year of 2007, I would have to let go of some things which also included people. I would not be able to change the thinking and destructive behaviors I were practicing, if I remained in relationships with some current friends. I could not be concerned with how anyone felt when I began to distant myself from them. When service was over and the New Year started I received many hugs before I left the church. I had no invitations for a midnight meal, so I began my short journey home. The message from the pastor was fresh in my mind and I felt strengthened by it. People on the street were saying "happy New Year" to those they passed. I was no different but I kept my distance and didn't break my stride. I could feel some stomach cramps indicating hunger. I felt regrets about not starting my meal earlier as I usually did on New Year's Eve. The regular street dealers were no where to be seen. They were probably at some party now but would be out here later. I was happy about that because they were the last people I had a Happy New Year for. My block was empty and quiet except for the distant gunfire. The hoods and some regular folks felt firing off their weapons was a good way to bring in another year. This was the only time some of them had a chance to even shoot off their pistols and rifles. "Ahhh home at last!" I cried softly as I put my key in the door. I ascended the next flight of steps and took a quick piss in the bathroom before I unlocked my apartment door and stepped inside. I kicked off my shoes and begin to shed my clothes. I felt aroused as I did this but fought back those erotic feelings. I was not going to let sex or drugs rule me this year. The two were so closely connected for me, that I had to stop both to get rid of one. I went into the kitchen and pulled out a twin pack of Cornish hens. I poured a half of bag of dried back eyed peas in a pot of water to soak with some added seasonings. I put a half a cup of white rice in a small pot and covered it up. I had a bag of frozen collar greens that I just sat on the sink. I took a half gallon bottle of cider and placed it in the freezer. I titled my kitchen blinds so that the sun would come through whenever it decided to arrive. I stepped out of the kitchen but left the light on. I picked up the clothes I had just worn from the bed and hung them up. I was satisfied now with my New Year's Day dinner selected and ready

ZEKE SMITH

to be prepared. I turned on the T.V. and watched some of the televised celebrations before dozing off to sleep. It was a good night and I prayed that it would also be a good day.

The sun crashed through my windows with fury. The brightness of it was shielded from my eyes with my hands, as I struggled to see the clock on the wall. My guess of 9 a.m. was confirmed, when my vision stopped being a blur. I rose out of the bed with an erect penis like some teen aged boy. I stumbled to the bathroom to release myself and get that overnight bad taste out of my mouth. I went back to my room for a wash cloth. I figured I might as well shower and get dressed before I started cooking. The water felt good cascading down my body as I began to lather up my rag. I had long finished pissing, but my penis was still erect, like it had been played with all this time. I started applying the soap suds to my neck and slowly worked my way down. I reached around the top and sides to clean my back. I placed the bar of soap in my rag again and began to wash the pole that was jutting out from my body. I felt waves of pleasure as the up and down motions of the soapy rag along my member excited me. I had not planned to play this game so early in the year but I couldn't resist the feelings that were being created. I wondered if I would be doomed to another year of masturbating if I continued. I thought about my wife and the fun we had in the shower. I thought about a deceased friend that seduced me in the shower, after inviting me, in to wash her back. I thought about the stranger I took off the street one night, and then washed her up like an infant child. I became more aggressive with the rag as my member began to cry out with joy and spray the area with cream. My body was convulsing now as I aimed to the drain and the stream turned to droplets. The soap had fallen from my hands and water had rinsed the suds from my body. I took the rag with its remaining lather and gently stroked my member. It began to calm down relax. It remained firm in anticipation of another round. "I'm sorry feller this is it. We have a meal to prepare." I did not wait for my penis to respond as I exited the shower still dripping with water. I didn't bring a towel so I would continue to use my rag to dry off. I had to wash and rinse it a number of times before all the soap and sperm were out of it. I peeked out the bathroom door to check the hallway. I found it empty so I darted into my room butt naked with my dirty clothes tucked under my arms. I stepped into the kitchen first to turn on the oven and also to start the greens before I got dressed. It would take me ten minutes to grease up my body because the penis begged for some extra attention. I wondered if this was the way to practice celibacy. I found some designer jeans and a warm sweatshirt to wear. I put on my cleanest sneakers and played my Aretha Franklin CD. I stepped back into the kitchen and started to do my thing. Three hours later my meal was finished and so was I. I turned on the T.V. and watched college football before dozing off to sleep.

I found myself in a dark room with the faint hum of machinery in the background. I slowly scanned the area to gain an understanding of my whereabouts. My mouth was and my eye lids were sticky. I rose up from my prone position and realized it was the living room. The nap I took was a long one because my wall clock was saying two o'clock. I hated these moments when I would wake up disorientated. The worst feeling in the world to me was not to know where I was at. I stumbled into the bathroom and released myself. I went into the kitchen after washing my hands. I flicked on the lights and began another survey to rekindle my memory. "Ah, I finished cooking but never ate! Well I'm going to eat my dinner now." I began to laugh out loud as I heard myself think. I needed a pet. I fixed a healthy plate with everything on it. I even put a couple of spoons of apple sauce on the side in a saucer. I put my food in the micro wave to heat up. I popped in a tape and sat down to eat when my food was ready. Emmm this was good and so were the images on my T.V. screen. I thought that it might be too much food to eat at this time, but I wasn't planning on sleeping for awhile. I began to think about what lied ahead for me. I was hopeful that this year would be better than the last. I took an inventory of my assets as I gobbled down my food. My situation wouldn't be that bad if the drugs and loose women stayed out of my life. I would have to gain some closer relationships with the members of my church. I would need to spend more time listening to my sister when she felt friendly. We both wanted companionship but were looking in the wrong places. I understood her turmoil and her desperation in finding a mate. She had to know that her choice was a faulty one but loneliness is a hurtful feeling. I thought about the other people I considered friends and knew that a lot of changes had to be made. I looked down at my plate and wondered where all the food had gone. If I wasn't home alone, I would have blamed someone else for eating some of it. I pushed the empty plate to the side and began to eat my apple sauce. I had even forgotten to pour myself something to drink. I sat there still for a moment, feeling full but not bloated. "Maybe it wasn't too much food to eat this late?" I said out loud as I pressed my hands on the table to help myself rise up. I cleared the table of my dishes and the other things left from my dinner preparation. I went into my cabinets to find some bowls for my food. It was time to put this food away if I expected to

ZEKE SMITH

eat any more of it. The only advantage to a cold apartment was your food didn't spoil, if it was left out too long on the stove. It took me about a half an hour to finish putting up the food and washing all my dishes. I even made sure they were dried and put away. I poured a drink of Bacardi and some cider. It was all I had and I wasn't complaining. I needed a cigarette now and the drink is a nice compliment. I turned the volume down on the T.V. and took another look at the images on the screen. "I wish they were here dancing like that." The tape playing was a favorite amateur video of mine. Those young women stripping and gyrating for the camera put me in the mood. I stepped out the kitchen to my living room slash bedroom. I grabbed myself a hat and jacket and headed quietly downstairs to smoke my cigarette.

The air was cold but my heart was warm. I thought about all the things I had to do in the upcoming days. My therapy sessions would resume because their holiday break was over. I had to contact my attorneys to see how my dual cases were progressing. I had to make a careful assessment of my finances to see how long I could go without some income. I took a deep pull from the cigarette in my hand and watched the creatures of the night go to and fro. There were lions, tigers, and bears to borrow a line from the Wizard of Oz. I even saw a few sultry pussy cats that looked inviting under the illumination of the street lamps. I even contemplated calling one over in hopes of mounting her. The thought left my mind just as quick as I envisioned the consequences that could result. The thought did last long enough to cause a growth in my pants that I began to massage. The smoke from my cigarette moved slowly through the air as if it was performing a ballet. I inhaled again while smoke leaked through my nostrils. I squirmed in my seat to give my butt cheeks a better position on the hard concrete that they rested on. I saw some movement under the trees diagonally across from me and realized that, all this time I was not alone on the block. The local dealers had concealed their presence well as they avoided detection unless you wanted their goods. I waved my hand in the air as if at a baseball game to indicate my awareness of their presence. They hollered back in unison; "Yo Zeke" defeating the whole purpose of being hidden. They were known more for their courage and not their intelligence. I started to feel the heat from the cigarette in my hand. It was a definite indication to put it out. I took one more pull from the filter pinched tightly between my fingers. I rubbed what was left across the stoop's pavement and flicked to the ground below me. I sat still for a moment feeling light headed. I then rose from my seated position satisfied about the time I had spent in the cold early morning air. I could see daybreak trying to make its debut. I stuck my key in the lock and let myself back in the house. I didn't wave as I left not wanting to hear another; "Yo Zeke." I immediately started to strip my clothes off when I entered the apartment. I was going to shower before I returned to my bed. I wanted to be fresh whenever I awakened to officially begin my day.

Monday came fast and left just as quick. In fact the days and weeks flew by as my routine had little variations. It was a brutal winter with plenty of snow. I kept my life simple and just maintained my medical appointments and found things to do in the house. I would occasionally arrange for my sister to make either an evening or an early morning money drop to pay my bills. These were not loans but resources I had accumulated while working. I feared my funds being seized with child support and other judgments hanging over my head. The Spring Season was a welcome sight when it finally arrived. My sister had intensified her relationship with the bad boy. It was against the best advice that all who loved her gave. She seemed very committed to pursue it regardless of the immediate consequences. One of those consequences was some long time friends reducing or eliminating contact with her. I remained loyal and faithful along with my other sisters. I just paid more attention to what else she was doing. I feared that the relationship may take her back to some habits that nearly destroyed her. I recall that it was a late March day when I found out from my cousin that she was planning to marry this guy. The fact that she didn't tell me was just as disturbing as the planned marriage itself. I couldn't digest this. She would be graduating from college soon with her Bachelor Degree. My sisters and I would be attending the ceremony in Upstate New York. The news of this marriage was interfering with the joy I had for her accomplishment. She deserved more than what this bum could give her but she lacked the patience for God to deliver. We all went to the ceremony as planned and took lots of pictures. We concealed our discontent for this individual that had clouded our sister's thinking. Yes he was present also which didn't make it any easier. We smiled a lot at the function and showered our sister with a lot of love and praise. We all cringed whenever they embraced wondering why this failure was the love of her life. We left happy for her success but sad for the upcoming wedding. The fact that just last year he was implicated in a local murder wasn't enough to stop her. The car I rode back in was quiet as everyone kept their thoughts to themselves.

The wedding was growing near as joy appeared daily on my big sister's face. My cousin kept me informed of the details because my sister Big

ZEKE SMITH

Mama wasn't talking. I was spending a lot of time at my cousin's house because of her need for a baby sitter. The first couple of times were charity because I enjoyed the children. The requests became more frequent as the household began to experience some prosperity. They had cable television which I didn't so I often staid up late watching it. The ride home wasn't difficult but the walk to the bus always aggravated my injured knee. The ten or twenty dollars I received was a big help to my budget. I had reached a place in my life where money wasn't the great motivator for the things I did. I trusted God to make a place for me and also to sustain me. I felt my condition was a result of my disobedience so I accepted what life and God with little complaints. My cousin Roberta also had some friends that I liked to be around and party with. It was wholesome fun and my righteousness was protected. My babysitting was elevated to a full time job when Roberta found some new employment. She was also attending college a Bachelor Degree in Sociology. Her husband was committed more to his vocation than the household so my presence became essential for the children's well being. It's always amazing how people seem to notice each others importance there's a need. We have a tendency to overlook each the value in a person if their resources are low or diminished. I avoid holding a person's character flaws against them and pray that my heart doesn't harden against them. This became my routine for most of the spring. I mixed it up with bus rides with my transit friend in the mornings. She was always a joy to be around and she liked to listen to how God was moving in my life. I continued to do my therapy but wasn't seeing any improvement in my physical condition. I was growing stronger in my spirituality and my faith in Jesus Christ. My cousin had joined the same church I was attending and was developing some faith of her own. She began to realize that she couldn't depend on her husband to be consistent in treating her fairly and properly. I refused to come between them or take sides. I would just agree with them both whenever they sought my advice or complained about each other to me. My cousin's husband Sam extended a few favors to me but he often times received more than he gave. It appeared that this was a goal of his in any relationship that he had with anyone.

My leg and back was not getting any better. I began to have my therapy sessions put some focus on my knee. I was walking with a cane which I didn't enjoy. The lawyers were collecting bills and other expenses, but weren't allocating any money. I was taking pain killers on a regular basis and felt that I was becoming dependent on them. I started to ride the stationary bicycle to develop some flexibility back into my knee. I saw major improvement in my physical state by the end of April but my emotional state deteriorated. My sister announced that she would be getting married the following month. There was nothing anyone could do. I grew tired of the babysitting because of the occasional turmoil in the household. I was becoming too concerned with their affairs and didn't want to be involved. The money was insufficient for the labor or for what they could afford to pay. I began to focus on getting back to work and off my dependency on pain killers. I began to exercise in the house and take long walks after dinner. I cut down on smoking the cigarettes and finally started using the patch to quit. I was successful and after my sister's tragic wedding I was cleared to return to work. The return to work was no simple task to endure. I wasn't completely healed but being at other people's mercy, had lasted long enough. I returned to the van service and to Pathmark in the same week. The healing of my leg took place one evening during rehearsal with the Men's Day Choir at church. If it had not been for that healing, I never would have been able to return to work. My welfare benefits were near the end. Their doctors said I was fully recovered and available for work. I was shifted to a job ready program and given all types of incentives to return to work. The fact that I had a job to return to didn't matter to them. I was still treated as anyone else unemployed on welfare. Now back to my healing. We were having evening rehearsals to prepare us for our Men's Day. We not only rehearsed but there was also good fellowship. This particular night my right leg was severely constricted. I was in a lot of pain and couldn't bend my knee at all. I was using my cane daily at this point but on this night, it wasn't much help. I refused to stay home because this was our last rehearsal. Plus I needed the fellowship to stay grounded with the Lord. I only had to walk two blocks to the church but it just as well been a mile. I grimaced in pain with every movement of my body. I hopped out my door with the cane in tow. I leaned on the banister, like it was a crutch, on the downstairs stairwell with my right leg held in the air. I slid and hopped, slid and hopped, until I reached the bottom of the stairs. I used up a lot of energy with that maneuver and was out of breath when I stepped outside. I repeated the action on the outside concrete stairs until I touched the ground below. I stepped out the front yard and leaned up against the fence surrounding it. The air was very chilly and I felt unprepared with the clothes I was wearing. There were no more banisters to lean on which made forward progress extremely unbearable. The cane did little to soften the impact of my weight shifting to my right leg as I inched forward. I received curious stares but offers of assistance as I made my way down the street.

ZEKE SMITH

"Emmm oh, Emmm oh" I cried out loud with each step that I took. I finally left the block that I lived on and could see the church in the distance. I paused with every few yards that I walked to catch my breath. This trip was a more painful undertaking, than what I had anticipated. I believed that the pain would go away and my knee would start functioning properly. It never happened so I continued on until I reached the front of the church. I felt some relief because there were no stairs to climb up or walk down. I immediately sat down when I stepped inside the church foyer. I began to massage my knee and alternately bent it slightly again hoping to bring back some flexibility in the joint. I didn't want my situation to be a distraction so I concealed it as much as possible when I entered the sanctuary. "Bro. Zeke come on down. Are you alright?" I looked at the deacon and nodded, to demonstrate that it wasn't as bad as it looked. I hugged and shook hands with the brothers present. The music minister was setting us up in our positions according to our voice. I was in the tenor section but could go deep when called upon. My focus on the music took my mind off the pain. We sung our songs and joked at some points. There was such an air of brotherhood and I could feel the presence of the Lord. God was moving in this place tonight because everyone had come to this rehearsal. There were times in the past when some men that had committed to singing weren't at the rehearsals. Tonight was much different with our singing being as good as the fellowshipping. It was a relief when we finished but I began to think about that trip home. I shared my affliction with the men and asked who could drive me home. They laughed because I lived so close but quickly understood when they saw the pain on my face. I couldn't hide it anymore as the knee started to throb this time. We ended our rehearsals the same way we started them, with a prayer circle. Requests were solicited but mine was for my sister because her marriage was so close. When the minister started to pray as we held hands, I felt a presence that caused me to raise my right leg, and put it in the circle. I felt my body go limp as I bent my left leg and stood completely still. I began to mumble a prayer of my own as the minister's voice faded from my hearing.

"Dear Father God, I come to you in the name of Jesus, asking that you forgive me for my sins and transgressions and hear my prayer. The pain in my joints is overwhelming and walking is difficult. I ask you Father God in the name of Jesus to heal me and relieve me of this affliction. You have kept me thus far Father and I'm grateful for the burdens you have lifted but again I need you Father. I need to return to work. I need to secure funds to provide for future needs. I can't rely on others Father. I rely only on you. Release me from this pain. Release me from this affliction. Restore my limps so that I can pass my physical and return to work. I trust in you Father and the name of Jesus." My leg grew heavy as the minister's voice became louder. I felt a tingling and my leg became lighter. I opened my eyes and watched the others as tears began to roll down my face. I heard my sister's name being called out as prayer continued. The brother next to me started to squeeze my hand tightly as I slowly lowered my leg. I raised my head to drain the tears that were clouding my vision. Then I heard the voice say; "In the name of Jesus we pray, Amen!" We all began to release the grip of the hands next to us. I stood motionless for a moment as I put more pressure on my knee. I straightened up my body while moving my leg from the broken circle. We began to hug one another and when I walked forward, there was no pain. I was a bit unsteady on my feet but I could bend my knee. "Wow I can bend my knee." I said again to myself but only I could hear. I raised my hands in the air and began to shout; "HALLELUJAH, HALLELUJAH, HALLELUJAH!" I began to walk some more with just a slight limp as all eyes were on me. I began to cry but from the joy of deliverance and not from any pain. A few understood the reason for my joy others were just moved by my emotion. The voices around me were faint in my ears as my focus was on the Lord and The Holy Spirit I felt pulsating through out my body. The deacon that committed to drive me home was dismayed when I told him that I decided to walk. A healing had taken place that night. Jesus had rescued me from my pain and the burden of unemployment. I walked up the aisle of the sanctuary unassisted by the cane I now carried. I continued to limp as I walked out the door. The closer I came to my house the less I limped. By the time I reached my front door I was walking as if nothing were ever wrong. I've often read in the scriptures the healings that Jesus and the other disciples performed but now I was a recipient in the modern world. I climbed the stairs in much less pain than when I had gone down. I stepped inside my house feeling resurrected from a dilemma I thought I couldn't escape. I searched my wardrobe for the proper attire for my big day tomorrow. I would have one opportunity to show myself approved for work. I had the documents from two sets of doctors that said I could work. I slept sound that night but not without the help of some porn to relax me.

I had to be in Queens at 10:00 a.m. The bus ride would be a short one. I was up at 8:00 a.m. to get myself ready. I took a nice hot shower with no fooling around. I wanted my limbs to be limber and my strength intact.

I ate a light breakfast of toast and oatmeal. I drank a large glass of juice to flush it down. The only pills I took were for my blood pressure. I wore pressed jeans, a collared shirt with a light weight sweater over it. I wore my black boots that I liked to drive in with my short black leather jacket. I slid a black wool skull cap over my head and stepped outside my door. I made sure both locks were on before walking down the stairs. The air was cold but the sun shined bright. It was 9:15 which gave me plenty of time to reach my destination on time. I could see two busses coming when I reached the bus-stop. I knew one would be mine so I dug in my pocket for the metro card to pay my fare. There was the usual activity on the streets for this time of day. There were school children and some parents racing about to catch their busses. I could see delivery men arriving with their loads to drop off. The laundry mat had its activity too with a small group in front talking about something, which was probably only important to them. The bus pulled up in front of me. A few people stepped off but I was the only one to get on. The neighbors that I usually rode with were long gone by this time. In fat they were probably taking their first breaks for the day by this time. I walked to the middle of the bus and sat down after swiping my card. The reader showed that I was good until Saturday. I was a little fidgety in my seat with so much time passed since I last took this ride. It took no time at all to reach my stop. There was very few school children left at this time. Those with jobs were already there except for the ones running late. I got off the stop indicated by the printed directions on the appointment card. I had been at this place once before when I first got the job. I looked across the street and saw the medical building. I took my time walking not wanting to aggravate my knee. I stepped inside unsure about the direction to go in. I went to the first receptionist desk I saw, only to learn that the one I needed was downstairs. It was five minutes before ten when I handed the young woman at the desk my card. She pulled some files and had me fill out some forms. When I was done she gave me a specimen cup and showed me where the bathroom was at. There were no visible controls to insure that the urine samples weren't doctored. It was what I expected from an outfit with low wages for a skilled job. The union was even a bigger sham which was confirmed during my absence. The provided me with no assistance and little information that I could use. I would not be apart of it a second time around. I returned to the desk with my urine but was told to hang on to it until the doctor called me. I was relieved that the wait was a short one because holding that container of warm piss was cramping my style.

I stepped into the doctor's spacious office and gave the nurse present my urine. She pointed to a wired basket in the corner of the room for me to place it in. She continued to go over the forms I had filled out and directed me to sit at her desk while she completed her survey. I was impressed with the cleanliness of the place and its neat design. It looked more like an office in Manhattan than in Queens. "Mr. Smith you are a diabetic?" She had a thick accent that was either Cuban or Columbian. In any case she was very beautiful and sounded good. I made her repeat the question before I answered, just to hear her voice again. "No it's in my family." The question was ambiguous the way it was written. She had to change my response before we could go on with the interview. This part of the exam was the most pleasant before the doctor came in and had me remove my shirt. He instructed me to sit on the examination table while he began to check my vital signs. He also tested my joints for pain and examined scars on my back. I spent more time with the nurse than with the doctor. I was then told that my job would contact me about the results of the examination. I was then given a paper to show that I was there to take to the job. I took the same bus to the job that I took to the doctor's office, just in the opposite direction. It took about twenty minutes from the time I left the doctor to the time it took to ride the bus to the job. I went inside to speak with the head dispatcher who was in charge of the office. It seemed disappointed that I didn't have more information to give him. He seemed more interested in my plans about legal actions for the accident. He began to negotiate a settlement if I would drop my case. He made this a condition of me returning to work so we began to pass numbers back in forth until we could agree on something. I began to recall our first conversation when I was hired. He was so cocky in explaining the conditions of employment. He mandated that I join the union which was just a front that took money but gave no benefits. I knew the talk he was having with me was illegal but I went along because I needed an income. I signed an agreement that he hastily wrote up on some typing paper. The payment would be in two parts with the bulk of it coming upfront. I even included a clause that would insure that I couldn't be fired once the final payments were made. He didn't realize it at the time but that was the strongest language that gave me an advantage.

I went back to work with everyone being curious about where I had been. They knew I was in an accident but they didn't know the out come. We were both forbidden to discuss the terms we agreed to. I took the bulk of the money and put it into my retirement fund. I had exhausted my resources during my time out of work. I spread the rest around my bank accounts and caught up my rent. I couldn't get my old route back so the job wasn't as attractive as it was before. I couldn't shake the feeling that they were trying to set me up in some kind of way. I knew these people were not going to let some black boy take the upper hand on them. I stayed alert and just waited for them to tip their hand. I was no longer getting the types of runs I had before. I mostly had to go to the Veterans Hospital. I spent more time waiting for pick ups than actually driving. I soon learned why they wanted my claim to disappear and the reason why they ducked responsibility for the accident so long. There company had another accident occur that was more severe than mine. It involved one of the veterans we picked up. This was a lucrative contract and one of the few they were able to hold on to. I was being sacrificed because two accidents so close together would send their premiums soaring. It had come to my attention that all of their vans were not always insured. They played this game of "coverage roulette". It was only during inspection time that a van was guaranteed to be fully covered. Like any game of chance the results can't be accurately predicted and their last roll came up snake eyes. In the mean time I was forced to suffer unduly and return to work while I trusted God and not medical attention to rehabilitate me.

My job at Pathmark was going much better. They respected the limitations placed on me from the accident. They also understood the amount of debt I had from being out of work. The union began to collect back dues from every pay check. The Family Court in New York under the direction of the state of Virginia had levied a judgment against me for child support. I was already paying a judgment from the credit cards I had with my wife. I was smart to have deductions made to my credit union, so my take home pay was just a few dollars over carfare. I was still receiving food stamps and welfare would pay my rent for the next six months. It was during this period that I made a real connection with Jesus and began to study God's word more intensely. I began to understand the rewards and blessings that came from faith and obedience. I began to recognize that praising God regardless of your circumstances was what God expected. My body grew stronger as The Word of God formed the foundation of my life. The situations I encountered began to be seen by me as revelations from God. I started to experience some profound visions during my sleep and would awaken at 3:00 a.m. regularly praising God. I felt the Lords presence almost constantly where ever I was at. I began to assist a woman with a project to start a non-profit that would help young men that had aged out of the foster care system in New York. It was a faith based organization and our fellowship with each other to realize her dream, brought me even closer to God. I gained a lot of knowledge about the process of grant writing and the tools needed to get a 501C Charter. I utilized my writing skills to draft her funding plea letters, mission statement and organizational structure. My past experience counseling enabled me to put a program of activities in place. We began to foster a strong bond of friendship and fellowship. My interaction with her gave my life purpose and direction. It also rekindled my love of mentoring the youth and provided me a path for redemption. We had a successful bus ride to a culturally historical institution out of state. I sold enough tickets to guarantee a profit and introduce enough family and friends to widen our base of support. The relationship began to shift when I started feeling over burdened by the amount of assignments she was giving me to do. I maintained intellectual support of her ideas but drew back my physical labor. I had a more pressing matter closer to home because my sister's wedding was coming up. I couldn't stop it but I also would not abandon her because of it.

The wedding was on a Friday afternoon. It was on this day because that's the only day she could use her church. There would be a reception in the Fellowship Hall immediately following the service. Our Pastor performed the ceremony with her son giving her away and her daughter was the maid of honor. The families of the bride and groom were well represented at the event. It was there that I learned that the groom's sisters were friends of mine from their early teenage years and I knew their children. This still didn't change my mind about what I thought of their brother. We took a lot of pictures at the wedding and the reception. I was given a seat at the children table which seemed to tickle everyone to death. We joked a lot about the marriage to take the edge off of our anger and disappointment. I remember when the preacher asked; "If anyone disagrees with this union speak now or forever hold your peace?" I began to rise but sat back down then my nephew made the same move and we all laughed quietly. A party was a party so I tried to have fun and show support for my sister. The atmosphere was festive but underneath it all you could sense a darker current was flowing. The reception lasted till late evening. When it was over my two other sisters headed back to their homes. My hose was busy and crowded. Big Mama's son and daughter, along with their combined six sons, were staying at the house.

I rose early the next Saturday morning as usual. The weather was sunny and pleasant as dawn turned into day. I fumbled around my apartment

ZEKE SMITH

making sure that nothing embarrassing was lying about. I just wanted to be prepared if someone wanted to visit. I knew my shower would be used so I wanted to make sure the rest of the place was available if needed. There was coolness in the air although the sun shined brightly in the air. I heard a lot of activity down stairs as I continued cleaning after taking my shower. I had already alerted my people on the block about my family visiting. They knew to mind their manners and other activities not to mar this day for my sister. When I finally was able to go outside, I learned the bride and groom was taking everyone to breakfast. I had already eaten and with my invitation being an after thought I declined. It was good to have my younger nephews around but I wasn't in the mood to be around the rest of them. I stepped across the street to mingle with my people while the breakfast entourage piled into two cars and drove off. In a short time later the landlord's home attendant arrived and was ranging the bell when I came across the street and let her in. I didn't return to my people but instead when back into the house. I noticed as I walked up the stairs to my apartment that my sister's apartment doors were left open and I could see disarray around the hall room and bathroom. I just thought to myself how one generation had bred another generation of untidy people. I was still feeling uneasy from the wedding and my first couple of weeks back to work. I opened up a beer and lit a cigarette in my kitchen while a porn tape entertained me. I was trying to shake what had a hold of me. The hidden anger inside me, prevented prayer from being an option. The visions on my small T.V. screen and the effects of the beer soon had me stimulating myself. It wasn't long before I climaxed and the energy started draining from my body. I finished off my beer and went into my other room. I popped in a DVD tape and before long had fallen off to sleep.

I was abruptly awakened by the sound of the door bell in the hallway. I stepped outside to find the home attendant trying to alert someone that she had to leave but would return. The landlord's son who was my next door neighbor, was either sleep or not at home. It didn't matter then because I was now up and just took the information. The house was still quiet so they probably had not returned from breakfast. I returned back to my apartment and went back to sleep.

It was the door bell again that awakened me from my sleep. This time I didn't have to get up because my deep sleeping neighbor had responded. I could hear his loud voice when I stuck my head out the door; "Wait a minute; I'm going to throw you the key." I continued on to use the bathroom, believing that sleep was no longer an option for me. I smoothed the wrinkles out my pants with my hands. I quickly cleaned up my kitchen again from the small snack I had before I had fell asleep. It must have been an hour that passed before I heard more noise in the hallway. The breakfast crew had returned and I heard some commotion about some missing jewelry. It was never a comfortable feeling to be around anyone that was missing something. In my early years my gambling habits caused me to pick up a lot of things that weren't mine. On a good night I was able to put money back before it was missed. When the dice didn't roll in my favor I was left either lying about the theft or making promises to pay it back. Just when everyone's memory was clear about those early years, my drug addiction set me off again but this time paying anything back became rare. The label of the thief stuck this time like crazy glue and I never shook it. I didn't wait for a visit this time but instead went downstairs to hear the details. They claimed that while they were out someone went into my sister's room where the door was left wide open and took her wedding ring. "What!" I exclaimed; "You think I'm the one that did? I got plenty of money and have no use for your ring. I haven't even been down stairs except to walk out the door or to answer the bell." The more I spoke the guiltier I appeared to everyone. My niece and sister quickly adopted the idea that it was me. They both were earlier victims of mine but my sister was in debt to me but never intends to pay it. I began to examine their claims to figure out if someone did come in here and rob the ring while I was sleep. I began to focus on the home attendant's earlier departure and thought that maybe that was the reason she left. She even accused me out loud because she lost some jewelry earlier that month and felt that I had it. It didn't matter to anyone that I never visited down stairs unless I stop for a moment to speak the landlady who was bed ridden. My nephew came upstairs to speak with me about the incident and he didn't even appear convinced of my innocence before he left. I refused to let this mar my day but what I wanted didn't matter. The incident hung over my head like a storm cloud. I spent the whole day and the rest of the week trying to figure out who could have done this. I never considered that he was a family member. I kept thinking that the home attendant was the guilty party. My sister shot murder stares at me whenever our paths crossed. She stopped speaking to me. Even at church she didn't communicate. I forced to tell people on the outside about this incident and some of them even questioned my innocence. The days my sister attended Bible Study were miserable and stole my joy. I began to use the scriptures during these sessions to communicate with her. It hurt so much that she would think that I would commit a crime like this on such a special day for her. I was the one in the family that demonstrated the most support for her marriage to this deadbeat. During this period of estrangement form my sister he grew closer to me. I never trusted him but did not want to distant myself from him. I told the area dealers to let me know if he ever copped drugs from him. A short time after the wedding he became unemployed and lazy. Now my sister was supporting him and the disappointment began to show on her face. We were an outlet for each other but now that was lost for us both. This vermin who was her husband continued to endear himself to me. He began to offer me beers when I came in from work. He always seemed to know when I was due because he would be sitting on the stoop waiting. He started driving my sister's jeep regularly. She even gave him the extra work at the Senior Citizen Center that she was the director of. Yeah her husband Barry became very comfortable with me and began to let go of some secrets that my sister didn't know about. He had her just where he wanted her, isolated from her friends and estranged from her brother.

My bosses at Pathmark had welcomed me back and so did most of the co-workers that I knew. There were still others because of their work ethics that I didn't associate with. It was these individuals that made my work day unpleasant. The accident had placed some physical limitations on my movement and endurance. I found myself in pain often because I would not accept that I couldn't do as much now as I did before. I quickly learned that driving was the most difficult part of the week because of my right knee. I would sometimes get excruciating pain from cramps and would be unable to bend my knee after driving any great distance. I only shared this discomfort with my doctors who couldn't do much about it because of the workman compensation laws. I would limp home every night after getting off the bus. I developed some close ties with a young bus driver and still had even a closer relationship with one nearly my age. The older one Huey kept me grounded in Christ and the younger one Slick tested my relationship with God by the proposals he always came up with. I couldn't convert Slick and should have put more distance between us. The older me that was killed off when I accepted Christ was always trying to find a way to be resurrected. Slick along with the local negative associations that I thought I needed gave the Old Man some life. The pain when I drove, the short hours at my night job and the lack of any steady female companionship, drove me back into the murky waters of sin. I started to contemplate dealing drugs again. I began to do my x-rated shows at the after hour clubs. The young and old women caught up in addiction became my toys. My focus shifted from securing my future to bringing pleasure to my present. I began to duck conversations with my daughter because often times my condition made it hard to speak. My lying increased to everyone around me. I would go to work in the morning after being up all night. Driving became a dangerous mission for me because of my fatigue. I started to blur the boundaries between the clients that I transported and myself. I accepted their gifts whenever offered and began to self-disclose my downward spiral to those that knew Jesus. In June it all started to come apart when I was involved in a minor suspicious fender bender. It appeared to be an accident that was set up to happen. I only had my gut instincts to go on because there was no other tangible proof. The accident and all the other issues that developed because of it resulted in my employment being terminated. I still had my night job at the store but the loss of the additional income put extreme pressure on my finances. The store allowed me some daytime hours which helped a lot. I risked some savings to put a package on the streets that only served to accelerate my drug use. I found myself being more involved with Barry my sister's new husband. I started to notice his behavior more and suspected that he was getting high and not just on weed and beer. The only ones that knew of my firing initially were my people on the streets. I stayed hidden behind closed doors during the day. I made sure that what ever I needed was in the house before daybreak. I began to experience paranoia during the day whenever my nights were filled with drugs. The summer was killing me but I couldn't stop it. I fell behind on my rent because my welfare subsidies stopped when I went back to work. The money I tucked away was rapidly disappearing. I was rarely communicating with my daughter and I began to miss her. I was making it to church for Sunday school and Worship service but my soul was tormented. My sister would not make eye contact with me whenever we crossed paths. She began to be ill often on Sundays and would not attend service. The marriage was a disappointment to her but she kept it to herself. I began to have strange dreams in August that caused me to stop drugging and staying up late at night. I changed my diet and began to take walks after eating. I bought some vitamins and received the nicotine patches from a program I heard on the radio. The settlement from the lawsuit against the tobacco industry allowed some states to fund programs to stop smoking. I cleaned myself up and distanced myself from the people, places, and things that caused me to get high. Church and the people in it became my foundation. I thought less of having women around me and more of studying the scriptures. I began hating Barry because he was the reason why my sister was faltering. I felt he was using her and I wanted him gone. I paid more attention to what he was doing around the neighborhood. I was getting my sleep but was waking up at early morning hours from my dreams. I started to sip beers at three in the morning on my stoop. It was a time when the house was quiet and I could keep an eye on my god brother. He had recently joined the boys on the block and revealed a side of him that I didn't know. It would have broken my godmother's heart so I kept his activities to myself. I still tried to inject some common sense into him and allowed him some protection when I was around. Yes waking up from my dreams and then going outside to sit on the stoop became a regular ritual.

The associate ministers at the church had been giving the sermons more regularly than our Pastor. The reason for our Pastor's absence was said to be that he was on a vacation. It was probably the second Sunday in July that the whole congregation was startled. The morning service started like any other that day. The devotional service was as energetic as ever as the church began to fill up. The choir was hitting their notes and I was moved by spirit that filled the air. I had my usual seat in the center of the sanctuary when our regular service started. The prayer had ended and the morning scripture was read, and that's when it happened. The announcer introduced our Pastor Reverend Dr. J. Parsons. A silence fell over the sanctuary as our Pastor was led up to the pulpit from the side entrance. He was being assisted by his wife as he took his seat in the pulpit. A thunderous applause erupted as the ministers and the entire congregation rose to their feet. I was startled by his appearance because he looked gaunt and tired. When the applause started to die down Pastor Parsons rose to his feet and slowly walked up to the pulpit. He began to sing his signature hymn while the musicians added their accompaniment. People began to rise and clap their hands adding more rhythm to the song. When he stopped singing he began to speak. The reason for his absence was because of illness. It was a personal matter and his family felt it was unnecessary to inform the members. He continued to explain that he was battling cancer and was uncertain about his prognosis. He apologized for being secretive and stated his presence here today was a necessary decision that he made. I began to hear the whispers and the muffled crying that stared. The Pastor appeared so heroic in his disclosure in the face of his pain. I also sensed the empathy of the congregation as they once again rose to their feet and began to applaud. We all so loved Pastor Parsons. We heaped enormous praise upon him for his leadership and insightfulness. I had developed a close bond with him and he took a personal interest in my walk with God. He was involved with the church for more than a few decades. He followed in the foot steps of the church's founder and had initiated programs that helped with its growth. The rest of the service was difficult after the Pastor was led off the pulpit and disappeared from view along with his wife. In the days that followed many different rumors circulated that angered members more. The more information that became available the anger of some turned to resentment. There were those that felt betrayed by not being informed of the Pastor's condition. My sister who was already dealing with some depression because of her marriage became even more depressed. The Pastor never returned to the pulpit again. The Lord called him home before the end of July. It was a grand homecoming celebration for The Rev. Dr. Joseph Parson. The days that followed were filled with grief and uncertainty. You never knew what to expect at the following Sunday services. The people continued to praise the man forgetting sometimes who had put him there. The membership began to express their discord by withholding their support of the church. The chairman of the deacon board was now in charge as spelled out in the church by-laws.

It was in the middle of August when The Lord would change my waking hours. It would be five in the morning and not three and I wouldn't be rushing to sit on the stoop. I was walking along Broadway in my neighborhood. The weather was hot for August and I was enjoying it. The rehab plan that I developed for myself was working. I was headed to the new chicken joint that had opened up. The businesses along this avenue were making a strong come back from the Blackout of 1977. I ran into a Deacon from my church that was pushing a baby carriage. He was headed to the supermarket so I deviated from my destination to walk with him. I was very familiar with him because my sister introduced us when I was locked up. He was a guard where I was at and offered some comfort and spiritual guidance during that time. The friendship increased and we grew closer. The dream I had the night before gave me more worry concerning my sister the minister and how she was relating to me. I refrained from discussing her and our relationship in the past but now felt a need to do so. I let him know that my sister wasn't speaking to me and the reason why. We kept company for about an hour as I related my concerns to him. He was not as alarmed as I was when I finished explaining things to him. I wanted him to understand that I felt she was risking God's judgment because she wasn't functioning as an obedient servant. There were too many stories of her being selective about the saints she embraced. There were my own

ZEKE SMITH

personal observations of contradictory behavior towards myself and others. I loved my sister dearly and my new understanding of the way God moves had me scared. The Deacon listened but he lacked the understanding to take action. I felt that his relationship with her would be a voice she would hear. The elevated train above us roared into the station and drowned out our voices. I had finished speaking and he was finished listening. We both continued on to our destination and I mumbled a prayer while I walked away. The rest of my day was uneventful. The house was kept orderly and I didn't succumb to any of my weaknesses that week.

The beginning of the third week in August I ran into my sister as she was leaving that morning for work. We made eye contact and I said "Good morning". She responded with a "Good morning" and I felt a great weight lifted up off me. It had been so ling since she had spoken to me. I knew my sister loved me; she was just caught up in a situation that she couldn't get out of. The rest of my day was filled with so much joy. My church was in an upheaval because of the Pastor's death but my spirit was uplifted and filled joy. I was working early in the afternoon on Mondays and Tuesdays and was off on Wednesday. I then had to work on Thursday and Friday from 4:00 p.m. to 8:00 p.m. I usually came home about five on the early shift but didn't get home until eight on the late shift. The neighborhood was used to seeing me arrive home about one in the morning, for those that were still awake. My apartment was located in the back so even when I was home you wouldn't know it by my lights. My buddies that did their hustling in the hood were planning a big cook-out in an area park. I was well known for my skill at the grill so I was asked to cook. They also wanted to have enough food to feed five hundred people so they called upon me to figure out what they needed to buy. It was a joint effort amongst at least five young men. The organizer was like a true brother to me whom I liked and admired a lot. He demonstrated real love towards me in spite of the conditions under which we met. We never refused to help one another even when it required some sacrifice. They had been planning this for over a month and now the event was only days away. I wasn't seeing too much of Barry my sister's husband that week. My young cutie next door though was a different matter. I was around early enough now to see a lot of her. We shared lunches and dinners, when I worked late. We shared beers at night when I worked early. We had experienced some discord between us because she misused some money I had given her. It felt too good being around her to late money come between us. What I did for her also showed how legit I was in the things we talked about.

This Friday I arrived home my usual time of 9:00 p.m. Barry stuck his head out the door as the fence gate slammed and I walked up the stairs. He went back inside as quickly as he had come out. When I reached the top of the stairs my little cutie came outside to smoke a cigarette. We spent a few minutes speaking before I noticed the landlord coming into the yard. It looked like he had been to the store by the size of the bag he carried. I continued to speak to Candy as she blew smoke in my face. I began to get aroused and didn't want to waste it now. I told her that I would be back out after I took a shower and would get us some beers. The landlord had reached the top of the steps by this time; and we walked into the door together. I didn't have a lot to say to him because he had been doing too much negative talking about me to others. The corner barber would always fill me in on his never ending rants about his dissatisfaction with me being there. He also grossly miscalculated the rent I owed. I took my time walking up the creaky steps to my apartment. The landlord stopped downstairs on the second floor to visit with his mother. This was a usual habit of his and besides he needed the rest after climbing a flight of stairs. I stepped inside and went straight to my bed and collapsed on top of it. I was tired and horny and wanted to get back outside as soon as possible. I rubbed myself to sleep without ever turning on a light, radio or television.

I rolled over on the bed and my eyes were struggling to open. The room was pitch black except for the dim moon light, which was peering thru the blinds. I raised myself up off the bed and noticed that my phone had a lot of missed calls. I reached over and picked up the phone and began to scan the alerts that were flashing. My landlord had called and I could see that the voicemail sign was lit up. There were two missed calls from the landlord and then I saw that my young Jamaican cutie had also called twice. I stumbled out into the hallway as I started to listen to the voicemail. The landlord was asking me to call him when I received this message. I wondered why he didn't just knock on my door. I then called my neighbor who was probably upset that I had not come back outside. The phone rang as I walked into the bathroom to release myself. It rang and rang until finally she answered. "Candy"; I said. "Are you sleeping?" What came next startled me. "Hey Zee I called to see what had happened to your sister. I saw the ambulance take her away." My body stiffened and I shuck myself off before returning my member back to its chamber. I flushed the toilet and walked back into the hallway. It was then that I noticed bright lights shining up from downstairs. "Candy, you said my sister left in an ambulance?" "Yeah Zee is she alright?" I then began to walk down the stairs

ZEKE SMITH

to see why there was so much activity in the house. "Candy I'll call you back later." We both disconnected the call and that's when I realized what time it was. It was 1:00 a.m. and the first call had come in at 11:45p.m from the landlord. Candy had just called shortly before I got up. I then began to walk slowly downstairs trying to shake the feeling of disorientation that had engulfed me. I went past the second floor and turned to descend the next flight of stairs. It was then that I saw the landlord sitting at the bottom of the landing, repeating over and over; "I never saw so much blood before. A female police captain came up and met me before I reached the bottom. "Sir, stop where you are and don't come any further!" She was very demanding in her tone and posture. I froze in my tracks and began to speak as my arms limply dropped to my sides. "What happened and where is my sister. I leaned over the banister to see bandages and blood littering the hallway floor. "Who are you sir and where did you come from?" I was not in the mood to answer questions but wanted answers to my own. "Where is my sister and what happened here?" I was the one being demanding now and I was fully awake. The police captain relaxed her tone as a detective came from outside and starting with questions of his own. I recognized him the incident last week when my god brother was shot. "Its okay captain I know him." The detective came to me and led me back upstairs to the second floor. He relaxed a bit and spoke softly as he began to respond to the questions I was asking the captain. "The woman downstairs was hurt and has been taken to the hospital. She has a very bad head injury." Anger immediately began to overtake me as I shouted out; "where's Barry?" The detective tried to calm me down as I asked again; "where's Barry?" "Barry rode to the hospital with an officer. "He should be in handcuffs; I know he's the one that did this." The detective didn't respond to my statement and instead started back up with his questions. "Where were you and did you hear anything?" I was becoming more and more annoyed. This was the same detective that had questioned me last week. He was a big black guy with a limited vocabulary. I was not enthusiastic about talking with him. Time was moving and I needed some answers. I knew enough about crime to understand that the first few hours are the most crucial. I asked myself; "Why wasn't someone here to preserve the crime scene? Why was there so much traffic in and out without collecting any evidence? My sister's room should have also been off limits or at least checked for clues to this vicious beating." I began to hear the coarse voice of the detective again in my ear. "Didn't I speak to you last week about that shooting?" "Yeah you spoke to me. I was upstairs when all this happened. I was sleep after coming home at 9:00 p.m. Barry was here and so was the landlord when I came home." I walked outside and reached into my pocket for my cell phone. I looked back at the big black detective and he began to speak again. "You always asleep when something happen around here; so do you ever know anything?" I couldn't tell if it was ignorance or sarcasm; and it didn't matter when I exploded. "That's my sister and you should be talking to Barry and not me. When are you going to start dusting for prints and stop people from walking around downstairs? No one should be in that kitchen or hallway until you guys search for evidence." I saw a look of discontent cross the face of the big black detective; in addition, he began to speak. "I know my job and forensic can't come until the morning." I continued walking outside as his words peppered my back. I was done listening to this person. I needed some help over here to protect this crime scene and console me. I called my baby sister first who was sleeping hard when she answered the phone. I had to stay on the line with her for a few minutes, just to make sure she was awake after I told her. I couldn't tell if she felt any pain initially but she agreed to get up and go to the hospital. I then called my cousin whom I often visited. I enjoyed caring for her children and her house was sometimes a refuge for me. I needed her over here with me to keep me company. I wanted to make sure that I held myself together under these extreme circumstances. My cousin knew my weaknesses and my strengths; she also loved my sister as much as I did. I continued making my calls as the one questioned everybody would ask me was; where's Barry? I forgot about the detective and he forgot about me. I made it downstairs and walked up the block. The streets were empty. The all night store that kept a crowd outside was empty too. I walked over there as I lit a cigarette. I stepped inside to speak with the owner named Skinny.

"Yo Zeke what happened?" He asked a question that I knew he had the answer to. I wanted to ask him what happened. He probably knew more than me at this point and I wanted to know all that he knew. "Yo Skinny where's everybody at? The streets have gotten real empty since my sister was beaten." I searched his face for any tell tale signs that would reveal what he might be thinking. I wasn't relying on just his words for information. I figured facial expressions and other body language would be more truthful. "Skinny gimme a pack of cigarettes and I'm getting two Heinekens from the box. Put everything in the book." I could have paid for my stuff but I was testing his reaction. I wanted to know if he had any hostile feelings towards me. I was about to launch a campaign to bring this store down and put it out of business. This store had a connection to my sister's attack.

I just didn't know in what way. Skinny wasn't excited about the credit I was asking for but he didn't protest or refuse me. "That's ah shame what happen to your sister; she is such a nice lady. It hasn't been too busy tonight around here Zeke. If I hear something I will let you know." I intentionally didn't give him any details about what happened. It was important to see what circulates in the streets on its own. "Okay Skinny, I'll see you later." I had told my cousin to come here and my baby sister to go to the hospital. I think enough time has passed for both of them to be at least out of the house. I began walking back towards my house taking inventory of all that I saw around me. I popped the cap on one of the beers and began to drink. The activity around the house was calming down. The police had left with the exception of a uniformed officer watching the house. Grief had not struck me at this point; I was just very angry. A car pulled up as I was trying to figure out who are these people that are hanging around the house. The landlord was constantly retelling his story about the way he found my sister lying on the floor. He was no longer acting stunned or shock but was very relaxed and enjoying the attention. He was already known as a gossiper that couldn't keep quiet about anything. There was a young black woman in the midst that showed a lot of interest in everything he was saying. She even questioned him at times for clarity. I walked up to her to find out who she was, while my cousin approached me from the cab she had arrived in. My cousin and I hugged and I gave her the other beer that I had. She began to ask questions too but I was unable to answer them right then. "One moment cousin I need to talk with this lady." My cousin walked to the stoop to hear the account that the landlord was giving. I finally had a chance to ask this woman who she was. She introduced herself as Peggy and she was a reporter from the New York Post. She was young and attractive so talking to her would be a pleasure. She had learned of the incident form the newswire. I was concerned that too much information would be given that could hinder the investigation. Peggy had already received a lot of details from the talkative landlord. I allowed her to interview me and promised her exclusive information in the future if she respected my wishes. I told her about most of what had taken place. I gave her detailed information about Barry's criminal background and the rocky marriage. I let her know who my sister was and the impact she had on the community and the people around her. She wanted to take some pictures which I refused. I paused for a moment to tell my brother in law the landlord, to stop talking about the attack. He didn't object and actually seemed relieved that someone had shut him up. Peggy was satisfied with the story I told. She then gave me her card and left to file her story. I went back t my cousin and we began to console each other. We both expressed anger towards Barry and disappointment in my sister's decision to marry him. We stayed outside and talked some more about past times and how this incident was affecting us. My cousin had to work the next day and I had a barbeque to attend. We separated after a few hours and I walked her to the bus-stop and waited until she boarded before leaving. It was 4:00 a.m. when my baby sister called from the hospital to update me on the Minister's condition. It was some gruesome details about the surgical procedure, which had to be performed to save our sister's life. The surgeon that performed it was delayed from leaving the hospital before my sister arrived. If he had left that night on time my sister would have died that morning. He was the only qualified to do what had to be done. God definitely had His Hand in this. I went upstairs to sleep trusting that the assigned officer would guard the crime scene. I never fell asleep but instead just bathed and dressed for the upcoming barbeque. I felt grateful that I had something to do, which would take my mind off of what had happened to my sister the minister.

IN GOD I TRUST

I T WAS AUGUST 24, 2007 and the morning sun was shining in its glory. I was up all night and still shaken by the events that had unfolded. In spite of my own circumstances, I was compelled to keep the commitment I made weeks ago. My partners in the neighborhood wanted to bless the area children with a huge free barbeque. I was going to be one of the cooks and I looked forward to being a part of an historic moment for the neighborhood. I knew the crime scene investigators were due to come this morning but I didn't have a specific time. I would have to use my ten speed bike to commute between the park and my home. It would be a challenge and I was confident that my faith in Jesus the Christ would provide the strength. The park was where the cook out would be held. It was only a five minute ride on my bike. I left the location with the assigned officer guarding the house. It was not the same one that was there over night. Took a moment to explain some details about what had happened and then I left. It was about 8:30 a.m. when I arrived. The crews were already out there setting up their grills and off-loading supplies from their vehicles. My partner was there and to my surprise he had someone there to get things started. Everybody who knew of my tragedy was offering their support. Anytime I gave any information about what happened, I would just break out in tears. My partner told me that he didn't expect me to help but I insisted that he give me something to do. I began to arrange the tables in his area and also brought out the rest of his supplies from his truck. I started to fill a little better as I offered suggestions and cleaned up the area. I then let him know that I would be going back and forth between here and my house. I told him about the crime scene investigators coming to dust for prints and gather any other evidence that they could. He was extremely compassionate about my situation, showing a side of himself that I never saw. When the crew started to light up their morning blunts, I got in the circle and took a few hits to ease my pain. I stayed an hour and a half before I realized the time. I took off on my bike and headed back to the house.

When I arrived back at the house, I learned to my surprise that the crime scene investigators had come and gone. The police officer guarding the residence had also left. I was very disappointed and questioned the landlord about what had taken place. He was not much use as he busily was cleaning up the blood. I went into the kitchen and looked around envisioning what my sister must have gone through. It was a very unsettling feeling as I viewed the blood splatters on the wall and the pools of blood on the floor. I was shaken and angry as I began to question the landlord again. "What did the police do while they were here? Did they lift any finger prints?" I looked directly at him as he started to answer. "I didn't watch while they were down here. I'm still having trouble believing what took place. I think they took finger prints. They didn't check the drains because people had used the sink before they came." I couldn't believe that he was that much of an idiot to allow anyone down here before the police came. I knew I should have stayed and waited. I trusted this man to call me when they arrived and he couldn't even do that. I began to believe that he had something to hide but couldn't put my finger on it. I thought about lashing out at him for his incompetence but knew that it wouldn't make a difference. I went upstairs to my apartment and sobbed uncontrollably for some time before returning to the park. I called the detectives first to get an update about Barry and to let them know where I would be at.

My people were busy with grills and the smell of charcoal was in the air. I still made them feel uncomfortable when I was around. I didn't have anything to do there but watch. I then realized that my help wasn't needed. I wondered if that still would have been the case if my sister had not been attacked. Time continued to move forward and an hour had passed when I noticed a car had drove right through the park up to where I was at. It was no mystery who the burly white men that got out of the car were. The people around me were nervous because the smell of weed was thick in the air. "Relax guys! Does anyone know where Zeke is at? We are not here for anything else so continue with your cook-out." I told everyone to chill out as I walked up to the officers. "Hey I'm Zeke." They began to explain to me that they needed me to come to the precinct. I could come on my own or ride with them. I asked my close friend who was like a brother to me to watch my bike. I didn't want them to say too much about why I was needed until I got into the car. I felt real special as they drove back through the crowd and out the park. They offered their sympathy and began to tell me about some evidence that might help identify who was responsible for my sister's condition. "We have a 911 tape and need you to hear and maybe identify the voice. We need to know if it was your sister calling." Wow they had a 911 tape recording! I thought to myself. Someone had called this in but didn't let me know. It was so common for Blacks in the hood to not get involved in these matters. We all had difficulty coming forward with any information about anything because we often feared becoming a suspect. We also didn't trust the police to keep our identity secret. I sat in the back of the car full of hope that this piece of evidence would tie Barry to the crime.

We pulled into the precinct parking lot and entered the building through the back door. It was unusual for me because I generally came in thru the front in handcuffs. It was the new style of building constructed to look more like a fortress than a location for public access. I followed the two detectives upstairs and entered a room filled with communication equipment. They began to explain to me that they needed to know if the voice on the tape was my sister's or a known person. The detectives summoned the technician to play the tape and I listened intently. "Hello someone has been hurt could you please send an ambulance." The voice then gave the location and hung up when the operator requested further information. This look of disappointment shown upon my face; then I began to speak. "Excuse me, could you play the tape again? The voice doesn't sound like my sister." The operator started to play the tape again and I listened even more intently, while praying to God to assist me in making the identification. There was a crackling sound in the background and the sound wasn't of the best quality. "It's definitely not my sister." I was more disappointed than the police. They were so hopeful that the call would make a major difference in the case. The first hours of an investigation is the most crucial because memories fade and evidence disappear. "Thank you sir, we appreciate you coming down. We will continue to work on this." I could see that they were genuinely concerned about the outcome of the case. It wasn't just about me but also about their numbers because the precinct was experiencing an upsurge of violent crime. The 911 call had come in at 11:45 p.m. and an officer did respond. When they arrived at the house no one answered and the second floor outside door was open. They could not enter the premises without being let in. They eventually dismissed the call as unfounded. They drove me back to the park where the cook out was in full swing. My people gave me something to eat and I continued to talk about my dismay at someone doing what they did to my family. I was not the only one angry. My people were also disgusted about the event because they had gotten to know my sister well. They said she was good people and never troubled them and always had a smile. I finished eating and took some pulls off a blunt before heading back home. When I arrived the home attendant for the landlady was helping to clean up the mess. I closed the door to my sister's apartment and went up to my mine own apartment. It didn't take long for me to fall asleep as I began to feel the effect of blunts that I had puffed on.

It was night fall when I awaken. I went to the bathroom and released myself. I splashed some water on my face and gargled slightly. The anger in me had vanished only to be replaced by sorrow. I grabbed my cigarette pack and went downstairs to smoke. The building was quiet. It seemed that I was the only one moving around. I looked at my cell phone and saw that it was just 11:00 p.m. The block was empty and quiet too. That seemed strange even with everything that had taken place. I sat there smoking and soon realized that the figure I was watching come up the block was Barry. "What the fuck is he doing here?" I said out loud. This brazen asshole continued to walk until he reached the house. I was upset at this point that my people had not given me the tool I had asked for. "Barry, what are you doing here?" I continued to scan the area checking for witnesses as I contemplated ending his life right now. I was standing straight up at the top of the steps as he climbed up the stairs. "Zeke man I've been up all day at the precinct and I'm tired." I stared him down before opening my mouth. "I don't give a fuck. Why didn't you go to your mother's house? My nephew is on his way here and I don't want you at this house." I kept looking around hoping for any of my people to show up and watch my back as I plotted his demise. "Man I need some sleep. I'll leave in the morning" I usually lock the door behind me when I sit on the stoop. This time I didn't so I allowed him to go inside while I walked to Skinny's store for a beer. I stood outside Skinny's drinking my beer not wanting to be in the same house as that mother. I was only at the store for a few minutes when I noticed some activity across from me. I watched a dark van pull up past my house and realized that my nephew had arrived. "Oh shit no Dee!" I raced across the street clutching the beer bottle tightly in my hand. My nephew was heading into the house while his sister's sons followed close behind. When I reached the house, I found out that his sister was already inside. I kept shouting for them to come outside and I could hear Barry screaming from inside the house. I was not going to get between them because they were a lot more upset than I was. Lights in the block started coming on as cries of pain filed the air. I was helpless at this point because they were not responding to my voice of reason. Just as fast my baby sister pulled up as if sent by God and I quickly filled her in. "Baby Sis they gonna kill him I can't let that happen." She tried to calm me down but to no avail. I couldn't let my family mess up their lives over this piece of shit. I called the police before trying to get into the house myself. Barry had barricaded himself in

ZEKE SMITH

the bathroom after fleeing from the beating they were putting on him. I was glad that his body wasn't stretched out on the floor. I started pulling some of the big bodies out the door while my sister became hysterical. She did not do well in these types of situations and I became more determined to bring it under control. I let them know the police were on the way to prevent them from doing any more damage. My sister was in the hospital fighting for her life and these fools were trying to damage theirs. I don't know how but my niece had got to the house before my nephew which began to look like a calculated plan. The police pulled up as I was getting my two tall younger nephews to leave the house so tat their aunt would calm down. I also let them know that if anyone had to do a bid for this, it would be me. Finally the voice of reason was heard. I went downstairs to let the police know what type of assistance was needed. They were well aware of the past events and were eager to help. They advised me that Barry could stay because it was his home. I advised them that if Barry stayed it would be his grave. They went inside and escorted him out of the house. He was anxious to take their suggestion to stay somewhere else because they would not be able to protect him. I told him to take everything he needed because he would not be allowed back inside. The police gave him a ride someplace and calm slowly returned. I was feeling something different now as I considered sacrificing my freedom to avenge the beating of my sister. I knew that I would do better in jail than anyone else present. My sister's children and grandchildren began to settle themselves in the house. My baby sister also had calmed herself down and we all had a good laugh about tonight's events. I offered my couch to my nephew but he refused. He had left his family home and would instead be sleeping cross town at a friend's house. I sat outside on the stoop foe awhile before finally retiring in my own apartment. The rest of the clan settled in Big Mama's place and Baby Sis returned home.

I awoke that morning after having an uneasy sleep. The hallway was filled with the smell of food cooking. I made myself a nice breakfast and ate before taking my shower. It was Sunday morning and church service was on my day's agenda. I had to go worship and give praise and glory to God for all the things that I went through and survived. I arrived early enough to help one of the trustees with cleaning up the front of the church and the parking lot. I felt I had to stay busy to relax and keep my mind off of my sister's tragedy. I often fought back tears and suppressed my grief as I kept reliving in my mind the attack on my sister. The article in the Post had made everyone aware who may not have already known, why my sister the minister would not be in church today. I finished up the outside cleaning and made my way upstairs to Sunday school. When I made my way into the large room, one of the older members whom I was fond of was already there. "Good morning Brother Zeke, how is Minister Easley doing?" She asked in her soft yet firm voice with genuine concern. "Not so good Sister Gloria. She hasn't regain consciousness and is in the fight of her life. I'm just trusting God to care for her right now." Sister Gloria was a very attractive woman and was aging with grace. I felt such a strong attraction towards her. It was not just about her maturity and grace, but more about her devotion for studying the word of God. I was still a married man and failed in previous attempts to get a divorce; however, I would not pass up the opportunity to court. She was not the type of woman I was accustomed to. She was the type of woman though that I needed in my life. "Brother Zeke my prayers are with you and your family." Sister Gloria was sitting when I entered the room. I was standing as we spoke, still uncertain about where I myself would sit. When she finished speaking she rose from her seat and faced me. I could feel the tears begin to roll down my cheeks. I began to pat my pockets in search of my handkerchief. She extended her arms towards me and I collapsed in her gentle embrace. I started to hear her voice as the relaxing scent of her perfume filled my nostrils. "It's going to be alright Brother Zeke; you just trust and believe in God's word. He will bring you through." My tears increased and my breathing became labored. I tried to respond to her comforting words but nothing would come out. She continued to hold me and I continued to cry. I started to question my decision to come to church with so much pain in me. I raised my arms forcing her to loosen the grip she had on me. She slid her hands down the sides of my arms and took a step back. I raised my head while her hands met mine and I too took a step back. "Thank you sister, thank you so much for your words and your concern." She returned to her seat and I took the one next to her at the table. I could hear some conversation in the hall outside the room as other members began entering the room. It was a good class; I just had trouble focusing as anger tried to take over. My thoughts were with my sister. When class was over we all departed but not before a prayer was uttered by the group for myself and family.

I stopped for refreshments before entering the sanctuary. I understood everyone's curiosity but it change my attitude about answering so many questions. The majority of the people just wanted details, so that they could retell the story to someone else. I shortened my stay in the refreshment area and entered the sanctuary, where the devotional service had started. Calm fell over the place as I entered and proceeded to my usual seat in the middle of the pews. I bowed my head immediately after sitting down. I began to pray for my sister's recovery and apprehension of her attacker. I also asked God to let justice prevail and not allow me to jeopardize my future by seeking revenge. I left church that day with a vague memory of what had taken place.

I returned home to find that the news reporters had visited the house again. I also learned that a few of the T.V. news networks had also came and conducted some interviews. I went to work the following day with everyone confronting me about the story in the Daily News. I had made the front page with a large photo of me in tears asking for the law and the Lord to deliver justice. My days became a non-stop routine of; going to work, visiting the hospital and searching for clues at night. I knew I couldn't keep this up but I maintained it for the next two weeks. Time was passing and the police were no closer to presenting a case to the grand jury, as they were on the first day of the crime. My sister had a police guard around the clock but I fought hard to get one removed who seemed preoccupied with other things. I had a few run inns with this officer until she was finally removed. Overall the guard detail was professional and courteous and often displayed compassion. My people bungled an opportunity to help make a case against Barry by delivering a beating instead of visiting a potential witness. They couldn't resist the chance they had after they had, when they unexpectantly caught him napping in the park. He showed up at church the following Sunday seeking sympathy and proclaiming his innocence. He was bruised but not bad enough. There was a group of church members that believed in him not being guilty and severed ties to those I became aware of. My birthday came but there was no celebrating. I just wanted my sister to open her eyes and speak. I wanted her to tell me what had happened that night. I wanted to hear from her the name of her assailant. If any of those things would happen, then I could celebrate a birthday.

The longer my sister laid in that bed comatose and unresponsive to stimuli, the more apparent it seemed that recovery was impossible. I believed in the power and might of Jesus the Christ and the healing power of his name. I also believed that God's plan was different from anything we all had hoped for. My sister had achieved a great deal and I was especially proud of her. We shared a common thread because of things in the world we both liked. She was my example that you can change if you trust Jesus. She began to take an interest in my salvation and I could see the glee in her eyes whenever she introduced me in church. I too had my demons that were a struggle to get rid of. God had stepped in and spared her life for other healings to take place around her. My beloved sister's greatest liability was relationships and I knew that Jesus was bringing her home to be with him. She finally would have a man that would treat her the way she deserved to be treated. I knew that Jesus would not desert her. I was comfortable knowing that "Big Mama" would not wake up. I continued my visits daily skipping only those days when someone took my place and begged me to stay home. I would read Psalm 86 to her while sitting at the foot of the bed. The hospital staff knew me well. The police officers at the 81st prescient also became very familiar with me. I began to utilize street pharmaceuticals to ease my pain and help me function daily. September was coming to end and I felt that my sister would not be here this Christmas.

I was moving around at a hectic pace. I began to wonder where all the energy came from and how long it would last. I realized that a combination of anger and love was the driving force that kept me going. The anger I felt was towards the police who couldn't do anything right and Barry who became bolder with his cries of innocence. I started using my vintage ten speed bike to get around. I assisted my nephew in getting the proper information, as he prepared to move his mother south for her recovery. He was not wiling to prepare for what seemed inevitable to me. I kept up my bedside vigil and cherished every moment that I could spend with my sister. I began to get some leads and a better picture of what might have happened that night. I was given some names of people that might have assisted Barry that night. My revelations to the police fell on deaf ears. The investigation of my sister's beating didn't prevent any officer from taking their time off. I was appalled at the circumstances that unfolded before me. I had another confrontation at the church when Barry once again showed up. This time my anger was unleashed at all those who permitted his continued presence there. The point I was making finally took root and he was barred from the premises until this matter was cleared. It was too little too late for me; because the insensitivity that was demonstrated, left a bitter tastes in my mouth, that wouldn't go away. My niece, who was my sister's oldest child, had to return home for some personal reasons. I continued to assist my nephew with whatever he was trying to do. He had a close relationship with his mother and if she didn't survive, it would crush him. I also was concerned about how her grandchildren would react. I was able to organize a group of her closest friends from our church to help me with visitation. The most important one being Sister Murphy who was

ZEKE SMITH

consistent in relieving me so I could either rest or go to work. I wanted to make sure that someone was always with her during visiting hours.

It was the last week in the month of September that her condition took a turn for the worst. She had been showing some signs life that suggested a miraculous recovery was about to take place. I even reversed my earlier thinking as I began to believe that God was going to show His power and might. I began to believe that all the prayers that were uttered on her behalf would be answered. I thought about talking my nephew out of moving her because she would receive more support if left in New York. My niece was on her back from the trip back home when the doctors gave me the news. It was the morning of September 29, 2007 when I got the news. I had gone home the night before feeling good about my sister's chances. The doctors said that something happened overnight that changed the prognosis. They couldn't name it but I said it was a combination of my sister's desire to live and god's will to bring her home. There was no longer any brain activity and the only thing that had her breathing was the respirator. I was shattered and grief stricken and began to cry uncontrollably. I could hardly speak as I began to make the phone calls to my family. My baby sister had visiting as often as I was and she didn't take the news too well. In a very short time the entire family was present as we waited for her daughter to return. It would have to be her children's decision about pulling the plug. The hospital's policy permitted someone to speak to us about donating any usable organs. We naturally became enraged. It was not just from anger because we felt disrespected but also from ignorance because of our grief. My niece arrived that afternoon along with her four sons. It was the saddest day of our lives and all the courage I showed up to that point just left me. I forgot about my love of Christ for a moment and the faith I had in God's will being done. The preaching I did about remaining calm and trusting the Lord was exchanged for cries of murder. I became the one to watch as my family wondered what moves I would make. I could hear them whispering to each other to keep an eye on me. My church family increased their attendance. I had allowed more of the membership to visit the hospital that week. I knew what she meant to them and what they meant to her. I turned away the curiosity seekers and allowed only the ones that genuinely had a relationship with her. I didn't care about how anyone felt at that time because I was seeking the power of prayer to reverse my sister's condition. I was shadowed where ever I went as my grief left me crippled. I didn't cry alone and I knew others w feeling just as bad. It was approximately 9:30 p.m. when they disconnected the respirator. It was a short time later that my sister the minister was pronounced dead.

The reality of things was difficult to digest. The minister's battle was over and mine had just begun. In recent weeks when I thought about the possibility of her death, I didn't see myself having trouble accepting it. I didn't see myself becoming so angry that the thought of forgiveness would elude me. I was ready to return to a former self to wreak havoc upon anyone I thought responsible. I was refusing to allow prayer to be an option. I was hurting more than ever and couldn't understand why. I regretted not speaking more truthful to my sister as she lied in that bed. I listened to the advice of my family who believed more in her recovery than I did. I hid my true feelings and thoughts from everyone but God and was now feeling this deep regret. I left the hospital alone not wanting any company. I didn't know where I was going or what I was going to do. My money was short so my choices were limited. I thanked the few friends that were present as I exited the floor. I did feel good about my decision to allow her church to visit during her final days against my family wishes.

It took some time for me to reach the neighborhood. I resisted the urge to lose control and act a fool. I went into my small cramped apartment and let the tears flow. I knew if my sister were here now counseling me, she would be able to guide me to a scripture to find relief. She wasn't here so I relied on the two that carried me since I had found Jesus. I read Psalm 27 for strength and Psalm 34 for gratitude. Psalm 34 had become even more special because my sister Big Mama would often quote from it before she started her sermons. "I will bless the lord at all times. His praise shall continually be in my mouth." I started to feel some relief as my anger and pain subsided. I began to pray for justice against those responsible. I told God that he would have to handle this and that I trusted Him to bring meaning to my sister's death. I asked God to comfort us all and foster unity amongst us. We had been battling each other with our different ideologies about the best course to take. There were different camps in place and each had a course of action that they thought should be followed. My sister didn't have a will and no one could recall any conversation about what she might have wanted. Her possessions were being claim even before her soul ascended to heaven. I was certain about where she would be residing at for now on. I was certain that now she was with a man that would love her for all eternity and never disappoint her. I was certain that she was with Jesus the Christ. "Hallelujah, hallelujah, hallelujah!" I shouted out loud as I felt the spirit of the lord fall upon me. I lay across my couch and buried my

ZEKE SMITH

head in my hands, as I fell off to sleep. My face kept sliding off my arms as the tears continued to flow. I was confident that there would be more joy in the morning.

The light started flickering thru the blinds as distant voices filled my ears. I took a moment to think about where I was and what day it was. I felt disorientated and the voices grew louder. I rose from my very comfortable position in the bed. I soon realized that I had passed out after returning from the hospital. Daybreak was fighting its way thru the blinds and my eye lids were struggling against, whatever substance matter this was that had the lids glued. I started smelling morning food and the voices downstairs grew louder and louder. It wasn't that they were getting closer but my level of consciousness was increasing. Using all my current available strength, I lifted myself off the bed and sat straight up. I quickly surveyed the room and concluded that nothing was out of place. I placed one foot on the floor and the other was dragged off the bed with the leg following close behind. The only thing that I reached for at this point was my dick as I headed to the hallway bathroom. The aroma of the food was even more pronounced now as I stepped into the bathroom. I took my time to aim accurately as my member found freedom in the gentleness of the bathroom atmosphere. I watched while a strong steady stream of a deeply colored yellow liquid flowed freely but forcefully from the small opening stuck at the tip of this swollen piece of meat in my hands. I could hear my niece voice announcing the readiness of the meal she had finished cooking. I listen for a voice to yell out my name, to summon me down for a sampling of the meal. I shook myself off as the final drops from my discharge of fluids had ended. I washed my hands before leaving the confines of the small bathroom and back into the narrow hallway. I still had not heard my name as I walked slowly back to my rooms. Yes, my apartment was just a series of rooms attached in no specific order that afforded me the illusion of being whole or being complete. I turned on the kitchen T.V. and prepared my self to watch some porn. I would be accessing my personal library because this T.V. was only able to show VCR tapes. I selected one of favorites of a beauty booty contest that had amateur stars showing their stuffs and talents to an eager audience of party goers. The girls were barely legal and in excellent condition with the right attitude. It was more than a treat for me because I could never be so fortunate to have attended one of these parties. The end of part 2 of this tape showed a set of twins that had the fattest lips that I ever seen. I'm talking about the other set of lips located downstairs. The area was all ways a place of interest for me especially if it was a tenderoni.

I started gathering my clothes together to put an outfit in place for the day. I wanted comfort with cuteness. I kept looking up at the screen to decide whether or not I should cum before or after my shower. I figured I could always rewind the tape to bring it back to a choice scene. I clothes for the day was selected and I started to strip down to expose my nakedness. I left the kitchen and put the clothes that I had removed in my dirty clothes bag. I looked around the room until I found my robe. I also reached for the jar of Vaseline as I returned to the kitchen. I laid my robe across the back of the chair that faced the television. The set of twins on the screen in front of me were busy exploring each other. They were both fine examples of the human form. Their supple forms were a delight to my sight. My member began to respond to what was before me. I looked down to watch its limp form transform to an erect object that protruded from my body. I removed the cover from the Vaseline and removed some of the contents with two fingers of my right hand. I became fixated on the images before me. I applied the grease from the jar to the length of my now stiff cock. The lips on the girls' pussy were fat and inviting. I began a slow massage of my member as the two assumed the 69 position. The seat I sat in wasn't close enough to the erotic vision before me. I rose from my seat with cock in hand for a closer look. I had watched this scene many times before but each time I looked seemed like the first. My dick felt good in my hands as I continued the massage in an up and down motion. The girls picked up their pace as they started to lick each other. I too picked up my pace as stood before them. The head of my cock gleamed in the light of day that flickered through the kitchen blinds. Oh how I wished that the girls were in my apartment with me. The absence of their physical bodies would not prevent me from enjoying them. I hands began to move faster as the grease slid through my fingers. "Ooooo, oh, emmm!" I moaned to myself as my cock reached its maximum length. I backed away from the front of the refrigerator that the T.V. sat upon. I turned my body slightly towards the window to my right but continued my stare at girls. I squeezed hard on my dick as the sensitivity of its head became more pronounced. "Damn girls the pussy looks good. I like what you're doing now make me cum." I spoke loudly as if they could hear the sounds of my pleasure. I started to instruct them on what I wanted to do as if they could respond. I was lost in my thoughts now while my imagination became a reality. My body stiffened and my toes curled as a clear thick liquid started oozing from the opening at the tip of my dick. I began to jerk as I fought back against my member wanting to free the semen from my body. My efforts were futile as

ZEKE SMITH

my body jerked and my grip tightened as a stream of cum headed towards the window. I didn't care at the time where it landed. I didn't care about what it might stain. I only cared about how good it felt as stream after stream of cum landed on the radiator, the curtains, and then finally on the floor. The girls had finished licking each other as a young male entered the scene with an erect cock of his own. The girls changed position and now lay alongside each other. They started spreading their legs and the lips of their pussy wide apart in anticipation of what was about to come. I was done and the voices in my hallway grew loud again. I would not watch this young buck fuck my girls because of jealousy. I would not watch anymore because too much time had elapsed and I needed a shower. I reached up with my left hand and stopped the tape. I turned off the T.V. and exited the kitchen. I looked back at my cum that was now fluid than what it was when it left my body. I grabbed a paper towel to clean my hand and cum that landed on the floor. I made my way to the bathroom to finish the clean-up. I thought about how nice it was to have pussy on demand even if I couldn't touch it.

The quick shower had done what I expected it to do. I felt fresh as I dressed after adding some scent to my body. I could clearly hear the conversations downstairs. It was naturally about the money. My sister was gone but not the bickering about her meager possessions. My grief didn't permit me to think about those things. I was now concerned with closure for myself and a forgetting of the ordeal that dominated my life for the past month or so. I wanted to make sure all her friends knew that her battle was over and where they could view her one last time. The visitations that I had allowed for many of the church members were now more relevant to me. It would have been more than a shame if those who cared the most for her, weren't allowed to see her before God claimed her soul. I knew that this morning she had no pain and was in good company. Now her children would have to come face to face with the reality that mama was gone. There would be no more opportunities for them to share any feelings with her and get a response. There would be no more lectures about how they were behaving from her. There would be no more opportunities for them to express thanks, gratitude, appreciation, or love with their mama. The window of opportunity was shut tight and any communication now with my sister would have to be in spirit. I knew that communicating in spirit would be their biggest obstacle to overcome. My own mother's death was the catalyses that sent me to Jesus the Christ. I prayed that the passing of the minister would do the same for her children.

I made my way downstairs feeling reluctant to see anybody. I knew I couldn't hide from what I was feeling for my niece and nephew. I knew the selfishness that both of them were displaying would not disappear. I just knew that I couldn't let them get into my head and disrupt my grieving process that was sure to last awhile. "Good morning family. Did everybody sleep alright last night?" I had to start somewhere and figured this was the most appropriate way for me to begin. I glanced over at the dining room table and saw my photographs being displayed. They brought back instant memories of my son's birth and the relationship I had with his mother. I saw so many of my life's memories before me and wondered how they were in the possession of my now deceased sister. The most startling revelation was that they were now being claimed by my niece. Even after I disclosed my ownership of those photos, she still refused to turn them ver. She claimed that they were now her property because of her mother's death. I didn't argue because it wasn't appropriate but it was the beginning of my displeasure with her actions. I had a hard time accepting her reasoning for claiming my photos. I couldn't even remember how my sister came into possession of them. I had petitioned my brothers of the men's ministry at my church for a love offering to cover my expenses for all the time I spent at the hospital caring for my sister and investigating her assault. I decided that this would be a good time, to follow up on that request. I left the house to go to the church. I also wanted to make sure that the church had information about the funeral arrangements. It was details like this that the rest of the family was slow to tend too. I was able to speak with the chairman of the Men's Ministry, who informed me that the funds that were collected were turned over to my sister's best friend. This was the same friend that reduced her socializing because of my sister's decision to marry Barry. Barry was the prime suspect in the eyes of the people for my sister's attack and subsequent death. I didn't believe any different but I refused to be the one to deliver justice. I continue to rely on the law and the Lord to do that. The family had omitted Barry and even his family from any participation in the process of planning my sister's homecoming. It didn't seem to matter to anyone that the money they were using, was from an insurance policy that he was the beneficiary of. This decision would come back to haunt them later. I had a new source of discontent to deal with after learning that the several hundred dollars that was collected on my behalf were not at my disposal. I didn't even understand how this self-appointed representative could act in this manner, without consulting with me. I realized the dilemma that the trustee chairman faced and did not hold him accountable.

ZEKE SMITH

It was Sunday morning and I was preparing myself for worship. I was the only one in the house that saw the need to be at church praising God. It had been a hectic past few days. The media was still involved in covering the story of my sister's demise. They wanted to take some graphic pictures which I didn't agree to. They respected my wishes and the reporter Mr. Gould, who was now a close friend and confidant assured me that any future coverage would be in good taste. I arrived at church feeling some relief that the worst was over. I felt an even greater relief that the suffering of my sister was over. I followed my normal routine of helping to clean the front of the church and the adjacent parking lot. Since the death of our pastor you never knew who would be preaching until you got there. I went to Sunday school which went as well as could be expected. My fellow believers were kind in their approach to me and I filled them in on the final minutes of my sister's life. I dispelled any rumors that might have been circulating and gave a more accurate account. I received some cards offering condolences and financial assistance. The prayer at the end of our lesson that day was devoted to me and my family. I also offered prayer for church unity and for gratitude concerning how I was embraced by the congregation. I stopped in the snack room before entering the sanctuary at the conclusion of Sunday school. When I came down the stairs from the snack room I couldn't help notice the bee hive of activity near the side exit door. There were curious looks on the faces of some of my friends as my attention continued to focus on the commotion at the door. I gasped when I realized what was going on. Barry was attempting to enter the church as he explained his displeasure at not being allowed to see his wife or participate in her funeral. I walked over and struggled to contain myself as others became alarmed by my arrival. "Yo Zeke, I didn't do it and your nephews beat me up the other day." He trembled as he spoke but still displayed certain arrogance as he delivered his lines. "What happened that day Barry? You didn't protect my sister if you didn't do it. I can't protect you and you don't need to be here." I stood face to face with him as a few of the deacons stood between me and him. I saw some bandages on his face and other bruises that weren't covered up. My nephews did a lousy job of whooping that ass. It just proved that should leave those things to the pros. I fought back the urge to reach through the small crowd and choke the life from him. I felt like if he loved my sister so much than he should be with her. I began to protest loudly about how he was still being allowed to come here. I didn't want to hear about Christian values or the concept of American justice. What I wanted was for this piece of shit to be gone out of my sight. I wanted these people here to understand that this ingrate was guilty of my sister's death regardless of what wasn't proven. I prayed that they would understand that I would hold anyone accountable that chose the wrong position in this matter.

Barry got the message and finally limped away but not without loudly voicing more of his disproval about his treatment. I burst into tears once he was out of my sight. I needed God now, so I left with tears still running down my face and entered the sanctuary. I too had a limp even after proclaiming my healing from accident I was in. It appeared that stress would aggravate the condition in my knee that had yet to be officially diagnosed. I made my way down the aisle and sat in my usual section that positioned me in front of whoever might be preaching. The service was uplifting and short and the walk back home seemed much longer. It seemed like the sun was always shining. I could not remember the last time it rained. The friends, neighbors, and strangers that I passed on my way home, all had smiling cheerful faces. I asked myself; was this for me and did all of them know about the turmoil inside me? I walked slowly up the stairs when I reached my house. I stopped momentarily to greet my landlady and put a smile on her face. I turned on the television once I was inside my apartment. I was hoping that Sunday football would divert my attention away from the pain inside me. I had to work this Sunday. I was saving my bereavement days for the funeral and burial, which now were only a few days away.

My daughter who lived in Virginia had known of my sister's attack and I had also informed my older son. They both lived in reach of one another. What neither knew at this time; was that my sister had died. I was so busy with my anger that I kept putting off telling them. I made the call to Legs and let her know that Big Mama had gone home. I told her first because I wanted to make sure that Z Baby had someone with her. My wife immediately made plans to attend the funeral. She didn't have a lot of time to plan and her resources were limited. I suggested that she contact my son and see if they could all travel together to save on the expense. My son's mother was always close to Big Mama and my own mother. I knew that she would not miss the funeral. It was strange how my wife whom had initially despised Carolyn for the way she treated my son had suddenly grown so close. I was satisfied beyond belief that both my children would be here to share the grief. I let Carolyn's mother know that my sister had passed and that they would be coming to New York soon. God has a way of bringing people together under some difficult circumstances and performing miraculous healings of their souls. My feelings towards my niece and nephew continue to harden because of neglect of anyone else's feelings besides their own. I just wanted this to be over so that I could plan the rest of my life. The last time my children were together was last year for Thanksgiving. It was at that time that my son let me know that he was grown and did not have to listen to me. My daughter got a big laugh at his defiance when he reused to eat the carrots I put on his plate. It was also the last time I saw my wife because she is the one that brought them on the train. I just mailed the money for them all to travel. My wife never did pay back the money she borrowed for her fare. She also wasn't very friendly towards me when she arrived. I began to make arrangements for their arrival, which would be one day before the funeral. Legs would likely stay with her best girlfriend, and my daughter would stay with me, when they arrive. Carolyn and my son would be close by because Carolyn's mother lived around the corner from me. I was tired now and decided that the best thing to do would be to go to bed early and pray for a better day tomorrow.

I was awaken by the songs of the birds giving God praise. The sun was flickering through the blinds and my eyes kept blinking in an attempt to clear the gunk from them. I sat straight up in the bed and swung my legs to plant them on the floor. I was excited about today because my daughter would be arriving along with her brother. Carolyn had contacted Legs so they were all traveling together. My wife would stay with her best friend so everyone would avoid the expense of a hotel. They would be traveling by car and I knew my daughter would alert me when they were close. I took a long shower as I pondered the events that were unfolding. I could only attribute the cooperation of both my babies' mama to the will of God. My Lord had begun to fill my life with purpose when I was released from Rikers Island the last time. I started my own ministry with the youth while I was there. I got reconnected with Christ to avoid any more drama in my life. Righteousness had always been a part of me but I didn't know what to call. It was always a struggle to be as low down as those around me. I even gave the suckers an even break. I rinsed off the soap and exited the shower. I picked out an outfit that would accent the areas of my body that had become more developed. I wanted to make a good impression on my arriving guests. I didn't want any signs of my struggles with the beast to show. I wanted to have a glow so that there would be no worry about me. My whole family would be present at the funeral and some friends that I hadn't seen for decades. I already had been receiving calls prayers from people that had followed the story in the paper. There was both the curious and concerned. I never tried to figure out which one was which. There were no more trips to be made or errands to run. I stayed in the neighborhood to assure everyone that I would stay out of trouble. Barry's sisters came by the house to drop off food and to offer their condolences. I had watched them both grow up and raise two boys without ever knowing the connection. I felt they were just as much a victim from their brother's actions and neither voiced support about his innocence. Their presence created tension in the house but I graciously accepted what they brought and explained how awkward the situation was. They both understood and departed without incident. I now felt empowered to bring calm and understanding amidst so much anger and confusion. I knew God step to his business and I also trusted NYPD not to make any more mistakes. Time was moving as morning quickly became noon. I was expecting my daughter to any minute to say that they were passing through New Jersey. I didn't have to wait long as a familiar ring tone echoed in my ear.

"Hey Z Baby, is that you?" I began to walk away from the house as I could hear a rushing sound in the background. There was a little static too as my baby responded to the question. "Hey Daddy, we are almost there. We are getting ready to enter the Holland Tunnel." A big smile could be seen spreading across my face as I continued to walk up the block away from the house. "Oh man it's so good to hear your voice. I can't wait for all of yawl to get here." I stopped in my tracks and leaned against the fence of the last house with a front yard. "Daddy I'm going to lose you because we are about to enter the tunnel." I started to respond when static filled my ear and the phone went dead. "Oh well, my baby will call back" I was speaking out loud with no one listening, as I raised myself off the fence, and walked back to the house. I rushed upstairs to make one last thorough inspection of my apartment. I didn't want my children to encounter any unexpected surprises.

I was back downstairs waiting anxiously for the car to pull up. It wasn't long before my phone rang and a familiar name popped up on my caller I.D. "Big Dee what's up?" I shouted into the receiver. "Hey Zeke, I'm near your block could you give me that address again?" This was my wife's best friend whom she would be staying with while in New York. "Where are you now Dee?" "I'm coming down Mother Gaston." She was right around the corner and didn't realize it. "Okay just keep on down to Broadway and make that double left and you will see me standing outside." They sure planned their arrival well. They would only be minutes apart from getting here. I guess my wife wasn't ready to spend any time alone with me while she waited for her friend. It was just a matter of minutes before I saw that familiar black jeep pull into the block. I walked up to the car and pointed to a parking spot. Big Dee stepped out and began a long hug. The friendship I had with Dee was one of the good things from my marriage. It had survived when everything else had failed. She was always a means of me knowing what my wife might have been going through without me. "Hey Dee, you looking well, Legs should be here any minute now." She smiled and began to explain how she couldn't remember the block from the last time she was here. "Hey girl, we all are getting old and the memory is the first to go." We both stood there chit chatting waiting for Legs and the rest of the gang to arrive. A very familiar car pulled into the block with a loud engine. The wait was over and I could see Z Baby crouched up in the back seat. I ran to the car and before Z Baby could get out; my wife exited the vehicle and gave me a long passionate hug. I was taken by surprise but it felt good. It had never happened this way on any of her previous trips here. In fact the last time she didn't even get out of the car. "Hey Kitten, I whispered into her ear. The funeral is tomorrow and I'm glad that you're here." She slowly released her grip on me and said; "I'm sorry for your loss. Big Mama was special to me too." Yes, Big Mama was special. She was the only sister that attended my wedding. She was very happy for me that day as we all went out to eat after the civil ceremony. Z Baby climbed out of the car as her brother made his way around too. Carolyn stayed inside as I gave her the instructions for tomorrow. I let her know what time my son should be around here because he would be riding in the family car. I let her know that I had my own limo so we all would be together. My family wanted to keep my grief as far away from them as possible. I was the emotional crier at such events as the rest of them tried to maintain a dignified posture. I hugged both my kids as everyone one else returned to their appropriate vehicles. I helped Z Baby carry her bags upstairs while both cars pulled off. It was nice to have my daughter back with me.

We both walked through the door with my mind still on my wife. Her body had felt so light and fragile. I some how thought that her condition was my fault. I should have been more stubborn when asked to leave the first time. I should have been more defiant when asked to leave the last time. We both had pledged that there would be no more separations but she reneged on that promise. She cut me out of the relocation plans even after I gave her the bulk of the money from the settlement. I still loved this money regardless of the condition of her health. I saw some satisfaction in my daughter's face when Legs and I hugged downstairs. "Z Baby, you can put your bags over there and you can either sleep on the couch or my bed." My daughter looked at me as I spoke and a new sadness fell over me. I realized how much she had grown without me being there to educate along the way. I thought about all the father daughter interaction that I missed. The interaction that fathers looked forward to each time they cradle their little girls in their arms. Z Baby had only recently asked me to move down there where she was at. She said I could easily get a job with all the things I knew how to do. It was a wonderful idea coming from an innocent child that didn't understand the other complexities of life that went with it. I told her I would give it some thought and she continued to campaign for it whenever we would speak. "Daddy you can take the bed and I don't mind sleeping on the couch. The bed would be better for you with the trouble you have with your knee." There she goes again always thinking about what's best for her dad. It was early evening and too soon for bed, so we settled down and starting scanning the tube for something to watch. I suggested some Chinese food for dinner and she agreed. I went right across the street from the house and returned with a large order of chicken wings and fried rice. When we finished eating it was well after 9p.m., so after cleaning up our mess, we went to bed. We both took the time though to lay out our outfits for tomorrow. "Good night daddy." "Good night Z Baby."

I rose early the next day before the sun crashed through the blinds. Z Baby was still sleep when I went into the bathroom to shower. It was nice waking up with my daughter in the room. She was missing her daddy and I was missing her too. I didn't spend a lot of time in the bathroom knowing that I had to share it with a girl. I grabbed my clothes after re-entering the apartment and went into the kitchen to dress. The daylight started sneaking a peek of the kitchen as I finished putting on my clothes and a fresh scent. I would make breakfast this morning to make my child a little more comfortable. Z Baby loved my pancakes and that's what I would be making for her. I went back into the room and stared making my bed and putting everything else in order. I was in stealth mode to ensure that I wouldn't wake up Z Baby prematurely. I picked up my phone and noticed that I had a few missed calls and some texts waiting to be read. They were well wishes and requests for funeral arrangements for Big Mama. I began to feel some sadness as I ponder the significance of the day. Daylight had picked up some momentum now and the sun was starting to flex its muscle. I began to hear Z Baby stirring in the other room and I shouted; "Good morning Z Baby, I'm making you some pancakes for breakfast!" Her response was quick and filled with excitement. "Okay daddy, I sure do miss your pancakes!" I knew I had picked the right thing to cook. I felt a sense of accomplishment at my daughter's approval of the menu. She continued to rise and was soon in the bathroom showering and getting dressed. The sun was now in its glory and I didn't need to use the lights in the house. The sun had the rooms fully illuminated and I went about the business of making breakfast. I would also have eggs and sausage on the menu and our old favorite grape Kool-Aid. I had to go to the church and make sure things were in order. I was too busy waiting for my children to check yesterday. The rest of the family had gone down yesterday and didn't mention that anything needed to change. The trustees had set 2 shifts to guard the body overnight. I believe this was more of a custom than an actual need for security. I mixed my batter while the sausage fried. I beat up three eggs and had them ready to hit the pan after the pancakes were done. I heard Z Baby come back into the apartment from the bathroom and knew I should pick up the pace. "How many pancakes you want?" I shouted out into the next room. "I just want two pancakes Daddy." I continued on making the breakfast as Z Baby cleaned up her area where she slept at.

"Come on baby, I'm putting the pancakes in the pan now. I guess you want your eggs scrambled?" I didn't like serving cold pancakes and I hated when you wasn't there to get them straight out the pan. "I heard you Daddy; I will be there in a minute." I wanted to hurry up and get to the church. I knew people from the past would be stopping by and I wanted to greet them. I realized that everyone would also not be attending the funeral and some family should be there to speak with them. My sister had a lot of friends and with the media attention; there would be more than a few that we both were friends with. Once upon a time before we knew The Lord our lives were entwined. The night life was something that we both enjoyed. There were instances when I was out doing my thing chasing money, that I ran into my sister attending bar. She was what was known as a "Starmaid." She even won top honors in a few of the nightlife publications. "Alright Z Baby your breakfast is in the plate." It was easy to hear what was happening in the next room, so I knew she would be rushing in soon. "I'm coming now Daddy!" I could hear some frustration in her voice but I didn't care. I wanted my breakfast eaten while it was hot. I began to pile food on to my plate as Z Baby stepped into the kitchen. I watched as Z Baby poured juice in the glasses that I had set down on the table. The kitchen was small and the over-sized table looked out of place when only food was on it. I said grace and we ate quickly, because there was a lot to do and I didn't want to miss anything.

I gripped the banister tight as my daughter and I descended the stairs. "Daddy, are you alright?" My little girl asked with deep concern in her voice. "I'm okay; it's just my knee that gives me trouble from time to time. I never fully recovered from the accident and you know the trouble I've had with getting treatment. I wasn't about to drag that story out about greedy insurance companies that hated to respond properly to claims. We made our way down the stairs and around the corner. I watched as my neighbors either stared or glared as we made our way to the church. I had not seen my sister since she was in the hospital. I was not anxious or filled with joy about seeing her in a coffin. We crossed the street and approached the converted movie house. Wayside Baptist Church was a magnificent structure. It had a mixed congregation from many walks of life and levels of income. I squeezed my daughter's hand as we stood in front of the main entrance. It was time to face the truth that my sister was now; Home with Jesus.

DELIVERENCE

I WAS FINALLY here to see my sister in her glory. I walked slowly through the church gripping my daughter's hand tightly. There was very little activity at this time, except for the few people gathered around the coffin. I soon noticed that a few of the members from the congregation were sitting in the pews. I continued the aisle with my daughter still at my side. There were silent hellos directed at me as I drew closer to the coffin. The few people that stood around began to clear the area and my heart beat quickened. My daughter released my hand and I went and knelt down in front of the coffin. I began to pray a final time before my sister and God. I wanted to make sure that the right people had cOme to claim her soul. She looked so beautiful in her attire. They had done a nice job considering the type of injuries that she had sustained. It still did not do her justice. I had planned to stay awhile after my inspection. I wanted to greet some of her friends that would be paying their respects. I wanted to stand guard one last time to ensure her peace. My sister's close friend Jocelyn was also their collecting cards and giving out information. My sister the minister, closest friends had distanced themselves from her, when her determination led to her marriage. I felt they should have drawn closer to her even if my sister had become difficult to be around. I imagine everyone had some guilt to deal with concerning their relationship with her. My grief began to over-take me and my daughter quickly came to my side. My tears were flowing freely now and began to dampen my shirt collar. My daughter Z Baby helped me to my feet and I stumbled to a nearby seat. I put my face in my hands as a mixture of snot and tears filled my palms. I continued to cry until there were no more tears to fall. I was handed a box of tissue which I used to clean myself up. "Daddy is you still going to stay?" I looked up at my daughter who looked so mature beyond her years. She seemed more like the care giver and I know she wanted me to leave. I tried to answer but words wouldn't leave my lips. Jocelyn walked up to assure me that she would handle things at the church until service started. She said she would collect the cards if any were left. I explained to her that the family members needed to receive the cards that were addressed to them. I rose to my feet and motioned to my daughter that we were leaving. The anger that I was feeling at this time gave me strength and took away the tears. I didn't like the job that Jocelyn was doing but this was not the place to voice it. We made our way back to the house and as we walked, I told my daughter not to leave me alone.

Time had no boundaries as it drew close to the funeral. The community affairs officer of the NYPD had arranged for a police presence during services. I didn't want the prime suspect in my sister's murder to come and disrupt things. My niece and nephew were functioning under stress because their mother's death was starting to hit them hard. I still had to maintain my own composure because the devil was still busy, trying to reclaim one of his own. My daughter was cooperative in keeping a close eye on her dad. She would even remind me of what I could lose if I lost control. I made contact with my wife to make sure that she would arrive on time to ride in the family car. We had plenty of limos to accommodate everyone. I received a few calls from friends of mine and the family as many expressed disbelief at what had happened. The Daily News coverage of the event had made many aware of my loss and reunited me with acquaintances from my past. The local crew that hustled on the block took up a collection for flowers. It was to my surprise that the money was turned over to my nephew. I couldn't understand how they made that decision, when it was my sister and I whom they had the relationship with. I thank them for the gesture any way; because I don't think they realized how much it hurt me. It was nearly time to start leaving the house so I began to change clothes along with my daughter. It was nice to have a female present to critique my look before I left the house. The time away from my daughter made it appear that she was growing up fast. I knew better though and gave thinks to my God keeping her while I was not there.

"Hey Z Baby, are you ready to leave?" I called out to her from the kitchen as I drank some juice. My little girl wasn't displaying any emotions and I didn't want to upset her. She was doing such a good job of babysitting me. "Give me a minute daddy and I will be." Great! I had not been downstairs to see how everyone else was doing since I came back into the house. I would not be going there to check until my daughter was ready to go with me. I rinsed out the glass I was drinking out of and placed it in the dish drain. It was about that time that I could hear the bell ringing downstairs. I went and stuck my head into the hallway outside my door, to make sure it was getting answered. The home attendant was answering the bell and I soon saw that it was my son along with his mother. "Hey you guys can wait downstairs because we getting ready to come down." They both were in the vestibule as I was yelling my instructions to them. I now started to wonder if my wife would be here on time and asked Z Baby to give her a call. I looked at myself in the mirror and saw a face filled with sadness. My eyes were red from crying and I couldn't force a smile on my face. I knew from history that the homecoming service for my sister would take its toll on me. I also knew that it was something that I had to do and I wrote a poem for Baby Sis to read.

Don't Weep For Me

I love all you people gathered in my name; with all you knowing I would do the same.

I'm now with a Man that I adore; who shows me love, and so much more.

I have become who I wanted to be, so all my people don't weep for me.

Weep for my children whom I loved so much; who can no longer feel my tender touch.

Weep for my sisters and the meals we'll miss; and all my grandchildren whom I can't kiss.

Weep for my brother and all his devotion; that even in heaven he created a commotion.

Weep for my friends that all through the years; helped me wipe away some of my tears.

Excuse me for a moment, they're playing my song; I'm looking at Jesus . . . I must move along.

Don't weep for me, for on this day; I now have a Man who will always stay.

There goes that music; "I love you Brother Z, just preserve my memory."

But don't weep for me.

It was heart felt words that The Lord gave me. My sister the minister, affectionately known as Big Mama was happier than I was when I found Jesus. She took pride in mentoring me and we both prayed that all our family would find comfort in the Lord. There were more things that we had in common than our differences. We both were side tracked from what we were raised to be, by false glamour that the night life held. We were always looking for that right love to complete our existence. She had now finally found hers and was on her way home to be with Him. I allowed my mind to drift back to what was most important. My daughter informed me that her mother had arrived and was waiting downstairs with Carolyn and Shawn. We left the apartment and made our way downstairs. I could hear a lot of conversation as we walked past the landlady's room on down to the main floor of the house. I looked around to see both of my families huddled together. My two sisters were there also with their children. My older sister Selena was there with her family and I know it was a sacrifice for all of them to be present. The eyes in the room began to focus on me. I was determined not to do or say anything that would add confusion or disruption to the atmosphere. I went over to my wife who looked frail but beautiful. I wished that she was here under different circumstances that would have allowed us to a joyful time together. I reached out for her and she responded with a gentle hug. It felt so good to have her in my arms. I could feel sadness returning to me but it had nothing to do with the death of my sister. It was the death of my marriage and the current separation from the love of my life, which had me feeling remorseful. I took a deep breath and let it out slowly as I released the grip on my wife's waist. "Hey, don't you all think it's time to leave for the church?" There was no response but the talking in the large living room did stop. I motioned for my people to follow me out the door and Legs and Z Baby took up positions on either side of me. Carolyn and Shawn followed closely behind us. I was still amazed at how my babies' mommas came together to travel here. I needed their presence and I know Big Mama was smiling down upon us. The limos stretched up the block outside the house. There were some onlookers gathered around to watch us enter the vehicles. My sister was a fixture in this neighborhood for a few decades and the area was a family strong hold because of my uncle's previous business. I also had developed some influence because of my street hustling and the different money making ventures that was created here. I also had my share of romantic conquests of the most popular and the relatively unknown. I never discriminated when it came to love. I enjoyed the outside but what a woman had on the inside made the difference. We began to pile into the cars for the short journey to the church. We probably could have walked there quicker than the ride, but my culture followed strict adherence to protocol during funerals.

We arrived at the church with a police escort. I didn't focus on faces as I went but I could see that there was standing room only. We made our way to the front and I stopped at the coffin to say a brief prayer. My daughter stayed at my side and we sat a couple of rows from the front. My younger niece sat on the other side of me. The rest of my family refused to sit too close to me because of my response to grief, and the emotions that were always let loose. It was something that we always laughed at later but nothing was funny to me during real time. The tears had started to flow while people were still being seated. This was a large church with a stable and impressive congregation. My sister the minister was the first female preacher to be ordained here. I was the first family member to join her as a member. She was very popular especially amongst the seniors. Our church was currently in mourning because our pastor had gone on to a greater glory just a few months prior. I looked up from my praying position with tears running down my face to who was here. I turned and looked behind me to see my son and my other sisters seated behind me. I was handed a box of tissues to help stem the flow of snot and tears that were covering my face. One of the associate ministers; who were a regular fixture at the hospital during my sister's battle was doing the service. He was my mentor and he refused any payment for what he was doing.

It was an uplifting highly spiritual homecoming. There were an endless number of people that came up and made thoughtful comments concerning the life that my sister had lived. One of friends from her sisterhood belted out a song that brought all those present to their feet. The chorus sung and the Reverend preached. I was moved by the effort that was put forth by our church to make this a joyous occasion. When it was time for Baby Sis to read the poem I wrote, she stepped up to the podium and delivered an emotion recitation. The whole audience was also moved by the words. I wanted to get up and say something along with the numerous speakers, but I stayed glued to my seat. I did rise up and shout some hallelujahs during the eulogy and stood during most of the singing. It was a great ceremony for a great lady who meant so much to people. When the service was over; the congregation filed out in front of us and I got a chance to see, all who had come to bid my sister the minister farewell. My face stayed wet with tears and the wrinkles increased as the pain I was in remained visible. The cards I received during this time were passed along to Carolyn to hold on to. The church had prepared for food the family and guests in our Fellowship Hall. I was uplifted when I saw that my best friend Roz had made it. I insisted that she remain and eat with my family. She was Z Baby's unofficial godmother because of all the support she gave from my child's birth. I remember how heads were turned when she showed up at the baby shower with an arm full of gifts.

When all the guests had departed we took our last views of my sister's body and that's when everybody present became emotional. The reality of her passing had sunk in and we knew that her physical presence would be no more. My attention turned towards her children and grandchildren and their out pouring of emotion overcame me. It hurt me even more to see the pain that they were in. I knew what she met to them and I feared how well would they do without her love and guidance. It was still a lot of hatred in their hearts because of the way she had died. They had not yet found the strength and wisdom to forgive. I was concerned if they could honor their mother more by coming to Jesus, instead of seeking retribution against those responsible for her death. I committed myself to keep them in my prayers and lead by example, in spite of my own struggle with forgiveness. I said I did forgive but I questioned whether or not it was in my heart. Funerals had a way of tearing families apart instead of bringing them together. Our situation was no different and I refused to be one of the problems. I let go of my displeasure and planned to forge a new relationship with the family members that had disappointed during this time.

It was time to go to the Fellowship Hall and join the others that stayed to offer further condolences. I was looking forward to seeing my fellow saints and friends whom I hadn't seen in awhile.

I left the sanctuary with my small entourage in tow. My daughter, wife, Roz, Shawn and his mother all left with me. When we got to the Fellowship Hall, it was buzzing with activity. We selected an area to sit where we all could be together. There were so many people that I wanted to have a private conversation with but I didn't want my wife to be uncomfortable. The members of my church made me feel like a rock star with all the attention they were giving me. In spite of this love that was being directed towards me, I still felt emptiness inside because my sister Minister Ealey was not here. I had officially arrived in the kingdom by the way I was conducting myself, since this tragedy had occurred. There were hugs, uplifting talks, promises of continued support and cards filled with added words; that let me know how much I met to them. I balanced my time between the visitors to our table and with the family seated around me. I watched my cousin, who was more like a niece; mingle with the saints on the other side of the room. She was my sister's hair dresser when ever she wanted braids. I know she was in a lot of pain because they had grown so close. My sister and I both rejoiced when my cousin joined the church. In fact; it was my sister who had performed her wedding ceremony. I waved at the sisterhood that my sister was a member of. It was just a group of Godly women; that had a great love for Jesus the Christ, whom were always there for each other. The Reverend that presided over the funeral service came over and wished me well and again pledged to assist me in any manner that was needed. The food began to arrive at the table by the ushers that were assigned the task. I knew them all as well as they knew me. When I first joined the church, I was always known as Minister Ealey's brother. She was so proud of her little brother and she didn't hide how good she felt about me being there. She flashes the brightest smile whenever she saw me at services. I wanted salvation for myself and I wanted to succeed in the ministry for her. The world I live in will be so very different without her. The marriage she was in caused a rift between us because of false accusations against me. She was too blind to see the truth because of love. She was now in a place where I would have no worry about how she was being treated. I think most of the people present that knew of her struggles were happy for her now. Even though death had sent her on a journey, it took her to place of peace, security and love. "Zeke, hey Zeke you want this plate now?" I had been in a daze as I watched the activity in the room. My wife was calling me to see if I was ready to eat. I looked over at her and began to shed a tear. I still had not responded to her question. "Honey, you want to eat now?" She asked the question again but in a much softer voice. I couldn't remember the last time she had called me honey. That was my pet name and I called her kitten. It was starting to feel like our separation had ended. I would be prepared to move back in with her if she let me. It would help to distract me from finding out all the people who were responsible for my sister's death. "Hey Kitten, yes I'm ready to eat. I was just having a moment. I know The Lord will strengthen me in these coming days and weeks and keep me covered in The Blood. Could someone please pass me a napkin so I can dry my face?" The table laughed gently because it was funny to them how in an instant tears would start rolling down my cheeks. I was so caught up in my grief that I didn't realize that Big Dee had joined us at the table. She was in church with my wife but I didn't see her when we left to eat. They had a true friendship and it was Big Dee whom I called on when my wife needed good advice. Big Dee had picked her up when she first arrived and that's where Legs had spent the night. I could always count on her to help out when it was needed. We spent a few hours down there and it was more like a banquet instead of a reprise. Nobody was in a hurry to leave. My daughter whispered in my ear that my wife was tired. I knew there were so health issues but no one gave any details. "I think it's time to go.

We all began to rise from the tables and started sharing hugs and farewells. The burial would be early the next morning. We had to travel across the river, so everyone was encouraged to be here before 9 a.m., if they planned on riding to the cemetery. The light had left and evening was upon us when we stepped outside. It had been a very long day and I was anxious to go to bed. It was times like these that a woman's company would have benefited me the most. I guess it's the need to be nurtured by my mother, which causes me to seek the attention of a woman. We were offered a ride home but I didn't see the point in that. The walk would do me good, as I continued to point things out to Z Baby while we walked. The weather was still mild for this time of year. The rest of the group had gone their separate ways. My niece and nephew went back to the house with some of the guests. I knew the neighbors would be stopping by and so would some other friends of the family. I didn't feel up to the type of gathering that would be taking place. I went straight to my apartment when we reached the house. I turned on the television and went to bed after saying good night to my daughter.

The sun crashed through the windows and hit me in the face. My eyes seemed glued together as the lids struggle to lift themselves up. I wiped the side of my hand across my face to clear some of the debris. I squinted to see the clock as adrenalin began to flow in me. "What time is it?" I shouted out loud to the air around me. I was still trying to figure out where I was at. There were no dreams last night just sound sleep and my head began to clear. I leaped out the bed and searched the walls for a clock. "I'm home now and the burial is today." I whispered to myself. "There it is and it's almost 8 a.m." the conversation with me continued until Z Baby started to stir. "We got to get Ready Z Baby! We don't have a lot of time." She stretched her arms in the before swinging her legs around to sit up on the couch. "Okay Daddy, I'm awake." It would be casual dress today. I didn't know about anyone else, I just wanted to be comfortable. It take us long to get dressed and we had enough time to go downstairs and search for leftovers. It looked like we were the last to arrive because the house was full. We began to go over the seating arrangements for the cars. We all left the house without incident and drove to the church. It was a short but emotional ceremony. People that didn't get a chance to say anything yesterday was able to speak now. It was a long ride to the cemetery in New Jersey. The procession took us past my old job in Newark. I allowed my mind to drift for a moment to think about a more prosperous time. The death of my mother and the depression that followed caused me to lose that job. I didn't have any regrets because I was tired of dealing with other people's problems. It took us about ninety minutes to get there with the time we spent chatting before leaving the church. We also had an unusually large number of cars in the procession. I started seeing more familiar sights as we came upon Rose Hill Cemetery. The cars snaked their through the grounds as the lead driver searched for our plot. The funeral director had already gone into the office with the necessary paperwork. We finally came to a stop and the bodies began to file out of the vehicles. I reserved comment on the conditions that I saw and just wondered how far my mother's grave was from where I stood. Everyone was just standing around waiting for the director to return and escort us to my sister's final resting place. The wait wasn't long as he appeared and pointed to an area we two grave diggers stood near a tent with about twenty folding chairs underneath. The ushers from the funeral home began to pass out flowers from the arrangements with instructions to either place them on the coffin or take them home for a keepsake. Once the chairs were filled up, I remained on the outskirts. I was tired of being judged for my emotions and I knew I could not hold together now. The pain had returned and I didn't need anything to distract me from what I was feeling. Death was so final and there was so much more that I wanted to say to my sister. The weather was mild and the sun shone brightly. The beauty of the day did nothing to make me fill any better. The closer we came to the end of this ceremony, the more sniffles and sobs could be heard. There were a few loud outbursts as the grandchildren fell apart. My daughter had separated from me once we stepped out of the limo. I didn't mind being alone. I didn't mind not having anyone near me to talk to. I heard the call for the flowers to be placed on the coffin. I remained where I was at and kept mine in my hand. The tears began to fall everywhere, when that coffin started its slow decent into the ground. My niece had to be restrained as her emotions took full control of her body. The worst part of it all was watching the little children trying to cope. It was time to leave because everything was finished but some still refused to depart. I began to walk back to my limo and motioned for the rest of my passengers to join me. The ride back to Brooklyn was not cheerful at all. The only thing I could think about was returning to the streets to get better information than what I had. I held off on my own investigation about my sister's death until she was buried. I now had to wait for the rest of the family to return back to their homes before I began to pressure my sources. The police was not doing a satisfactory job. I needed to know about anything and anybody tat was connected to this. I would not rest until I knew the truth.

We arrived at the house in less time than it took to leave. There were some neighbors and church members inside heating up the food. My neighbors began bringing other dishes and some gave me cards. This was the time when everyone could focus more on the joy of a loved one's pain ending. It was a time when it was okay to have a festive atmosphere. There would be drinking and a lot of story telling. My sister was a minister and didn't indulge and I reminded everyone of that before the bottles started coming out. I knew people and some of my family would be getting twisted; it just wasn't going to happen here. It was plenty of food and people present to serve it. I hung out sharing tales of our early up bringing and some of the other things that made us laugh. This was no time to hate. We needed to celebrate my sister's life and the good she was able to do before going home with Jesus. We spent a lot of hours downstairs. My daughter got an earful of the life her daddy had lived before she arrived. I stayed as long as I could. I wanted to get some rest because I was going to church in the morning. I went upstairs and fell fast asleep. It was almost daybreak when I awaken to find Z Baby sleeping on the couch. I never considered getting her up to go to church because I knew she was tired. She had been spending a lot of time chatting with her cousins. They all made me feel so old with the way they had all grown up. I took my shower after selecting an outfit to wear. I never had a problem getting clean because I believed in keeping a tight wardrobe. It also felt good when a woman would comment on how good I looked. While I was taking my shower, I thought about the mornings when I could hear my sister praying downstairs. She put in a lot work for god to hear her. There were very few people that she left out as she made her supplications to The Lord. I would never hear those prayers again and wondered if I should now take up the practice? The sun had made its grand entrance through the venetian blinds. I must have been in that bathroom longer than it seemed. I grabbed my underwear and the pants to my suit and stepped into the kitchen. I had to go back into the outer room for my cosmetics. There was no sense I taking a shower if you couldn't smell good afterwards. I had to pick up my pace if I wanted to get to Sunday school on time. The closer I came to leaving for church; the more depressed I became at the thought of it. I never had a service where I didn't shed any tears. When I began my worship, the grace and mercy of God always overwhelmed me. The journey that brought me to this point was long, hard, and painful. I always gave thanks to The Lord for being patient enough to wait on me to come to Him. My body was now well scented and lubricated so it was time to add the clothes. It didn't take long to finish the process and I was now ready to leave. Z Baby rose long enough to see me leave as I gave her instructions on what she could eat for breakfast. I closed and locked the door behind me. I started my descent down the stairs and past my sister's old living quarters. The current inhabitants were all asleep and the only sounds were from the home attendant getting the bathroom ready for Mama Mary. She was the landlady and the grandmother of my nephew. I stepped outside and the weather was still being kind. The sidewalk crew was still absent from their usual perch. Guess the neighborhood was still reeling from the loss of one of their own. The few people I walk past avoided eye contact. Their behavior only made me add them to my list of suspects. I stopped paying attention to those around and just looked straight ahead until I arrived at the church. I didn't think that staying home was what God wanted. I needed to find out early how I would feel being here without my sister the minister present. I wanted to think the congregation for support. I wanted to be with my fellow saints and feel the love they had for me. I was really disappointed that none of Big Mama's children would be attending. I was especially disappointed at my nephew because of the money that was turned over to him to pay off some bills. In spite of my hurried departure from the house, I was not the first at Sunday school. My teacher was present along with a sizable group of other members. I received hugs when I walked in and hugs from those who arrived later. I cried often as I tried to focus on the lesson. I was given many opportunities to speak along with others as we shared memories of the minister. She wasn't liked by everyone but she was loved by all. They even passed a card around for those present to sign and the envelope was filled with money. Everybody knew about the time I missed at work while guarding my sister's privacy at the hospital. Everybody knew about the time I spent roaming the streets at night searching for the information that the police couldn't get. They all knew the joy I felt at being where my sister was at as we worship God together. The service after Sunday school was just as intense and I was given an opportunity to address the congregation again before the service ended. The following worship services were not much different than this one. The pain, the love, the questions, and the answers I gave became a ritual as we all tried to weather this storm.

I spent a lot of time on the stoop that Sunday. My daughter and the rest of the bunch spent more time outside than inside. My neighbor next door had made me some food. She was so sweet. She had even viewed the body before the funeral. She gave as much support as she could because she took my sister's death hard. I couldn't spend as much time with as I normally would. She had made some advances towards one of my nephews which upset me. I had to check him so he wouldn't respond to it. I went upstairs early that even and fell asleep on the couch. I was awakening long enough by Z Baby to see her leave. Her mother came to get her with Donna driving. I was too tired to walk with her but I did rise up to give her a hug. They would be sleeping over at Donna's house before driving back with Carolyn and Shawn on Monday.

The days went fast and the weeks went even faster. I was back to my regular routine minus the drugs. I even cut back on smoking cigarettes. I wanted to keep a clear head as I put myself in some dangerous situations to get answers. The police investigation had crawled to a halt. There were some dedicated officers that I had met who kept me informed. I learned some new information in the streets that I didn't share with anyone. I knew who was guilty and I knew he didn't act alone. I also knew that I was betrayed by friends that were supposed to be helping me protect my sister. I continued to wait on God because I was confident that He would handle this matter. I had proof from my own past history, that I was shadowed by The Lord wherever I went. My friends were blessed and my enemies were cursed. The best news came a few weeks after the burial when Barry was arrested for some muggings in Manhattan. It seems women were a favorite target of his and one of them spotted him on the street. She had the wisdom to immediately alert an officer and he was arrested. The newspaper account listed a number of victims that pointed him out of a line up. The revelation of this news brought joy and satisfaction to the family and community. I lifted up my hands to God and praised him for delivering justice. It seemed that the week before and the week after that my sister was attacked, he was busy robbing women in Harlem. The Manhattan District Attorney's office was nothing like the one in Brooklyn. I knew justice would come swiftly and be precise. I made sure that they knew he was suspected of killing my sister and another neighbor two years earlier. My people wanted to reach inside the bars and not wait for the system to deliver judgment. He was easy to track with the many contacts that I had on both sides of the law. I held fast to my faith that God was in charge and that I would continue to trust in Him. I knew that God could guide hands and influence minds. There were some members of my congregation that became guilt ridden. They couldn't trust the first hand knowledge that I had from the beginning. They wanted to believe this corrupt individual based on who he was before he snapped as a teenager. I witnessed the first carnage that he was responsible for. The prison system didn't reform him; it just made him a wiser animal. He toyed with the notion of seeking salvation only to gain favor from those around him. I now had a better testimony than before when it came to trusting God and having faith. I forgave him from the beginning s I could function. I didn't try to counsel anyone else on the subject. I now had to get past the anger in me for my friends betraying. I learned to late about him buying drugs after my sister left for work. I started watching Barry more closely, after he stopped working less than two weeks after the wedding. The pawn ticket was found for the ring my sister accused me of taking. There was even more damaging items found that gave evidence to his activities. The nursing home my sister ran gave graphic details of the treatment she received from him. The spoke of missing items when he was around and the uneasiness the residents felt when he was present. He found an angel in my sister, but she didn't realize until too late, that he was the devil. I didn't mind talking when people asked me; how are you doing Zeke? The weeks became better and I spoke regularly with my daughter. I felt God had rewarded me once again for my patience and obedience. I continued to stay dry and avoided the triggers that set me off. I stayed off the stoop after midnight and kept away from my porn collection. I began to sleep easy at night and began preparing for Thanksgiving. I wanted to cook me a small meal in hopes that could get a righteous woman to join me. It was just two weeks away so I started bringing home a few items each night from work.

My job was relatively easy and my body was responding to the therapy that I giving it. I was exercising regularly and my hours had been changed at work to cover the day shift. This would have been nice if I could have gotten more hours. I met a young guy who was a hard worker. He also was a college student that had his head on right. Our friendship helped me to deal with the pain I was in and it provided a distraction. We worked well together and shared the work equally. This was a new venture for me because most young people ducked work and hid as much as they could. My spirits was uplifted even more when I read in the paper that Barry had received a sentence of 45 years to life for those Manhattan muggings. He was a three time loser so any sentence had to have life behind it. The 45 year minimum guaranteed that he would never see the streets again. There were other things happening in the hood that showed me how God was moving swiftly to deliver judgment. God was delivering judgment on those who dared to defile His people.

I came in one day from like I normally do and checked the mail before going upstairs. I grabbed the bunch of envelopes taking those with my name and leaving the rest in the hallway. I plopped them down on my kitchen table and started taking inventory of my food. I wanted to see if all was in place for my upcoming meal. Thanksgiving was now two days away and my rent was just paid and money was tight. I would keep my meal as simple as possible. I had a tendency to over do it when it came to cooking. I would use Stove Top Stuffing Mix and add some onions, green peppers, and turkey giblets to enhance it. My job gave me a turkey and I had another one from my church. I sat down at the table and began to check the mail. There was one envelope that stood out because it just had my name on it with no stamp and only Donna's name for a return address. I quickly tore it apart and began to read it. The more I read the sadder I became. I was expecting some news from my wife but this message caught me off guard. She started out by telling me about problems she had been having with her health since last year. The recent tests they had taken along with the x-rays had discovered a growth on her lungs and liver. It was cancer and it had her scared. She pleaded with me to relocate to Virginia. She wanted me to pack up immediately and leave everything else behind. She said the doctors had given her a year at most and her greatest concern was for Z Baby. She felt that I could come down there and establish myself, so that Z Baby would not have to move if the worst happened. Legs did not want to die and she vowed to fight this illness. I was in shock and not just from her diagnosis but from the invitation. My daughter had been trying to get me to move down there for some time. She wanted to have some place else to go when things became unbearable for her at home. Z Baby was a developing teen so all her feelings were natural and expected. She just didn't understand that and Legs was always too busy with her own issues to explain it. I had told Z baby that I wanted to move in January but not out of New York. You see; I had promised myself that I would never leave New York without being a success. I had left many times before during my life time whenever things got to hot for me. I was always able to survive in New York with the wisdom that God and the streets had blessed me with. Legs wanted an answer right away. She promised that I could stay with her until I got my own place and that she would help me find a job. She didn't explain in her letter why she chose to communicate this way. I could only speculate that she feared rejection if she came direct. I began to feel responsible in some way for her situation. I should have never let her go it alone. I should have been more forceful in keeping our marriage intact. I should have held her more accountable for the agreements she made whenever we reunited. I used to voice my displeasure to God about the way she treated me during our separations. I never wished or expected this type of judgment to be handed down. It was a lot that she was asking me to do. It was not an easy decision to make. I began to recall the dream I had earlier that year and the poem that I awaken with in my heart. I pledged never to return to her again because the last separation was too painful. I had lost too much when she turned me back out to ever trust her again. The letter she wrote me never mentioned any of her needs. She focused only on our daughter Z Baby. She knew that was enough to sway me. What she didn't know that my love of Jesus and my commitment to love her forever, was enough to get me packing. There was no date on the letter so I couldn't tell when it was written or dropped off. I called Donna to get some details before I would call Legs with my response.

"Hey Donna I got the letter. What is this all about and when did you bring this here?" Donna had answered the phone on the first ring and she was eager to talk to me. Donna knew that my love and concern had never diminished that much for my wife. It was Donna that I would call whenever I wanted to know how she was doing or when I suspected that she wasn't doing right. "Zeke, Legs called me last week and asked me to bring this letter to you. She had mailed it to me to bring to you." She continued to tell me how weak my wife was and that she couldn't work anymore. I let Donna know that I would be there. I couldn't sleep that night. The neighborhood had returned back to normal with the night life keeping pace. I was avoiding my crew up to this point because I didn't want to be around those I held responsible for contributing to my sister's demise. It was well after midnight when I stepped outside in search of the one I considered my brother. We even favored each other enough to pass for blood kin. I threw my hands in the air when I hit the sidewalk and he stepped out of the shadows. "Yo wouldn't believe what has happened? I got a letter from my wife and she wants me to move down there." My main man looked at me with a slight smile on his face. He heard my stories of the betrayals and the conflicts she sometimes created. He also knew of the pain I was in and the difficulty had being a Christian in the hood. "Well Zeke, what you going to do?" He had a serious look on his while he waited for my response. It was just the two of us out there right now; as I began to give him an answer, while sobbing uncontrollably. "Yo she has cancer and may not be here next year. She wants me to set myself up down there so I can take care of my daughter. I know she feels alone right now or else she wouldn't be sending for me. You know I had told you that my daughter wanted to move down there before." I had to stop speaking for a moment to get the snot and tears off my face. He stepped away for a minute to handle some traffic that had passed through. "Damn Zeke that some deep shit! I know you gonna go because of your daughter, right?" I gave the traffic another minute to die down before I spoke again. I also needed more time to calm myself down because now I was overwhelmed with emotion. "Yo I got to go but not because of her but for the love of Jesus. I know this is God talking to me and He is sending me on this mission. He wouldn't be sending me just for my family. I know there are other things for me to do there." I told him a lot but not everything that I was feeling. I knew that God was lifting me up out of this valley I was in. He was sending me to a place where I could worship and praise Him without the distractions that I had here. He knew what was on my heart and the desires that I had. God was making a way when I thought there was no way. I was being delivered and I believe that my friend felt the same thing. "Zeke that's good. Let me know what I can do to help. When are you leaving?" The response gave was the one you would expect from a friend that has love in their heart. There were many mornings that I made breakfast for him. It was a way to show my love and it became a way for me to eat too. It was my treat at first but then he started giving me the money. The rest of the crew seemed jealous until they were included at a cost. I would miss him and always prayed that he too would get delivered from this madness. "Hey man thanks for the offer and I don't know when I'm leaving. I just paid rent so I have to start hustling up some money. I give myself about 3 weeks. I got a lot of stuff to get rid of, that I can't take with me. "Don't worry Zeke I got your back. I got some money for you when its time for you to leave." He was sincere and I knew that I could take him at his word. "Good look! I need you to help me stay clean until I get out of here." I didn't want to lose focus on the mission and the opportunities it was creating. I had to stay away from the head hunters and cheap thrills. I couldn't get caught back up just because I was leaving. I could not let any obstacles exist that would block or delay my departure. "Yo Black, I need to borrow your phone to call my wife."

I knew it was late but I didn't have a choice. My phone was still cut off and it would be a day or two before it could be back on. The phone rang a few times before someone answered. "Hey Kitten, it's me!" In today's world a strange number went unanswered at this hour. "I'm gonna come down there; it will just be a few weeks before I leave. I have a lot of stuff to get rid of and I need to put some money together." I could hear her labored breathing in the phone as I spoke. "Honey, you don't have to bring anything with you. You can throw all that stuff away. I will take care of you. I'm positive that I can get you a job. I had to stop working and I'm waiting for my disability to start." It now became clearer to me, the reason for the sense of urgency to get me down there. She needed me for the present as much as she spoke about the future. I had to get off this phone anyway and I had heard enough for now. "Okay Kitten, you can reach me at this number if it's an emergency. I will talk to you later." I gave my people back their phone and made my way back upstairs. The traffic moving around out there was tempting me to get involved. I had to focus on packing and getting me some paper. I wasn't going to be in New York for Christmas. It was easy for me to fall asleep; even though, daybreak would be here in a couple of hours.

The morning felt good and I was excited about waking up to see another day. I looked around the room to see what I could live without. I would have to travel by Greyhound and I knew I couldn't take a lot of things with me. I would have to start collecting my boxes at work tonight. I was back on evenings and it was working out for me. I would also have to work on Thanksgiving but at least I wouldn't get off as late as usual. I had to get myself together so I could meet my close friend Rhonda from transit. She usually passed by my block about 8 a.m. so I would have to hurry. We had developed a sincere friendship and I never had ambitions about making her my girl. She was always somebody I could talk honestly with and not be judged. She also did a good job of keeping me correct because she didn't admire the thug life. I never had to worry about falling into sin when I was with her. The times that I spent riding her route with her was a healthy social event for me. I was anxious to tell her about the reunion with my wife and my decision to relocate to Virginia. She knew my whole story. I mean we had been friends for almost as long as she was a bus driver. We met one Mother's Day and remained friends ever sense. I left the house and made it to the bus-stop on time. I knew she would be coming soon because she was good at keeping her schedule. I had another close friend that also drove a bus. In fact, I knew quite a few drivers because I had spent a lot of time riding when I had the two jobs. This line rode through Queens and Brooklyn. It also stopped close to the depot in Queens where you could get the busses to Long Island. Yep here she comes now! "Hey Rhonda, I got a lot to talk about today!" She smiled as she said hello. She was such a beautiful young woman with a lot of determination. She shared a house with her sister, which was left to them by their mother. I was always trying to get her to let me upgrade it for them. There are always times in my life when I met people that I just want to do things for. I believe God brings me before others to bless them in ways they don't believe could happen to them. It is not always about riches and material things. There are people that never experienced a true friendship or they never received anything without having to give something in return. I feel strong about God using me to just give others hope; that people do good things just for the love of God. The bus only had three passengers which wasn't unusual for this time of morning. We were headed to the last stop on the Brooklyn side. "So Zeke, what's this stuff you got to talk about? You always got something deep coming out your mouth, so what is it now?" My girl Rhonda was being inpatient. I was waiting till we made the last stop and took that 3 minute break. I didn't want to start talking with passengers on the bus. I knew the topic might break me up because I was already feeling queasy. The bus started to make that turn off Broadway to the last stop of the line. I started talking just as the last passenger exited the bus. "My wife sent me a letter by her girlfriend and she wants me to move down there." I didn't need to say anything else before Rhonda let go of her response. "WOW ZEKE THAT'S GOOD!" Rhonda would always tell me that I'm still in love with my wife whenever I spoke about my past. She knew how much I feared my daughter being a teenager without me being closer by. My eyes watered as I began to tell her the rest of the story about the cancer. I didn't stop talking until she knew everything about my situation. I let her know that I needed money and some extra work to be able to make this move. I asked her if she wanted anything out of my house because all of it had to go. I would only be able to take my clothes and tools with me. Rhonda wasn't smiling as much but she was still excited. "Man Zeke, that's awful. I will give you something next week when I get paid. How is Z Baby doing?" She had spoken to my daughter over the phone and I was always showing her pictures. Her oldest son was about the same age so she understood my challenges. "Right now Z Baby is doing better than me and she understands what's happening with her mother." Rhonda stepped off the bus and disappeared into the store across from us. I knew she was picking up her snacks and maybe using the bathroom. This was the first part of her run so she had a long way to go. I stayed on the bus and made the trip with her to Queens. I did the round trip back to Brooklyn and got off in front of my block. My time with her was a good thing for me. It was almost noon time so I decided to go visit with my Godmother and let her know what was going on.

My Godmother only lived a few blocks from me so my walk didn't take long. I tapped on the window until I got somebody's attention. I could see thru the blinds that Moms was alone. She took short steps until she reached the door and let me in. "Zeke what brings you down here? I got some grits left and some coffee. You just have to make yourself an egg to go with it." I could always count on food, shelter, work, and some good advice from Moms. She didn't become my godmother until after my own mother died. She had long been a friend and was known for opening up her house to people in need. She had a large heart and loved family and friends and showed it. "That sounds real good Mrs. Gee and I got some things I need to tell you" Moms sat down at the table and put her glasses back on. There were a lot of memories at this house. This was the one person left in my life that I loved as much as my mother. If the world didn't acknowledge me for whom I was, Mrs. Gee did. She was hand picked by my mother to fill the gap. When my own mother went on to glory, it took me awhile to return to this house. Each time that I stepped in the door and relaxed at the kitchen table, I would be overcome with grief. The tears would flow like a water fall and all I could talk about was my mother's absence. Whenever I thought that I had adjusted to my mother's death, a visit here would bring back the pain. It took months for me to return to normality. I looked at Mrs. Gee and I could see how time had claimed her body and some of her mind. She was still vibrant and robust but her movements slowed along with her thinking. The one thing I knew about Mrs. Gee; was that she would live her life fully until God called her home. I put a light under the coffee pot and added a little water to the brew. This was always the special part of my visit. Preparing a meal for either one or the both of us and then eating it while we chatted. "Moms I'm still feeling the pain from my sister's but they did catch the guy. He was robbing women up in Harlem before and after he attacked my sister. God found a way to deliver justice; even though, he was never charged with my sister's death." Mrs. Gee began to shake her head and offered some opinions on what she just heard. I took two eggs out of the fridge and continued to tell her the reason for my visit. "I got a letter from my wife and she wants me to move down there with her and Z Baby. She has lung cancer Moms and she wants to make sure Z Baby will be taken care of if the worst happens." The joy of being reunited with my wife was taken by the pain of her illness. Mrs. Gee looked at me and took her time to express what she was feeling now. "Zeke, I know you going to go because of Z Baby. I also know how much you miss your wife and you never took anyone after her. I think this is a good time for you to leave New York. You can go there and make a fresh start with your family. The doctors don't always know, so you just trust in God." I had returned to my seat at the table when Mrs. Gee started talking. I had buried my head in my hands as the tears began to flow. I began to feel God's power fill with wisdom about his purpose for me. She was right about it being a good time for me to leave. I had trouble sleeping at night as demons assaulted me in my sleep. I stopped trusting my neighbors because they knew more than they told me. I would be able to lift my family up and serve God without the distractions I encountered every day. I slowly calmed down as the smell of coffee filled the air. Mrs. Gee was smiling now as if the news that I brought had given her some relief. I stood up and stated to cook my eggs and make toast. I gave her the rest of my plans about giving away my furnishings and finding extra work to raise money for the trip. I also asked her to hold on to any money that I did get, until it was time for me to leave. She then gave me a list of things that I could do for her before I left, that would put some money in my kitty. We finished our talk while I ate. I felt real good when I left her house. I also felt strengthen by the Lord.

Thanksgiving came and left without any extra dinner guests. My baby sister came and picked a plate. I know she will be missing my care packages after I leave. I focused on packing clothes I didn't need and organizing my tools for travel. I gave away the entire collection of porn first, which made it easier to focus on the task at hand. I packed up my other movies and music for shipping. I selected some items for sale but only to my closest friends or associates. This was a major undertaking and I was excited about it being done.

It was now Saturday morning and all my holidays in Brooklyn had come to an end. The next one would be Christmas and I planned to be in Virginia for that one. The more I thought about being reunited with my wife one more time, the more I felt relief from the opportunity that the Lord had given me. I contacted my regular midnight bus driver and let him know about my plans. He had just taken over the house his mother had left which his sister had been living in. It seems that she had let it run down and work needed to be done. I convinced him that I was the man for the job. He already knew that this was a field of mine but he wondered if I was capable of such a big undertaking. I had another bus driver that I usually saw when I was going to work. He was younger than and not as responsible as the other. He made a lot of promises that he didn't keep but I maintained the relationship anyway. Our conversations usually focused on the social work that I did on the streets. He gave some support when I was involved in helping another woman launch a program that addressed the issue of young men being released from foster care when they became too old. The fund raiser was a success but the relationship I had with her soured. I gave him my collection of porn with no regrets because he was so eager to receive it. I went to work that night and found some good boxes to bring home. My friend was the one driving when I went home that night. I called him Godfather because he was working on renovating a vintage Eldorado. He lived in the Bronx and he was my male link to sanity. I could get real with him about my struggles with life and the changes I was trying to make. We spoke a lot about the job he wanted me to do as drove his route. We decided on me checking out the house when he got off work. I would meet him back at the depot when he got off. I looked forward to leaving the area for a night and made sure that my absence wasn't noticed. I was still having trouble sleeping at night and my plans to relocate weren't making it any easier. "Yo Godfather, I've been having quite a day. I can't wait to get out of here." He remained focused on the rode as the nearly empty bus made its way along the route. "I hear you Zoe, change can make a difference" Godfather was almost a decade younger than me but he understood all that I was going through. We had been friends for a few years so he knew about all my jobs and the places I lived. We got close because he would have to wake me up when it was time for me to get off. He knew the streets as well as I did, but he had escaped its clutches a long time ago. My stop was about to come up so I stood and started surveying the streets. It was the normal traffic for a Saturday night. It was after midnight and the all night store had the regular crowd outside. "Okay Godfather, I will see you in about an hour." The bus pulled up in front of the store and the doors flung open. "Okay Zoe, be careful!" I hobbled down the steps with my boxes in hand. I looked back at my friend as the bus drove away. I thought to myself how good God was the way he put the necessary people in my life at the right times. I stood at the curb waiting for the traffic to die down enough for me to cross the street. "Zeke are you alright?" I heard the familiar voice behind me cry out behind me. I shouted back without turning around; "Yeah I'm good." They were one of the reasons that staying clean was so difficult. They didn't care about me and didn't have enough respect to leave me alone. I skipped across the as distant car lights grew nearer. I couldn't remember the last time I was able to run with the shape my knees were in. I took my time walking up the stairs to my apartment. There was no joy in coming back here. I would be getting a break from this tonight. I would be sleeping somewhere else and I couldn't wait to leave. I stepped inside my door and put the boxes down. I looked and didn't see anything that I needed to do before I left. I packed a small tool bag and fixed a quick snack. If I moved fast enough I would be able catch Godfather on his return trip to the depot. I had my phone back on now and made sure it was in my pocket when I stepped back outside to meet Godfather. I didn't have to wait long for him to arrive at the stop.

"What's up Zoe, I didn't expect you to be here. I thought you were going to meet me outside the depot?" This was not the original plan but I just needed to be gone. I sat down and stayed quiet. I was deep in thought as I contemplated what my expenses would be and how much I could make off this job. I wanted to at make $400 but I would first have to see what he wanted me to do. I was very good at rehabilitating old houses because of the experience I gained when I first started this. I had a good track record and a long list of satisfied customers. It was easy for me to set a price, because my basic charge for labor was 3x the cost of materials. "Yeah Godfather, I left right away to make sure I didn't fall asleep. You know how it is when it's this late!" Godfather took his time making the short trip to make sure he didn't get there too early. He made three turns before he could see the line of buses he had to get behind. I stayed on the bus until it was time for him to pull into the garage. I knew most of the dispatchers and quite a few of the drivers. I walked across the street and stood beside his car until he came out. He took the long route home to avoid any tolls going to the Bronx. I watched intently to learn the way as I fought back the urge to sleep. We stepped into the house and I quickly dropped my tool bag after removing my coat. "Hey this is nice and the neighborhood seems good as well." The place was filled with old furniture and for the most part it was in disarray. I walked through the rooms on the main floor and inspected the floors and ceilings as I went. The most challenging thing appeared to be the large wall mirror, which would have to be removed when painted. The walls were in good shape but were filled with pictures and other hangings. "Well Zoe, what do you think? Can you do the job and how much will it cost me?" Godfather had a slight smile on his face as he finished his sentence. This is how it was when I did jobs for friends. It didn't matter how good I was and I was never the first choice when they had real money to spend. I had seen that look many times before. Money would not be an issue because my time was too short to be picky. I had already set my departure date and I needed to stay busy until it was time to leave. "I'm not going to break you but I need to get started on this right away." It was time for him to really start laughing as I began to smile. I set the price that I wanted and I would be able to start this weekend. He wanted the upstairs bedrooms painted and the kitchen. He wanted more work done but didn't have the money for it now. We both retired for the night and I slept in the cluttered living room on the couch. The next morning we went out and brought supplies and

ZEKE SMITH

I spent the whole weekend painting. The work lasted until that Monday afternoon when it was time for him to go to work. We settled on a routine of me going home with him at night and returning home when he left for work. I got everything done that first week and had two more to go before moving time. He was astounded at the skills I had. He paid me and I gave that money to my Godmother to hold on to. The days that I didn't have to work at Pathmark, I would work on the things at Mrs. Gee house. I definitely kept myself busy. I began to disburse my belongings throughout the neighborhood. I wasn't charging but some gave large donations when they understood why I was leaving. These were real friends that found a way to repay me for years of service to them. I had one special neighbor that knew my family and her son had disappeared years ago. We grew even closer after that tragedy as I tried to make up for her loss. I made sure that she received the best I could offer if she wanted it. I gave my plants to my godmother and one of her friends that I teased a lot got my mural of the Last Supper. I packed up everything that I would ship and added towels, linen, and clothing to the bunch. Things were progressing at a good pace and I was satisfied at my progress. I made regular nightly phone calls to my daughter to keep her posted about my progress. She would tell me how excited her mother had become about me moving down there with them. I was happy to hear that and felt reassured that God was already working on improving her health. I had a week to go when I went out and purchased my Greyhound Bus ticket. I would need extra money to pay the baggage I had over their limit. I made arrangements to finish all the renovations for the rest of Godfather's house. He had recently gotten married and his wife would be moving from Brooklyn to the Bronx. I helped them make that move along with the other work that I did. He couldn't pay me now but would mail the money next year when he got his income tax refund. I sold some things to a few church members that would benefit their children. I would also have to wait for that money to be mailed to me after I left. When I had just days to go I began downsizing some more because I still had too much left. I donated a lot of clothing to the men's shelter that the Salvation Army ran. I gave my 10 speed bike to one of the kids in the area. My electronic equipment went to one of my god sisters reluctantly because I was asking for some kind of money. I was making deliveries up to the last minute as I began to change my address with everyone that I did business with. I took a leave of absence from my union to protect my job and membership. I had all my military records transferred to Virginia and was able to secure my G.I. Bill loan voucher before I left. The last weekend in New York was filled with tension and sadness. I left that Sunday night to catch a 1 a.m. bus. I missed an opportunity to hit my number big with so much going on. The date of my departure came out in New York State pick four, on the day that I purchased ticket. I played too late and I believe that it was divine intervention. If I had hit that number, it may have delayed or even prevented my departure. I was forced to use a local crack head to help me to the bus station. I had to dump some more of my clothes minutes before heading to the subway station. It amazed me how so few of my fellow saints were willing to drive me to Manhattan or even the few blocks to the subway station. I had to keep my eye on the help to make sure that he didn't leave anything behind. The journey to subway was torture because of the rain falling and the weight of the bags. The ride to Manhattan was only a short rest because it of the long walk to the terminal after getting off the train. I had to do some more negotiating to get the price lowered for my extra bags. I was happy to pay the help off and watch him leave. He did well for a rainy Sunday. The money I gave him wouldn't last as long as he wanted it too. I spent the time riding with venting my feelings about how the landlord had treated me. I knew he would carry the information back with him and use it to get paid again. I told him to keep whatever I left behind because I knew he would be the one cleaning the place up. I left the house after saying good-bye at the very last minute. I guess he thought I had nowhere else to go. I would miss Mother Mary but not her son. I got my bags tagged and scanned the area for whom ever might be riding with me. The tools I brought with me caused the most problems for me but I couldn't leave them behind. I was planning on using my renovation skills to eat until I became employed. I sat still for a moment and recalled all that I had been through for the past year. I could not take credit for surviving. I had to give God the glory.

The bus pulled out with a full load. In fact there were some passengers left waiting for the next bus. It seems that the one I was on was overbooked. I was told when I brought my ticket to get there early. I made sure that I had a bus I didn't have to switch. I knew with the amount of baggage I had that changing buses would definitely create some problems. I surrendered my window seat to a young blond. I was too tired to be talkative and I was still the processing information concerning my move. My seat was located in the middle of the bus which gave me a good vantage point of the luggage compartment outside. There would be stops along the way but the buses would not be changed. There was some confusion before we left so it was nearly 2 a.m. before we pulled out of the terminal. I was traveling with about ten cigarettes in my pack. Yeah that last day in Brooklyn was tough so I needed a relaxer and cigarettes were the safest. The young woman seated next to me was very attractive and she had brought a pillow with her. Whenever our eyes made contact we just smiled at each other without speaking. I had to fight back fantasies that were building up in my head. I didn't need any more tests of temptation. What I needed was opportunities to preach the gospel of Jesus the Christ to strengthen my bond and stay connected. I stretched out my right leg as much as I could and then leaned towards the aisle. I placed my left arm on the armrest and laid my head on my forearm. It was uncomfortable but it didn't keep me from falling asleep.

I felt the bus churning to a stop as I peeled my face off my arm. It was still dark and I had no idea what time it was. The bus was making a rest stop along the New Jersey turnpike. I patted my pockets to make sure the cigarettes were there and I stood up waiting for the bus to completely stop. I looked over at the blond next to me and wondered if she would be getting off too. She still had her head pressed into the pillow that was propped up against the window. The bus finally came to a full stop and I quickly exited. I didn't know how long we would be stopped and I wanted to get this tobacco in my lungs. I found a place off to the side and lit up. It's amazing how something so bad for you can feel so good. That was actually the problem with sin. It felt so good to sin and it made a harsh world feel desirable but the consequences were so cruel. I smoked this cigarette knowing that it could lead to my death yet I continued to smoke. There would be moments of abstinence to clear out my lungs yet I would go back to smoking again. I knew I had to immerse myself in Jesus if I had any hope of recovering from my addictions and afflictions. I continued to puff until only a flicker of fire remained. I tossed the bud and returned to the bus. I knew the evidence of what I had just done was lingering about me. I reached into the small leather bag beneath me and pulled out some cologne. I sprayed some gently underneath my chin and on my outer garments. I returned the bottle to my bag and sat upright and rigid in my seat. I turned my attention towards the passenger seated next to me and imagined whom she might be. She was casually dressed and the clothing did a bad job of concealing her curves. The lamp light from the outside illuminated her body even more. I sat there staring at her as I pretended to be looking out the window. She rolled her head off the pillow and sat directly up and began to stare back at me. I couldn't break the gaze upon her and remained quiet. A smile broke across her face as she began to speak. "Hey stranger, what's your name? They call me Destiny." She had the gentlest of voices and a pleasant smell was emanating from her body. I viewed all that the light and her body's position would allow me to see. She was a fair maiden and I was glad to be in her company. Her smile and hello was inviting, so I began to respond. "Destiny your name sounds nice. My name is Zeke and I'm relocating to Virginia. Where are you headed?" There was something so alluring about Destiny and I figured this was test of my sincerity from God. I felt the warmth in my pants created from just the sound of her voice. I was not going to act on those feelings but instead I started giving her my testimony. The bus started pulling off as she tried to speak. "I'm going to do a show in . . . ." I interrupted her because I didn't want to lose track. I had to vent because I was filled with so much emotion from the pain I was in. I had finally given up on my hometown, even though it was for a good cause. "I was born and raised in Brooklyn and I'm leaving to live permanently somewhere else. I've been separated from my wife off and on for the past six years. She ahs cancer now and wants me with her to help take better care of our teen age daughter. I had to give up everything I had except what I could carry to do this. I'm going only because that's what Jesus wants me to do." Destiny sat silent for a long time. I imagined she was trying to comprehend what I had said. She was probably wondering why a complete stranger would confide in her like this. Tears had started rolling down my cheeks and I started sniffling. She reached over and held my hands drawing me a little closer. The other passengers all seemed to be asleep as the bus made its way down the highway. I watched as her eyes started to glisten and she began to speak. "That is really a remarkable thing that you're doing. I don't know of anyone that would have done the same. You are a wonderful and you must be in love with your wife. I know she is going to appreciate you coming and you do whatever you can for her." She then paused for a moment and began searching her bag for something. She pulled out a magazine and started thumbing through the pages. She finally stopped and handed the magazine to me. Destiny then began to me some of her story. "I model for the men's magazines. This is one my photo spreads that you're looking at. I'm headed home to Texas but I'm doing shows along the way. Do you ever look at these magazines?" My mind was adrift as I look at what she had given me. It was a definite distraction from the sorrow I was feeling. I knew there was something different about her. She was white and she didn't mind me being black. "I used to look at these things but it has been a long time. Wow, you are the first model I ever met." We continued to share stories about our lives as the bus moved on. We never fell back to sleep and was good company for each other. She had

her problems too and was missing her own daughter. We sat talking until daylight sneaked through the windows. We forged a friendship during that ride and even had prayer together. We had a lay over in Chesapeake before the bus continued on to Newport News. We had to separate at that point but she gave me an autographed nude picture of her. She signed it wishing me the brightest blessings. I had passed the test of temptation by ministering to this woman instead of lusting after her. I felt very prepared to do what the Lord had sent me to do. My cigarettes had lasted until it was time to make the last leg of the trip. I called Sprint to change my address before the bus left. It was the final act to complete my transition from Northerner to Southerner. My face stayed glued to the window as the bus pulled out of the lot. We had lost most of the passengers and I figured it was time to call my wife. Z Baby had said that Legs would be picking me up but I should call when I got close. I knew very little about this region when it came to driving. I called Legs and told her where I was. She said that I was close and that I should call when the bus arrived. My mind started drifting again as I thought about my little Jamaican friend. I didn't get a chance to say goodbye because she was ducking me. She was in my debt which caused me to stop being so nice. I never understood how the girls thought that my generosity was some type of weakness. They didn't understand that I gave such honor to them because of my up bringing. I had a long stretch of years when what my mama taught me had gone out the window. I wasn't going to return to that place so I made sure that I gave before I tried to receive. It felt good being nice and I didn't have to look over my shoulder or worry about public opinion. I knew if nothing else, God would take notice. I came back to reality and saw that the streets had changed. We were no longer on the highway and I figured we would be stopping soon. The bus came to a stop at a red light and I started to call Legs back again. "Hey Kitten, the bus is on Warwick Blvd and it looks like it's getting ready to stop." There was silence as I waited for a response. I thought we had a broken connection until she started talking. "Okay Honey, I'm not that far away. I'm going to leave the house now. Just wait there for me." Just wait there for you? What else did she think I would do? The bus pulled into this little tiny station on the main street. I grabbed the bags I had on the bus with me and stepped outside. I went around to the side of the bus and began unloading all my stuff. It was quite a bit and it left me tired. I couldn't wait to eat but most of all I couldn't wait to see Legs.

I stood there waiting to see the little short that my wife. I got a chance to ride in it last year when I came down for Z Baby's middle school graduation.

I had made romantic overtures then but Kitten didn't bite. The weather was incredible down here. It felt more like September or April than December. I continue to stand guard over my bags as I watched the cars go by. I had no idea which direction Legs would be coming from, so I was looking both ways. My bladder started to talk to me and I began pray out loud for Legs to come. I watched a car pull up into the lot and figured it was for someone else; after all, I was not the only one waiting for a ride. It was an emerald green economy model and looked real good. "Nah that can't be her;" I thought out loud. I had worn my leather coat that my Godfather had given me, when I renovated his house. I had slung it over my bags while I turned to face the car that had just arrived. The driver stepped out and a huge smile flashed across their, as they turned to look in my direction. "Kitten;" I yelled out and began walking towards her. I tried to stay composed as my feelings engulfed me. The sun was shining on her and she looked like an angel. She looked like she had spent some time getting herself ready. She was always self conscious about how she looked in public. I walked faster to meet her as she came from the other side of the car. I reached out and pulled her towards me and gave her a hug. She felt so light and frail in my arms. The joy I had was being threatened by the sadness I started to feel. Her face was a little gaunt and the make-up couldn't conceal all the lines in her face. My age was showing too with a head full of grey hair and a bald spot to match. My Kitten had to remind about the reason why she was here. I released my hold on her as she instructed me to put the bags in the car. I stopped her from helping but she insisted on grabbing something. She pointed to a small shopping mall across from where we stood and told me that was the church I visited before. I began to recognize the area now because I had went to the K-Mart next to it, when I had brought her a gift on my last visit. "Hey girl nice ride, you doing real good for yourself;" she blushed as I put the last bag in the car. We both climbed inside and started the journey home. "Z Baby wanted to stay home from school to me you but I said no." It had been a long time since she had shared any parenting wisdom with me. I only heard from her about Z Baby if she was met with some resistance from her. "Yeah you were right; it was no need to miss school for this." The rest of the ride was in silence as I surveyed the areas we rode through. I continued to feel amazed that we were back together again. I continued to be amazed that I had moved out of New York with no plans to return. We finally made a left turn off the main street we were on sandwiched between two gas stations. She began to drive much slower as we came to a small driveway and she made another left turn. We drove

ZEKE SMITH

over a couple of speed bumps before she made a half turn and pull in front of some apartments. The construction down here was much different than New York. The apartments looked expensive with their parking spaces and balconies. The landscape looked well maintained and I didn't notice any rubbish. There were large dumpsters located along the side boundary of the property for garbage. There were also a number of small garages circling the back and side. Legs got out first and reached back to take my coat with her. I still couldn't believe how hot it was outside. I made a few trips back and forth to the car as I removed all my baggage. I would be expecting the rest of my stuff to arrive by mail. I finally had a chance to settle down in the apartment. I sat quietly in the living room as searched my memory for the descriptions Z Baby had given me. I recalled the storms and the lights out. I thought back on how she would be forced to stay in her room when her mother had company. I recognized most of the furniture because I had brought it. The rest of the things were foreign and I wondered what had happened to some of the things we had in New York. My wife offered me something to eat as I sat there staring out the balcony doors. I was in a lot of emotional pain but I wouldn't let it show. I just wanted to unpack and get more information about my wife's condition.

Legs had gone to the back bedroom and began to clean up. She said she would make some room in her closet for my clothes. The house was neat but untidy. The dishwasher was filled with dishes and the fridge had boxes of various fast foods. I see not much had changed when it came to the household. I worked my way around the kitchen and started making me some eggs and turkey bacon. There was also some fresh spinach in there that I cooked up with the eggs. I made enough for Legs because I would have to help her eat and gain weight if she were going to survive. I did not think of myself as a husband or a father at this point. I was just a servant sent here to serve. I would exercise total obedience and not try to exercise any control. I had to learn what the situation has been like without me being here. I would only be able to learn that, if I remained submissive and silent. I went right to work doing the things that I was known for. I started cleaning the first and worked my way backwards through the living room and Z Baby's bedroom. I wasn't surprised at the conditions because I had always kept the house in order. My wife seemed so happy in spite of her health condition. She kept me company talking as I went about putting things in order. She insisted that I not touch her room because she would take care of it. We took a break from chatting as we ate the food that I had prepared. I was feeling good too about what I was doing. The subject of money didn't come up but I let her know that I had some to give her. I had a little more than $200 in my pockets when I arrived. I split that with her above her objections. She had money but I wanted to give what I had before I got broke. I couldn't think of anything at the time besides Christmas, so I didn't think that I needed much money in my pocket. My step daughter Pauline had a job referral for me where she worked at; I just had to do the application on line before her boss could pull it. Time had gone by pretty quick with all the talking and cleaning going on. Legs had spent some time on the phone letting everyone know that her husband was home. I kept wondering what had happened to the guy she was supposed to marry. She had been pressing me for a divorce just last year so I knew she had gotten serious with someone. I wouldn't bring up the subject now but I didn't let the information leave my memory. I had to go dump the garbage and while I was out there, she wanted me to introduce myself to the development manager. Legs wanted me to pitch for a job on the maintenance crew there since I had those skills. I walked over towards the office after dumping the garbage while Legs stood outside on the balcony. The manager happened to be going to her car and Legs then called out to her. "Hi Sandy, that's my husband." I walked up to her and introduced myself. I also let her know about the things I was capable of doing. It was a brief conversation but in that short time she gave Legs a lot of praise. She thought the world of Legs because of brashness and New York attitude. I made my way back upstairs while Legs stayed outside and smoked a cigarette on the balcony. It was almost time for Z Baby to come home so I just fell back on the couch for a minute's rest.

"Daddy get up, we getting ready to go food shopping;" Z Baby was home and urging me to rise. I looked up at her as I tried to remember where I was at. I was having one hell of a dream and was wishing that I was still sleep. "Hey kid you home now?" I asked in a sheepish voice. "Daddy I've been home for two hours now and I finished doing my homework. You were sleeping so good that I didn't want to wake you. Mommy wants to go to Wal-Mart and get some food before it gets too late." I got up and went to the hall bathroom to relieve myself. I didn't make it here when I was doing my cleaning but the bathrooms would be first tomorrow. It was dark outside and the house felt a little chilly. It might have been hot earlier but the night air brought the cold. We all got ourselves together and piled into the car. We had to step around a small group of kids that had camped out on the steps outside our door. My wife drove and I sat next to her in the front seat. It didn't take long to get to the store. It seems that we were

ZEKE SMITH

located right in the middle of everything. We went up and down the aisles grabbing this and grabbing that. I had no preferences for anything and just paid attention to what they were getting. When we got to the meat section my wife had me make the choices because she said I would be doing the cooking. Z Baby was happy to hear that because they usually ate mostly fast food. Legs had to pick up a prescription and while at the pharmacy she introduced me to her friends. She got to know them all very well since she had become ill. One of the girls looked like Fantasia the singer so much that my wife only called her that. I could see that everybody liked her and she introduced me to everyone that she saw. She seemed to feel real good about having her husband with her. She even bragged about me coming down here to take care of her. This was pretty much how it was the first week back home. I traveled with her during the day to all her appointments and errands and she took me around to meet everyone she did business with. I walked Z Baby to her bus-stop around the corner from us because she was usually the first one there and it was still dark. I remember how we used to talk on the phone when she first started taking the bus to High School. She was afraid being alone out there because public housing was located right across from the stop. My wife had me feeling like a celebrity as she showed me around. The rest of her family had not started coming around yet. I didn't know what to expect when they did. I know that no one made me feel welcome when I came to Z Baby's graduation except my wife. I shifted things around in z baby's room to space for my clothes. I was able to put my tools and papers away in a large storage closet that was located on the balcony. I spent my first week sleeping on the couch as my tried to adjust to me being there. I did visit with her during the day as we watched Judge Judy and Divorce Court in the mornings. I took Z Baby to bible study that Wednesday and we all went to church on Sunday. I got to meet her pastor for the first time because I had met the first lady the last time I visited Z Baby. Christmas was coming up and be both focused on doing things for Z Baby. Legs wanted this one to be special because she didn't think she would be around for the next one.

The second week had a more relaxed atmosphere as I was allowed to assume control of the household. My wife didn't allow my role to be diminished and I began to feel that I was there more for her than Z Baby. I was happy to see that she was eating and Z Baby was happy to have home cooked meals when she came home. I had to send to New York for money to get my license switched over. Legs argued about giving me enough money for six years and wanted me to do it for a shorter time.

That exchange brought up some old feelings in both of us but it upset the atmosphere too much. I also was told that I had to speak with Pauline my step daughter because she had some issues with me from New York that never got resolved. I really didn't want to travel down this road and felt immaturity and a lack of respect was bringing this on. My wife always tried too hard to please her family and do what they wanted. It was difficult for her to stand up for herself because of her past. They just wouldn't let her forget especially if she ran into difficulties. Her recovery didn't have the solid foundation that mine did because she never allowed herself to transition to a sober life style. Our strengths supported each others' weaknesses and I always needed her love once she had given it to me. I lasted as long as I did and prospered only because of her. I had stopped everyone from eating fast food and no more dishwashers. My money arrived from New York from my Godfather. I went the same day and had my license changed over to Virginia. I didn't want to lose my CDL class B after all I went through to get it. It was also good that I was able to show that type of connection with the people I left. I even had a referral letter from my church to show that I left in good standings and only because I was moving. I was being patient about finding a job because there was so much to do at the house. I wanted to get things in order at home and establish a routine so I would know what shift I should work. Since I was here now everyone backed off from whatever it was that they were doing for Legs before I came. I did not come to bury my wife. I came to help her live. We all spent a lot of time with each other. I started meeting my neighbors and the children that lived in the complex. I met the young woman that lived under us whom my wife treated as a daughter. Her name was Toni and she teased me about my heavy foot steps across the floor so early in the morning. We went out and got decorations for the tree that we had while in New York. Legs and I went and brought a digital camera for Z Baby for Christmas. Our child wasn't caught up about receiving anything because she knew how things were. The only thing that troubled me, amongst all the joy I felt about having my family back; that there was too much focus on the possibility of death. We made a trip to meet Legs friend that had a beauty salon close to the house. I felt right at home as I walked through the door because her friend made me feel so welcome. "Honey this is my best girl Meedy." Legs then walked over to her friend and they started hugging. Meedy was smiling but I could still sense some worry in the tone of her voice. "Legs this is your husband?" Yep was Legs quick reply as a broad smile filled her face. "Girl I know you happy he is here! Your wife is always talking about you. How long are you going to be here?" Meedy was a very attractive young woman and much younger than my wife. She was talkative and seemed genuinely in love with my wife. Legs were good at forging good relationships with people. She had a little trouble walking but that didn't take the smile off her face. I started to answer Meedy but Legs cut me off. "I'm sorry, this is Zeke and he moved down here to take care of me and Z Baby. This is his home now." Meedy began to stare a bit at me and that worried look she had quickly disappeared. "Zeke your wife is crazy and I'm so glad you are here. Legs my girl and I know she has been having a hard time lately." Legs began to fill her in on what was happening with her health. She let her know that she had to stop work and was waiting on her disability to be approved. I chimed in a few times to let Meedy know what Legs had meant to me. I also let her know that I was looking for work and was a good handy man. I told her that I was good at painting and renovating houses. We visited with her for about an hour before Legs started to tire and we made our way back home. Legs had been home bound before I came. She had become afraid to drive by herself and always stayed off the interstate highways. This made getting around even more difficult because other routes were either too long or just impossible. I now saw that my first task would be to get Legs to start living again and not think about the inevitability of death.

One afternoon after returning from my wife's doctor's appointment we made a stop at Wal-Mart to pick up a few things. Legs caught me off guard by telling me to pick out a Christmas gift. We were both feeling good after receiving a favorable doctor's report. Well Lags and Z Baby had been bugging me about cutting my hair. It had taken me three years to grow what I had. One side of my head grew hair faster than the other and the whole head grew slow. My bald spot was there but it wasn't so noticeable. I also didn't mind the grey hair because I had begun to accept the aging process in spite of my good looks. I was tired being untruthful about my age and viewed my grey hair as a sign of wisdom and survival. The girls didn't see it that way and felt that I looked like an old man. Legs certainly didn't want any attention drawn to how old she might actually. She still had super model beauty and a petite body. I found a nice inexpensive hair cutting set that included blades for shaving. I slipped off from her for a minute and brought a piece of jewelry that I thought she would like. I went into a small reserve of cash that I had held back. She had no idea about my purchase so it would be a big surprise on Christmas. My last Christmas was still fresh in my memory so I was committed to sacrificing and bringing others joy. I noticed how quickly Legs would lose her energy in the afternoon. I realized that any activities that we did would have to take place in the morning. She spent most of her time in the bed and lacked the drive to do much else. I recall the day Pauline was coming to visit and Legs instructed me to sit down with her when she arrived. Legs explained that Pauline needed to vent some feelings she had towards me and begged me to cooperate. I quickly became annoyed at Legs worrying about Pauline with all the health issues she had to deal with. I thought back at the interference Pauline created in New York before she left, when I was trying to patch things up with my wife, after one of our separations. My wife spent a lot of energy trying to get Pauline and me to get along with each other. I never understood why or when the bad blood started. I accepted her as my child from the beginning and made it a precondition before things got serious with Legs. I took time out to give her driving lessons when she wanted a license. I brought her a leather jacket. I made myself available when she struggle with the emotions of a teenager. I gave her a lot more respect than she gave me. When she had her first child, I took extra measures to forge a good relationship with her. One day something just clicked in her and the relationship slowly and steadily deteriorated. Pauline's daughter immediately became attached to me and would follow me around whenever they visited. She called me daddy during one period of time. Now again with all this stuff going on I had to take time out to speak with this woman about her feelings. Pauline came into the house that day feeling jovial and upbeat. Legs reminded me about her request so I went and sat in the dining room adjacent to the kitchen. Pauline was already sitting there and it had been years since we were this close to each other. I was the one Legs called when her furniture that she left behind in New York had to be removed. She had moved around the corner from us at that time and her life was in turmoil. Things were not working out with her baby daddy so she decided to move one day. It wasn't planned that well because she had left a lot behind, including her college education. I stepped up to the plate even though I was living out of my car then. "What's up Pauline? Do you have the information about the job you told me about?" I wanted to deflect from the issue for a moment just to prepare myself for some humility. I would definitely need to put my acting skills to use because this was a bunch of bullshit. "Hi Zeke, you look good. I guess you going to need a job before you can get your own place. Who knows, you might even find you a nice woman down here. I have this air mattress if you need something to sleep on. I know it will be more comfortable than the couch." I sat stunned at her words without revealing what I was feeling. I put a big grin on my face and continued to listen to her. It was nothing new that she was beefing about. It appeared that she was trying to get information more than she was trying to settle something. I knew if Legs just wanted her husband back with her to help, she could not tell her family that. I don't care what might have happened between couples, one should not condemn reconciliations. People should never be afraid to be truthful to their families about the love they may have for their spouses. I went through the same thing with some of my kin. Everyone did not outright support my decision to move south. They knew what had transcribed between me and Legs and they didn't like it. They didn't like the fact that Legs snuck out of New York without telling them. They never mistreated her and yet she cut them off too. I just sat there listening and agreeing until she felt satisfied. My response was my testimony about my faith and the good relationship that I had with the Lord. I spoke about some truths and how the gospel had propelled me forward to survive in spite of the obstacles that were placed in my path. I let her know that I was here to take care of my family and that included my wife. When I finished speaking Pauline looked at me and said; "You have God's favor."

My sister-in-law whom I always communicated with was lower key but was still acting with authority. I knew that after being here two weeks that I was not welcomed by all. It seems that all the plans they had made for wife's possible demise never included me being here. I continued to give everyone a break and stayed glued to my wife. We decorated the tree and started putting gifts underneath. We brought some cookie dough so Z Baby could make her cookies for Santa Claus. The house was full of the Christmas spirit. The day before Christmas we received the surprise of our life. I answered the door that morning when a small group of people came asking for Legs and Z Baby. I thought they were Mormons. I called legs to the door and they started asking her where they should put the gifts. These people had come with a mini van full of electronics, computers, stuffed animals and clothes. They had an envelope with gift cards and other things. Z Baby had been adopted by one of the large corporations down here. They knew of Legs condition but they didn't know of mine. I helped bring some things into the house and they thought I was the grandfather. I still had my head full of hair with most of it being grey. I made sure I cut it that night. The gifts were wrapped and already had names on them. I waited until they left before I started crying but Legs let it loose right away. I felt hurt that a gift wasn't there for me. I felt hurt that the whole world didn't know I was coming. I even met the old boyfriend that week.

The one she was supposed to marry whom went back to his wife after his son died. I knew who he was but Legs wasn't prepared to be honest when she asked my permission if he could come by. It was a brief visit and I put on my phony friendly face. I knew it was a case of show and tell for both of them. Legs was anxious to show the man that quit on her; that she still had someone who loved her and was prepared to show it. I would think that he wanted to see this person he had heard so much about in the flesh. When he came he wasn't a bearer of gifts. I didn't give them any privacy as I tried to hear the things that weren't being said. I fell back on my training and experience as an investigator to know the truth that wasn't outwardly being revealed. This was quite a time leading up to Christmas. God had revealed His power and might in so many ways. He had demonstrated His love for me and revealed the purpose He had for my life. I was a willing recipient of His grace and mercy. I knew I had a part to play in this and I didn't allow myself to be distracted. I had no more excuses to use for not giving God all the glory and praise that he deserved. I humbled myself as I felt His presence around me. I had become a good student when it came to studying the scriptures, so I knew all the promises that God had made for believers. Z Baby came home from school that day and walked into a house filled with joy. Legs and I had finished transforming the home into a clean and orderly environment. I was filled with happiness that eclipsed my joy. I stopped for a moment and hugged the two females in my life. I was filled with content and felt certain that God would continue to bless me as long as I remained obedient to His word. Z Baby made her cookies that night for Santa and I started a dinner for tomorrow. We all stayed in Legs' room and watched television that night. We all wore our pajamas as we waited anxiously for day break to start opening the gifts. I had to place my clippers under the tree, even though I had used them to cut my hair. Z Baby told me to sleep in her room that night. I welcomed the invitation as I let humility win over pride. My body had been through a lot on the couch. It now felt like home. I became more assertive in establishing routines and order in the household. I would spend a lot of time just talking with Legs about some of the things I went through. She enjoyed hearing my stories of survival on the streets of Brooklyn. I didn't speak of any sexual activities or relationships with women that I might have been involved in. We both avoided certain topics to prevent any bad memories from coming up. We grew closer and closer and the time spent worshiping at church made things even better. I was being viewed as a saint by so many because I had come back home to care for my wife. Legs would make sure that I had money for the offering. We were back in the house of the Lord sitting side by side. I still felt the pain of my existence whenever their chorus would sing. They had sons that I was unfamiliar which that would just draw all my hurt and sorrow out of me. There were some that couldn't believe that we were back together under these circumstances. Then there were those that tried to get more information about than what I was giving up. It was a small congregation that had trouble keeping members. It was not unusual for the sermon to be based on that very subject. It didn't matter much to me because I was here to worship God and support my wife through her ordeal.

My bags that I shipped ahead of me began to arrive. I received my video tapes and DVDs. The clothes and linen that I sent ahead came too. We began to relive some old memories in the house, as Legs and Z Baby watched me the boxes get unwrapped. I developed a relationship with the mailman because of the amount of packages I received. I let him know about my family's history in the post office. He spoke about his own desire to relocate to Florida. I then let him know about my desire to stay rooted in Virginia. I stopped using my receipts to claim my packages after becoming so familiar with my carrier. It was a mistake because I never received the box that contained my CD tapes.

HOME SWEET HOME

IT WAS STILL dark outside when the girls came into the room and woke me up. My wife wanted to make sure I captured Z Baby's happiness when she started opening her gifts. I recalled how in the past that, this was always the most cherished moment for us and I would always tape my little girl's response. She was no longer my little and this could be the last Christmas that we would all be together. I didn't have a video camera to use but my phone made up for it. Z Baby dove into the pile and started pulling the wrappings off the boxes. She had to be the happiest child in the world on this Christmas day. I know I was the happiest dad watching her. My little girl always expressed joy and made you fill well about anything you did for her. She was astounded at the amount of gifts and the type of gifts. She wondered where all this money had come from but she didn't asked. Legs and I both kept receiving hugs as Z Baby became overwhelmed with joy. Legs also had a chance to be blessed, when she revealed the gifts that bore her name. I felt a little sadness because nothing new was there for me. I just quickly remembered why I was there and the sadness turned to joy. Z Baby had received a computer complete with programs and printer. She loved that most of all because the one she had was a dinosaur; that had been passed down to her. We would continue the tradition of going to the movies on Christmas. I had missed this most of all, during our separations in the past. My son Shawn lived in Portsmouth with his stepfather. The marriage his mother was in dissolved and I thought of her complaints to me about feeling alienated, because she didn't have any family in Virginia. Her husband had even complained to me about her. It was a joke to listen to both of them; especially since they both tried to diminish my role. I returned to bed as Z Baby and Legs continue to examine and play with the things they received. My little girl was a teenager now and I was happy to see her child like exhilaration. I needed a nap to be alert while on the drive to Portsmouth.

The nap I took was short but it served its purpose. I went straight to my Legs bathroom and took my shower. They knew I was strict about being on time and I didn't want to be the one who was late. I searched through my clothes and found something jiggy for today's outing. My main man from Brooklyn had blessed me with an extensive casual wardrobe of name brand goods. I was looking real youthful in my Roca Wear with the bald head to match. I went and finish preparing dinner while the girls started to get themselves together. Pauline and her husband John had come over to see the fresh bounty from Santa and exchange their gifts. Legs had made sure she brought the grandchildren something and some gifts for Z Baby had the tags switched to accommodate the oldest one. John was able to set-up the computer for Z Baby while he was there. I continued to get the meal ready after exchanging some holiday greetings. We were headed to Hampton for the movie and had to leave soon because we had to pick up Shawn along the way. My money was short and I couldn't afford to treat anyone. Legs were in control of the dollars and I had to be humble to avoid any friction. I made sure Shawn was bringing some money with him so that his fun wouldn't be spoiled. I had to speak with his step father Dan to get clear directions to the house. The ride to pick up Shawn was a lot of fun and I had Z Baby ring the bell after we got there. The neighborhood was dismal and the house he owned was shabby. I was glad to leave once Shawn had gotten into the car. We were now off to Hampton and decided to watch the new movie "The Great Debaters" after we got there. We had a good time at the movie but I could see that the long day was having a toll on Legs. Darkness had fallen when we started our ride back to Portsmouth. We didn't incur any trouble getting there but when it was time for us to return home problems started. Legs had lost any patience and wanted to be home. I wanted to get her there but a series of wrong turns were delaying out arrival. The folks in the South didn't believe in remembering streets. I didn't pay enough attention going to be able get back easily. I was busy talking with my children and just enjoying the fact that we were all together. The movie we watched also gave us things to talk about as I tried to use it as an educational tool. I started to become a little unglued because no one in the car could get me back on the right rode. Z Baby was having the time of her life laughing at her mother and I argue about my driving. Legs took offense at one point because she thought Z Baby was laughing at her. Legs were having even more difficulty because it was now way past her time to take her medication. All the humor had now left me and I started driving faster in hopes that I would see something that would click and get me headed home. Z Baby spotted a street that would take us to Newport News the long way. The long way or the short way didn't matter to me as long as it was the way. When we finally made it home, everyone was tired and aggravated. It was little conversation in the house as I tried to calm Legs down and let her know that no one was laughing at her. I talked

Legs into eating something before she started swallowing pills. I sat at the table with Z Baby and ate before settling on the couch in front of the TV. It was a fun day after all, and I got a kick out of watching Z Baby laugh so much. I slept on the couch while the TV watched me, until Z Baby came and chased me to bed.

The rest of the week was filled with some old fashion family activity. The days were spent visiting friends that Legs wanted me to meet; and the evenings had Z Baby teaching me about computers. I was able to make a resume and I even got myself an email. The name just flowed out my mouth as if God was speaking. It was z savior and it said a lot about who I had become. I was fascinated by all things that you could do with a computer. Z Baby then showed me how to use Micro Soft Word and I was able to do a resume. I was like a little kid with a new toy. Z Baby was getting a kick out of watching her dad discover technology. We all had a lot of fun with each other that week and then we started to prepare for the New Year celebration. Legs said she would do the cooking this time so it was back to Wal-Mart again. I liked shopping at Wal-Mart because it reminded me of my last job in New York. I worked at Pathmark which also was a large retail store. In fact every time Wal-Mart tried to open a store there they received stiff opposition from the unions and were always unsuccessful. We would be having a traditional soul food meal that consisted of; hog maws and chittlings, black eyed peas, collard greens, my special boiled egg gravy, potato salad, yams and a small turkey. We got all the things we needed and I met some more friends of both Legs and Z Baby. I had my bald head now so I wasn't looking so old. I made it a point when we got home that day to let Legs know that I would be going out job searching after the holidays. I was ready now since I had made myself that resume on the computer.

I had been to church for two straight Sundays and I never saw them open the doors of the church for membership or do any other alter. I found that very strange because I was going to join. I didn't want a new year to come in without me being attached to a congregation. "Legs, how come they don't do alter calls at your church?" Legs looked puzzled when I asked her. "What do you mean by that Honey?" Now it was my time to look puzzled. Legs had been at Bridge Street for more than five years so I knew she understood the process of inviting people to join. "Oh I know what you mean now. The Pastor only does that if he knows someone wants to join. I'll say something this Sunday when we go." That was the strangest thing I ever heard but I didn't say anything. I figured it wasn't d them with any big deal even though it looked more like a lack of faith. I did wind up joining that Sunday and I presented them with my introduction letter from my past church. I let them know then that I was interested in their hospitality ministry since I was an excellent cook. I became very involved in the activities of the church because it was lacking some leadership amongst the males. I took the lead in volunteering to almost anything and was faithful in my tithing. My wife didn't have the strength to do as much as she used to but her attendance was good. We attended the watch service on New Years Eve and that following week I went to a Temp Agency that Legs had told me about. I told them about her struggles with her health and they all spoke so highly of her. They acknowledged the sacrifice I had made in relocating and pledged to find me something suitable real soon. I just needed to make daily phone calls to check for possible positions. Their process was much didn't than what I knew of the Temp Agencies in New York. I quickly learned that the whole employment issue down here was much different than New York. I continued to trust God because I knew He was my keeper. When I got back home that day, I told Legs how well everyone had spoke about her at Express Employment. The news made her smile and she gave me more information about her dealings with them. She said she wasn't with them long before she had landed her job at Canon through another source. The job at Canon was something that paid well after she had been laid off by the Community Service Board. She then told me that she had spoken with her old bosses at Canon and that she wanted to go visit them tomorrow. They were having a small party before the New Year and wanted her to attend.

We left early that morning on Tuesday to attend the office party. Legs were very excited about the trip as she paid special attention to the way she looked before leaving. We were all in the car and Legs did the driving. It seemed like a long ride and we went into areas I had not seen yet. I couldn't wait for these holidays to be over so that Legs could get back to her normal routine. All these activities on a daily basis were visibly wearing her down. Her next treatment would be on Thursday and that was fine with me. We pulled into a gravel filled driveway and drove a short distance until we came upon some trailers. The area looked liked a construction site with a lot of work left to do. We went inside and I realized that the trailer was actually an office that had a dining room, conference room, and a bathroom inside. One by one we greeted everyone we past as we were directed to go to the back. Everyone we past flashed a big smile and greeted us with "Happy Holidays." Mostly everyone male and female hugged Legs as she introduced me by name and title. There was a layout of food and a nice size group of people there to eat. Legs were busy talking and filling everyone in on what she has been going through since having to leave the job. It was no secret about her health and they were just glad to see her. One of her bosses called her and Z Baby into an office and had a brief conversation with them. I could hear Z Baby telling them about some of the things she had gotten for Christmas. While the three of them were walking back out into the area where I was sitting alone, the gentleman gave Legs and Z Baby an envelope and said Merry Christmas to both of them. They both hugged and thanked him. I was eager to know what was in the envelope but Legs said she would wait until we left. She continued to fellowship with her co-workers and catch up on the company gossip. She introduced me to the person she trained to take her place. The time finally came for us to leave. I took a few more goodies with me to eat since no one had given me an envelope. The ride home seemed faster than the one going. We didn't make any stops on the way back and I was glad for that. It was coming up on 3:00 p.m. and we all looked like we were ready for a nap. When we got home the girls opened their envelopes. They both gave out yells at the contents inside. Legs had seven one hundred dollar bills and Z Baby had two. They both stood in the middle of the floor grinning. Legs were happy that now she would be able to pay the rent on time. I stood there waiting for someone to hand me some money but it never happened. It was okay though because the girls expressed the most joy I had seen since Christmas. It was clear to me that my wife had made quite an impression on the people here in Virginia. The people, whom she worked with; from all the jobs she had since moving here, were still friends with her. The one thing I always told my wife; was that she was high functioning at work. We became close in the beginning because of our jobs and I was helping her be better at it. When her income had dropped she winded up working two jobs and the second one was at Dillard's. She fell in love with that part-time position which ended up being full-time. I met a few of the friends she had because everyone was checking on her for the holidays. It was only recent months that she had become too tired to maintain any type of employment. We were still waiting for an answer from Social Security about her disability request. We all went to the evening service at church to bring in the New Year. Z Baby thought that since I was there we would go to a party. I quickly reminded her that daddy was saved and sanctified, and church is where I've been for the past five New Years. She laughed as we finally got ourselves together to leave.

ZEKE SMITH

The church had a large gathering of regulars and more than a few strangers. They had a radio ministry which also brought in first time worshippers. They also boasted a large amount of youth but were in need of a stronger ministry to keep them engaged. I don't know how it was before I came but I kept my daughter next to me during service. It was a moving service with the congregation being given the opportunity to give their testimonies. I didn't hesitate to stand up because my faith in Jesus had healed my knee. I wanted to talk about the love I had for my wife and thank God for reuniting us when we both thought all hope was lost. I never passed on an opportunity to speak about the goodness of the Lord or the power of faith. My words were well received that night as the atmosphere became filled with people's emotions. I shouted hallelujah as my wife squeezed my hand. I sat down when my words became too muffled because of my own emotion. The preacher's words were able to touch everyone and the message was relevant for the season. My wife and I both stood up to receive prayer at the end of the service. The alter call was made but no one came forward on this day. My wife was still shedding tears as we approached the front of the sanctuary. We went home that night full of the spirit. I saw my wife becoming more relaxed about her situation. I spent most of New Year's Day finishing up the apartment. It was pretty much in the condition that I liked now. I made it a point not to have anything dirty around when a new year came in. I fell short this year and used the occasion to demonstrate tolerance for others short comings. I was not a perfect being myself; and I realized that it would take some time for Z Baby to adjust to a routine that she had as a child. We had an uneventful weekend with only a few visitors coming by. Legs made it for it with the time she spent talking on the phone. She began to spend less time in bed and more time socializing. We generally watched TV together in the living and rented movies from Blockbuster.

I got up early as usual on Monday. I made me some oatmeal and started pulling out clothes to be washed. It was real convenient having a washer and dryer and we still had our other washer from New York moth balled in the kitchen. Z Baby had some cereal before we left out together for her bus-stop. We would usually spend time talking about how we stayed connected when I wasn't a part of her household. The picture I had in my mind about the area was nothing like the reality of it. I teased Z Baby about her exaggeration of dangers that she faced walking alone to her bus-stop. She was not receptive to my joking. That was the last time I teased her about her fears. I gave my usual wave when she got on the bus. I couldn't get a hug because she thought that it was too babyish. I fixed Legs some breakfast when I got back home so she could take her Meds. I cleaned up my room or actually Z Baby's room and made the bed up. Z Baby was sleeping with her mom now because I couldn't take the couch anymore. It was okay for now as I was working my way back to the master bedroom. I called New York to check on Godfather to make sure my renovations were holding up. I still didn't get any construction work down here, which made me second guess lugging all those tools this far. I made my call to Express Employment to see if anything was available. You had to call everyday to let them know you were available to work. The phone calls really made the difference. I needed something that would allow me to work at my own pace without supervision. I had cleared their background check and drug screening. It was now up to them to come with something. I was eager to demonstrate what a valuable worker I was and how much pride and quality I put into my labor. I got good news when I made my call this morning. They had a position in Williamsburg that had just come in. They wanted to explain the position to me and give me traveling directions. I was hoping before I left to see them that the job wouldn't coincide with Legs' medical appointments or treatments. I watched Judge Judy with Legs before I left for Express Employment. The ride to their office took longer than usual because I got lost going. I was still getting used too the main traveling routes. I would sometimes get confused about my turns and wound up on the interstate. The way the area here was developed never made sense to me. It was only two main connecting streets so a wrong turn into a neighborhood would have you traveling in circles. I finally made it to the office and was greeted by the receptionist. I generally was greeted with smiles whenever I entered the office. My wife had made a profound impact on them and the fact that I came to care for her made them accept me even more. They were all very friendly towards me and treated me as if I had a more lengthy relationship with them. I thanked God for who He had led me to. I totally trusted them with my future here because I felt our meeting was divine intervention. All my business and social contacts were based on whom Legs had introduced me to. She was so diligent in making me comfortable and in helping me to have some success. I was directed to speak with Marsha whose desk was located in the main area of the small store front office. It was a neat and well maintained area. The atmosphere had a pleasant scent in the air and the place was painted in warm subtle colors. Marsha told me about the job and gave me a detailed map on how to get there. I explained that I needed the straight route because any type of short cut would only confuse me. I was very excited about the job she started to tell me about. It was almost a month to the day of my arrival and my first contact had yielded success. It was a janitorial position at a pet resort that also had an adjacent animal hospital. The request for a staff person had come from a personal friend of Randy. Randy was a high ranking staff person of the business who I had spoken with on my first visit. "Mr. Smith, how do you feel about dogs and cats?" "I love animals Marsha and I used to train and breed Belgium Shepherds. I'm not that in love with cats. I don't like the way they like to rub up against you. I'm much better with dogs and don't have any fears about them." She laughed at some of the things I said and continued on with a description of my duties. "They mainly need you to do the cleaning overnight but you will have to have some contact with the animals while you are there. This is why I asked you about your feelings towards animals. The hours are from 10 p.m. to 8 a.m. four days a week. I know you are taking care of Legs now, so this should help you with being home during the day." I began a silent prayer thanking God for His love and compassion. This was truly a perfect job for me at this time. I would be able to work without supervision at a pace that wouldn't offer any additional physical challenges. "Oh thank you Jesus Marsha, this is good. When do I start and how much is the pay?" Marsha sat still for a moment without speaking. She appeared to be calculating something in her head. "You will start at $8 an hour and if they like you, they will hire you permanently after ninety days. That's when you will get a raise but I don't exactly know for how much at this time. It's a night job but your first week will be in the day so that they can teach you how to work with the animals." I was okay with everything; I just needed to work something out with my sister-in-law Coco. Legs would need somebody to go with her on the next two appointments until my night shift started. "Okay Marsha, thank you so much. I won't let you guys down." I left the office feeling so empowered and filled with gratitude for what the Lord had just provided. I couldn't wait to get home and give Legs the good news. Now I was feeling like the man again, because I would be able to make a meaningful contribution to the household. I would not have to keep relying on phone calls to New York or Legs spotty generosity to put money in my pocket.

The ride home was uneventful this time. I rushed upstairs after parking the car, eager to tell Legs how good God had been. Legs were in her bedroom napping with the TV on. I hesitated to wake her but decided that my news was too important to hang on to. I didn't have to shake her because the sound of me entering the room had alerted her to my presence. She rolled over and looked at me before asking; "How did it go Honey?" I didn't waste a second before responding; "I got a job Kitten!" Legs sat straight up in the bed and began to clear her throat. I watched as she pushed the covers off of herself and swung her legs around to hang off the side of the bed. I went over and sat next to her and put my arms around her waist. I felt that familiar tingle in my lions as I gave her a soft kiss on the cheek. She looked at me and said; "Okay Honey, you know I can't do anything!" I let go of a hardy laugh and stood in front of her as my hand slipped from around her waist. She started smiling as I began to tell her about the job and when I would be starting. She began to show more happiness than me as I helped her rise up off the bed. She went into the bathroom and returned after a short time. "I think it's a good idea for me to go there now so I don't get lost tomorrow." She agreed with me and asked how much money I would be making. I gave her the numbers and she was still smiling. "Well that's a start. If the job hires you after the first ninety days you will automatically get a raise of at least one dollar an hour." She understood the process with the temp agencies here because that's how she had gotten all her jobs. I gave her another kiss before leaving to start my journey. "Be careful driving Honey and call me when you're on your way back." I accepted the advice she gave without a comment. I was learning how to be a better husband this time around. I didn't feel a need to assert my authority or become defensive about anything she might say to me. I was seeing a much more mature woman than the one I had married. I began to get the feeling that it was more about being here for her rather than someone else. I went to the job with no problem. It was an easy set of directions to follow because the route was along some main highways. It was located right next to Eastern State Hospital. I didn't go inside the place; and instead just drove past it and made a U Turn down the block from it. I called Legs as I waited in front of a stop sign and let her know that I was headed back. "Wow Honey that was quick!" I thought the same thing to myself as we ended the call and I began my journey back home. When Z Baby came home that afternoon, she too became excited about me starting a new job. The news didn't stay inside the house long, as Legs began to make her calls telling everyone that her husband had a job. I used the rest of the day making sure that the house was in order. I wouldn't have the time to clean everyday with a job to go to now. I spoke with Z Baby and let her know, that she would have to do a better job keeping the bathroom clean. I also told her to keep our room clean and not to leave her clothes lying around. She smiled and then laughed at what I told her. I made myself a lunch with some of the left-over food from the fridge. I put together an outfit for tomorrow and retired early.

It was the first Tuesday in 2008 and I had a job to go to. I was the first one up and used the hall bathroom to shower. I made myself some oatmeal after I got dressed. I watched the news while I ate and waited on Z Baby to get ready to leave. I had a good feeling in me since getting out of the bed. I took a moment to say my morning prayer and asked God to forgive me for being late. I usually prayed in the morning as soon as my feet hit the floor. I was excited today that I was more focused on going to work than I was on thanking God for the opportunity. When Z Baby finally was ready to leave, I went and said goodbye to Legs because I wasn't coming back to the house. I drove the car to the bus stop just around the corner, and we both waited inside until her bus came. I was not trying to be late on my first day. I did not know what the traffic would be like at this time of morning. I headed east when I got to route 143 and entered interstate 64 just after the Wal-Mart exit. It was busy but the cars were zooming. I had to be at the job at 8 a.m. and the time now was 7 a.m., so I knew I wouldn't be late. I got to work at 7:45 and had to wait for the manager to arrive that was going to train me. There was a young sister sitting at their front desk that was responsible for booking the animals that came in. It was pretty busy as both dogs and cats were getting check into their quarters. Most of the animals were coming to stay for the day until their masters returned from work. There were other then just some dogs coming in for exercise and to play for a couple of hours in an outside yard. The lobby area was very clean and the tile floors had a shine. I was directed to their lounge area that had a refrigerator, coffee machine, and an exercise chair. It also contained some long tables that stretched almost the length of the rooms with a variety of chairs sitting around them. It was after 8 a.m. and the manager still had not come. The receptionist in the front began to tell me a few things about the business and what to expect. I listened intently because I wanted to succeed at this employment opportunity. I thought briefly about how my daughter would tell me, when she was a little girl; "Daddy you can do anything!" I found myself at different times in life utilizing various skills and talents in order to eat. I never scrutinized what I had to do to make a living. I didn't think about glamour or prestige and there were those instances when my work wasn't legal. Those days of throwing bricks and taking risky chances were over. Now here I was again fulfilling a child's prophecy that; her daddy could do anything. I continue examining the space as the receptionist spoke.

She said her name was Angel and that she was married with two children. She also had relocated years ago from a northern state. I immediately felt comfortable with her because of that common ground. The facility was well organized and properly constructed to serve the purpose it was designed for. It had a retail area in the front that stocked all types of items related to pet's care and maintenance. There were multiple egresses to go either to the second floor or the back area that housed the animals. You could also go through another set of doors to access the adjacent animal hospital. I never considered becoming a veterinarian but now the thought was entering my mind. I turned quickly around when the front door chimes went off indicating that someone was entering the building. A young petite woman rushed inside and stepped up to the front desk. She then went around the counter and performed some tasks on the computer, while at the same time greeting me with a hello. When she finished she disappeared into the back for only a moment. "Hi my name is Gina, are you Zeke?" She was cute and looked very young. She stood before me a little out of breath as I wondered if this was the manager I was waiting for. I expected to see someone much older for the position. I had even expected to see a man. "Hi Gina and yes I'm Zeke." Gina spoke very proper with an accent that I had not encountered since being down here. She informed me that I had to go and take a drug test before I would start. She then told me that she was the supervisor and I would meet the office manager at a later time. We went into a small room that was located off from the front desk. It was used to process the incoming pets for the resort. It also doubled as an office when privacy was needed. She began to orientate me about the business and the work I would be doing. I didn't need any training concerning the cleaning but I had to know what responsibilities I would have and the way they wanted them done. I also needed to know how to handle the dogs and cats in there care and some of the other exotic pets that might be their responsibility. She then began to give me some travel directions as she prepared the paperwork for the drug test. During the time I was time I was in the front speaking with Angel, I watched numerous females of various ages and sizes come in. They all gave friendly hellos as they walked in. Most of them stopped in the lounge before continuing on to the other side. I began to ask myself; "Where are the men?"

I needed detail information to get to this medical facility where I would take the drug screening. I knew nothing of the area and the streets she was naming. In the south or at least since I was in Virginia; directions always included landmarks and other fixtures instead of streets and intersections.

It made getting to a place easy but it made returning to where you started at hard. I learned to drop my bread crumbs and leave myself a trail to keep from getting lost. It took me a couple of hours to do what I had to do. When I returned, I was ready to start my training as a veterinarian assistant. I gave Gina the paperwork from the medical facility. This was a normal routine for them to send new hires for drug screening. I had no reason to be concerned about a drug test. My piss was clean enough to nurse a baby. She filed the papers after a careful examination of them and proceeded to show me how to clock in. I then showed her the time sheets that Express had given me in order for me to get paid. Gina didn't realize at the time that I was a referral from a temp agency. I explained the whole situation to her and suggested that her boss would explain things to her. The owner of the business was away at the time so she would have to speak to the facility manager. Gina was in charge of the resort side of the business. I was a fast learner; as she took me through all the motions, for me to understand my responsibilities to the care of the animals. The first week was exciting as I was taught to administer medications, clean the pens and cages, and how to read the charts to probably feed the pets. I gained a lot of respect from my in-laws by getting a decent job so fast. My little grand daughter was amused as I explained my new job to her. She especially thought it was funny as told a tale of my interaction with a cat. I switched over to the night shift the following week after assuring them that I understood my duties well enough to be left alone. The manager was especially pleased with the way things were going after my second week of employment. He was a close friend and neighbor of Randy. I was glad that things were going so well and felt that it was a match orchestrated in heaven. I received my first pay check that week. Gina had instructed me not to let anyone know that I was from a temp agency and that she would be the one signing my time sheet. She still had me clocking in like everyone else. It was quiet working at night. The last person usually left when I came in. They only stayed if there were some unfinished business that wasn't taken care of. I finally met another male besides the office manager. He was Gina's brother and he was the one cleaning at night before I came. When I had worked there for a month, I began to receive a lot of praise for the job I was doing. The work was tedious because I had a lot to do before 6 a.m. when I would have to start feeding and letting the pets out to walk. The cats didn't get any exercise from me and I would make sure that they were all back in their cages, before I started. Legs had started getting her disability check so we were doing well financially. It felt good having my own money and paying my own tithes. We had pizza on occasion and even started going to the movies on weekends. I became more active at church as I tried to do more for God and His people. I continued to cook and go with Legs on her medical appointments. We found time to hang out on the days I didn't have to work. We began having more conversations about our past difficulties and some times they were heated. It wasn't easy but we both finally understood that talk was necessary for us both to heal. We shared honestly and openly about everything that troubled us. Legs began to gain a little weight and I watched her curves start to get plump again. Valentine Day was coming up and Legs told that she wanted to go to our churches annual luncheon on that day. She said the year before she just served because she had no one to go with. She explained how in the past her sister Coco and her husband had gone with her. The tickets were $50 per couple for church members and $25 for non members. This was one of the ways to get the community involved in their activities. Legs and I kept perfect attendance at Sunday service. We also went to Bible study during the week unless Legs were feeling too bad, and then I would go with just Z Baby. They had such a large amount of youth in the church that they were able to have a separate Bible study for them. I continued to progress at work and had started sending money to my credit union up north. It was good that Express had direct deposit so I was able to split funds between my bank and credit union. I was offered $100 to open an account at one of the larger banks because I was a recent resident to Virginia. I took advantage of that because I no longer feared having my money confiscated. Legs then put me on her account since I was handling all the bill paying. The trust we had in each other had come a long way and was even better than when we first got married. The household was functioning with a lot of love and harmony. Z Baby continued to do well in school. I had established myself as a competent worker and I was getting along with the other associates there. I had even developed some close relationships with a number of them. Compliments about my labor and personality were common place at work, in the community, and at my church; which we attended regularly. Legs and I attended the Valentine's Day luncheon and the love and commitment that was present in our marriage now became public. Couples that were having difficulty in their relationships began to seek our advice on how to remedy their problems. Our lives couldn't have been much better and it showed with the way Z Baby performed at school. I became A little discontent at my sleeping arrangements and before I told Legs, I spoke with Z Baby about. She was very receptive to the things I said to her.

I even told her about difficulty I had when she was a child that wouldn't sleep in her own bed. She took me very serious this time and there was no laughter. On that night I moved into the bedroom with my wife. We had now gone full circle in our present reunion. Initially there was tension the first few nights we slept together. I imagine that the memories we had of others that we slept with came to mind. I know at first those were the things that I was feeling. I can't speak for Legs but I didn't think it was much different. Those days that followed after Valentine's Day; saw our maturity with each other develop progressively. I was experiencing such a high that week as I looked forward to my next payday. I was accustomed to giving Legs $100 and I would fill the car up with gas; which usually cost me about $50. When you added the deduction that I had going to my credit union account I was left with $75 in my pocket. I was content with this arrangement because all my past experiences while living a part from my wife, left me feeling very grateful. I never brought any sadness into the house. I usually took care of that at work. The grief and sorrow that I felt because of my wife's illness and the feelings of remorse from our separation was processed at work. I did all my crying and praising as I performed my chores with only other people's pets as my witnesses. I prayed when I arrived and prayed before I left. I communicated with my God regularly. My language and conversations at work was all about the gospel and how God was moving in my life. It was no fluke and those around me began to accept it as being a part. My fellow associates who only included females became mindful of the language they used around me. I saw that not only my labor and the quality of it was affecting people but also my belief system was having an impact. When I saw my pay check that week, the peace that I had become accustomed to was disturbed. A major portion of my check had been taken out by child support. I was used to a much smaller amount being deducted while in New York. The amount being taken now left me with very little to work with. I went home and complained to Legs about why this order was still in effect with me living there. She became defensive which in turn caused me to become offensive. This situation was threatening to become a major issue and a source of hostility. It took me more than a moment to calm down because Legs were denying that she was receiving anything. I showed her my check and the stub for proof and she still wouldn't acknowledge it. I asked her to have the support order stopped and she refused. I slept on the couch that night and prayed that things would be better tomorrow. It was an uneasy sleep since I had gotten used to being in a bed.

I awoke the next morning feeling cranky but not upset. It just took a night's sleep for me to remember why I was here. I began to view my wife as a hero because she had developed a positive attitude about her situation. She had struggled through all those harsh feelings towards me and was displaying her love daily. We had started laughing together and she had stopped focusing on her illness. She had become more cooperative during her chemotherapy. The nurses found her pleasant most days as opposed to being evil all the time; which forced me to make apologies behind her back. The nurses were accustomed to patients having anger because of their sickness but I wasn't used to legs being that way. If she felt more secure in me paying child support by payroll deductions that was imposed by the courts; then I should not be in opposition to that, and allow her to have that peace. I didn't have to go to work until the following evening, so I went and made breakfast for everybody and pulled some meat from the freezer to thaw. I made pancakes, eggs, and sausage to everyone's delight. I would cook a nice dinner to help put the house back in order. My wife Legs, continued to gain weight and she began to notice it. I gave her breakfast in bed that morning; and told her that I was sorry I didn't sleep with her, because my back was killing me. She laughed out loud signaling an end to the hostilities and reached out for me to hug her. I had to move her food to the side to keep from getting any syrup on me. I went and sat at the table to eat my food with Z Baby. I had to make sure that none of the girls felt neglected because they both were spoiled and jealous.

I found myself becoming more and more involved in the church's activities. I especially was paying attention to its physical condition. I became a part of their maintenance committee and hospitality. I wasn't allowed to cook but I did help serve and keep the kitchen clean. I developed close relationships with more of the members. I avoided the women and clung to the men. I was finished with the new member's class so I was able to officially become a part of the different ministries. The job started to become more of a challenge also at this time. It had only been two months since I started but they were already trying to hire me permanently. They even suggested that I quit the agency I was with and they would rehire me right away. I would not be a party to such deception and didn't mind waiting the extra time for a raise. My decision only confirmed to them who I belonged too and I began to receive more respect as a Christian. There was one associate at work who worked two jobs and she took special care in teaching me everything I needed to know. Her heart was in her work and she often complained to me about the lonely life she was living. Katie enjoyed working with animals and was good at it. It was great when she was with me because I didn't have to deal with the pets. She had trained me for the night shift because she had done it for so long herself. There was the only other male that worked there who split the days with her. Katie was much more thorough than him but neither was as thorough as me. I didn't take any short cuts. I changed my mop water often as I moved from one area to another. I took pride in removing the dog's poop from their outside areas and when ever they soiled their pens. It was a lot of work to do which explains why everything didn't get done before I started. The only blessing was that I didn't have to worry about buffing and waxing any floors because outside contractors took care of that. My relationship with Katie began to sour when she was over looked for a manager's position. She often told how she had trained so many other managers before and that she never considered applying for the position herself. The person that hired me was let go by the boss for a number of reasons. The boss then decided to split the position in two and have separate managers for each part of her business. Gina, who initially had orientated me, was given the position at the resort side. This angered Katie because she wasn't offered the position. It didn't seem to matter to her that she never wanted it. She allowed that anger to fester and grow and it began to affect her job performance. She also became a difficult person to work with because she started to do less and expect me to do more. I started to distance myself but remained cordial and professional. I had always found comfort in the things I did at work. I was now faced with some things that made me uncomfortable. There was a deaf associate and I was given a pad to communicate with her. I only encountered her once and sometimes twice week. We only had a couple of hours to spend working together because she came in the morning. I began to feel the pressure of all the responsibilities I had at home, the church and my community. I spend my nights at work praying and crying because it was the most effective way for me to release the tension. When my fellow co-workers began to create problems things became more unbearable. There was some misunderstanding in my written communication with the deaf associate and it was blown out of proportion. Then I was being pressured to do things for the pets that I was unable to do. I only received any guidance or understanding from a few. I was forced to ask the associates at the hospital to help; which they did gladly. I was now harboring resentments and all I could do was pray about it. I couldn't even discuss these things with my wife because she had enough to deal with. I would spend the whole time with her during her chemotherapy and she had begun to develop a "there's no hope attitude." She would experience emotional highs and lows and finally it was addressed with medication. I found myself leaning more and more on Angel at work. She built me up and expressed a lot of gratitude for what I was doing. Angel would compliment me for always having such a positive attitude about everything. She thanked me for daily smile and look of contentment when I did my work. Angel told me, that no one before me had kept the place as clean as I did. Whenever I needed to talk she made herself available. She had her own struggles to deal with but she still found time to help me with mine.

In late February we began to experience plenty of prosperity in the household. Legs had been receiving over $1,000 a month from Social Security plus my weekly donations for child support. My future employment was pretty much guaranteed because of the satisfaction with my job performance. The temp agency was receiving excellent reports from my supervisors on a weekly basis. Z Baby had always wanted a puppy since she fell in love with the one her cousin had. Even while I was living in New York she spoke of her desire to have a small dog. I thought it was a great idea but I questioned her ability to care for one. I let her know that I had dogs as a teenager and it was no simple task. She began to talk about wanting a dog again since I had been working with them. The tales I told about my interactions with the animals not only amused my grand daughter but it amused Z Baby also. I had fallen in love with this cute little white puppy at work. He was the cutest pup with this large black nose and deep black eyes. The dog's name was Mr. Lucky and he would always wipe his feet after doing his business on the grass. I only saw him early in the mornings when ever I had to walk and feed the pets that were over night patients at the hospital. I started looking forward to seeing this pup. He used to get so excited when I came to walk him. His presence in my life began to have a therapeutic effect as I was dealing with the challenge of caring for my wife. I started sharing my love of the pup with the hospital associates and found out that he was a rescue dog. Rescue animals were those that had been abused either by their owners or were those found abandoned in the street. I inquired about being able to take this pup home; and after waiting about a week, I was given permission by the veterinarian caring for him. Z Baby became so excited when I arrived home one day with the news. We went shopping for a cage for the pup to sleep in. Legs didn't get as excited about the dog coming as Z Baby did but she knew that I had a history of having dogs before. His name was Lucky because he had survived some really harsh conditions. He was in bad shape and frighten, when he first came to the hospital. They nursed him back to perfect health at the hospital with no visible signs of his past neglect. When I brought him home, my daughter wasted n time in changing his name. She had fallen immediately in love with him. Legs did not want him no where near her but she too thought he was cute. Z Baby named him Bean and I used to call him Mr. Bean. She argued about me adding the mister and I quickly got used to calling him Bean. Bean was an instant hit in the Smith household. He was a happy pup and didn't require a lot of attention. Bean added joy to the house and around the same time he came, I received some additional bad news.

I was home resting and watching television with Legs. I received a phone call from Carolyn that disrupted my peace. We had become friendlier towards each other since my sister's funeral. I respected and appreciated the way she had responded. She called to tell me that Shawn had been hit by a truck and was in critical condition at a hospital in Norfolk, Virginia. She had sketchy details about the circumstances of how it had happened. She was living in another state at this time and could not respond to his needs. She needed me to go to the hospital and she would join me later. This was not the first time she had called me about our son. Her marriage was in disarray and she was separated from her husband. I was not pleased with the call because Shawn's living situation had changed without my knowledge. I went to my knees and began to pray. I couldn't understand why the Lord allowed additional burdens to come upon me at this time. I was surviving enough of a struggle and started falling a part again after hearing this news. I had no idea where this place was at. Legs would not be able to travel with me because of her condition. The only thing that was in my favor this morning was the weather. I called the number Carolyn had given after I finished praying. I was crying uncontrollably as I tried to dial the number. I was in the other room when Legs entered to ask me what was wrong. In my shaken state I had not even informed her of what had just happened with Shawn. My son had been through a lot since birth. He was afflicted with so many health issues that his survival and joy was a true testament to the power of Jesus. He was saved as a teenager and was connected with a loving church. It was this church that gave him the resources to remain in contact with me in New York. I had no control over the events that caused our separation but I always without question, responded to his needs. I let know Legs know what was happening and she offered to make the call as I tried to regain my composure. She gave me the directions to the hospital after speaking with a nurse. She couldn't get any information about Shawn except that he was brought in that morning as an accident victim. I put Bean in his cage and left out immediately. It was a straight run to the hospital in Norfolk. I didn't need to make any turns or worry about taking the wrong highway. Legs had received good directions from the nurse; and were able to give me additional travel instructions that made it even simpler. It took me about 45 minutes to get there and Shawn was still in the emergency room when I arrived. I was able to get some detailed information about what had happened from Shawn. He was in a lot of pain but it wasn't being expressed on his face. Shawn had learned to be tolerant of his short comings. There was not much that I was allowed to do when he was growing up. I too had learned to be tolerant of life's short comings. I didn't want hi to speak but he was determined to express his anger and disbelief at being struck by a truck. "Dad that truck ran the light. He didn't stop for me. I had the light dad. The truck didn't stop for me." I had to turn away from him because it was too painful for me to watch. There were so many things that he never understood, about the world he lived in. On top of being diagnosed with epilepsy at six months of age; he also had to content with being bi-polar which made socializing difficult. He was easy to like and love because it took a lot for him to see the bad in people. He loved family and he loved Jesus. Shawn had been saved since a teenager and his church did a good job of caring for him. Now he was lying on this bed with multiple fractures and didn't understand how he could be at fault. "Its okay son, try not to speak right now. Your mother told me what happened." They had to cut his clothes off him and Shawn was complaining about that. I had to explain to him it was necessary to treat his injuries. I knew it would be a while before his mother came so I made sure they had his health history and I gave my information for contact. The nurses told me the extent of his injuries and I almost passed out when I got the full report. He was hit by a truck while crossing in the middle of the street. He had just got off one bus and was rushing to get the next one waiting across the street. Shawn was on his way to school; to be taught something he couldn't learn, at a job that would never hire him. It was sad about the amount of people that had taken advantage of him starting with his mother. She started out by changing his last name to make it easier for her to get welfare. We had a rocky relationship from the time she was six months pregnant. While we were out following leads to get our own apartment, she informed me that I wouldn't be living with her. When I heard that it was the beginning of my end. I wiped the tears from my face and went back to Shawn. I was not going to leave him until he was settled

ZEKE SMITH

in a room. Knew that God stepped in and saved him because if he had fallen backwards he would be dead. The impact from the truck fractured his pelvis and shifted his spine. He broke his jaw and nose when he hit the ground. He also injured his hands in the fall. He was still coherent and not screaming out in pain but he was hurting. He lost some teeth and cracks one or two others. I stayed with him until they finished his x-rays and checked him into a room. It was way past noon by the time they finished processing him. I was told that I should try to leave now since I lived in Newport News and had to go over the water. They said the traffic got real bad at 3:00 and there was no need for me to stay. They gave him some pain medication that put him to sleep. I was exhausted when I left and I promised him that I would be back before he fell asleep. I spent the ride home questioning God about all the burdens I was carrying and when would it end.

When I walked into the house from my long ride home, Legs were seated in the living room watching TV. I started telling her all the things that was wrong with Shawn and the pain he was in. This was the first time that she listened to me without interrupting with questions. She had been steadily improving and I didn't want this new situation to cause her any relapse. Legs had been exhibiting a good attitude and were doing more things around the house. She wasn't in the bed so much and began to let the dog out when she was up and about. This was the best sign she gave that her health was improving. She had the body that I had fell in love except for a slight bulge in her belly. I tried hard to maintain my composure as I started to describe to her Shawn's injuries. It was at this time that she started to ask questions about where his mother was at. I then began to lose the battle of staying calm. I started visualizing the scene in the emergency room. The anger in me that tried to rise was subdued by my sorrow and grief. I sobbed uncontrollably as I finished giving Legs the information. She rose from the couch as I started walking around the room in circles. Legs then grabbed me from behind and held me tightly. She didn't talk but her actions were speaking volumes. I realized that she was feeling helpless and just wanted to comfort me. She led me to the bedroom as I continued my sobbing. I just couldn't stop crying. I feared losing my son as I fought to hold on to hold on to my wife. There were just too many depressing things going on at one time. The world around me would get bearable and then something always seemed to occur that would interfere with my joy. We nestled up close in the bed as we both fell asleep. We both laid there until Z Baby woke us up to ask me if I had to work that night. Z Baby was my alarm clock by default. She had become accustomed to my daily schedule and watched the times I rose to leave for work. She knew my days better than I did. I looked at the clock on the wall and saw that it was 8:00 p.m. Wow we had been sleeping for over three hours. I up and thanked Z Baby and started telling her bout the accident Shawn was in. Z Baby had become closer to her brother since I moved down here. During the first six years of her life, Shawn made it a point to send her a Christmas gift; which was usually a doll baby. Now she was returning that early love and devotion to her by checking on him. When she had saw his living conditions in Portsmouth, she asked me if I would let him live with us. I said no at the time because I didn't think we had the room to support another grown man in the house. She became visibly disturbed about his situation. I regretted telling her at this time because I would be leaving for work soon. She asked for further details; but I had to stop talking, in order to shower before leaving for work. On the nights that I went to work Z Baby would sleep with her mother. I didn't mind because it didn't interfere with Legs and I sleeping together. I felt good now about it because they could comfort each other, while dealing with their feelings about Shawn.

I got to work a little early this night. I was happy to see that Rosie was working when I came thru the door. Rosie was an evening associate who had been working there for a long time. She knew everything about everybody and didn't mind telling it. She was amongst some of the mature females that worked there. Although she wasn't in a minority group, we had hit it off and were good friends. She was my outlet to vent about my struggles and I listen to the difficulties she had in life. She had a young adult daughter that was sometimes there when I came to work. The only handicap with her was the fears she had about being there alone once day light left. She experienced those visions depicted in horror movies because the place was surrounded by woods. She gave me a hug when I told her about the additional trauma that was now a part of my life. She made an extra effort to put things in order before she left, so that my shift would be easier. I made my rounds checking on the animals and turning out the lights. Rosie had it looking like 42nd Street in there with all the lights on. I let her leave early as I settled in the employee lounge area to calm my nerves. I rested long enough for my mind to be clear of the things that were upsetting me. I said my prayers before I began my routine of cleaning, starting first with the kennel area. The dogs were making a lot of noise as I vacuumed and then mopped the floors. I checked their door tags to see who might need special attention. I used the remote to turn off the televisions

ZEKE SMITH

that were still on. I next tackled the back areas and side rooms where the cats were housed at. Rosie would always make sure that none were left out playing because she knew of my fear of them. These were not usually the cats that I was used to seeing. Some of these cats were huge and aggressive. I think some were even unaccustomed to having someone like me around. I took a short break as I changed my mop water and wiped down some counters. I then moved my cleaning equipment to the other side after double checking the doors to make sure they were locked. Sometimes the evening associates would forget to check the side exits of the hospital. I didn't want any unexpected visitors with a mental hospital so close. I too had my own fears because I generally worked in a daze as I meditated on the Lord. The time had passed into a new day and my body was telling me to sit down. The problem with my knees and feet dictated that I not do so much so soon. I didn't always pay attention to that when I got caught up in my cleaning. Cleaning my house was one of the ways that I dealt with any emotional situations; because it gave me such a peace to make things look fresh. When I was at work time went by fast, as I broke up my routine for the most efficiency. There was a TV in the lounge that I thought was broken and that you could watch tapes on it. All the channels were snowy with only static for sound. I had a lot of extra time on my hands this night so I tried to make an antenna after I finished eating my lunch. I was able to get a station and there was some type of religious program playing. On this night I discovered the TBN. It had to be the work of God because I was delivered that night at work from my emotional burdens. I now had an outlet while I was at work that gave me peace and understanding. I included watching the programs on TBN as part of my nightly routine. It was truly a miracle because the environment that had started showing some signs of hostility; was now the most peaceful place on earth to me. I was being spiritually fed by the programs I watched. It helped to make me a more informed and committed Christian. The troubles with my son became mute after I listened to others witness on TBN. The situation with my wife became more inspirational than depressing. I met the challenge of getting along with all my coworkers with ease. It was as if God stayed at my side at work. My level of integrity rose and I truly began to labor to please the Lord. The days and nights disappeared quickly as I cared for Legs while making regular visits to see Shawn at the hospital. Carolyn had finally showed up and she stayed with a friend for a while to make more visits to see her son. Z Baby would travel with me when I visited Shawn on the weekends. The world around me had gotten better again in spite of the trials and tribulations. I stood every Sunday after service, for additional prayer with my wife. I counseled another member who was still trying to get back with his wife. The month of March was drawing close to its end and I had a lot to shout about. My experience with joy and happiness told me that things were just too good to remain the same. I prepared myself for a change in my situation and the new challenge from God that was sure to come.

Shawn's injuries were severe and he needed rehabilitation. He was unable to walk and had to use a wheel chair. His jaw was wired shut so the only food he ate was liquid. There was a concern about food getting trapped in his mouth and causing an infection. He had to be taught how to use a Waterpik in order to keep his mouth clean. There were so many new things that he had to adjust to. He had been hospitalized for more than a month and the doctors were ready to discharge. The major problem that we faced was caring for him. He was very independent and hard headed. Shawn always had a problem with taking advice from anyone that wasn't attached to his church. I had major problems of my own that I was still adjusting to. He would not be able to live alone and his housing had to be able to accommodate a wheel chair. The house he lived in was not suitable although his stepfather Dan said that he would have it renovated. If Shawn couldn't find a place to live with someone who could care for him, he would have to be placed in a state institution until he could. Carolyn did not want to take him and suggested that he be placed in a home. My hands were tied and if he went back home Dan could still not help because he was already confined to a wheel chair. There were also questionable activities at the house that would place Shawn at risk. I was prepared to leave it to God until one morning my son made a passionate plea; "Dad don't let mommy put me in a home!" I looked in his eyes and saw sadness that he never displayed before. I did not believe that I would be able to handle this additional responsible. Shawn received SSI and with his disability he would not be able to handle his affairs. I also had to think of his mental state and stubbornness if I did take it on. "Shawn I don't know if I can help because you can't go back to Dan's house." I spoke with his doctors, physical therapist, and the social worker assigned to him. I told them the situation that I had at home and they understood the problems I faced. They even shifted their attention towards me for awhile because of my daily emotional break downs. I was made aware of some resources that I could access to help me cope better and maintain my mental stability. "Shawn I got to go now but I will be back tomorrow." He looked up at me again and repeated his plea; "Dad please don't let mommy put me in a home." I left that day very shaken up. I received more encouragement from the nurses as I stepped into the elevator. I was in no hurry to get home as I tried to work this thing out. I drove home in a daze in the slow lane, as I whispered prayers to my savior; Jesus. The traffic congestion that I encountered along the way had no effect on me. I finally arrived at my complex and watched the playing outside as I drove slowly over the two speed bumps. I pulled into my parking space and exited the vehicle. I returned some hellos before climbing my stairs. "Kitten they want to discharge Shawn!" I shouted out as I entered the apartment. I continued walking to the back and Kitten met me in the hallway outside the bathroom. "They're ready to discharge Shawn but he still can't walk. He has problems with his right leg too. We don't have enough room for him here because he can't go back to that house in Portsmouth!" I was speaking so rapidly that Leg's could hardly keep up or process what I saying. She wrapped her arms around me and asked me to be quiet for a moment. She tightened her embrace and we just stood there silently together for a moment. My eyes began to water as I closed them shut. I tried to pull away from Leg's to sit down but she held on and stood her ground. I soon gave up and began to cry. "Let it all out; we will deal with this together. Shawn can get a one bedroom apartment here and you will be able to watch him much easier. He doesn't have to live with us." I started to calm down and she finally allowed me to go into the bedroom. The words she spoke made more since than the thoughts of over crowding that I had in my head. Legs returned to the bed as I went into the bathroom to wash my face and hands. I came out and lay down across the foot of the bed and we both watched the TV until Z Baby came home.

Z Baby came in and we both started telling her about the situation with her brother. She didn't hesitate about offering a place for him to stay. I was shocked and overwhelmed that my little girl had grown up and was thinking about someone else. She displayed a lot of maturity and was prepared to make any sacrifice for her brother. She had seen firsthand the conditions he was living under and agreed that he shouldn't go back. The following day I spoke with our housing management and they promised to make an apartment available. I just needed to put up a $200 deposit and pay the first month's rent on the first of April. I then left for the hospital after making the arrangements. I knew that Shawn would be excited and I prepared myself for the extra labor that I would endure. I knew that God would see me through this by giving me the strength and resources to accomplish this mission. When I arrived at the hospital I first spoke with the social worker before seeing Shawn. She helped me to secure the necessary paperwork to become Shawn's payee. She also helped me arrange supportive services in my neighbor to reduce traveling expenses. Shawn was not happy about signing the letter that gave me control over his resources. He signed the letter under protest after I explained to him that it was the only way I would accept responsibility for his welfare. Carolyn didn't like it either when she showed up because she had to be made aware of the document. She had arrived at the hospital late and missed the conversations I had with the social worker. "Zeke, thanks for taking Shawn. I will get him when I find a better place to live." She had finally let me know how much disarray her own life was in. I brought Shawn home that afternoon and he only had to stay with me for a few days before an apartment was ready for him. He didn't have any furniture, so wife's sister Coco was able to let me pick some out at the agency she worked at. The deacon at my church provided the transportation to pick up the things that Saturday. The rest of the week was difficult at work as I juggled caring for both Shawn and my wife. Time passed as Shawn became adjusted to his new living quarters. The job of watching him was split between Z Baby and me. We had to shop for him and prepare his meals. After two weeks and just before Easter Sunday, I was able to get him a home attendant to help bath him and the hospital had arranged for a visiting nurse to attend to his dressings and teach him how to care for his leg. The money I had to spend now really put a strain on my budget. I found myself spending the money that I was trying to save. I began complaining to Legs about the money I was giving her. I wanted to get this support order cancelled but she still refused. I accused her of hiding resources and not being honest with me. The conversation that followed made me realize, how much she had changed and was now devoted to me. "Honey how you could accuse me of that. I wouldn't hide anything from you. Look at all that we through and now we are back together. Don't you think that God had something to do with this since we never got a divorce? I let you know everything thing that I have. If it will make you feel better I will go and get the order removed." This was the first time that I really saw my wife stand up for herself. It was the first time since I had arrived down here that she said she loved me with conviction. I stood there feeling stupid that I had pushed her to that point. It would have never happened if I didn't have all this added pressure on me. She had been doing great. She was getting out more on her own again and wasn't complaining about pain. She had started looking forward to finishing her chemo treatment and doing the customary dance at the hospital. "I'm sorry Kitten, I believe you." I went and hugged her as she sat on the bed in her bathrobe. She was gently crying as I kept repeating how sorry I was.

We began to prepare for Easter Sunday and Shawn's situation continued to stretch the resources of labor and money. I was focused on Legs whose emotional state had begun to deteriorate. I was forced to give Z Baby some of the responsibility of caring for Shawn. She had to check on him before going to school and when she came home. I was officially hired at my job and no longer worked for Express. This made it possible for me to take on extra work at other locations, when assignments were available. We attended service on Easter Sunday which was an emotional experience for all of us. When the alter call was made for prayer even Z Baby stood up to be touched. I was still taking Legs to her treatments but now I also had to take Shawn to his. I held church every night at work to keep my spirit. The naps I took on my lunch breaks were getting longer. I didn't know how long I could go on like this. Coco surprised us one day when she brought Legs a motorize wheel chair to get around in. It was funny watching Legs learn how to operate but it was a big help. She now had the ability to get around in the area without my assistance and without having to drive. We had a scare on early evening as we all went to the store together for ice cream. We had to cross a main thoroughfare and Legs had became confused about how to go forward and backwards. I had to grab the controls to get us out of the streets. That was the last time she tried to cross that street. The time continues moving forward and so did I but Legs regression didn't stop. I noticed physical changes in her face and in her weight. She returned to her antisocial behavior at the hospital. There were occasions when I almost had to force her to go for her treatments. On her of my days off during the week, Z Baby came home and rousted me from my sleep. She started asking me where was Legs. "She is probably down stairs with her friend." Z Baby went down stairs but she wasn't there. Z Baby was becoming a little more upset when she realized that the car was gone. "I don't know Z Baby she was here when I fell asleep. She wasn't talking about going any where." Z Baby couldn't function and neither could I. We made phone calls but she didn't answer. We called her friends that she might have gone to see but she wasn't there. We exhausted all possibilities and just sat in the living room, hoping that she would return soon. It wasn't until night that she finally walked through the door beaming with excitement and acting like a child at Christmas. I was the first to speak and Z Baby followed right behind me. "Kitten where were you? We have been worried sick." "Yeah ma, why didn't you answer your phone?" Legs looked at both us as if we had done something wrong. She continued smiling and started pulling objects from the bags she had brought in. "Look at all the stuff I got from Dillard's! I was there all day hanging out with the girls. I had a good time. I got tired of being stuck in the house. Honey I didn't wake you up because you would have stopped me. I wanted to drive by myself." She was sounding like a little girl. It never occurred to her that someone might be worried. She then told us how she never heard her phone. I knew then that she needed more attention than what I was giving her. I had to give her more outlets for fun and entertainment. I understood what she was saying. I was always pressing her to get better. She argued with me about the certainty of her death. I tried to get her to understand that people were dying without cancer and that I could still go before her. I argued that our days are numbered but we didn't know the time or place. Legs would then snap back that I didn't have cancer. She was right and I had nothing to say behind that. When I had gotten over being afraid that something had happened to her, I began to share in her joy. "Look I brought something for everybody. I didn't have to pay for this stuff. It was given to me and some things I just stuffed into my bags." We started laughing because we knew how Legs would always try to get something extra whenever we stayed at hotels and even when she was at the hospital. We had soap, blankets, towels and an assortment of other things that came from her sticky fingers. She never thought of it as stealing. She had a lot of cosmetics and perfume. She gave me a few bottles of cologne and a watch. I was glad to see how happy she was and she was very happy. Z Baby went through the things and said; "Mommy, you are something else!" When the laughter stopped and the excitement died down Legs was walked quietly to her room. I knew she was tired and so did Z Baby. I went around the corner to check on Shawn while Z Baby went to her room to do her homework. I was glad I didn't have to go to work on this night because I was tired too. I stayed with Shawn until well after midnight. I had fallen asleep while watching TV. I went back home after taking out some meat to cook for Shawn later. The house was quiet when I went in. I took the dog for a walk to clear my head and give him a break. His presence in the house did make a difference. Sometimes I would come home and find him in the bed with Legs. She never liked the idea of him being in a cage. Z Baby was doing well with both the dog and Shawn, but I could see some evidence of the strain it was putting on her. I never complained about anything she did. I tried to compensate for the extra labor and other responsibility. I allowed her more free time with her friends without question. There was just too much sickness! Express called me one

ZEKE SMITH

morning and offered me a job at Prime Outlets. It was paying good money by their standards and it wouldn't affect my other job. I took on the assignment and it made a difference. I met a brother there whose wife had passed and he was raising his children alone. The second job became a source of therapy and it made me aware of some stores that I knew nothing about. Coco gave Legs an opportunity to buy two big screen televisions from her job. This was good therapy for Legs because it made her feel vital in the family. She had been steadily regressing and the cancer had started to spread. They increased the dosage of chemo which caused her more pain. It was a downward spiral for her health. The more treatment, the more pain; the more pain the more medicine. The more medicine, the more side affects that sometimes led to more new drugs. The job at Prime Outlet was only for a month. I didn't mind because I couldn't keep up the pace much longer than that. I was named employee of the month for May by Express. Legs were filled with joy and yet she had trouble showing her happiness. We received even worst news on the next doctor's visit. It was revealed that the cancer had started growing again in her liver. It had also spread to her brain. We all gathered at the hospital on this day because Legs had become very ill. The options that were available didn't please legs and she refused to go any further. I didn't want her to give up but she had decided to turn it over to God. When she was first diagnosed all the preparations that were made never considered that I would be there. Legs had painted such a negative picture of me that no one believed we would ever be together again. Legs had sent for me because she needed someone. She had her family believing that it was only because of Z Baby. I didn't fault her because I knew through the years of our marriage she could never be totally honest with her family. I guess the baggage she carried from past relationships, and the other mistakes she made in life, made it even more difficult. Legs asked for my advice when I returned to the room. I had stepped out because grief had overwhelmed me and I didn't want Legs to see it. "It's up to you Kitten. I will support whatever you decide. I stepped out again and took a short walk outside. I didn't want to lose what God had given back. I didn't want to accept that this truly was the beginning of her end. Coco came out and spoke with me offering some comfort. We went back inside where Pauline, Z Baby and Legs were sitting inside. The doctor was very straight forward in giving his prognosis. Legs decided not to pursue any more treatment. There was already procedures set-up by Coco for this moment. Legs had made her the medical proxy so she started making phone calls. I stayed inside until we left out together. Coco contacted Hospice and let me know that they would be to the house in the morning. I began to feel like an outsider. I didn't want to argue about the decisions that were being made so I remained silent. I went to work that night with the heaviest emotional burden since my arrival. I now began to think more of Z Baby's future with her mother gone. My own body had started giving me trouble with all the work that I was doing. I had to take longer and longer breaks at work to recover from my assignments. The lawyers still could not reach a settlement with the insurance company about my injuries from the accident. The compensation board was lagging in getting me a date to be heard. The massage chair at work became my best friend. I found additional comfort in my contacts from New York. Godfather had sent me the money for the work I did on his house. I was able to send a portion of that to my credit union and the rest was used around the house. The money from Legs tax refund was long gone. It was everyone's belief that an insurance policy was in place to cover burial expenses. The focus was switched from recovery and life to making comfort and death.

The following morning I went home without delay from work. I let my friend Angel at work know the situation with my wife. The other workers at the animal hospital were also told. Everyone was very supportive as I continually broke down crying. The owner had difficulty listening because she was very sensitive to these types of situations. She still was supportive and offered her help. I was now limping by the time I left work. When I arrived home that morning I first check to see that Legs had taken her medications. I then went around the corner with our dog Bean to start Shawn's dinner. I had a lot of anxieties about what laid ahead. I was fighting depression and exhaustion which wasn't a good mix. It was ten 'o clock by the time I made it back upstairs. Coco called me and asked; "If I would call her when Hospice arrived." She went on to say; "I have important business at work which might prevent me from being there. If I can't come could you put your phone on speaker so I can follow everything?" I didn't see any problems with that. I knew what Hospice did but I was never on this side of the arrangements. "Sure Coco I will call you." Shortly after Coco called, I received one from Pauline my wife's oldest daughter. "Good morning Zeke' how is mommy doing?" "Well she is still in the bed and is experiencing some pain, but otherwise she's okay." I didn't mind the calls but there were so many things I was trying to do at the time. I wish they would just come by. I continue to listen to Pauline on the phone as my mind wondered. "I will be there soon to help out." Pauline ended her call and I went back to trying to clean up the house and fix Legs some breakfast. I also had the clean Legs' bathroom real good and move some of her clothes around so that her closet door would close. When Legs finally got up she had an upbeat mood. She was feeling some relief; that she didn't have to do the treatments any more. She was feeling some relief; that there were no more doctor visits and she could just chill at home. She was fearful of dying and yet she felt okay about not fighting this disease any more. Pauline arrived way before the Hospice so she had time to speak with her mother. I continued doing the things that I had to do in the house. My relationship with Pauline was still not what Legs had hoped for, yet I tried to maintain peace between us. Bean was running around the house doing what dogs do. It looked like he sensed something because he would come into Legs bedroom and just sit near the end of the bed. He had become accustomed to being in there and Legs welcomed his presence. I had set up his cage in Z Baby's room and she would put him in the bed with her at night. The knock on the door brought loud barks from Bean. He had a big bark for such a small dog. It was the nurses from Hospice. They arrived with their bags filled with information and some supplies. I let them in and put Bean in his cage. I led them to Legs who was still sitting up in the bed speaking with Pauline. I called Coco to alert her that Hospice had arrived. They began to ask Legs questions about her health and what she knew of Hospice. They took her vitals and wanted to know what meds she was on. I was able to give them that information as I pointed to the bottles lined up on the dresser. They then asked for Coco because that's the name they had in their paperwork. During this time no one had actually asked who I was and I never identified myself. The lead nurse Karen made it clear that Coco had to be present for the meeting to continue. I called Coco to inform her and she said she would be there soon. She had a little distance to travel so I estimated that it might take about half an hour. They rearranged their agenda to cover some things that didn't require Coco's presence or signature. It was during this time that they learned; I was the husband as they listed the close family members involved in her care. I was expecting them to come much earlier than they did so my routine was thrown off a little. It was a depressing atmosphere for me and I had to keep leaving the room to calm myself. They were asking about some things concerning Legs and Pauline was answering questions before I could respond. What I had to say didn't matter and it upset Legs that we were having this exchange. I took the high road and left the room after telling Pauline that it didn't matter to me. Shortly after this Coco arrived and I explained to her what had just taken place. Then Z Baby came in from school. Coco encouraged me to come back inside and discuss it. I did not want to say anything because I had too much resentment about what was taking place. I was left out of the whole decision making process concerning my wife. I felt that out of respect I should have been brought up to date about what they had decided to do. Legs didn't even want to tell me anything. She had hid the paperwork when I took her to pick it up from the lawyer's office. I didn't give it much thought because I knew I had not surrendered any of my rights as her husband. I didn't come to change anything because I did think that any plans made would include me. Tensions were high in the room. Legs were visibly upset as Z Baby sat emotionless on the bed. When Coco had finished speaking she too encouraged me to respond. When I started talking they didn't anticipate what I would be saying. "I didn't want my wife to give up but she made that decision. I would have not involved Hospice at this but Coco made the call before I could object. There were a lot of plans made before I got here. I understand that her sister is her medical proxy and was given power of attorney but I'm her husband." Coco was upset and angry now because no one understood the level of Legs commitment to me. They didn't understand that we had mended our broken fence and would not desert each other. They started realizing that I was called to be with my wife and not my child. Legs had become concerned with her health and future and she felt that I could provide more comfort than anyone. She had become ashamed of her body and wouldn't let me see her naked but I continued to tell her how beautiful she was to me. I continued to let her know that I would love her forever. I recalled how she would put everyone before me as I continue to make her first in my life. I even checked on her during the many separations making sure that she was alright. I recalled how during our last brief reunion after my birthday party I lavished some expensive gifts upon her. She remained silent during my exchange. She remained silent as opposing views were offered and Pauline left the room. She remained silent until the head nurse Karen asked a question. "Who are the contact person and next of kin to make decisions for you?" Legs didn't hesitate to say Zeke my husband. The nurse asked a second question. "Who is the second person Legs?" Legs again she didn't hesitate and said; "My daughter Z Baby." Coco got up mad at what had taken place saying that she didn't have to be here. Pauline left later as she continued speaking with her sister and mother. The nurse explained that as her husband I always had the authority to make the decisions and that I would be responsible for Z Baby. I agreed and said that I knew this but didn't want to upset the flow of things. We discussed the process of Hospice further. She told a story of one patient that lived for eight years on Hospice. I was given contact information and told that Legs would be receiving a visiting nurse to monitor her vitals. She explained that the goal of hospice was to provide comfort for their patient and did not make any medical decisions. She stated that it was important for us to know that Hospice took no action to prolong life. Coco had asked before she left that if Legs condition had worsened to near death, she wanted the family members that lived out of town to be able to arrive before she died. The nurse answered that question now and clarified that; Hospice could not do anything that would hinder the natural course of death. When everyone had finally left, Legs were very sad about the way family relationships were going. She didn't understand that she had played a part in it by not disclosing her full intentions. I didn't have a problem because she was facing death and nothing else in this world was more important to me than her satisfaction. In the days ahead as the nurses made their visits, and Legs routine began to change; I began to ask Legs to take a more active role in preparing Z Baby for the life ahead of her. I wanted Legs to start having the conversations with her child that mothers do. I wanted legs to give Z Baby some orderly direction while she was here. I didn't want the job to remain solely on me. I knew the consequences of people losing loved ones and then having to deal with the things that were never said. I wanted Legs to start the dialog between her daughters to lessen the impact of her death on Z Baby and Pauline. It took a lot of courage for Legs to discuss the subject of her immortality because her death had now become certain and the time was close at hand.

Our wedding anniversary was on May 14, and this year of 2008 was the first time we celebrated in six years, while actually together. I didn't have any money for a lavish gift and had to settle on a $30 piece of silver jewelry from Wal-Mart. It was a floating heart on a necklace and she cherished that more than anything else I had ever given her God had been good to us in allowing this reunion at such a crucial time in both our lives. I had smothered my wife with so much love and attention that she would beg me to take a day off from worrying about her. The only friend that I had which I didn't inherit from Legs network was my co-worker Angel. I began to lean on her more as she guided me through my troubles. We had time to share our problems because she too was going things. Once we had lunch outside in the court yard at work. I was really able to share some things that I couldn't speak about inside. I was still juggling responsibilities and had to pay more attention to the medicines Legs were taking. She started receiving stronger pain killers which left her almost comatose for much of the day. She was falling asleep during church services and would often wake up disorientated. Z Baby found humor in this and I eventually let her sit with her friends. It was easy for me to monitor legs if Z Baby wasn't there causing laughter. It was just one of the ways that Z Baby was able to deal with all that was going on. We finally had to get a wheel chair for Legs to get around. She tired too easily and the walk to from the car to the sanctuary became almost impossible. I didn't want Legs to feel stuck at home and not a part of the family routines. I was not ashamed of her but she was feeling some shame for herself. She started receiving more attention from the church as the membership so her slowly fading away. She would get angry at the Pastor talking about healing when she was slowly marching towards death. The church was generous in their out pouring of love and support; both emotionally and sometimes financially. I was an active participant in the maintenance of the church. I was generous in my donations also. I saw them making a great effort for me to see how much they loved my wife. She too had been active until her jobs and then her health had curtailed her involvement. They had watched Z Baby develop during her tender years before adolescence. I had constant breakdowns during all our Sunday services. I went to Bible study whenever Legs didn't mind being left alone or I would just take Z Baby if I stayed at home. We were holding it together as a family and some of the bitterness from Coco and Pauline had died down. I saw my wife as a hero and a great example of someone that had to deal with their impending demise.

My wife had said during the first week of my arrival that she didn't think she would be around for next Christmas. She now just wanted to be around for her birthday on June 24th. She started asking me about what I wanted for Father's Day. I would always answer; you baby. Her two closest friends had made plans to visit her. Donna and Mary had been her running partners in the projects. They came to all the gatherings we had back in New York. I was also usually the only spouse attending most of the functions that they gave. She had other friends but these were the two closest. It had been arranged that they would all stay at Coco's house because she had the room. They also wanted o have a sleep over the way they did yearly in New York. I had taken another temporary assignment from Express. They were so good at thinking of me first whenever they had something that I could do. They had become an extended family of mine whom always had an attentive ear to listen when I needed to talk. This job had me working at a nursing home in Williamsburg that wasn't as far from the house as my regular job. The girls arrived in Virginia during the week of Father's Day. I sat up with Legs as she waited for someone to pick her up that Friday night. She fell asleep waiting as we both reminisced about our times in New York. She was very tired by the time Coco came to get her but she was still excited. It was decided not to take her wheel chair with her because she wouldn't be traveling much. She was very sick during the visit and her energy level was low but she had fun. They took her out shopping and they had their sleepover with them all in the same bed. I was happy for her. I was surprised that Saturday with some gifts for Father's Day that Legs had picked out. I had two short sets and some cologne. She always made it a point to buy me cologne. I picked her up that night from Coco's house because she wanted to sleep in her bed. The many drugs she was taking were affecting her judgment. She didn't always know where she was at or what time of day it was. When I went to pick her up they second guessed not having the wheel chair because they realize how impaired her mobility was. I parked in front of the house and rang the bell to announce my arrival. Legs had assistance when she came to the door. They all talked about the things they did and how much fun they had. I was as happy as Legs because of her friends' visit. They stood wondering if she could make it to the car; that's when I picked her up into my arms and took her to the car. They were all spellbound and even Legs were caught off guard. We went home and I put her to bed. The next day was Father's Day and they would be honoring the men, much the same way they did for the women on Mother's Day.

We went to church and the service was moving. I felt especially proud because of all the things I had been able to do for my family and the community around me. God had resurrected me from the ashes that were my life. He had placed me in a place that allowed me to grow closer to him. I was filled with the Holy Spirit as I carried out my assignment from the Lord. I was paying bills and donating to charities without being able to trace where the money was coming from. The confusion didn't last long as He revealed to me in visions that it was Him. My testimony of faith was louder and heard more often. I sought to inspire others not to give up on love or difficult circumstances. I didn't have to review the scriptures to know how powerful God was or how certain was His promises. I was living proof here on earth. My baby was all dolled up in a nice yellow dress with flowery prints for church. She stood out amongst all the women, because she had fashioned a matching hand band that gave her a European look. Loved it ad in spite of her apparent handicap, she was the most beautiful woman in the house today. She received a lot of hugs and well wishes that Sunday. I too returned a lot of hand shakes. There were those that approached out of concern and then there were also just the curious. Z Baby had a difficult time accepting her mother being in a wheel chair. I constantly explained to her that it was necessary because even she saw how quickly her mother would tire. When we got home I went and carried Legs upstairs and sat her on the couch, before returning to the car to get the wheel chair. We had stayed over at the church to eat and everybody seemed tired. We stayed in the living room watching TV. I welcomed any opportunity for Legs to be in the living room. She spent so much time in the bed and I felt that it added to her unhappiness. She was definitely a fighter and continued to be my role model. I couldn't help but think about the same courage my mother had shown when she had her first heart attack. During her hospital stay she would talk about her preparation for death and imagined how her children would respond to it. In spite of the gloomy nature of the topic she was able to add humor to make it digestible. It was now the same way with Legs. We stayed out there talking about the visit with her friends. They had stayed up Friday night telling stories and she had me laughing about how she kept dozing off. We both fell asleep on that couch before Z Baby finally woke us both up to go to be. I assisted her to the bathroom before helping her to the bed. I gave her meds after she came out. Her excuse for taking so long in there was because she was freshening up. I just laughed and took my turn inside. I did much the same thing too except I cleaned up the bathroom before I left. I know my knack for trying to keep everything perfect around me annoyed some people. I didn't care because it gave honor to God and my mother, and it gave me an outlet to vent my sorrow. If I was feeling bad about anything, all I had to do was start cleaning and those bad feelings were slowly replaced with joy.

I came out the bathroom to find Legs with her arms outstretched lying on the bed and still fully dressed. She had not even removed her head band. The lights in the room were dim with only the dull lamp light on. I removed my suit and hung it up before helping Legs undress. I took my time removing her garments as she moaned softly in pain with each motion. I took off her dress and slip and left her with just the undergarments. I reached for her head band but she wanted to leave it on. She was slurring her speech as she talked to me. "Here Honey this is what I have for you for Father's Day. Just be gentle with me because I'm still feeling the pain." I was moved by this gesture. I was only joking about wanting her on this day but she took it seriously. I don't know if it was her need or was she just trying to satisfy me. I carefully peeled off the rest of her clothes as I got naked with her. The lights were casting a sensual glow in the room. I put in a tape of the music that we listen too early in our marriage. I stroked her gently as I viewed her nakedness for the first time in years. Even though she had lost a lot of weight and her face was a little gaunt; I still saw nothing but beauty before me. The curves of her body still stood out and the nipples on her small breasts were erect. I too began to respond to this vision before me but was in no hurry to make her a prisoner of my embrace. I continued my fore play stroking and rubbing her body as I licked across her nipples. I knew I couldn't put any weight on her body so my knees and elbows allowed me to hover above her. I began to experience pain of my own but I endured for the greater prize that lay ahead. I wanted to give the meds she had just taken time to kick in. I didn't want to withdraw once I entered her. I watched as she seemed to be in a daze. Yes it was no time to claim my prize. I stepped up to her receptionist's desk and let them no why I was here. I identified myself by sliding my I.D. card through the slot. I was immediately recognized and allowed to enter. There was some resistance when I started to browse through the selection. It seemed like everyone present didn't recognize me because it was a long time ago that I was there. I continue to walk up and down the hallways and smiles became common place. I began to search the premises more rapidly as the receptionist encouraged me to check out all the selections. It began to feel real good in this place and I made myself comfortable. The building began to rock as I continued my search. The floors around became slippery but I kept my balance. The rhythm of my walk was not interrupted and I could move at an even quicker pace. I wanted to leave the shop but the receptionist cried out for help and put a tight grip on my body. The more I struggled to get free the better it felt to stay. I was confused until the people let out shouts of their own. "Hallelujah, hallelujah thank you thank you." I then responded in unison with shouts of my own; "yes, yes, thank you thank you baby it's so good." I began to slow my browsing down as the receptionist let go of her grip. The building stop rocking but you could still hear the foundation squeaking. I stayed inside while everyone began to calm down and disappear. I body relaxed enough for me to think about leaving. I backed up and left as I slid my I.D. card back out of the slot. I thought about letting stay overnight until I saw all the juice that was left around me. The receptionist smiled and winked at me as I left. They closed the store and that was the last time I was able to visit it. The love making night was the most incredible of our 15 year marriage. It demonstrated what sacrifice in the face of adversity is all about. It left a lasting impression on me as I went about with the business of enjoying the last days of my wife's life. I usually looked forward to going to work because of the solace and peace I received from being alone. I would the TBN network and receive extra spiritual guidance. I would sit in the massage chair and have my body healed. I found it to be the perfect environment for me to escape my reality without using drugs or alcohol. This was not the case tonight. I wanted to stay home and cuddle up with my wife. She was sleeping peacefully when I rose up out of the bed. She continued to sleep when I went and took a quick shower. I didn't have a lot of time to prepare; so in my haste to get dress, I made some noise. The sounds still didn't disturb Legs and she continued to sleep. I woke up Z Baby to let her know that I was leaving and that I had filled the pill boxes with Legs dosages for the week. I had developed this system when Legs became unable to recall when or what medicines she had taken. I arrived at work late but didn't cause any problems. My friend was on duty that always looked out for me. I jumped right into my shift and being briefed. I began my tour and took notes along the way. I was on a cloud that was created from making love to my wife. I was on a cloud because I saw an end to some of my suffering in sight. I felt an even greater high when I thought about how good I was able to make my wife feel. She thought that she lost the ability to have an orgasm but I proved her wrong. The night went away fast as I moved from one area to another cleaning without taking a break. I wasn't hungry because I had been fed by the bread of life. I felt the presence of the Lord as He working things out. Legs had a great weekend and so did I. Shawn was adjusting and became less dependent on Z Baby going around there to help. He had a home attendant that bathed him and kept the house clean. He had a therapist that came to help him rehabilitate. They had removed the wires from his jaw so he was able to eat solid foods again. Everyone at the job knew of my situation so with there good mornings some gave hugs. When I would arrive at work I would pray before leaving my car. When I left to go home I prayed and called Legs to let her know I was on the way. I never would panic if she didn't answer. I knew no matter what was going on she was in God's hands. I arrived home to find Legs struggling to clean herself up. She was afraid to take a shower because her pain patches might get wet. She wouldn't take a bath because she couldn't get in or out of the tub. She was too ashamed to let me bathe her and Z Baby mainly helped her on the weekends. I called our nurse that morning and arranged for someone to come everyday and wash her. It was not something that she readily accepted and it took a few slips and an

ZEKE SMITH

uncomfortable feeling about her hygiene for her to cooperate. She now had a staff of people that was concerned only with her comfort and general welfare. Once she got used to all the service that she was receiving, she began to display a better attitude. It was the next weekend after Father's Day and Legs woke up acting like her old self. I had one more week to work on my second job, which the Express Employment Agency gave me. I began calling her friends to have a surprise birthday party for her at the house. I couldn't believe how good she was looking and feeling. It was as if she was healed completely overnight. Legs had gone through a rough time that Friday. I was up let consoling and looking after her. I wanted her co-workers from Dillard's to surprise her and they thought it was a good idea. Coco had stopped by that morning to check on her sister. When she left I told her about my plans and she thought it was a good idea too. Once everything was set up I let Z Baby know because I had to leave for work. The people at the nursing home had fell in love with me. I enjoyed serving them and hearing their stories. I didn't have any elders left in my family that I had access to. The ones I was the closest to had went on to a greater glory. Hey were not happy to here that I would be leaving soon. The director was considering hiring me but I let him know that the wages were too low. I returned home that evening as the party was breaking up. Legs started smiling when I walked through the door. They had put together a real celebration on such a short notice. Legs were overcome with joy as she showed me the gifts that they had brought. I was so grateful for what they had done. I knew Legs had a special connection with the people she met there. I remember how much she loved that job from the few times we spoke while I was living in New York. I gave God all the credit because only He could orchestrate such a feat. There were a lot of tears as they were leaving. I thanked them all individually as I fought back my own tears. Legs were still looking and sounding good when we went to church that Sunday. It continued on even when I left for work that night. When I came home that Monday morning the nurses had to order oxygen because she was having too much difficulty breathing. I began preparing for the end because I didn't think she could hold on much longer. It started to have an effect on Z Baby as Legs weight loss became very noticeable. The nurses passed out literature to help us understand the dying process. I began alerting the family her family that the end was close. I wanted them to have a chance to see her alive because I didn't think that she would make it to her birthday. Some were grateful for the information and some had set dates to come; still others didn't want to have to make two trips. I had to start leaving work a little early because Z Baby could no longer handle giving her mother the medicine in the morning. It was always a lot to ask of her so I didn't object. Legs began to take pills whenever she hurt and sometimes took too much. She didn't want to just ease the pain she wanted to be high. I couldn't argue if it brought her peace and this was always a risk because of the potency of the drugs. I had alerted the staff in the beginning when started her chemo that we both were recovering addicts. I didn't want my wife to die addicted to any drug because that was an addict's goal. June 21 came on a Sunday and Legs were too sick to make it to church. We all stayed home that Sunday because our Pastor and first lady had visited with us prior. They saw the toll that the cancer had taken on my wife's body and mind. I didn't allow visits from everybody outside of the family. I didn't need curious onlookers coming by. I called her close friend from the church to come and sit with her while I went to work that night. I didn't like her being alone until she had fallen asleep. Z Baby already had seen enough suffering and I wanted to spare her too. The following morning Z Baby called me with a frantic call. Legs were in distress and Z Baby didn't know what to do. I notified my s the front desk and left immediately. I wasn't concerned with getting a ticket but I didn't want to be delayed by a traffic cop. I got home in record time and found Legs to be incoherent and crying out in pain. I began calling the family after I had sent for the nurses. There was a prescribed process in place that I had to follow and I did. I called the nurses a second time because they weren't arriving fast enough. The rest of the family came as soon as they could. We all had gathered in the room believing that Legs were ready to go home. The nurse began the exercises and started to do the tests to see what phase of the death process that she was in. They tried to create an atmosphere of peace and comfort that would allow Legs to move on. They had soft music playing and essence playing and after a long wait when was thinking that Legs were ready to leave us. She sat up alertly and shouted out; "Damn I was almost there. I saw the angels coming for me." We all bust out laughing and that broke the tension and grief that had filled the room. The eventually left and told us what to do if her condition worsened again. Legs spent the rest of the day sleeping and Pauline along with her husband stayed to look after her. Pauline was going to spend the night but changed her mind at the last minute and said she would return in the morning. I didn't go to work that night and stayed home instead. I didn't want Z Baby to be there alone. When we all had retired that night Legs became distressed again. It wasn't anything I could not handle. She fell back to sleep in my arms after I changed her pajamas.

Z Baby stayed home too and I let her go to her best friend's mother shop to get her nails done. I got up and gave Legs her medicine; and lay back down next to her after I washed and dressed. I was awakening from my nap by the dog's barking and heard someone at the door. Pauline had returned as promised. The day before Legs continued to ask for the family to have peace. She never liked the idea that Pauline and I wasn't getting along. They felt that it was one of the reasons why she was holding on. Legs older sister was leaving New York after the phone call but she couldn't leave right away. My family was waiting along with some others for the actual funeral date to be known. When I got up Legs mouth was wide open and I cold hear her heavy breathing. I answered the door and Pauline came in with the baby grand. She wanted to discuss our relationship before I returned back to the room. We spent a lot of time going back and forth listening and talking to each other. I had the locks on the doors changed when I signed a new lease on June first. I also had the carpet cleaned at that time and now the apartment was also in my name. I didn't inform anyone so the keys that they had were no longer useful and that was a problem for Pauline. She couldn't understand why she couldn't have a key to my apartment if her mother had given her one. Coco felt that I should have informed her before I did it. This only made the divide between us greater. Now here we were again discussing our relationship while my wife was on her death bed. We finally ended our talk and I returned to the room. I saw that Legs position had not changed so I made a more close up inspection. I then realized that the breathing I heard was the oxygen going into her mouth. My wife had died in my arms while we slept. Z Baby was entering the apartment as I began to shout Hallelujah. Pauline came and saw what I saw and suggested keeping it from Z Baby for her protection. "She's been here from the beginning so that won't be necessary Pauline." I continued expressing my joy that my wife had finally found peace. Z Baby came and watched her moms as I removed the oxygen. I noted the time and called Hospice. Her older sister Nicole was on the way. It was too bad they she couldn't arrive sooner but I didn't think that she wanted to. It was no need for me to miss any more work until the funeral. I didn't have time to take but they allowed me two days off with pay. It turned out to be a short term loan because they asked for the money back later. It took less than three hours for Hospice to inspect the body and Legs removed. This is when Coco found out that there was no insurance. The policy had only been started that year and the payments were behind. Nicole came and took care of everything in my honor. It felt good the way she treated me even though I had no money to bury my wife. The funeral was held at our church. The pastor had promised to help pay the expenses but only provided the church and clergy at no charge. Everyone that wanted to be there had made it. We had a video diary of Legs life at the church. There was a large funeral as friends, family, co-workers, and some of the people she served came and honored her. There were a lot tears at the funeral and burial. Some handled the events better than others. The tensions that were created between the people who loved her most soon subsided. Legs were courageous from the beginning to the end. She was able to live out her last days in spite of the pain with some joy. She touched many lives since moving to Virginia and most of them came to say goodbye. I said one thing when we snuggled up for the last time; "Forever, that's how long I'm going to love you." My wife died one day short of her 52nd birthday.